FAIR PLAY

Scott B. Lancaster

Prentice
Hall Press

This publication is designed to provide accurate and authoritative information in regard to the subject matter covered. It is sold with the understanding that the publisher is not engaged in rendering legal, accounting, or other professional services. If you require legal advice or other expert assistance, you should seek the services of a competent professional.

 A member of Penguin Putnam Inc.
375 Hudson Street
New York, New York, 10014

http://www.penguinputnam.com

Prentice Hall Press edition: September 2002

Library of Congress Cataloging-in-Publication Data
Lancaster, Scott B.
  Fair play : pro football's radical program that's successfully changing the future of youth sports / Scott B. Lancaster ; foreword by Bill Walsh.
    p.   cm.
  Includes index.
  ISBN 0-7352-0360-1
  1. Sports for children—Coaching. 2. Parent and child.
  3. Sportsmanship. I. Title.

GV709.24 .L36 2003
796'.07'7—dc21

                                                    2002072275

Printed in the United States of America

           10   9   8   7   6   5   4   3   2   1

To Mom and Dad

ACKNOWLEDGMENTS

Throughout this book I refer to the journey of a child's sports experience rather than the final results. The creation of this book was no different.

The enjoyment I experienced in writing this book comes in large part due to the support I received. And I received no stronger support than from the person that is always my inspiration, my wife, Susan.

I approached this project knowing that I needed a strong team of individuals to bring this important message and model to parents and coaches everywhere. And in keeping with the Fair Play philosophy, everyone played an equally important role.

I'm forever grateful to Patti DeMatteo, who made the project happen from the beginning with her willingness to contribute her time and keen business knowledge. Stephen Weiss was instrumental in the organization and the clarity he brought to editing my work while teaching me the finer points of writing. Jennifer Prosek's energy and expertise were vital.

For their diligence in helping me gather information and the people necessary to make this project complete, I thank Lee Becker and Jerry Horowitz.

I also want to thank Bill Walsh, Pete Carroll, and Boomer Esiason for their collective wisdom and passion for youth football and youth sports and the invaluable career guidance they have provided.

None of this philosophy would have been possible without the fortunate experience I had with my coach, Mike Woicik. Mike's innovative methods and volumes of knowledge paid major dividends for me in my career.

For the success of all our NFL Youth Programs there are too many to mention. However, I must thank my past and present staff—Matt Gliebe, Vida Hsu, Jennifer Magner, Jennifer Semien, Lynn DiNanno, Pam Perlman, Billie Christie, and Sola Winley—in addition to the NFL support I received over the years from Roger Goodell, Neil Glat, Mark Holtzman, Seth Rabinowitz, and Gene Washington.

To everyone at Prentice Hall, with special thanks to Debbie Yost and Barry Richardson for making my first book experience a rewarding and enjoyable one.

For my friends who would always come through with a timely phone call, I thank Richie Kotite, Pat Kirwan, David Doty, Lisa Anastos, Ellen Zavian, Paul Deen, Elliot Katzman, and Alan Littman.

Most of all, I thank my family, for being the balance and cornerstone for everything I do.

CONTENTS

FOREWORD
On Fair Play

Youth sports and activities are not as enjoyable, productive, or valuable as they might seem.

There are many high-sounding references made to youth sports and to learning the value of communication with others and mastering the fundamental skills. There is also much to be desired in the approach taken by many of those who consider themselves experts and those who have had years of experience in dealing with kids.

A youngster's sports experience should be directed toward enjoyment, gratification, and learning. Unfortunately, for every youngster who does gain the gratification and learns the lessons that are so valuable in later life, there are many others who have poor experiences that can affect them negatively for years.

My nephew is an example. His dream in early life was to be a wide receiver on a high school football team and then perhaps play on a college or professional team. A tall, angular athlete with great potential, he was in great condition. When he went to his first practice in youth football, the coach told the parents that he hoped they wouldn't stay around because they wouldn't like what they were going to see. That was the first experience my sister and her husband had with organized youth sports. After two days of being mistreated and ridiculed, my nephew stopped going to practice and became a soccer player. He had an outstanding career in high school and college soccer, and is now a soccer coach. This is an example of what can occur in any highly competitive youth sport.

I have known Scott Lancaster for several years. We have spent long hours discussing sports programs for young people geared toward enhancing the overall experience, making it instructional and enjoyable at the same time. Scott has been instrumental in building up the youth football program for the National Football League, but his solid ideas are applicable to all sports.

Fair Play takes a different approach to youth sports. The focus is not on winning and losing but on the advancement of every individual. Boys and girls learn to play and enjoy sports through a healthy and fulfilling experience. Fair Play describes a new philosophy with practical methods that can be applied to your child's sports experience through an all-encompassing learning model that results in gratification for every child who chooses to participate.

So much time is spent in organizing, planning, and then playing team sports that learning the skills of the game is sacrificed. This eliminates the vital opportunity for young athletes to take pride in learning, developing, and enhancing those skills to a point where they can formulate their own style and way to best compete. Often youth coaches are less concerned about the skills and fundamentals than they are on game planning. They then see themselves operating at the highest level, emulating college or professional coaches.

Those youngsters who can take pride and gratification in learning skills and at the same time thoroughly enjoy the experience are those who profit the most. They are the ones who carry on with a sports career that reaches their own level of potential. At some point these same athletes can look back with great pride and satisfaction on those early experiences.

The very thought of youth brings images of unbridled enthusiasm and energy, but with that also comes fragility and sensitivity. When children are enrolled in sports at an early age, they are impressionable in so many ways. The fact that those impressions often turn negative defeats the purpose of participation.

Young men and women are very susceptible to criticism and negativism from authority figures. Just as these youngsters are developing an appreciation for a sport or are in the beginning stages of learning the nuances of competition and team interaction, they often are degraded by the cynicism of their own coaches. The result is that they drop the sport forever, learn to dislike it, or simply satisfy their parents by continuing to participate until at some point they can make their own decision to quit.

This happens in individual sports such as swimming and tennis, and it also happens in youth team sports. Football, in particular, has had its problems with coaches who have identified themselves with the sport rather than with the teaching and developing of athletes.

Coaches who are concerned with developing their own image, identity, and self-confidence are not the people best suited to developing and enhancing the sports experience for young people. In my view, there are too many ego-driven coaches who identify themselves as the central figure and make sure they are surrounded by a group of people who are obligated to follow their directions regardless of what they are. The focus is placed on satisfying the coach rather than on teaching and allowing the kids to learn more about themselves and to develop skills they can use throughout their lives.

The qualities of any good coach include the ability to care first about every athlete as a person, followed by organization skills and creativity. Fair Play provides parents and coaches with the blueprint to incorporate all these qualities into your child's sports program.

Fair Play will benefit and assist all those who want to make youth sports, both individual and team, an enjoyable and gratifying experience. Everyone involved in youth sports should strive for experiences that allow young people to develop their own self-confidence and self-esteem, experiences through which the lessons of life are learned. Fair Play creates the environment in which young people learn to work in groups or teams to accomplish something to the point where the performance of a teammate begins to mean nearly as much as their own performance. These are always the most important values in sports education and sports experiences for young people.

It is of vital importance that parents personally observe how their children are being treated as young members of a sports team. They should feel that it is a positive experience. They should be able to see that the coach is competent and knowledgeable in offering the kind of direction that meets the needs of the youngsters and makes sports participation part of their journey toward becoming successful adults.

Fair Play should be part of every parent's evaluation of their youngster's experience because the enjoyment and the satisfaction of learning a skill, interacting with others, and actually playing are the essence of youth sports.

—BILL WALSH
San Francisco 49ers

Prologue

STARTING OVER

I work and live in New York City, the most competitive and largest professional sports city in the world. Many people only dream of working in professional sports; I am blessed with the opportunity.

I've spent most of my adult career working to develop youth sports programs, first at the U.S. Soccer Federation and now with the National Football League. As the NFL's Senior Director of Youth Football Development, I was hired to develop a strategy to increase participation in youth football.

Even after all my years of experience in building and turning around national youth sports programs, I never imagined I would write a book with the goal of transforming youth sports in America—that is, until a fall weekend two years ago awakened my senses and sent me down this path.

A WALK IN THE PARK

I live in Brooklyn, adjacent to the entrance of New York Harbor. The Verrazano Narrows Bridge, the suspension bridge that hosts the dramatic start of the New York City Marathon every year, majestically shadows our house. It also overlooks Shore Park, which is often filled with kids playing soccer.

My wife, Susan, and I were taking a walk through that park one Sunday with our ten-month-old son. I was mulling over a tricky problem, and I hoped to find solace in my wife's incredible listening skills. Her patience amazes me, and she always responds to my concerns with sensible advice.

The conflict that I was explaining to her focused on the high school football experience of my oldest son, Keith. Keith had played soccer growing up, and unlike most kids, he continued to play in high school, becoming the captain of his freshman team. But he dropped out. Boredom and poor coaching drove him away. Not ready to give up on organized sports, he tried out for football his sophomore year. His body had been developing quickly, and after some weight lifting he was big enough to feel comfortable playing football.

Before Keith joined the team, I met with the coach. I liked him and his philosophy. He believed in playing every kid, no matter what his experience, and he had still racked up plenty of winning seasons. That's my kind of coach! Unfortunately, he retired after that season, and Keith started his junior year with a new coach. This new person, a teacher who was elevated from assistant coach, was following a legend.

The team was stacked, with more than sixty players on the roster for each varsity game. A football game typically allows a coach to play three different units during a game; eleven on offense, eleven on defense, and eleven on special teams. But unlike his predecessor, the new coach chose to play a core squad of only fifteen boys. Except for one kicker, the other fourteen played offense, defense, and special teams, rotating in and out of the game. That left forty-five kids standing on the sidelines of each game with nothing to do but watch.

This new coach's competitive style was to run up the score on opposing teams by using only his top fifteen players. By halftime they were usually up by thirty points or more. Yet the coach would begin the second half with the same core players; they would stay in the game until halfway through the fourth quarter. At this time the coach made a few substitutions, and a lucky handful played out the remaining minutes of a lopsided contest.

The forty-five non-core players began each game standing on the sideline, cheering on their teammates enthusiastically. By the second half, when victory was well secured, they still stood on the sideline, but now their postures drooped and their chins hung.

My son, who had just learned the game the prior year, was not disappointed that he did not start. However, along with some of the other boys, he possessed ample size and had proven in practice that he was ready to play. He was therefore really excited when he was named the practice player of the week—until the coach "rewarded" him by letting him play the last two minutes of the game. Even more troubling for both of us was that none of his other friends, a group with plenty of talent, even got in the game.

As a parent you want to confront the coach immediately and demand answers. I knew, though, that would not rectify the situation. While I did think he needed to understand the effect he was having on the players, I had no right to tell him how to run his team.

This was a real predicament considering my position at the NFL. I was not only a concerned parent but also the person charged with increasing participation in youth football and training youth coaches. I knew all too well that high school coaches like this one were driving kids away by the thousands each year.

To his credit, my son approached the coach himself, but he was given the royal brush-off and told his time would come.

Nothing improved during the season. After spending the summer agonizing over his experience, Keith decided not to return to the team his senior year, and a majority of his friends did the same—all because of one misguided coach.

I have always felt that a teacher is there to teach, and that should not stop when the school bell rings—especially if the teacher is also involved in an athletic program. This particular instructor abandoned his responsibility when classes ended each day. Instead of continuing to teach and giving each player equal time, his ego told him to run up the score. Only a few select kids were privileged to learn and grow.

After listening to me rant, my wife calmly said, "This should only motivate you further."

I knew she was right, but it still irked me that I was powerless to help my son and others like him.

As we continued to walk, we came upon some six- and seven-year-old kids in uniforms playing a soccer game. Out on the field, half the players were gathered near one goal, laughing, chasing each other, and searching in the grass for insects. Down at the other goal, the rest of the players swarmed around the soccer ball. Suddenly, someone kicked the ball up the field. The preoccupied bunch hardly noticed, so the coach began to scream at them.

"Wake up!" he raged while racing toward them, his arms raised, his face fixed in anger. "What the hell are you doing? You're all a bunch of idiots!"

The players froze in their tracks, and a look of horror spread over their faces. They watched the berserk man scream at them as though he were a professional coach with a multimillion-dollar contract on the line. Some of the children began to cry. Their day was certainly ruined. Hopefully their athletic careers would not be.

I turned to my wife in disbelief. Without hesitation Susan said, "You'd better get started."

I knew I had to get the word out. I knew I had to write this book.

STARTING OUT

Most people who work or have worked for the NFL can describe the sense of awe that accompanies their first several weeks on the job. After all, the National Football League is the most successful and prestigious professional sports league in the world. Imagine my surprise and excitement on my second day at the NFL when I was handed an airline ticket to San Francisco and told that I was going to visit with the legendary Bill Walsh.

Walsh is widely recognized as one of the most innovative and successful football coaches in the history of the game. He won three Super Bowls as head coach of the San Francisco 49ers, and served two stints as head coach for Stanford University. Some of the very best coaches in the NFL, including Mike Holmgren, Steve Mariucci, Dick Vermeil, George Seifert, and Pete Carroll, have worked with and been mentored by Bill. In 1993, Walsh was inducted into the Pro Football Hall of Fame.

I was hired by the NFL because of my extensive experience in creating player development programs for soccer. The NFL gave me the specific task of rebuilding youth football from the foundation up. My discussion with Bill Walsh that day gave me the confidence to begin creating the next generation's football experience. I will always remember that it was Bill who gave me the encouragement that second day on my new job to be innovative within football's traditional system. He told me to create programs that always had a child's well-being in mind. Years later, after numerous conversations and visits in which I bounced new ideas and concepts off him, I returned to discuss with Bill my ideas about this book.

WHEN FUN MATTERED

No matter the season, my own childhood was an unbroken string of pickup games.

I grew up in the sleepy New England town of Cumberland, Rhode Island. After school, on summer vacations, and every weekend I would throw on my grass-stained jeans and go out to play with my friends. Depending on the season and our mood, we would play baseball, football, basketball, or ice or street hockey. It didn't matter if we had eighteen kids or two. We adjusted and made up our own rules and variations of games.

We took advantage of every ray of sunlight and moved our games under the streetlights when it got dark. Most of the time we forgot the score halfway through the game, and we always let everybody play. We played for the pure love of the game, and to our delight, the adults just left us alone.

Sports have always been my sanctuary, the constant that has carried me through difficult personal times and eventually gave me the vision to change youth sports.

My mother and father always encouraged the sports endeavors of my two younger brothers and me. If we were interested in playing a particular sport, they told us to sign up. For years the two of them spent many early mornings standing in freezing ice rinks supporting us. They carpooled to and from baseball practices and journeyed to distant track meets. Our family's busy schedule placed more wear and tear on our mom than I thought. Later, in high school, I discovered that she had been fighting cancer all those years. Despite the rigors of bringing up three boys, she never let on or let up.

Our parents didn't quiz us on our fielding errors or how we missed that pass outside the crease. They were more concerned with our academics than our athletics. But when the homework was done, they gave us total freedom to play. When we were intimidated, they were supportive.

I vividly remember thinking about trying out for Little League baseball as an eight-year-old. My friends explained to me that we would be tested in our hitting as well as our fielding of grounders and fly balls. I was terrified.

This would be my first sports tryout. When I had joined youth hockey, everyone made the team and everyone played. If you paid the price to register, you were in. It also helped that I had confidence in my hockey abilities. I had honed my skating skills in my backyard where a pond froze every winter.

I will never forget the morning of the Little League tryout. I was standing in the kitchen with my father who was waiting patiently, car keys in hand. Suddenly, I burst into tears and confided to my parents that I did not want to try out. I was scared out of my mind. Even then I could not fathom being humiliated in front of all my friends and sent home without being selected. My mom calmed me down, and my dad comforted me by saying he would work with me for a year, until I felt more confident about trying out.

In the end, even though my father and I played endless hours of catch, I did not try out for baseball until I was in junior high school. By that time the majority of the Little Leaguers who played when I was eight had already quit baseball, deflated and discouraged. I, however, went on to start for championship squads throughout high school.

SPORTS AS ESCAPE

As a youngster, you sometimes sense when things are not right at home, especially if it concerns your mom. I must have been eleven or twelve when I noticed that my mother's energy was beginning to disappear. Perhaps in my subconscious I knew there was something terribly wrong, but rather than face it, I sought my comfort zones. Playing sports was one of them.

Since I was my mom's firstborn child, she naturally found much joy in my accomplishments. I sensed there would be limited time to provide her with such joy, so I focused on what was important to her—my grades—and soon became an honor roll student. But what I enjoyed most and what became my magical escape from it all was sports. I loved playing them, and I loved being a fan.

My release came from watching and listening to Red Sox, Bruins, and Celtics games. It is no secret among Boston Red Sox fans that we must all appreciate the smaller accomplishments that a season brings rather than the ultimate results. This no doubt had an influence on the Fair Play philosophy.

I am sad to say my grandfather never lived to see his beloved Red Sox win it all, and I'm becoming more concerned that I may never get that opportunity, either. But we both loved every minute of those seasons. Each home run, strikeout, and double play made an imprint in my mind. The 1967, 1975, and 1986 teams went as far as they could go, only to disappoint us all in the World Series. But we were never disappointed enough not to appreciate the entire season.

They say boyhood dreams die hard. In my case, I always wanted to be a professional athlete. I pictured myself playing for the Red Sox, but my .200 batting average in high school vanquished those ambitions.

I had good speed, but so far it had surfaced only in hockey and football. Like my son, my football experience started early in high school when I began playing in my freshman year. Though I had no prior experience, a physical education teacher persuaded me to join his freshman football team.

"You'll see plenty of playing time with that speed," he told me. He repeated this every time I saw him—until I showed up for the first day of practice.

As a new player I needed plenty of instruction, but I didn't see a minute of time on the field. I watched from the sideline until my sophomore year. When I realized that nonstarting players would not receive any coaching, I knew my efforts were futile.

I then turned my attention to baseball and track, using my speed to become a state sprint champion. From there I went to Syracuse University and ran varsity track as a middle-distance runner. I earned four letters and saw my fair share of glory by running in the Penn Relays at Franklin Field in Philadelphia and the Millrose Games at Madison Square Garden in New York City.

Sadly, the majority of my athletic accomplishments came after I turned seventeen and my mom was already gone.

AN EARLY LESSON

The roots of Fair Play can also be traced to my experiences in becoming a baseball umpire at the age of seventeen. Despite playing on the high school varsity team as a starting outfielder, I still had strong feelings about baseball's youth leagues and liked the idea of being involved. But even at that young age I could see there were some underlying problems.

First of all, young players were judged on one tryout and were generally placed in a single position so they learned only one dimension of the game. They inevitably became labeled as an outfielder, catcher, first baseman, or benchwarmer.

Youth league games were boring beyond belief. You waited endlessly while some poor kid tried to pitch the ball over the plate. It wasn't his fault if he couldn't pitch, because no one had the knowledge or had taken the time to teach him the proper pitching mechanics. The limited instruction that coaches gave players was outweighed tenfold by the pride these adults took when by chance their team won a game. Parents set up their lawn chairs and voiced their opinions like a pack of disappointed season-ticket holders. It was only a game, after all, but for the grown-ups there seemed always to be more on the line.

This was such a contrast to my own backyard and empty lot games where everyone played and we constantly switched positions. Then we didn't need a scoreboard to have fun.

Still, being an umpire taught me a lesson I'll never forget. Given what was going on at home and my high school baseball experience, at seventeen I had a lot of knowledge of the game. I also had a seasoned thick skin. I therefore tried to remain unfazed during games when I heard people holler at me: "Are you blind?" and "What are you looking at? Get in the game!" One of my family members had prepared me for the job by introducing me to a major-league umpire. The man explained, "Remember, as an umpire, you are never the star. People will always hassle you, and you have to ignore it." I had the knack.

But then one day I made a call that nearly caused a riot. I can't recollect whether it was a strike when it should have been a ball or vice versa, but somehow I made a mistake and blew the call. One of the coaches ran up to me and started poking his finger into my chest. I asked him to stop, but he didn't, so I threw him out of the game. All of a sudden I began to feel hard objects stinging my back and legs. The parents in the stands were throwing rocks at me. They harassed me until the end of the game and even followed me as I walked to my car in the parking lot.

Considering the current state of violence in youth sports, I'm grateful nothing more serious happened. At least I didn't have to go to the emergency room. It was a scary, miserable experience, and I made this mental note: Something is very wrong with this picture, and somebody ought to do something about it. Little did I know that it would become my career.

WORKING IN SPORTS

I graduated from Syracuse in 1982 with a bachelor's degree in broadcast journalism. If I wasn't going to play professionally, I wanted to report on sports and do play-by-play. But I soon learned that finding a job like that was as rare as landing a starring role in a movie.

In 1986, after working at several advertising agencies in New York City, I landed a job that truly launched my career in youth sports development. I became the director of the United States Soccer Federation's marketing arm, Soccer USA Partners. There I developed marketing plans for the U.S. National and World Cup teams.

The job led me to found my own firm, called City Block Sports, through which I marketed the U.S. Women's National Soccer team. At City Block I represented such players as Mia Hamm, the world's best known and most talented female soccer player. I also created and directed City Block Soccer, an inner-city player development program for boys and girls ages five to fourteen. Mia and her teammates, including Kristine Lilly, Carla Overbeck, and Shannon Higgins, were of great assistance with the program.

We pulled off an unprecedented feat by holding a completely free one-week camp for girls from communities in need throughout New York City. All the instructors were members of the World Championship team. The program we set up eventually ran in all five boroughs of New York City and in Boston, Baltimore, and Chicago, and it attracted more than fifteen thousand boys and girls.

While continuing my soccer activities I joined what I believe is one of the best active lifestyle magazines in the business, *Outside,* as marketing director. Larry Burke, the owner and then publisher, had a vision to launch a kid's version of his magazine. *Outside Kids* would celebrate the free play of children.

Larry's forward-thinking ideas and energy attracted me to the project, but two years into the venture I received a surprise call from the NFL. It was an offer I could not pass up. *Outside Kids,* after struggling in a volatile business climate, was absorbed into the special issues department after I left. To this day I still believe that Larry was right on target in his mission to give kids the chance to read about other kids enjoying outside activities.

Despite playing a role in soccer's emergence in the 1980s and 1990s, I was hungry to do more for youth sports. When the NFL offered me the job opportunity, I knew I would have the resources and the credibility to do some very special things. From Pete Rozelle to Paul Tagliabue, the NFL has personified leadership both on and off the athletic field.

When I started at the NFL in 1995, there were 250,000 kids registered for "Punt, Pass & Kick," the skills competition. If you were into football as a kid, you probably remember competing in local "PP&K" contests or watching the finalists from around the country compete during a nationally televised playoff game.

Today, approximately *four million* kids nationwide are registered in one of five NFL Youth Programs. Our success has been focused primarily on providing alternative ways for kids to learn and play the game. We also give coaches easy access to programs and tools to run these programs. Today it is not uncommon to see as many girls as boys participating in NFL programs, and a growing number of women and moms are coaching.

The NFL provided me with a larger stage to incorporate the Fair Play philosophy that had been developing in my mind over the years. If the concepts of Fair Play can turn around a sport that is as steeped in tradition as football, I believe it can work for any child.

WHY I WROTE THIS BOOK

When my time is up, I want to be known as someone who tried to accomplish things for kids and make their lives better. We have all been painfully reminded, very close to home, that life is fragile and brief. As adults it is our responsibility to restore one of the lost treasures of childhood—free play.

The adult structures we have all adhered to in the past and have subjected our kids to are outdated and broken. If we don't fix the youth sports experience, it will be your child who gets cheated. Fair Play can be the blueprint for positive change.

I didn't write this book to persuade you to place your children in football programs. I hope our NFL youth programs serve that goal. I wrote it to extend the principles of Fair Play to kids nationwide. No matter what sport your children play, Fair Play will change their youth sports experience for the better. It provides a method for every child to improve, regardless of athletic ability. Your children will make their own decisions about which position to play. And they will no longer lose interest in sports and turn into couch potatoes, victims of today's sedentary lifestyle.

Over the past two decades I have created, tested, tinkered with, and perfected a philosophy of structural change for youth sports. Fair Play provides proven, innovative, and easy-to-incorporate methods that will improve your child's sports experience.

The idea for this book was born that day in the park with my wife and infant son. I knew the philosophy worked, and I knew it could affect many children positively, including my very own toddler. The only way I knew to reach out to you, a parent, was to write this book.

After discussing *Fair Play* with friends, I decided to donate my portion of the proceeds to the Boomer Esiason Foundation to fight cystic fibrosis. Boomer, a former Cincinnati Bengal, New York Jet, and Arizona Cardinals quarterback, is now a national radio and television NFL commentator and analyst. He has been a steadfast supporter not only of youth football but also of the fight to find a cure for CF. Boomer's son, Gunnar, is afflicted with the disease. Along with many of Boomer's friends, I am committed to helping in any way I can to find that cure in Gunnar's lifetime.

What follows is dedicated to my children and yours. May they all rediscover the joys of fair play throughout their lifetimes.

—Scott Lancaster
August 2002

1

UNLEASH THE REVOLUTION:
The Time for Change and Action in Youth Sports

Poor quality of play, inequitable playing time, little or no emphasis on fundamental skills, a lack of qualified coaches, plus adult interference, intimidation, and overinvolvement. All organized youth sports face problems that are eroding their participation base and ultimately robbing kids of the opportunity to achieve and improve—and to just have fun.

My goal in *Fair Play* is to provide solutions to these problems and others by offering a new model for youth sports. If you are a parent with kids involved in sports, this book will give you a blueprint for dramatically improving your children's overall experience. By learning the new approaches laid out in these chapters and sharing them with other parents, you will be able to create a better learning environment for young athletes. Whether you are a dad or mom coaching your child's sports team or a parent who just enjoys watching your kids play, this book will show you how to become better informed and make your children's participation in sports more enjoyable.

THE NEED FOR A BRAND-NEW APPROACH

There are many factors that make it difficult for parents to truly get involved in kids' sports, such as time constraints, personal commitments, and a perceived lack of knowledge. *Fair Play* takes all of these factors into consideration and provides an easy-to-follow plan that will give you and your child the tools to properly learn the basics of a sport, produce positive experiences, and achieve lifelong results.

Perhaps, like me, you are the parent of a young child, and worry about how your child will fare when he or she is ready to participate in sports. With all the negative stories we hear today about what is taking place on our children's playing fields, the time has come for a new and proven structure that removes the negative aspects from youth sports and substitutes positive ones.

There is already more than enough conversation and editorial comment about what is wrong with youth sports. In the past few years there have been several high-profile examples of how adults have all but ruined sports for children. In the 2001 Little League World Series, a parent deliberately falsified his son's birth certificate, allowing the fourteen-year-old to play in a twelve-and-under international tournament. In another shocking incident a parent in Massachusetts beat a hockey coach to death after a practice. Yet even with all these unsettling stories, there is still no positive action. You will still spend many hours driving your kids to practices and games, and instead of standing on a field of dreams, you will experience disappointment, frustration, and possibly fear.

Without a doubt the world is more dangerous today than when we were children, and we are not as comfortable as our parents were about sending our kids off unsupervised. Unfortunately, the joy of casual play has suffered as a result. Organized sports need to make up the difference by providing safe learning environments without stifling the joys of spontaneous play. But the way many parents and coaches behave has made this all but impossible.

Youth sports activists have made many attempts to institute certain reforms by lecturing parents and children on how to behave at games and practices. In fact, "Silent Sundays" have been instituted by some leagues where parents must sit on their hands and button their lips so as not to disrupt athletic events. In these programs, parents are asked to take courses in ethics and sign pledges to be models of spectator decorum.

While efforts like these are noble in intent, they have yet to produce any measurable results primarily because the problems they seek to resolve run far deeper than organizers care to admit. The very structure of how team sports are organized, taught, and implemented is at the root of the appalling widespread difficulties we have read about and witnessed. The most compelling evidence can be found in the fact that your kids and their friends continue to experience:

- No significant improvement in their skills and on-field performance.

- Practices that are disorganized and boring.

- Warming the bench without an equal opportunity to play and sometimes not playing at all.

- A 15 percent chance that violence will break out at their games or practices.

- A 75 percent chance that they will drop out of sports by the age of twelve.

Youth sports are, unfortunately, a monumental stage for adult entertainment and fulfillment. Whether it's to relive their childhood or erase their past athletic disappointments, some parents expect their children to excel at sports in order to right their own pasts. Until we demand that our children not be pawns in our own or someone else's personal interactive drama, we have failed them.

In order to improve youth sports and eliminate the negatives, kids must not be forced to play adult versions of games. We must change the structure of how kids learn and play. That structure is Fair Play.

This is not a gimmick. Fair Play does not require you to sign codes of proper behavior or attend workshops in applying common sense. Fair Play is a blueprint of practical applications that have been proven to work. You can acquire these methods from these pages and begin using them today, not only to improve youth sports but also to improve your child's athletic capabilities and attitudes toward participating now and in the future.

Fair Play will teach you a brand-new way to change youth sports in your community that will improve your child's athletic ability and overall experience. Your family will find new enjoyment in the time you spend together involved in sports.

THE SEVEN PRINCIPLES OF FAIR PLAY

Many years ago, prior to joining the NFL, I developed seven principles that guided me in the development of youth sports programs. These principles, the heart of the Fair Play philosophy, became the foundation for the programs I created in soccer and football. They can provide the structure needed to change today's ineffective youth programs. Incorporate the seven principles, and you will revolutionize the sports experience for your child and others.

Principle One: Make It Fun

Principle one is the primary objective and cornerstone of the entire philosophy. Every moment of the experience, from practices to games, should be fun. We will discuss how to be well organized and creative in designing drills to test skill development that are more contemporary than the traditional methods used since we were children.

Principle Two: Limit Standing Around

Idle time spent standing around is a common problem in youth sports. It ultimately turns kids off and ruins the first principle: Make it fun. Many professional teams and coaches place a major emphasis on fast-paced interactive practices that eliminate downtime. The secret is to have a plan and to be well organized every time you step on the field. This book provides examples and methods that apply to any sport.

Principle Three: Everyone Plays

Youth sports should be an inclusive experience. It is never fun to sit and watch others play while waiting for the distant opportunity to get in the game if the situation arises. The Fair Play structure eliminates first, second, and third strings, and allows everyone to play equally and receive more playing time than any traditional youth program.

Principle Four: Teach Every Position to Every Participant

Don't pigeonhole kids into one particular position because of their physical size or ability. In order to provide each participant a full experience and an appreciation for the game that lasts a lifetime, you should teach each player every position. If kids are taught the fundamentals of each position, over time they will find the position where they belong naturally, rather than having an adult dictate where they will play.

Principle Five: Emphasize the Fundamentals

A classic mistake made in many youth programs, even at the elite level, is that coaches become overly concerned with scheming and scrimmaging but forget to teach. Ralph Friedgen, University of Maryland's head football coach and the 2001 NCAA Coach of the Year, describes it best: "Coaches at every level of the game at times lose focus on how important the fundamentals of football are. We all become involved in drawing the X's and O's and scrimmaging when we need to get back to teaching blocking and tackling, the basics of the game."

Build a foundation that will never crack by teaching the basics properly. Learning the fundamentals and perfecting the basics at every level are essential to future success.

Principle Six: Incorporate a Progression of Skill Development for Every Participant

Regardless of skill level, every child should be provided a learning environment that measures and assures improvement. It's no secret that when kids experience improvement, no matter their athletic ability, they will continue to participate and return to learn more in order to build on their progress. Fair Play provides tools for coaches and youth teams to improve everyone's skill level.

Principle Seven: Yell Encouragement; Whisper Constructive Criticism

Keep it positive. Coaches, volunteers, and parents should not tolerate negative comments from anyone involved in the program. Kids realize when they have made a mistake. What they don't need is to have mistakes compounded by negative feedback and comments. Instead, they need instruction on how to correct mistakes that is supported by positive encouragement.

ARE YOU READY TO TRY SOMETHING DIFFERENT?

Whether you are a coach, parent, teacher, or an individual who volunteers your time to assist kids in sports, try to approach this book with an open mind. Many of the concepts are quite different from what you experienced growing up, what your children presently experience, and what we all are accustomed to when watching our favorite professional team compete.

We all have been brought up believing the notion that youth sports must replicate what we see in the pros. A majority of youth sports quickly advance to the adult version of the game in order to satisfy our desire to experience what we watch on television. We forget the extraordinary length of time it takes a professional athlete to prepare for each season and the countless hours spent on the fundamentals throughout the year.

There is a lot we don't see or understand that goes on behind the scenes in professional sports, such as repetitive drills, scoreless scrimmages, and hours spent in front of a chalkboard or watching videotaped games. We also forget that what we see on television is a form of entertainment. Our desire to be entertained by sports has led to harmful methods of coaching and, ultimately, poor results.

It is time to open your mind to alternative methods. Forget about recording three outs, three strikes, four balls, and errors. Don't expect to see first downs, touchdowns, or penalty flags. Eliminate from your mind offsides, penalty kicks, and yellow cards. And, most important, forget first, second, and third strings. The single most dreaded aspect of all youth sports is "the bench."

The concepts you will learn and read about in this book are designed to allow equal play and learning. The least talented will be instructed and play as much as the most talented, and each child will progress at his or her own pace, never at the expense of another.

Stop measuring success in runs, touchdowns, goals, or baskets. Instead, measure success when everyone on your team and in your league experiences improvement regardless of athletic ability. Imagine everyone on your team and in your entire league experiencing all aspects of the sport equally while receiving more attempts and repetitions than any traditional "adult-oriented" setting would ever allow.

The goal is to let kids improve and develop in all aspects of a sport, to introduce each participant to every position, and to allow each child to determine independently which position he or she would like to play. The methods described here will give kids the opportunity to test themselves individually and in group situations, and under consistent instructional supervision that responds as quickly to success as to failure. The lessons must be continually reinforced through positive feedback.

HOW TO USE THIS BOOK

There are multiple ways for you to use this book. Parents should discuss some or all of the alternative methods with their children's coaches and league administrators, and apply these lessons to your own kids in your backyard or neighborhood park. If you're a youth coach or league administrator, you can use *Fair Play* as a model for restructuring your entire program or simply take selected parts that fit your needs. If you're a baseball coach or league manager, for example, you may want to apply the concepts of this book to an off-season fall or winter program.

I recommend that all youth sports programs begin to restructure their methods to emphasize progression of skill development for every participant through fun, kid-friendly instruction, drills, and competitions. The adult version of sports does not produce maximum results for a majority of kids. I have spent the past fourteen years developing youth sports programs for the nation's largest sports organizations. I have spent the past seven years with the country's most recognized professional sports organization, the National Football League. At the NFL we discovered that even a sport steeped in tradition needs to reinvent itself at the youth level in order to pass along its legacy to the next generation.

To a large extent youth sports have been taught in the same way for the past century, but kids have obviously changed over the years. The challenge for traditional sports such as baseball, football, and basketball has been to keep the games contemporary in their approach to teaching. Though sports fundamentals remain essentially the same, the methods used to teach or play them do not.

Let's take, for example, the recent success of individual action sports or so-called extreme sports such as skateboarding, BMX biking, and snowboarding. The common link of these sports that attract hundreds of thousands of kids is their individualism; in addition, they engross kids in fundamentals. Children spend hours attempting to execute complex routines by breaking them down into a progression of fundamental elements. This is today's version of athletic development for kids, and every traditional team and individual sport must learn from it in order to stay current.

If you watch skateboarders, snowboarders, or BMX riders at play, you will discover that they spend hours practicing one skill over and over, never seeming to get bored. The secret is that they measure success by experiencing improvement in their skill through the pride of trying, not through the fear of failing. Very often they receive positive reinforcement from their peers. If you go to any skate park in the country, you will witness intense conversations taking place among the participants about the fundamental executions of skills.

I will show you how to borrow the approach of these contemporary sports to skill development and apply them to traditional youth sports. By helping kids work on fundamental skills you will become successful as a coach, involved parent, teacher, or youth volunteer. As adults we seem to miss the message that kids enjoy focusing on the fundamentals in order to improve in a way that makes sense to them. *Fair Play* introduces a new, more entertaining approach to teaching fundamentals that allows each participant to progress at his or her own pace. It incorporates the old playground adage of "the do-over."

WHAT WILL WE ACCOMPLISH?

Traditional youth sports have always been based on an adult model—the "draft" system and the anxiety-provoking pressure to win—that is entirely inappropriate for children. They have neither the musculature nor the cognitive ability to play adult games with any hope of success. Our new model takes as its starting point children's developing bodies and emotional vulnerabilities.

Wouldn't it be nice to stop talking about doing something to improve youth sports and actually start building programs that eliminate the problems? Wouldn't it be wonderful if our children could participate in programs that do not have to police out-of-control coaches and parents? With nothing to win or lose, there would be little for adults to fight about. By adopting the basic philosophies of Fair Play—everyone plays and learns every position, points are awarded for improvement, the instant do-over becomes the norm, and there is no scoreboard—you will see a real difference in how everyone behaves and reacts. You can look forward to the following:

- Kids will have more fun and will be more likely to stay involved.

- Parents will see improvement in their kids' skill development and competitive performance.

- Parents will have more realistic hopes for their children.

- Violence and inappropriate behavior will be eliminated.

- Youth sports will become a place to reinforce life skill messages.

- Total time spent will be reduced and more effectively spent.

One challenge to implementing this alternative to youth sports lies in the hands of a few adults. There will always be those who refuse to coach anything other than the "adult version" of a sport, no matter what age group they are coaching. These people get no satisfaction out of coaching in a setting that does not allow them to playact the role of a professional coach. This is where you as a parent must believe in the alternative structure and find others like you who are committed to implementing the methods prescribed in this book. Remember, anyone who disagrees will have plenty of opportunity to coach or place their children elsewhere.

One of the worst scenarios in youth sports involves an adult who insists on having his way, often for his own satisfaction and at the expense of the experience of the kids. You can avoid these issues as a coach, parent, or youth league organizer by establishing in specific detail the objectives of the structure to be used and the boundaries within which you will be working. The proven structures in this book will give you all the parameters needed to run a successful program.

If you are serious about providing your children with the highest quality sports program, you will find that Fair Play is an easy-to-use plan that:

- Improves the skills and performance of all participants.

- Allows for more effective use of your time.

- Eliminates the negative aspects of sports that we continue to read about and witness.

2

REGAINING THE ROAD:
Sports and the Journey Through Childhood

Your children's athletic development should be thought of as a journey, one that begins when they first participate in sports and continues throughout their lives. What they experience along the way should include a strong sense of camaraderie with their teammates, a sustained improvement of their skills, and an appreciation for even the smallest of accomplishments, whether they be individual, group, or team. But the momentum that will carry them forward is their enjoyment of each moment they spend engaged in the sport.

Children in their developmental athletic years, ages six to fourteen, should never despise going to practice or fear participating in a game. Yet most kids, even the best athletes, have given their parents a hard time about going to practice. This is a clear sign that the current system is failing. For all the positive reasons we want our children to participate in sports, a majority of the time these values are ineffectively provided, resulting in kids walking away from sports altogether.

EVEN TRACK PRACTICE CAN BE FUN

I mentioned earlier that I ran on the track team at Syracuse University. It was tremendously exciting to compete at the college level, especially at Syracuse, a Division One program that competes against many of the best teams in the nation. But I will never forget the awful anticipation I felt before each practice.

You might wonder how anyone could actually ever enjoy track practice. At that time I believed in the popular saying "No pain, no gain." That was until I encountered a coach I came to truly admire, a man who launched me on the path to developing alternative and nontraditional methods of participating in sports. That person is Mike Woicik, whom I still proudly consider my coach. Mike is currently the strength and conditioning coach for the New England Patriots, and served in the same capacity with the New Orleans Saints and the Dallas Cowboys. But before Mike coached at the professional level, he was an assistant track coach at Syracuse.

When I first joined the track team at Syracuse, our head coach easily could have been labeled the "Bobby Knight of track and field." His style of coaching included unpredictable verbal outbursts, ceaseless profanity, and "in-your-face" tactics he would call motivation but the rest of us considered pure intimidation. If he was displeased with the performance of any of his athletes, he would intentionally ignore the person in front of the whole team; he would do the same if the person tried to speak with him in private.

Here we were, college athletes far away from home, dedicating all our nonacademic time to training and fighting for the top spots on the team, and our coach played childish head games with us if we had a single bad day. Practices were completely predictable—always the same schedule for each day of the week—and they were always brutally difficult. As a result, when it came time for the actual meets, the entire team looked flat, felt unmotivated, and never ran well. By the middle of the season, practices had become unbearable, and the team was in complete disarray. In order to run well at meets, many of the athletes began to fake injuries during the week just to rest up for their races.

That all changed when Mike Woicik joined the team as the assistant coach my sophomore year; he was assigned specifically to work with the field athletes. I remember the jealousy all the runners felt when we witnessed how much fun the field athletes were having with Mike. Not only did their practices become something they all looked forward to, but their performances began to improve dramatically.

Mike brought to Syracuse a training routine of plyometrics and circuit training that increased strength, speed, and agility. At the time the unorthodox method of plyometrics was a combination of jumping and leaping drills designed to increase explosiveness in specific muscle groups, improving an athlete's overall speed and power. In addition to introducing new training techniques, Mike led his practices in an organized fashion designed to be fun while still accomplishing major goals for each athlete.

The circuit training was a way of structuring a practice whereby athletes could focus with maximum effort on different muscle groups by participating in a number of different drills with little rest in between. The practices were fast-paced and nontraditional, and did not consist of the same repetitive exercises that we were accustomed to in a traditional track practice.

Both plyometrics and circuit training are widespread in gyms across the country today, but back then they were being taught on only a limited basis.

When our head coach went away on a recruiting trip, we runners finally were given the opportunity to work with Mike. He created a training routine for us that worked on all phases of our athletic abilities and used alternative methods to achieve the results that our traditional training routines had failed to produce. Practices became competitive in a fun way, and we focused on different aspects or functions of our bodies for a specific period of time before switching to another drill. Despite the strange looks that the Syracuse basketball team would give us while they practiced simultaneously at Manley Field House, you could often find us at practice jumping up and down onto boxes of different heights, or in skipping, leaping, and bounding drills. And to break it up, Mike would incorporate different competitive games between small groups that worked together throughout practice.

As a direct result of Mike's innovations, we became better overall athletes. We performed better at meets, and, most important, our attitudes improved.

Suddenly, it was fun to go to practice because we didn't know what new training routine or competition Mike would introduce on any given day. Mike used alternative methods at the elite level of a sport to transform what had been an extremely traditional training regimen into an entirely enjoyable experience. Soon even the basketball team adopted Mike's training routine.

More important than the new training methods he introduced was the fact that Mike cared about each one of us as athletes and as people. He successfully created an entire journey that we could recall with fondness for the rest of our lives.

START THE JOURNEY RIGHT

As a college athlete I witnessed firsthand the impact that good coaching and innovative training techniques had on my performance and experience. But the importance of such a positive journey for young athletes is multiplied. If they are discouraged or are not engaged in all aspects of their activity, they will not learn, improve, or receive the many benefits that sports can deliver over a lifetime.

Fair Play offers a program structure that allows all children the opportunity to enjoy every practice, every game, and every moment of their journey.

Skeptics might question how this is possible. To these people, sports must have those who succeed and those who fail, those who start and those who rarely play. There must be winners and losers; otherwise, is there any point to playing?

The answer is yes. Just because almost every youth program subscribes to the "adult model" of the sport does not mean it is the right way to teach our children. There is a proven "kids model" that does not distinguish who plays or gets the most instruction. There is a model where no first, second, or third strings exist, yet the kids experience more firsthand competition than they ever would in other programs. Even more important, there is a way in which no final score is posted on a scoreboard to give adults a reason to judge their children. In our programs everyone succeeds by improving his or her skills beyond what any traditional youth program could achieve.

The new structure is based on a philosophy taken from my fourteen years in youth sports development, which also included studying with, working with, and borrowing from the best methods of some of the greatest coaches and teachers in sports, including such individuals as:

BILL WALSH, three-time Super Bowl Championship coach of the San Francisco 49ers.

JOHN WOODEN, fabled former head basketball coach of UCLA and winner of an unrivaled ten National Championships (including seven in a row).

PETE CARROLL, head football coach of the University of Southern California and former head coach of the New York Jets and New England Patriots.

PAUL PASQUALONI, head football coach of Syracuse University.

JOE PATERNO, head football coach of two-time National Champion Pennsylvania State University, with more than three hundred career victories and the only college coach to win nineteen bowl games.

We will discuss how these successful coaches use creative and nontraditional methods with their teams and athletes. They will explain why what you see at the highest levels of competition is not necessarily what your children should experience to get the best results.

MAKING SPORTS FUN

What do you recall from your own sports experiences as a child? Can you even remember your team's league record? Probably not. Instead, you might remember hitting a line drive off the sweet spot of a bat, making a challenging fingertip catch, watching your long-range jump shot drop magically through the net, or hearing the ball fly off the club when you hit a perfect golf shot.

If you were very fortunate, you had the opportunity to experience those moments in real competition. The majority of us, however, executed these great moves while playing around with our friends in our backyards or local courts. If you played organized sports, most likely you remember being unable to hit a curve ball, missing tackles, not fully understanding the defensive plan, or missing a wide-open layup. A great number of us remember that no one ever really taught us or gave us enough time to learn how to execute these skills. If someone had, perhaps we would have been able to recreate the fun we had in our informal backyard experiences while playing organized sports.

Fair Play, the program that eliminates negative elements and emphasizes positive experiences, can be applied to any sport. Whether your child is involved in a team sport, such as basketball, baseball, lacrosse, or soccer, or an individual sport, such as tennis, swimming, or track and field, Fair Play's methods will show how it is possible to change your child's sports experience for the better. When one young player is transformed positively by an athletic experience, so are the other members of his team and ultimately his community.

I have had the opportunity to study many aspects of youth behavior and trends in sports during my career. I've also examined a mountain of literature on the subject. One of the most compelling items I've come across is a 1999 *Sports Illustrated for Kids* trend study tracking kids' participation in sports. One of the questions posed to the children in the study was "Why do you play sports?" The answers they provided may surprise you:

It's fun	75%
For exercise	22%
To be with friends	18%
For fitness	12%
For the competition	9%
To stay out of trouble	7%
To be popular	6%

Fun is the overwhelming reason that kids choose to play sports, and competition is nearly the least important. No matter how much a parent encourages or pushes a child to participate in sports, the kids will get involved because they want to have fun with their friends. The trouble for kids begins when they start playing and find that they are not having a good time. Over the years I've asked the kids I work with what they dislike about sports. Their answers include the following:

Too much standing around.
Never get to play as much as others.
Practices are boring.
Never improve or learn anything.
Parents and coaches are too focused on winning.

Unfortunately, we register our kids in programs that are taught by coaches whose primary qualification is that their own child is on the team. In other words, we register our children in programs to have fun and learn new skills, but we place them in situations that are bound to disappoint and discourage them.

The *Sports Illustrated for Kids* study reported that only 20 percent of youth coaches had any training. A National Alliance for Youth Sports study found that the average youth sports coach spends eighty hours per season with his players. So four out of five of all youth coaches have no training whatsoever, yet they spend eighty hours instructing our children. This is clearly a recipe for disaster. The problems are compounded when our children sign up for contact sports such as football, lacrosse, and hockey. Would you bring your child to a karate school to be taught by an instructor whose only qualification is that he watches Bruce Lee films?

Back in the late 1980s and early 1990s, when soccer participation was beginning to grow in large numbers, I worked with members of the U.S. Women's National Soccer Team to develop youth programs at a grassroots level. During this period I often asked kids why they chose to play soccer over other sports. The most common answer was that their parents did not understand the sport, so they could not be as critical of them when they played.

The rise in individual nontraditional action sports should come as no surprise to anyone. Kids nationwide have found refuge in such sporting activities as skateboarding, BMX biking, and snowboarding. Consider the elements in these activities that appeal to kids more than traditional sports programs:

- No need to register to participate

- No required practices

- No adults telling them what to do or not do

- No scoreboard

- No sitting on the bench watching while others deemed worthier participate

There is also a great freedom about these activities that allows participants to be creative in developing their own individual styles of play while using the fundamentals of the sport as their foundation. Kids who participate in these sports seem to have a more widespread dedication to learning the basics and perfecting them alone or with the help of friends. Even more important, they always find ways to make the entire process fun.

Participating in these sports seems to be the new generation's version of free play. Kids gather by the dozens at parks, schoolyards, and parking lots to spend hours perfecting specific moves and working on the basics of their individual technique. More and more communities, through their parks and recreation departments, have built skate parks for kids to use for skateboarding and in-line trick skating. Though none of these activities seems organized or has official schedules or practices, they are very organized on an individual basis. Kids show up consistently in pairs, groups, or individually. They progress at their own pace without the presence of their parents or a coach.

How should you translate the trends and contemporary methods that have captured the attention of today's youth and apply them to your child's traditional sports experience? By carefully examining the problems in traditional youth sports and restructuring programs that work for today's kids. We can achieve success by developing new tools for parents, coaches, and youth organizers. The lessons of Fair Play can be incorporated into programs for kids that also preserve an important adult commodity—time.

Let's explore an approach to teaching that allows even the youngest of players to grasp the fundamentals of team sports while still having a great time on the field.

TEACHING DIFFERENT AGE GROUPS

The basic concepts of a sport apply no matter what the age of the athlete. In fact, most professionals participate in many of the same drills as youth players. But age is a critical factor when it comes to teaching and explaining the skills and the methods used to conduct the drills.

Ages Five to Eight: Getting Started

For children under eight, skill development should be introduced in the form of fun games, and limited instruction should be applied in short sessions. At the NFL we needed to find an appropriate entry-level activity for kids ages five to eight to teach the concepts of football. We determined that helmets, pads, and any type of contact were unsuitable for this age group. As an alternative, we adopted a game used by many college football teams as a fun break from the everyday drag of practices that is also a useful conditioning activity.

We call the game NFL Ultimate, and one of the reasons we use it is because any number of players can be actively involved in the game at the same time. No maximum or minimum number of players is needed, every player gets to touch the ball, and there are no set positions. Yet the game still incorporates the basic execution of football skills such as passing, catching, handing off, running with the ball, and getting open. NFL Ultimate borrows from many different sports, including soccer, basketball, rugby (minus the contact), ultimate Frisbee, and football. Coaches are on the field to make corrections and maintain the flow of the game, but they are also there to make sure that everyone is having fun.

NFL Ultimate is played on a field fifty yards long by about thirty yards wide with as many as twenty kids on the field at any one time. A team must move a junior-size rubber football continuously from teammate to teammate by throwing or handing off in any direction. There is no line of scrimmage, and the object is to score a touchdown in the opposite end zone. Once a player receives the ball, she can move only two steps before passing it along. Change of possession takes place when the team on offense drops the ball or throws or drops the ball out of bounds, or the ball is intercepted.

In NFL Ultimate, everyone learns basic skills and competes equally, and the game is simple enough for all to understand. For children at this age level even flag football can be too challenging with its set strategies and complicated passing plays. In NFL Ultimate, every kid can learn, execute, and enjoy success.

Ages Nine to Eleven: Imitating Their Heroes

Ages nine to eleven mark another important milestone in the development of young players. At these ages, kids are much more aware of the world around them. Their coordination and comprehension improves, and their skills develop more rapidly. However, these also can be very difficult ages to coach. These kids are less likely to listen properly to what adults want them to do, and they begin exploring their own way of doing things. Coaches and parents must be smart and creative in order for the players to feel a sense of independence while still following directions and learning.

This is also the first stage in which imitation becomes a helpful teaching tool. Kids begin to mimic what they watch on television, like Ken Griffey's baseball swing or Mia Hamm's soccer dribbling technique. Take advantage of this newfound awareness and teach through proper demonstration of skills. As a coach it is essential that you understand fully the concept you are demonstrating. Be smart: Either find someone who can demonstrate properly or videotape a professional performing the same skill so the children have a proper model to emulate. But remember, don't overdo the process. Allow for plenty of playing time between instructional sessions. Although this is the first stage of advanced awareness, the children are still quite young.

Though this may be the stage of advancing skill development, it is not necessarily a time to begin playing traditional adult games. Too often in traditional games kids sit and watch while others perform, or they play in the game but are kept away from the action, as with outfielders in baseball or defenders in soccer and lacrosse.

Kids at this stage want to be active and have fun learning. You should teach skills in short, easy-to-understand segments that account for short attention spans. As you will find throughout this book, you can begin to introduce fundamental skills through a fast-paced instructional phase followed by a game or a competitive segment that involves everyone equally, with no one standing around watching while others perform.

Ages Twelve to Fifteen: Staying Involved

The next significant stage of development occurs in the twelve-to fifteen-year-old age group. Unfortunately, due to bad past experiences or changing interests, 75 percent of all kids drop out of organized sports by the age of twelve. Hopefully, we can reverse this trend through Fair Play's alternative program structures. We need to find ways to encourage kids to continue to participate rather than give up their athletic endeavors at such a young age.

As a coach and parent you should recognize the importance of providing consistent positive encouragement to children at this age. Most participants will reach puberty during this stage, and it is important to factor this into any sport equation. For example, a twelve-year-old boy may go through a drastic change in size, coordination, and overall athletic ability in a short period of time. It is important not to prejudge anyone at this age level.

At the same time, children in this age group are more receptive to coaching and are able to retain more information. Practices should be well organized and have a designated purpose that illustrates exactly what each participant is attempting to achieve. Each practice should be broken into small progressive segments to achieve specific goals of knowledge and ability. The newfound skills should then be applied in competitions that allow all participants to replicate what each has learned in real game situations.

Anyone serious about a career in coaching or having a positive impact on athletes should make a personal commitment to coach this age group. It is the best opportunity to impart to young athletes such crucial life skills as self-control, sportsmanship, responsibility, and setting goals. Though kids should be taught life skills throughout their development, this age level calls for a more sophisticated approach, one that we've had much success in applying. Later on, I will illustrate methods by which parents and coaches can weave these lessons into on-field development, creating a lasting impact on all participants.

The NFL's Junior Player Development program is based on the alternative methods and structures discussed throughout this book. Junior Player Development (JPD) was specifically designed for kids in the sixth to ninth grades (twelve to fifteen years old) who have never played football, as well as for first-time coaches learning to teach all aspects of the game. Our results include over 80 percent of our participants from more than thirty sites nationwide moving on to play high school football. After three years of training, many of our players have gone on to become starters and potential college athletes. We've also seen coaches who started in this program move on to head coaching positions at high schools. The middle school football system of the city of Houston—the heartland of football—uses all aspects of the program. New Orleans is launching a new junior high school football program through JPD. And we never played a single game of traditional football.

GOALS YOU CAN ACHIEVE

In the following chapters we will discuss specific ways to accomplish a number of goals that will fix or drastically improve your child's sports program. Your child will experience improvement in his fundamental skills and overall performance while having fun during both practice and competition.

Chapter 3 presents a blueprint of the NFL's Junior Player Development program. JPD represents the application of the Fair Play philosophy in a vibrant, hugely successful nationwide program. Players are introduced to the game of tackle football in an environment that eliminates intimidation, promotes individualism, and forsakes the traditional eleven-on-eleven game. Instead, as many as 144 kids at any one time become members of a single team that learns together, and the lessons are reinforced with competition segments that reward improvement. JPD can serve as a model for using Fair Play in your own sports program.

Chapter 4 discusses the elimination of negative coaching and poor parental behavior. We have all witnessed adult coaches and spectators standing on the sidelines acting negatively. Yet kids respond best to positive reinforcement, and if it is incorporated in a child's program, you will witness an accelerated improvement in her development. This chapter describes how to involve more parents in specific roles, how to change the role of the head coach and coaches in general, and how to restructure an entire league's season objectives by redesigning practices and changing the concept of the traditional game.

Chapter 5 hits at the core of the revolutionary changes we can make in children's sports programs. Here you will find a method of coaching that benefits all participants, no matter their skill level, by providing the experience needed to apply their fundamental skills in competition. Everyone is instructed and plays equally, and yet everyone receives more real game experience than in any program available to kids today.

This chapter debates the often-used draft system that kids experience when registering for a program. I question the relevance of the draft system and provide alternative methods to eliminate judgments before children receive appropriate training. It is time to challenge the present-day mind-set of a need to win, a philosophy primarily enjoyed by adults. In our programs, victories are measured through learning and collective improvement as a team.

Chapter 6 offers to keep an entire team's interest all season and for every practice. Often kids who participate on teams find themselves being neglected because they're not considered the most talented. Or the naturally talented child fails to receive adequate attention because the coach spends too much time helping weaker players. Due to time constraints and limited coaching experience, youth league coaches find that they neglect to engage everyone in learning and, as a result, fail to achieve team and individual goals for the season. This chapter explains in detail how to improve everyone's skill level through new organizational methods and an easy-to-implement structure.

Chapter 7 shows how there can be improvement for all levels of participants from beginners to "naturals." Kids lose interest and drop out in large numbers if they experience neither improvement nor positive reinforcement. This chapter focuses on how parents and coaches can apply the alternative methods in their backyards or at organized practices and games. You will see how the fundamentals of any sport can be broken down in an entertaining way, with the goal of producing significant improvement in a child's skill progression, regardless of his athletic ability. And, even more important, I explain how you can incorporate these methods in all aspects of the game for an entire team.

Chapter 8 discusses the leap that women can make from the stands to the sidelines. For too long dads have ruled the sidelines as their private domains. Women can offer a tremendous amount to youth sports as coaches, and we're going to need them if we hope to save organized sports for our children. In innovative programs such as the one we set up in Somers, New York, women are already learning how to coach tackle football. We'll talk to Mary DeCesare, the first female head football coach in New York, about her experiences running her program. I provide seven tips for those who want to coach but don't think they have the knowledge. Finally, we look at the challenges and opportunities of instructing the other gender, with the help of Terry Liskevych, who coached the U.S. Women's Volleyball Team for twelve years.

Chapter 9 looks at the rapid increase in sports participation among girls and how parents can navigate and circumvent the issues that have arisen from that growth. Soccer superstar Mia

Hamm describes what makes for a good coach and what she learned from playing with boys when she was growing up. Girls and boys learn and play together in different ways and may require different approaches from their coach.

Also, women's lacrosse world champion and Stanford head coach Michele Uhlfelder discusses athletic scholarships for girls and says college coaches may avoid an athlete who has pushy parents.

Chapter 10 covers the important topic of fulfilling the missed opportunity of life skill development. Conventional wisdom leads us to believe that sports teach kids important life messages. Unfortunately, this does not hold true for a majority of kids involved in youth programs today. Many teaching opportunities are missed or ruined when bad behavior and negative elements become more the norm than the exception. This chapter examines the successful incorporation of sportsmanship, responsibility, leadership, and other life skill messages into all aspects of practice and competitions and how this has produced successful results for kids nationwide.

FIXING THE JOURNEY

We live in a society that has made it necessary for parents to know where their children are and what they are doing at all times. As a result, kids are registered in expensive organized sports programs that lack the sense of freedom we enjoyed as kids through the joys of recreational play.

Because parents have become so closely involved in their children's activities, they often want to control the action on the field and the results of the game. Parents who are themselves driven to succeed every day in the workplace frequently put pressure on their children to do the same, forgetting that sports should be fun. As a result, parents can no longer distinguish their children's experiences from their own and fail to recognize that sports should be introduced, taught, and conducted differently when it comes to kids. Parents are sometimes filled with the belief that they must raise winners, beginning at the earliest levels of youth sports. They forget about the developmental stages and progression of learning that must take place in order for kids to perform in a capacity that will eventually produce adult achievements.

The good news is that there are ways for you as a parent to stay involved—and in a much more productive and interactive manner than in the current system. The structure and philosophy described in Fair Play will show you how to become involved without disrupting the fun that kids seek. Youth organizations now have the tools available to produce a program that specifically addresses the issues kids have with sports, a program that has been proven to achieve all the goals we want for our children via a richer, more fulfilling journey.

3

BLUEPRINT FOR CHANGE:
The NFL Junior Player Development Model

If there is one sport that exemplifies the issues confronting organized youth athletics today, it is football. In 1995 the NFL examined the state of the game at the youth level. Our results were not only alarming but confusing. Although kids identified football as their number one fan sport, very few actually played organized tackle football. Rather, they were involved in other organized sports, such as soccer, baseball, and basketball.

More than any other game, soccer is turning kids on. The reason will become apparent as you read on.

WHY SOCCER THRIVES

Prior to joining the NFL, I spent seven years developing youth soccer programs with the marketing arm of the United States Soccer Federation and independently with members of the U.S. Women's National Soccer Team. While developing programs in conjunction with top female athletes such as Mia Hamm and Kristine Lilly in the early to mid-1990s, I witnessed firsthand the growth of a sport on the grassroots level.

Soccer embodies everything that is right about youth sports. Everyone plays, positions are interchangeable, and there is plenty of continuous movement and action. The low-key nature and lack of pressure that accompanies the sport appeals to kids, and soccer has grown quickly in popularity.

In any given soccer match, even among the top players in the world, dozens of errors are committed. The very nature of continuous uninterrupted play creates these errors, yet the flow of the game allows all to forget the past sequence as players move on immediately to the next series of touches on the ball.

Because soccer was still so new to organized youth sports (and parents) in the United States, we found we could try almost anything in our programs. One thing we tried was soccer camps for girls only. Back in the early 1990s these were very difficult for parents to find. Within our camps we experimented further by not playing any eleven-on-eleven scrimmages or official games. Instead, we held competitions that focused on skills such as passing, in which three or five girls played on a short field against the same number of defenders. A team was not allowed to take a shot on goal until every player had touched the ball once or sometimes two or three times.

In the early stages of youth soccer, coaching was minimal; the game felt and looked like organized free play. Adults were present, but they had little to say or do but watch. The sport benefited from the fact that it was foreign to most adults. Rather than a group of critical parents showing up every weekend to disrupt the game with negative comments and actions, youth soccer became more of a community outing than any organized youth sports program.

Moms in lawn chairs and dads on the sidelines spent time observing but also caught up with neighbors and friends while their kids had fun entertaining themselves. As a result of all the positive experiences people were having, the sport thrived, and the number of participants today dwarfs that of most other organized sports.

TACKLING YOUTH FOOTBALL

Unlike soccer, youth football suffers perceptual problems that discourage a majority of parents from ever considering registering their child to play. Mothers especially, and many fathers as well, see football as too rough, too aggressive, and too likely to result in serious injury. In addition, many kids are turned away before they even start because youth football programs discriminate by imposing weight limits that either prevent a child from playing specific positions or disqualify the child from playing altogether.

When it comes to learning the game, practices provide no training in the fundamentals, and kids become frustrated when they fail to improve.

Even worse is the physical and brutal treatment many coaches place on their athletes, which at times borders on abuse. As former NFL quarterback Boomer Esiason remembers, "One of the greatest errors in coaching I ever witnessed was when I was nine years old. Our coach had us run thirty yards with another player on our back. That was our conditioning. I understand that you want to hammer home the important points of being physical and tough, but at nine years old it's just not about that. It made me want to quit the game, and I almost did."

It is not uncommon to see coaches lining young kids up ten yards apart for their first time in pads and telling them to run at each other and hit their teammates as hard as possible. In the coaches' minds this distinguishes who is tough enough to play, with no consideration for the fundamentals. Coaches like these do not spend any time teaching technique or introducing the elements of tackling; it's line them up and make them hit.

Jerry Horowitz, a successful Bronx high school coach for the past thirty years with several New York City and New York State championships to his credit, compared this practice to "taking a kid who has never learned how to swim and trying to teach him how to dive first. Can you imagine standing on top of a high board, unable to swim, and being told to jump into the pool? You would think the person telling you to do so was crazy. But that's what we do to kids in tackle football, and then we expect them to stick with the game."

These are all examples of why things have to change. And they will.

THE ROOTS OF JUNIOR PLAYER DEVELOPMENT

Assigned the task of turning around a sport steeped in tradition but handicapped by perception and reality, we created a program called NFL Junior Player Development. JPD is an introductory tackle football program that addresses a majority of the issues challenging not only football but most other youth sports as well.

Before we started JPD, we held numerous discussions with high school coaches, college recruiters, and college coaches, people who witnessed the sport firsthand every day and understood its basic issues. They agreed overwhelmingly that the feeder system which should have been producing trained football players was nonexistent, that the quality and football knowledge of potential players entering high school was poor, and that the number of next-generation coaches who were unprepared and unqualified was alarming. This seemed like an exaggerated perspective until we discovered that only 19 percent of all middle or junior high schools nationwide offer football programs, forcing coaches at the high school level to go back to the basics.

As Domenick Laurendi, head coach of Xaverian High School in Brooklyn, explained, "We are now faced with dedicating an entire practice to how to put the equipment on properly. Most incoming freshmen have never worn a helmet and pads or been taught the basics of tackling and blocking. We are essentially playing the role of the youth coach. No wonder our quality of play has suffered leaguewide."

Jerry Horowitz added, "Once, if you wanted to coach high school football, you had to get in line to fill out an application. This is no longer the case. Today you almost have to beg people to commit to coaching. There isn't even any official training or qualifications required to coach football. It's rather scary."

The coaches' message called for drastic changes to the traditional youth football structure and methods used to introduce, teach, and play the game. This meant redefining the role of the football coach by emphasizing the importance of teaching all the basics of the game. We took under consideration what kids enjoy and challenged every adult involved to produce an environment that encourages all participants to want to return. In essence we developed a structure that was nontraditional when compared to the one in which we had all participated as kids. But we also provided the tools that allowed coaches (whom we prefer to call instructors) to focus solely on teaching the fundamentals of all aspects of the game. In the end we created an organized system to train and recruit coaches for the youth level as well as provide a feeder system into higher levels of coaching.

The underlying problems we found in youth football are the same ones that face all organized youth sports today: poor quality of play, little emphasis on fundamentals, a lack of qualified coaches, unequal treatment, and a decline in participation. Even soccer, that wholesome activity that parents couldn't figure out just ten years ago, is now plagued with issues similar to every other sport.

I've certainly learned a lot from what we've experienced and developed at the NFL to improve youth football, and now I feel that Junior Player Development, along with other programs, can serve as a model to rescue and improve the majority of organized youth sports.

The JPD model can benefit every sport and player. It will engage all athletes and produce improvement in their skills and overall performance through a solid foundation of athletic appreciation that will last into adulthood. This revolutionary structure can make a difference for all parents who have issues with their kids' sports experience or have kids who have dropped out of sports and no longer seem interested.

THE MODEL FOR CHANGE

Football's established traditions provide an important background to the problems we continue to confront, including these:

■ The art of preparing for a fall season of games

- The essence of controlled violence through the act of using one's body or equipment as an instrument to stop or pass through an opponent

- The emphasis on touchdowns, first downs, elaborate schemes, and game planning

These are the integral parts that attract millions of fans each week to gather at NFL stadiums, not to mention the tens of millions who watch the games on television. Adult coaches attracted to youth football mimic these same elements. Imagine attempting to change this mind-set by radically changing the role for youth coaches. With this in mind you can put into perspective our challenge. It's likely you will face the same challenge when trying to adapt change in youth sports in your own community. Through the methods used in JPD, I have seen tradition-bound football accomplish significant change with results that have begun to turn around youth football from a gradual decline to a broad-based resurgence. You can certainly apply similar methods and structural changes to your child's youth sports program. The results will provide your children with a fulfilling experience in which they enjoy significant improvement in their athletic abilities and performances.

You don't have to take my word for it. Let's look at some of the kids who have gone through the JPD program successfully.

REAL-LIFE TESTIMONIALS

I met Seyit Tabaru at a JPD program at Lincoln High School in Brooklyn. He was by far the biggest kid on the field, and it was nearly impossible to find a helmet that fit him. Seyit, who is

Turkish, had never played football before he came to JPD. Now, as a high school sophomore, he is a starter on his varsity team and is passionate about the game.

"At first I didn't know anything about football," Seyit said. "Once I started JPD, they showed me the meaning of responsibility and leadership, and how football can help a person out. Learning the fundamentals at JPD was incredibly important to me because it got me ready for the next step in my life, high school. Before that I didn't know how to get into my stance or anything like that. After the very first day when I met everybody and joined the team, football just became my life. It's the thing I think about the most now. At JPD, children from all over New York became friends, helped each other, and respected each other. My parents really appreciated that."

Twelve-year-old Kareem Barros, from Providence, Rhode Island, had played Pop Warner football since he was eight years old. A big kid, Kareem was allowed to play only defensive tackle or defensive end. "They would teach you the same position year after year, all year long, and I began to lose interest," he told us. Kareem found JPD a welcome change. By learning a number of different positions he never became bored and became knowledgeable about every aspect of the game.

Anthony Wiseman went through the JPD program in Washington, D.C. "JPD was great, I really learned a lot," he said. "Before I started the program, I didn't know a whole lot about football. Once I got into JPD, I learned all about technique. I had played some football at the Boys and Girls Club, but they really didn't teach me to understand the game. JPD provided great instruction and taught me a lot.

"It was great that the program was so well organized. The coaches made it fun, real, and never boring. They made it very exciting, and that made me want to go there every day. The coaches always tried to keep everybody's head up, told us what we needed to do on the next play, and voiced encouragement.

"The techniques they taught me I carried over to high school. I use those techniques at the game level now, and they made me a better player overall. I've improved in every aspect, from my stance to my attitude toward the game.

"My parents thought it was great because I always had a good attitude when I arrived home from practice. While they were watching, they could see I was having a great time."

Anthony's brother, Darren Wiseman, came to watch him play every day at JPD. He echoed his brother's words and added, "I like the unity of JPD, the team aspect of it. It is not an individual sport, and the coaches really emphasized helping each other. If one player understood something better than another player, he would try to explain it to him. At JPD they really want you to have an understanding of the game."

We've collected thousands of stories just like these over the past four years. Using this input from the kids who have gone through our program, we designed JPD specifically to address the issues they raised and others that plague youth sports and turn off kids.

A DAY AT JPD

To get a picture of a typical day at a program like JPD, imagine as many as 144 kids, some who have never played before and others with more experience, meeting on one playing field to learn all the fundamental skills of every position. The sport could be baseball, lacrosse, soccer, softball, or volleyball, but in this case it's youth football.

Kids are organized into six groups or teams of twenty-four, with each team equally matched in size and weight. Four instructors are assigned to each group, and each instructor is responsible for six participants divided into pairs by size and ability.

Once kids are assigned to a team, the so-called season begins. It is not a traditionally defined season of games, practices, playoffs, and championships. Instead, the season consists of two ninety-minute sessions per week for six to eight weeks. Learning occurs through drills reinforced with individual and group competitions that allow each participant to gauge his progress. Not a single traditional game is played, yet the kids have fun improving while playing equally and more often than they would in any other traditional sports program.

At a time when field space is sparse and too many hours are wasted driving from one game and practice to another, this structure allows an entire league to conduct a full season on one playing field, taking up a total of only three hours per week.

Over four years JPD has reached more than ten thousand kids between the ages of twelve and fourteen in thirty-five different towns. Approximately 90 percent of them never played football before. Our success can be measured by the fact that 80 percent of our players went on to participate in high school football programs.

I feel our success at JPD was achieved by incorporating solutions to issues kids had expressed as major concerns and as the reasons why they had either never tried, had given up, or were never interested in the game. These concerns were the building blocks that formed the key elements of the JPD program.

DEVELOPING INDIVIDUALISM

Junior Player Development promotes the individualism of every child involved. Rather than make an immediate judgment based on a particular child's size/weight or ability and pigeonhole the child in a particular position, JPD requires that every child learn every position. Once the child has had a chance to do this, he makes a decision about which position to pursue rather than having this decision dictated by a coach.

We've had kids who weighed as much as three hundred pounds participating in JPD with kids as little as seventy-five pounds. The structure is such that they never come into contact with each other, but they both learn how to play the quarterback, wide receiver, and running back positions as well as center, tackle, and linebacker. We allow kids the opportunity to experience and learn all aspects of the game before we ask them to decide what positions they feel most comfortable with as they progress to the next level.

As fourteen-year-old Ricardo McCoy, a JPD player from Maryland, recalled, "I was taught every position on the football field, and I was taught facts about life at every practice. We set personal goals every week to become better people in life and on the football field.

"I play running back and linebacker for DeMatha High School. In JPD I learned how to read the offense from the linebacker position. But I also got a lot out of learning the other positions. I learned pre-snap reads from the quarterback position and picked up a lot of tips from all the positions.

"JPD also teaches players that you have to be students, not just grow up to play football, but be obedient to your parents and the people around you, and be street smart."

Rico's father, Reggie McCoy, Sr., added, "Both of my boys went through the program. They got to see what an organized program looks like, with its structure, continual flow, playing different positions, and moving from one training area to the next without confusion. It was totally organized. Every day they were taught life skills, which was really nice. Our family is pretty tight, but some of the kids come from broken families where they may not get that support every day. It's a big help to the kids and to everyone around them. One interesting thing about it was kids from so many different cultures and neighborhoods coming together. They got to display some of the skills they had and made a lot of new friends."

PRODUCING A SUCCESSFUL JOURNEY

Junior Player Development promotes the entire journey of the sports experience, allowing more kids the opportunity to learn and progress through the sport. More emphasis is placed on proper preparation than on wins and losses. JPD emphasizes fundamental skill preparation, which engages every participant by applying contemporary twists to drills that appeal and capture each participant's attention.

For example, in the process of teaching every position, we break down each skill and reinforce what was just learned. We do this in a game by awarding points to every participant and allowing each one the opportunity to understand how to apply the newly learned skill.

Kareem Barros explained it this way: "We didn't need to play games with touchdowns and first downs. We competed every day by showing our coaches what we had learned. Instead of touchdowns we got points for doing a drill correctly. Not everyone gets to score touchdowns in a game. In JPD we all got the chance to score points and get better at all the positions at the same time."

In our programs we recognize every accomplishment by every individual. Results are not based solely on an arbitrary final team score. All competitions are designed to allow each participant to gauge his own progress.

ELIMINATING INTIMIDATION

Too often in sports the more mature and bigger kids are allowed to dominate a program, leaving kids who have yet to blossom discouraged and uninterested in pursuing a sport. The JPD structure eliminates all types of participant intimidation by introducing every part of the game gradually and providing a comfort level for every participant.

Youth leagues tend to begin a season by taking all interested kids and testing their skills without actually teaching those skills first. The results are often a disaster.

When a child shows up to register for a baseball league, she is immediately asked to field a ground ball to test her skill level. Has it ever occurred to the adults running this program that maybe no one ever demonstrated or taught that skill to this child? The answer is usually no, which results in that child's being judged immediately as having little or no potential.

I would argue that the fact the child showed up to register shows an interest, which is the first sign of potential. Anyone who is eager to learn can prosper from good instruction, but many sports programs ignore this basic concept, probably due to their lack of understanding child development.

In youth football there have been far too many cases of intimidation. Coaches tell kids to hit each other before teaching them anything. In JPD we eliminate this phenomenon of bypassing the fundamentals and instead teach a progression of every skill necessary to play. When we teach blocking and tackling, for example, we take every kid, experienced or not, and line them up six inches apart. Then, after they have executed each phase consistently and accurately, we slowly move them farther and farther apart until they are performing the skills at full speed. This is a prescribed formula of crawling, walking, jogging, and running through each fundamental skill. By taking a gradual approach we produce safer results along with the development of fundamentally sound players over a relatively short period of time.

ENGAGING EVERYONE

You may wonder how we can avoid boring these kids and losing their interest in the process of teaching and breaking down every fundamental skill. From my experience JPD actually prevents boredom. Children do not have a long attention span, so in JPD we teach everything in ten-minute segments. We break down entire skills into segments that are each explained, demonstrated, and then performed.

For example, if we are introducing and teaching the receiver position for the first time, we teach all the basics over nine ten-minute segments. The first segment covers their stance, a basic yet critical first component. The stance is important because it also coordinates the basics of the start, or the timing of the first step taken after the ball is snapped, in conjunction with the proper alignment or correct position the receiver must place himself in relation to the ball on the line of scrimmage. This is all explained, demonstrated, and taught through hands-on instruction within a ten-minute segment.

One secret of the program's success is the precise yet fast-paced segments that make up an entire season of teaching. Each of the segments promotes learning and holds an entire team's attention.

Even frigid March evenings couldn't keep kids like Adam Gaddie of the Bronx from showing up for JPD. "Even in the freezing cold, all the players in our JPD program showed up," he said. "We don't get that many opportunities to play organized football in New York and for free. Kids saw an open door and were smart enough to take a chance on it. The kids liked it that the coaches knew what they were doing. Everything was so planned out. Every time the whistle blew, we were learning something different."

IMPROVING OVERALL COACHING

By breaking down organized instruction into small parts we have been able to produce better coaches throughout our programs. A majority of college and professional football teams run their practice sessions exactly this way.

"Teaching the game's techniques and fundamentals remains one of the most rewarding parts of coaching," explained Pete Carroll, University of Southern California head coach and former head coach of the NFL's New York Jets and New England Patriots. "The system of breaking down our practices into short segments in order to drill each player in the fundamentals is essential to effective teaching. It keeps the players on the field for a set but short period of time in which we can achieve maximum results. And it provides coaching staffs with a structure that produces faster learning."

A key to this success, and something that improves a coach's ability to teach effectively and equally to the entire team, is the proper setup and organization of each segment. In JPD we take as many as twenty-four kids on a team and teach all of them the same position during ninety-minute sessions. The secret is pairing up the participants during each practice by equal size and ability and then dividing them into three different groups on the field. This allows for easier observation and hands-on corrections throughout each drill. Rather than game-planning formations, we stress proper drill setup. The result is more than 140 kids on one football field learning and interacting at the same time, with no one standing around for the entire ninety minutes.

Andre Ford, a postal worker in Washington, D.C.'s struggling southeast section, is another one of the many success stories of JPD. He adapted the coaching techniques and philosophies he learned at JPD to the Pop Warner program he supervises in his free time. Last year he took his team to the Pop Warner Super Bowl. He exemplifies the role of coach as teacher and always treats his team members as people first, athletes second.

As he said, "I like the fast pace of JPD, trying to get everything into ten-minute segments. This is something good that high school, college, and pro teams have done for years. But at the lower levels you go to a youth practice and see most of the kids standing around while a handful of their teammates practice. Everything drags as the coach goes over the same play for forty-five minutes.

"Another thing we picked up from JPD was the 'rah-rah' aspect. Whenever we get together, there is a lot of clapping and a serious camaraderie. Anytime there is a small success, we celebrate.

"With my coaches, JPD is mandatory. I have twenty-five coaches in my program. I had a coach who came in late to replace another coach two years ago, so he didn't have a chance to attend JPD his first year. He had some success, but last year he attended JPD and then made it to the regional championships. He also kept all his kids on the team for the whole year. That's a big thing for us. I tell my coaches that they're successful if they keep 95 percent of their roster. That coach attributes his success to JPD. It gave him more discipline as a coach and reminded him of why he was out there. Sometimes youth coaches get away from that and forget why they're out there.

"JPD has no weight restrictions, which is very positive. It gives kids who wouldn't be able to even put equipment on until high school a chance to play."

Boomer Esiason believes the JPD model can and should be used in other sports. "The key to JPD," he said, "is that it provides the correct structure in which to learn an entire sport and properly prepares you to advance to the next level. It truly is the template to be replicated in other sports in order to maintain interest and build a broader feeder system of talent."

ELIMINATING FIRST, SECOND, AND THIRD STRINGS

No matter what the sport, the following scene occurs all too often at youth practices: One group of kids is engaged and receiving the full attention of their coach, while the remainder of the team looks on, not engaged in anything. If you are not considered a member of the "starting team," you don't receive equal attention in practices or games; therefore, you don't learn, improve, or have any fun. This is always the point at which kids lose interest and quit.

JPD addresses this issue by eliminating first, second, and third strings. No one gets ignored, everyone plays and learns equally, and initial talent is not a factor. When a child registers to participate, no one is prejudged or is asked to audition in order to be drafted by a specific team due to athletic ability. Everyone begins the program on a level playing field, and, uniquely, all players remain as equals throughout the program. For example, all participants get to progress at their own pace, learning and competing with kids who are of similar size and ability.

Because everyone learns every position, the participants usually find their own strengths and the aspects of the game in which they can excel. They therefore become empowered by the overall experience. Each player is paired up and receives hands-on instruction through a one-to-six instructor-to-participant ratio.

Paul Pasqualoni, head football coach at Syracuse University, which is consistently ranked among the top twenty-five teams in the country, advised us throughout the development process of the JPD program. "The emphasis on fundamentals is the most important part of this program," Pasqualoni said. "It allows kids to truly learn the game in a comfortable environment that does not test their courage but advances them quickly into fundamentally sound football players. It also produces better overall coaches by eliminating the responsibility and focus on winning. At the youth level the focus should always be on teaching the game properly. JPD accomplishes this in a contemporary way that addresses a broad base of kids' needs and uses other creative alternatives that produce greater results than traditional games."

SATISFYING PARENTAL CONCERNS

Watching your child participate in youth sports can be a gut-wrenching experience. Often it is the first time your child is placed in a situation where she must perform in front of others. The experience can be stressful and uncomfortable for you and your child.

The philosophy of JPD was deliberately designed to take outside influences that often disrupt a youth sports experience—such as disgruntled parents, disputed officiating calls, and heckling from the sidelines—and prevent them from penetrating JPD's structure. When developing this program, I wanted to design a template that would lead youth sports in a new and positive direction by eliminating all the negative aspects that intrude on our children's experiences.

The mission of changing how youth sports are presented and executed became the backbone of JPD. We addressed all parental concerns by providing every participant equal yet maximum playing and learning time. Everyone learned and performed at every position, and parents witnessed their children improving. Kids had fun, were never bored, and always felt a sense of accomplishment.

One key to eliminating negative sideline behavior is the absence of the scoreboard. In every competition we award points for both group and individual accomplishments involving execution of fundamentals. When the program eventually progresses to group competitions and participants are executing skills in gamelike situations, the structure consists of coaches on the field correcting and encouraging players as well as assigning points. It is impossible for anyone observing from the sidelines to disagree with calls or become upset with unequal treatment. Three sets of forty-eight kids, continuously flowing in and out of competitions every four plays, with each set of three changing positions on a rotating basis, demonstrates that everyone is playing equally and more often, and is having an opportunity to perform a number of positions. All the action is conducted under close supervision and constant instruction both on and off the field.

In our programs, parents no longer discuss final scores but rather how much their kids have learned and improved. The total focus is on preparation and finding satisfaction through planning effectively. The results are based on the achievements of individuals as well as the contributions they make to group accomplishments, reinforced by a productive and positive accounting of their mistakes and the areas in which they need to improve.

INCORPORATING LIFE LESSONS

Sports can provide important lessons that can be carried through life. Hundreds of books have been written that focus on this subject. In my experience, however, youth sports programs generally do not incorporate life skills. There are certainly many programs that make an attempt, but these efforts are often halfhearted and address the subject only briefly.

Some programs recognize the importance of life skill accomplishments such as good grades but do nothing to assist a child in improving. Recognizing academic success is important, but it does little to raise the level of those who need assistance when the organization does not actually contribute to that success.

Many organizations claim that they promote life skills but never attempt to actually play any significant role in the process.

Sports provide the perfect opportunity to work with children to correct, as well as prevent, future problems.

As with most life skills, parents obviously play the most important role, but sports can provide positive reinforcement to a parent's message. A sport can demonstrate firsthand on the playing field the important traits and the specific tools required to overcome poor performance in the classroom.

For example, when we conduct drills in JPD, we also take time to explain what responsibility is and how it affects the kids and their families, friends, and teammates. We demonstrate the importance of setting goals and preparing properly to achieve them in the short and long term. We stress the importance of making smart moves. The children witness firsthand how a wrong decision can have a ripple effect and impact many different aspects of life.

Rafael Richardson went through the JPD program before playing football in high school. Now that he's graduated, he helps out as an instructor at JPD and wants to pursue a degree in coaching.

He said, "Life skills were good because kids had a new goal for each other each week. At the end everything comes into play. One week it would be team leadership, how everyone had to stick together. As a group those life skills stay with them as they go on to graduate, enter college, and go into the world. And it really makes for success in high school."

Adam Gaddie added, "For life skills the coaches touched on different topics to be applied in football and in life. They showed us how we can use discipline on the field to control ourselves and then use it in the classroom or with our families. It was very helpful. I had some problems with self-control, but when I started playing football, I obtained more discipline and began to think more about school and my parents."

These are just a few of the life skill messages that we intertwine in our on-field skill sessions. Coaches are provided with the tools and guidance materials to communicate in such a way that these messages are not perceived to have been preached but rather demonstrated naturally in real-time athletic situations.

WHAT JPD HAS ACCOMPLISHED

JPD is conducted at as many as thirty-five sites nationwide. In addition, several school district athletic departments (including the Houston Independent School District and the New Orleans Parish Schools) have adopted the entire program. In every one of our programs, stories can be told of how kids absorb not only the athletic portion of the program but also the life skill messages, and how they have begun to apply them.

Some of our programs are conducted on well-manicured fields while others resemble a dust bowl with little or no green anywhere in the vicinity. That's where we found thirteen-year-olds Daryl Cassell and Kareem Barros from Providence, Rhode Island. Both attended the JPD program at the Joslin Park and Recreation Department, nestled in the Federal Hill section of Providence. Infested with crime and poverty, this neighborhood offers little hope for many of its young people. As a native of Rhode Island, I know that no town in the state is very far from downtown Providence, yet the racial divide of the haves and have-nots can at times be immeasurable. I'm proud to say that this was one of several JPD sites where we were able to build bridges between the races. Both Daryl and Kareem felt that they had benefited and grown from participating in JPD.

"It's great. We have both seen a big difference in all the kids over the last few weeks," Daryl remarked. "They won't get mad at you and fight you over some little foul or when you try to correct them. They won't say, 'Oh, you ain't my friend.' They will just accept you. Everybody helps each other. We don't try to help ourselves; we ask each other how to do things. We're competing, but then again everybody wants to help each other. They don't jump on each other's backs."

"It's not about who's better than this, who's better than that," added Kareem. "There are a lot of good people here. We might all be different, but we're all one team and we have to work together. It's like the coach says, 'We're one team. Our shirts don't just say Patriots, Colts, Raiders. They say JPD. We're all family.' That's what we are. One family."

Other program accomplishments include having trained and now graduated three JPD instructors, including one woman, who are now in high school football head coaching positions. Later in the book I will discuss women as youth coaches in all sports as well as how the JPD model is unique to the development of female athletes.

As you read through this book, you will see how you can apply to your own child's sports program all the elements that make JPD a success.

4

SPORTS ARE FOR KIDS:
Eliminating Negative Coaching and Poor Parental Behavior

It's shocking but true: Associated Press sportswriter Tim Dahlberg reported on June 2, 2001, that several members of a Las Vegas youth football team were poisoned by a teammate's dad.

"Eight boys, ages 12 to 14, were soon vomiting violently— victims of poisoning, and casualties of an epidemic of parental rage sweeping through youth sports," Dahlberg wrote.

The parent, trying to get back at a player who picked on his twelve-year-old son, put a vomit-inducing herbal extract in his son's juice and instructed him to have the teammate drink it. The team didn't have enough to drink at practice that day, however, and other players ended up drinking the juice, too. The father was given six months house arrest and ordered to perform a year of community service. Although none of the players became seriously ill, one was so traumatized by the incident that he dropped out of sports.

In Reading, Massachusetts, another real tragedy occurred a year earlier when a father beat a father/coach to death during an argument over rough play at hockey practice. Thomas Junta was convicted of involuntary manslaughter and sentenced to six to ten years in state prison for killing Michael Costin, a father of four.

Reading newspaper and magazine articles and watching TV news reports about parents assaulting kids, coaches, and other parents at games and practices horrifies us. Yet it happens all the time. Sadly, we've all probably witnessed some type of poor parental behavior that borders on violence or abuse.

WELL-MEANING BUT MISGUIDED EFFORTS

No one has experienced abusive parents more often than youth sports officials. The increase in verbal and physical threats and actions has prompted the National Association of Sports Officials to offer assault insurance to its nineteen thousand members. Typical cases of abuse range from name-calling and shoving to officials' vehicles being run off the road by irate parents.

Organizers have tried desperately to implement new methods to correct deleterious adult behavior, from "Silent Sundays"—where parents must remain quiet at all times on the sidelines—to requiring that each parent sign a pledge of good behavior. Some youth leagues and organizations provide coaches with sensitivity training on such subjects as how to control their emotions and those of their players during competition and how to deal with problem parents. All attempts are genuine in their mission, but few produce effective long-term results.

One method that I take particular exception to is the "Silent Sunday." One Silent Sunday program was instituted in 1999 in the Northern Ohio Girls Soccer League. The league ordered parents to keep their lips buttoned throughout the entire game, which included cheering as well as shouting. The move prompted one youth sports organization leader to proclaim it "the greatest time-out in American sports."

Give me a break.

It may have been the greatest gimmick tried in youth sports—an effective public relations tool. And it may have had a positive effect in the short term due to the shock value of kids participating in front of a group of mute adults. But it certainly should not be considered a worthwhile long-term solution. Kids want to have fun, and one important way to have fun is to be reinforced with cheers from the spectators. To eliminate cheering and place restrictions on *positive* behavior is ludicrous.

The same holds true for ethics courses and signed pledges imploring parents and coaches to behave. Such present-day remedies, though noble in their intentions, serve only as a Band-Aid on a critical wound. Though courses, workshops, and clinics are helpful, they don't stop the poor behavior exemplified by adults when winning and losing are at stake.

WHAT KIDS WANT

What makes adults carry on like this? More than anything else it's our adult infatuation with winning. What many parents don't realize—and are often shocked when I tell them—is research studies have found that 90 percent of young male athletes would rather have an opportunity to play on a losing team than sit on the bench of a winning team.

The problem, however, goes deeper than the desire to win. The entire structure in which kids play today is a catalyst for bad behavior among all involved. Ideally, competition should not be the focal point but rather the means whereby kids achieve personal athletic skills while simultaneously developing crucial life skills.

The Positive Coaching Alliance (PCA), an organization created and housed at Stanford University, holds one of the few workshops that encourage coaches to deemphasize winning and stress the importance of adults as positive role models in youth sports. The PCA instructs coaches, parents, and youth sports organizers to develop a "double-goal" approach. The first goal is to try to win, which is important. But positive coaches also have a second, more important goal: to use sports to develop positive character traits and teach life lessons.

Jim Thompson, founder of PCA, said, "A positive coach helps players redefine what it means to be a winner. Rather than focusing solely on the scoreboard, players learn to focus on what we call the ELM Tree of Mastery. It emphasizes E for Effort, L for Learning and improving, and M for developing the courage to make Mistakes and rebound from them."

PCA also works with youth leagues around the United States to incorporate "Honoring the Game" into the organization's culture to prevent poor adult behavior at games. Thompson explained, "One step in developing a positive youth sports culture is to make Honoring the Game an integral part of the program. Honoring the Game requires coaches, parents, and athletes to demonstrate respect for the rules, opponents, officials, teammates, and one's self. Through this program the youth leagues we work with nationwide designate one or more parent from each team to be the 'Culture Keeper.' Each team's Culture Keeper is assigned the responsibility of gently reminding parents who begin to yell at officials to honor the game. They also hand out stickers and a card outlining the kind of behavior that is expected of adults at competitions."

Thompson added, "Culture is simply the way we do things here. The youth sports organizations we work with make it clear to adults what is expected and what is not tolerated in terms of their behavior. The results have been reduced misconduct among both coaches and parents, which means kids have more fun playing the games they love."

Most parents and coaches don't realize it, but kids approach sports with a viewpoint very different from adults. Adults promote structured programs that include tryouts, drafts, starting teams (whose players receive the majority of the coach's time at practices and games), and an overemphasis on league standings. From my experience there are too many parents who encourage and even force their children to participate in sports and then place an inordinate amount of pressure on them to succeed because they believe that somehow it will elevate their family's status. It's as if adults receive recognition in their community based on the achievements of their kids.

Too many stories have been told about families raising an athletic prodigy and attempting to ride their child's success. A classic example is top-ranked tennis star Jennifer Capriati, who showed so much talent at an early age that her father/coach Stefano became obsessed with turning her into a superstar. By age sixteen Capriati was world famous but nearly burned out on the sport she once loved to play. It was only much later in her career, when she found a reason to win for herself, that Capriati began to enjoy the game again and find true success.

HOW PARENTS CAN HELP

Adults need to approach youth sports in a fashion that is best for kids. Design a program around what kids want rather than what adults want, and I guarantee you'll witness an immediate reduction in negative coaching and poor parental behavior.

As a parent this is the question you need to ask yourself: Can I participate in and contribute to a totally new approach to sports? It is difficult for any parent to break away from the mind-set that focuses only on winning. Every day we are surrounded by images from professional and collegiate sports that set a tone for what competition should signify. So it's easy for us to lose sight of the true meaning of competition and totally miss the values it teaches everyone who participates.

WHAT KIDS SAY

After fourteen years of working with hundreds of thousands of kids, I can say without a doubt that winning a particular game has little or no long-term consequence or value to a child. In fact, it may be the least important part of a child's sports experience. Yet for many adults winning is the primary focus. The result is poor coaching and inappropriate parental behavior.

Another thing I discovered is that kids do not place much importance on their coach. For them it is more important to have fun with their friends and challenge themselves to improve their skills. Unfortunately, however, well-meaning adults deprive kids of these experiences by following the dictates of sports as we know them today. They seek the most talented and tell kids which position they will play, thus dictating what their experience will be throughout the season.

In reality kids don't want to be stressed over the order in which they will be selected to a team or whether or not they will be chosen at all. Most of all they don't want to endure the negative criticism dished out by coaches and parents who view competition as the primary goal. Where's the positive reinforcement? It's hard to find—if it's there at all.

Few children join a sport to have their self-worth diminished by a coach. They certainly don't place the same importance as their coach on what the final score will be or in what place the team will finish the season. To them winning is a nice by-product of their total sports experience, but it should not happen at the expense of having a bad experience.

Kids, as I've discovered, actually prefer to be left alone to make up the rules and determine their own sense of achievement. What they desire most is a great experience. Of course, kids still need supervision. But if you want a program that eliminates what turns kids off (negative coaches and pushy parents) and instills what they love (fun and positive reinforcement), it's time to re-think the way we approach youth sports today.

Fair Play, the philosophy I have incorporated in national soc-cer programs and NFL youth programs, is designed to embrace what kids want and provide adults with the tools to correct the things that turn kids off. It's also designed to shield players, par-ents, and coaches from the negative influences that can destroy programs and ruin kids' attitudes toward participation.

CHANGING THE STRUCTURE

Kids today experience their youth very differently from the way we did. They live in a world of interactive entertainment and niche products designed to fulfill their every whim. Our children devote the majority of their time to contemporary diversions such as video games, the Web, DVD players, and five hundred–channel television, to name just a few. In their fast-paced technical world, traditional organized sports have become as stale as last week's bread.

Until we begin to act creatively to rethink and update the experiences of our children, we will continue to witness more and more kids developing a dislike for sports and eventually dropping out. It not only threatens the rich entitlements that our children deserve to experience but even puts their health at risk. Most parents echo the concern that their children are not active enough, but herein lies the irony: We are concerned about our children's inactivity and attraction to nonphysical pursuits, yet when it comes to sports, we push them away with our actions and attitudes—no matter how well intended we may be.

We can't compare the kids today to the kids of yesterday. When we were kids, we had limited distractions (no MTV) to divert our attention. We relied on sports and playing with our friends, and had plenty of free time and free play to make up games with our own rules and boundaries. We welcomed the fabled do-over until we mastered an at-bat or successful series of free throws. And there were no adults around to ruin the experience.

Even though we faced negative situations when we participated in organized sports run by adults, we always had the ability to return to the streets, empty lots, or someone's backyard to play the way we wanted with our friends. These places were our sanctuaries, coveted places where we could go with our friends to recapture the pure "love of the game."

As parents you want your children to have the best sports experiences possible. So if you want to create an experience they will enjoy—one that builds a healthy foundation for an active lifestyle and offers all children the opportunity to perform at their own pace and measure their accomplishments without being judged by intrusive adults—you are ready to change the structure of youth sports. You are ready for Fair Play.

A BOLD NEW WAY OF THINKING

The beauty of the Fair Play philosophy and its tools and techniques is that you can approach it in three different ways: You can incorporate it slowly in phases, you can cherry-pick specific elements, or you can adopt the entire program. My own experience with the NFL's Junior Player Development has proven that a complete adoption of the philosophy is the best way to control and even eliminate all the negative elements that have infested youth sports.

Whether your child is the team star or rarely sees playing time, she will surely benefit from Fair Play's alternative approach to the playing field. I can promise that you will see measurably improved results and at a faster pace.

If your child is receiving one-on-one instruction from a professional and is completely happy and totally engaged in a sport, perhaps this philosophy is not necessary. But most kids do not get that type of opportunity. I believe that any child—whether shortstop, pitcher, quarterback, running back, center, midfielder, or goalie, starter or reserve—would benefit from Fair Play. It's a structure that's been proven to work. It produces maximum results in performance and fosters a lifelong appreciation for a healthy lifestyle.

My program is not meant to be a knock on youth coaches. These coaches dedicate hours of their free time to work with kids. Rather, the program is a call to arms against a current-day youth sports system that is trapped in the outdated practices of the past.

Currently, today's coaches have only the traditional adult model to emulate. It's what they grew up with; it's what they know. They are further challenged by a limited amount of time and the pressures of having to please the parents of every player. Fair Play will actually save coaches valuable time, provide them with a model that will satisfy parents, make them effective teachers of the game, and show them how to devote themselves to every child equally.

Convinced? Good. Then let's roll.

SEVEN STEPS BACK TO REALITY

I would be remiss if I did not first present this radical new approach to how youth sports should be taught and played in its totality, since this is the way it has been proven to work best. You may be tempted to adopt only certain elements or use them to make adjustments to your current program. However, I encourage you to take it all the way. Only by applying all the elements will players, coaches, and parents experience complete success and satisfaction.

Youth tackle football historically has been burdened as the poster child of "in your face" drill-sergeant-type coaching. Images of coaches grabbing and pulling at a child's face mask have perpetuated the poor perception that parents, and especially mothers, have of football. For some youth coaches and parents the violent nature of the sports we watch each weekend on television seems to translate into a license to act violently in front of and even toward the kids.

Of all sports, football still suffers the most from poor perception when it comes to adversarial coaching and negative parental behavior. This was the challenge I faced as the person responsible for rebuilding youth football, starting at the grass roots level. Although the design of the program initially came from my soccer experiences and was tested in youth football, it can be used in any sport. The result will be the same: better coaching and positive parents. We found success with the seven-step program that follows.

1. Recruit all parents.

The idea here is to engage parents as teachers of the game when they would ordinarily spend that time standing on the sidelines watching. This doesn't mean just designating which parent should bring the team snack. Rather, assign parents to different teaching responsibilities at each practice.

In soccer, for example, ask a pair of parents to teach dribbling and ball handling techniques throughout the season. This would be their only focused responsibility. At each practice these parents would run a dribbling station through which small groups of players would rotate.

If you provide parents with the proper tools to teach one or two skills within an organized structure, you will create an additional and useful group of enthusiastic supporters rather than a handful of disruptive and critical sideline parents.

We found that when parents became part of the overall experience and felt they had some ownership in the process, they were much less likely to act negatively.

2. Hold leaguewide practices and clinics.

A key concept we implemented when I designed camps for the U.S. Women's 1991 World Champion Soccer Team was to hold regular practices that broke down the divisions of an entire league of teams and instructed all players together. The concept proved to be so successful that we recently incorporated it into NFL Flag, a national flag football program for kids between the ages of six and fourteen. We adopted it as a proactive measure to combat combative parents.

In NFL Flag we recommend that each of the more than seven hundred leagues around the country set aside one day or evening each week in which the entire league gets together and conducts a skill-oriented practice or clinic session. Parents are encouraged to attend. The ninety-minute session is a fun way for players to learn new skills and improve on the basics along with members of other teams. The session is intended to be a substitute for single team practices.

The NFL provides the structure and curriculum, and encourages parents to assist coaches by running specific skill stations. In so doing, parents get involved in honing skills and achieving goals (both individual and team)—exclusive of winning games.

A good example of the skills we teach is how to snap the ball from the center to the quarterback. To snap, or begin play, the center must toss the ball five to seven yards behind him without it touching the ground. A team that can snap well will have more success moving the ball down the field.

We run a regular drill in which players practice snaps. They pair off and snap the ball to each other for a specific period of time. The object of the drill is to learn, apply, and then perform the skill through a series of fun games.

For your own team, weekly leaguewide practices is a proven way to help teach parents that traditional games do not need to be the sole focus of a child's experience or the only venue in which she can experience success. Parents who participate in these clinics learn to recognize that winning is not the paramount goal for kids. The leaguewide weekly practices or clinics are the place where parents and coaches can witness kids having fun learning and truly building a love for the game without the pressure of worrying about the scoreboard.

3. Eliminate traditional league play.

Forget tradition. Plan an entire season without league games. Instead, schedule a season of leaguewide clinics and competitions that teach kids the fundamentals of the game. In each session include individual and group competitions that allow everyone to apply what they have learned. Measure progress by keeping both individual and group scores throughout the entire season.

Radical? Yes. But think about what happens in a typical season of traditional play. Games and practices in any organized sport focus primarily on the entitled players deemed by coaches as superior athletes when compared to their teammates. This small percentage of elite players often starts and plays the majority of the games and receives the lion's share of attention at practice. Meanwhile, their teammates sit around and watch. So a majority of the kids—who may not have matured completely for their age or need additional individual attention to blossom—don't get an opportunity to truly participate in a complete program. The favoritism that takes place only creates conflict and disappointment among parents who believe their child deserves the right to participate as much as others.

The alternative season of clinics and competitions allows kids to learn equally and improve at their own pace. We've found that this type of structure improves the skills of *all* participants, including the most talented athletes, faster and more effectively than any traditional youth league experience.

The other payoff is that parents behave better, especially when they participate and see firsthand the attention their children get

and the progress they make. The only thing it does not do is satisfy the adult thirst to compare their child's or team's performance
with that of the pros.

I recommend that children hone their skills through a clinics
and competitions structure that continues until they reach high
school. This gives them the time to mature and receive a sufficient
amount of fundamental skill training. Only then are they ready to
progress to adultlike games. Their future experience will be the
better for it.

As a substitute for games, allow kids the opportunity of specific "free time" (a period during weekly practices and clinics) in
which they can play "pick-up" games without adult input or restrictions. While still under adult supervision, this allows a component that is missing from kids' lives today. A productive coaching
tip or tool would be to observe from afar without comment and
later address and incorporate corrections during structured drills.

If you decide to take on a season of clinics and competitions,
don't give up this philosophy once you resume traditional play.
Hold clinic sessions weekly.

Every sport experiences a different maturation rate due to
physical and cognitive requirements. In youth football, for example, none of the programs we've developed at the NFL for youth
tackle football begin before the age of twelve. The physical abilities
required to achieve success in the fundamentals of the game are
unrealistic for a majority of kids before they reach this age. We also
recommend a comprehensive amount of training in all the fundamentals for a minimum of two years prior to participating in
eleven-on-eleven traditional football.

Many of today's youth football organizations actually begin
the traditional eleven-on-eleven tackle game as young as six or
seven. Unfortunately, forcing kids to play like adults has pushed

many children out of the game by age ten because of their frustration from experiencing little or no improvement, limited playing time, and hardly any fun.

4. Let kids decide.

Individualism and creativity are missing from traditional organized sports, which is another reason kids get disenchanted and drop out. Letting them create their own games or work on the skill of their desire gives them a stake in their own development. They feel empowered. It makes for happy kids and happy parents.

You can give kids the opportunity to express their creativity by allowing them to run a portion of practice. This is best done during the weekly leaguewide clinics and competitions.

For a coach this approach is an additional teaching tool. We've found that when kids are given the choice to practice what they want, they have better recall of recently taught skills. I tested this concept in one NFL program with a group of kids who had been instructed for the first time in three positions—quarterback, center, and wide receiver. All instruction took place in a series of ninety-minute clinic or competition sessions. Later I had instructors ask their players to create a skill game that would best help them perform and remember a newly learned skill. One of the twelve-year-olds came up with a game to test the quarterback, center, and wide receiver skills. Players split into groups of three to practice snapping, throwing, and catching the ball. He awarded the group one point for a successful snap, one if the quarterback dropped back into a proper throwing position, and one if the receiver caught the ball.

The drill he invented was simple but effective. As all three players rotated through the positions, they had to work together to accumulate points. They also competed against the other groups to see who could get the most points.

The results were astounding. Kids were executing drills correctly immediately following instruction, and over 80 percent recalled and properly executed the same fundamentals days after the drill was originally taught.

Rather than a Silent Sunday in which parents deliberately keep their mouths shut, it is much more productive to give kids the freedom to play their own games with their own sets of rules. When parents cannot relate to what is going on but witness their kids having fun and learning at the same time, they have little to complain about and no reason to interfere.

A proven example of this takes place on any given day at any skate park. It is fascinating to observe parents while their kids attempt new moves or tricks using their own creativity. You do not hear parents screaming at their children, since they can't pass judgment on something they don't understand. What you do see are parents supporting their children by simply being there.

It is your challenge as a coach or parent working with kids to create an environment in which learning is fun for everyone. Remember, it is the journey that matters for kids, not the final score or league standing.

5. Eliminate head coaches.

Negative coaching has also played a leading role in ruining a child's sports experience. One tactic that has proven successful is to organize a team or league without using the title of head coach. If you are the head coach of a team, rename yourself the team coordinator. Your role will be to organize and manage the team and at the same time recruit as many other parents as possible to perform specific instructional roles.

Rather than take on the entire responsibility of coaching yourself, empower other parents to share and contribute. The roles should focus primarily on teaching and improving everyone's fundamental skills. By including others it is easier to create a more supportive and helpful group of advocates who assist you and allow for a greater emphasis on instruction. It is crucial, however, to create an atmosphere that welcomes all parents and makes it easy for them to stay involved. This will help foster a spirit of community. A rotation of parents helping out on a limited basis goes a long way in providing a higher quality of learning experience for kids.

The person assigned to be the team coordinator must emphasize organization. Youth coaching takes up a tremendous amount of time, but sharing duties, cuts down on time and makes more people feel involved.

The secret to making this approach successful is to plan thoroughly before the season starts. If you are the driver of this idea (team coordinator), the first step is to gather everyone involved—players and parents—set goals, and get everyone to agree.

A Little League baseball team might agree to dedicate one season to fielding skills and allow the players to select three different positions to learn. Each coach or instructor would be assigned a specific role. If you have six parents and twelve players, each pair of parents teaches two out of the six positions: outfielders, first base, third base, second base or shortstop, catcher, and pitcher. Granted, this is a best-case scenario. But whatever the circumstances, assign no more than four players per position to each group, allowing for an instructor-to-player ratio of one to two. The concept also works with as few as three instructors for twelve kids, or a one-to-four ratio.

Plan an entire season of practices prior to the start of the program and design each practice so that it has a specific goal. In my baseball example, one practice for the shortstop and second base group might be devoted to progressing from fielding grounders to improving footwork to turning a double play. This concept saves time, improves overall effectiveness in skill development, and takes the pressure off each individual to be the center of every parent's attention.

6. Take coaches off the sidelines.

The most important role of any coach is to teach and prepare players for eventual competition. To me, nothing is more frustrating than watching a youth coach scour the sidelines in imitation of an NFL or NBA head coach.

We have all witnessed a coach (possibly at a game as insignificant as a six-year-old's soccer match) screaming and carrying on as if he were on the verge of a World Cup berth for his team. Ironically enough, a head soccer coach for a national team playing in the World Cup is not even allowed to coach from the sidelines. Yet a weekend does not go by in this country when you can't find raging lunatics coaching from the sidelines of a youth soccer game.

I firmly believe that keeping coaches away from the sidelines will correct the negative aspects of coaching in youth sports. If the game is taught properly, there is no need for coaches to hang close at game time.

At our first annual NFL Flag National Championships in November 2000, we instituted a rule that coaches could not be on the sidelines or communicate with their team during the game other than at halftime. They were relegated to the stands with other parents to cheer and provide positive support.

When we announced the rule at a meeting the night before the tournament, the kids applauded openly and were clearly pleased. The coaches' reaction was mixed. A good percentage viewed it as positive. Some of the others, however, waited until game time to try to ignore the rule and made a scene when we asked them to leave the sideline.

The intent of the "disappearing coach" is to emphasize that games are for kids, not adults. We gave the tournament back to the kids because it is their place to perform. Coaches should be teachers and supporters, not the focus of attention.

I asked former Bengals and Jets quarterback Boomer Esiason, whose son Gunnar plays NFL Flag, what he thought when we benched the coaches. He said, "It was terrific. Putting kids in charge of their own team and the decision-making on the field, especially in flag football, is a great opportunity to create a level of responsibility that people may not associate with youth football. Football can be such a coach-driven sport because of the sheer numbers of people playing."

He continued, "NFL Flag allows kids to play with and among themselves. Kids learn from the responsibility of being prepared. To be willing, ready, and able to play, and to communicate offensive and defensive plays and formations, is an added bonus to what you're doing. It takes out that screaming coach in the midst of it all."

It may come as a surprise, but it was not until 1967 that sideline coaching was officially sanctioned in college football. The early rulers of the game were so opposed that a member of the 1902 Harvard College faculty athletic committee spoke for all advocates of "amateur purity" when he classified "sideline coaching" as among the "shady practices" that violated true sport.

At the youth level I couldn't agree more. Sometimes you must go back in history to move a sport forward. Youth sports are certainly important enough to deserve a return to a sense of purity.

7. Identify teaching moments.

A vital piece of advice that I would give any youth coach trying to improve her effectiveness and reduce negative reactions from players and parents is to always identify "teaching moments." They can offer some of the best lessons ever learned.

A successful coach is someone who can spot a mistake or miscue and turn it into opportunity—a moment to learn by example. Sports are the perfect place for this opportunity because they tend to present these moments much more often than ordinary lifetime activities. Smart coaches are always on the lookout to capture these moments during practice or play.

The approach is simple and effective: A coach spots the mistake, stops play, gathers the players together, and points out a positive aspect of the guilty player's (or players') ability. He then explains the error, notes that it is a common mistake anyone can make, and proceeds to correct the problem with a practical demonstration. By discussing the solution with the team, the players get hands-on experience in a positive setting.

A mistake acknowledged through positive reinforcement can have a positive and lasting effect on the entire team and be a rewarding experience for the player who bungled the play.

It's a win-win solution.

We designed NFL Junior Player Development to provide an entire season of "teaching moments." Each session throughout the season is designed to break down every fundamental aspect of a particular position under close supervision and consistent explanation.

We use competitions to apply and test each child's knowledge, but just as important are the corrections they learn from their mistakes. This is where real learning takes place. The structure ensures teaching moments all season long by preoccupying each coach, not with a win-loss record but with teaching and therefore advancing each individual.

Use these seven methods together or select several to adapt to your league or coaching philosophy. You will then be able to build a program that proactively prevents the types of horror stories we read about daily concerning youth sports.

5

EVERYBOY PLAYS:
Produce a Democratic Experience and Eliminate Prejudgments

I t was the first week in August. Kristi, my step-daughter, was excited when she sat down to eat her breakfast. "We have soccer registration today," she announced. "The fall soccer season starts this early?" I asked my wife. "I was told they had a mandatory registration day on Saturday," she yelled back from the kitchen.

I was curious. Having been involved in soccer for a number of years, I had never heard of registration on the first Saturday in August. But this was Kristi's first year in a new age group of nine- and ten-year-olds. Maybe they did things differently in Brooklyn.

FIRSTHAND EXPERIENCE

As we pulled up to the dusty field scorched by that summer's relentless rays, there must have been fifty boys and girls waiting with their parents. While we stood on the sideline with the other parents and anxious kids, I noticed two rows of five orange cones about seven yards apart. I hadn't expected that there would be a

95

practice today. Luckily for us, Kristi, who is usually accessorized to the nines with a store's worth of trinkets hanging from and wrapped around her body, was ready to go with soccer cleats and shorts.

On the field I noticed six serious-looking men equipped with clipboards and pens. They called the kids into a semicircle and explained that in order to register they must go through a tryout. After the tryout they would be drafted to a team. At that moment you would have thought fifty bladders were about to explode. Kids were nervously looking for soccer balls to warm up; some ran to their parents with confused looks on their faces.

Yes, this group of six soccer "experts" was ready to use its keen scouting abilities to put together a thorough draft report on the kids. Would they later retire to a smoky back room and barter the futures of their new young stars? I may be wrong, but it did not appear to me that any of the six had kicked a soccer ball in quite a while, if ever. Two lines were formed immediately, about twenty-five players deep. The in-depth evaluation would include dribbling the soccer ball around five cones and returning to the starting line. That's it! We could all go home.

As the kids dribbled, our six coaching maestros were feverishly jotting down detailed observations. These insightful reports would be studied before announcing who would play on which team. Imagine. This little exercise orchestrated by six inexperienced volunteers would determine these youngsters' first sports experience.

Don't get me wrong. I, more than most, appreciate people who volunteer their time to coach youth sports. But the volunteer coaches I respect are the ones who are there for the sake of the *kids*.

As these coaches studied their notes and attempted to discover the potential "diamonds in the rough," they showed little concern for the emotions of the kids. They were clueless as to the real reason fifty kids showed up on the field that day. They were there to have fun. To play with their friends. To joke about the colors they'd get to wear. They couldn't have cared less about "getting drafted"—if they even understood what it meant.

OUT WITH THE DRAFT

I will never understand why coaches use a draft system in youth sports. What difference does it make at these young ages?

Some people argue that drafting is necessary to prevent coaches from building a dynasty of talent to dominate an entire season. To these people I say: *You have lost the real meaning of youth sports.*

Draft day. It is literally the beginning of the end. To me it's the very moment when youth programs fail. And it happens before the season even begins. Without any formal training, eight- and nine-year-olds are asked to try out, to be judged and labeled. It's like asking kids to take the final exam before the course begins.

Such a misguided system is a guaranteed failure. Yet we allow adults with little or no training to judge young players before teaching a single skill. How can we determine the physical ability of a child still in the early stages of physical and psychological development? The answer is simple: We can't.

LET ALL PLAYERS PLAY

Many of today's kids face reduced or nonexistent physical education programs and after-school sports programs prior to reaching high school in depleted school systems. This has become a disturbing trend in all communities nationwide. Kids and families are left with few options other than relying on community-based leagues and programs to find training and a fun venue to play. Unfortunately, our children do not find a quality experience—where they receive proper training and programs that are run fairly—in our communities, either.

Eight- and nine-year-olds often participate with kids who are older and more physically mature. Community leagues such as youth baseball often have teams with ages ranging from eight to twelve. After having their abilities judged and labeled and their egos bruised during a tryout, many of these younger athletes are left to sit idly at practices and games without receiving the training necessary to improve.

Practices in many youth programs are generally disorganized and accomplish little. Let's face it, many coaches look to just get through the practices and often see them as a nuisance. That's because most men and women who volunteer to coach already have busy lives. They don't have the time to prepare properly for practice and may not even have the experience. They may know how the game is played, but practice? The result is the most common home remedy in youth sports: "Let's just play," also known as the scrimmage.

The scrimmage is the easiest practice to conduct, the simplest way to avoid real coaching or teaching—and the swiftest way to disappoint every child. It produces an environment that focuses only on the starting team while the other players just sit around, not learning a thing.

Scrimmages that follow a real lesson can be very helpful, but most coaches skip the instruction and just resort to a scrimmage. Some may argue that real games at practice are what kids want.

Many will say that kids don't want to spend the time learning the fundamentals. But in reality nobody benefits when a scrimmage is used as a substitute for an effective practice.

Eight- and nine-year-olds go from practice to game with little or no instruction only to watch their older or more gifted teammates play. On game day they watch from the bench. If they are suddenly called into action, they are unfairly required to perform and execute skills that may be totally foreign to them. The result? Disappointed and disillusioned kids. Then we are puzzled when our kids choose instead to sit on the couch and ingest a steady diet of television and video games.

The most common mistake youth coaches make is not to prepare for their practices. They should arrive at each practice armed with one or two goals that include every participant on the team. Practices need to be fun, fast-paced sessions that engage everyone and challenge them to learn. *Fair Play* addresses this specifically in Chapter 6, which includes tools that any parent or youth coach can use.

THE GIFTED GET CHEATED, TOO

Even parents who believe they have an athletic prodigy on their hands often find their children are victims of unfair youth league methods. The naturally talented are frequently asked to take on the bulk of responsibility to win. Their natural talent places them at the focal point of the team. Coaches expect these players to deliver the victory for their team. If they are unsuccessful, they are perceived to have failed for the entire team.

Gifted athletes are often asked to attempt feats that their abilities and maturity allow them to do before their peers. Take a talented youth baseball pitcher in a twelve-and-under league as an example. This youngster may be large for his age and have the ability to throw a curve ball or slider. In order to win games, he may be called upon to throw these pitches more often than he can physically handle. The result can be an injury or physical and psychological burnout. It also means that he is cheated out of the full experience of learning the entire game.

Eventually, these athletes will face equally if not more talented peers as they advance in age and competitive level. Without the right training in every aspect of the game, they'll be handicapped because they won't have the flexibility to switch to another position.

I can't stress enough the importance of proper training during the early stages for developing players. Without it, the cards are stacked against their being able to contribute and continue playing at higher levels. Unfortunately for most of our children, the present-day youth sports program ignores this responsibility.

A BETTER WAY TO SORT PLAYERS

The first and probably most crucial period in youth sports is the introduction of the player to the game. A youth draft or tryout should not be the first rung on the ladder of a lifetime sports experience.

If your children are between the ages of five and nine or are new to a sport, they should never be subjected to a tryout. If your children are already playing in a league with drafts and tryouts, this book will show you how to adjust your league's current methods to make them fair for all kids.

Young participants just learning a sport or any child under the age of ten should not be asked to try out for a team. Though many leagues never turn anyone away, they do draft in order of ability, which gives a child an immediate label that is difficult to shed. When a coach is pressed for time, he cuts corners by ignoring the last group of kids picked.

Most youth coaches assume, without regard for a child's welfare, that there are some on the team who will not contribute to winning and are thus not worth instructing. These players never get a fair share of time in games. It is much easier to instruct a talented athlete. Most youth coaches are limited in their ability to teach the basics of the game, so they cannot handle the challenge of instructing the majority of the team; therefore, they don't. This is not done maliciously. Most coaches have had no formal training, yet they have taken their time to volunteer to work with kids. Many coaches likely don't realize how detrimental their methods are to the kids. And as a result they unknowingly underestimate the impact it has on the rest of the kids' lives.

That's where Fair Play comes in.

In the NFL Junior Player Development program (with as many as 144 kids at any one time between twelve and fourteen), we divide the players into six teams, mixing the experienced players with the newcomers (beginners in tackle football may be much older than beginners in other sports).

We never see the kids play before arranging the team rosters, so it's impossible to choose players based on ability alone. The only determining factor is weight. The six lightest players are the first assigned to the six teams. The others are divided equally by weight among the teams and so on until the six heaviest kids are placed.

This allows for a proper match of the lightest to the heaviest players to compete against each other during each session.

Everyone makes a team, and the only prejudgment we use—the weight of the player—is strictly to keep the children safe while they learn the game.

JPD gives kids a democratic experience: Since there are no traditional games, everyone learns and plays equally. It is a true instructional program in that it advances every participant's ability. Everyone on the team is taught the same skill at the same time, and then we test the proper execution of that skill through competitions.

For example, one team of twenty-four may spend a segment of its practice learning the correct fundamentals of tackling. All twenty-four kids learn together, go through the segments of instruction together, and practice actual tackling techniques together. Then they proceed to a mini-competition segment with another team that has learned the proper techniques of taking a handoff and running with the ball. Before they compete, the players on the two teams are matched by weight.

We pay special attention to the structure of each drill. First we walk the players through the exercise, emphasizing the proper techniques without applying body-to-body impact. Learning how to tackle and get hit is complicated, and there is no need to rush the players into contact.

Our coaches supervise all drill competitions closely and control the tempo. They monitor the techniques and provide instant hands-on feedback to reinforce what they've just taught. As the technique of the players improves, the speed of the drill increases. Meanwhile, coaches continue to observe the players closely and provide feedback. They keep score for each participant by awarding points for proper execution. Everyone learns, no one gets ignored, and all players are given the opportunity to advance at their own pace. The mini-competitions serve as a barometer of individual progress despite the fact that no games are being played.

Coaches use common sense to split up mismatched players and fairly match players by their ability. It is the main objective of all JPD coaches to provide an experience that encourages all participants to want to come back to every practice.

One great example of making commonsense decisions occurred during a JPD program I observed in Providence, Rhode Island. It was a few weeks into the program, a time when competitions in specific skills had advanced to nearly full speed. Across the field I heard the crunch of shoulder pads, but the drill was conducted safely and a real, true competition was taking place. One pair of players was executing perfectly, with all-out vigor. I was not surprised by their performance until one of the helmets came off and a fourteen-year-old girl appeared. The coach told me that he constantly moved her around to find appropriate matches because her skills were advancing so rapidly, she was beating the boys her size too easily. "If one of those boys is discouraged," the coach told me, "he will probably never return because his friends will razz him."

A youth coach should not place a child in a situation where he cannot achieve some type of success. Negative results are detrimental to confidence building.

DODGING THE DRAFT

In the NFL's youth tackle football program, we have overcome the draft phenomenon and the mind-set that real games must be played. It's an approach that can be reproduced in any sport.

Let me prescribe a solution to my stepdaughter's soccer try-out and the season of unfair games and meaningless league standings that followed it. Her season was one in which, unfortunately, very little was learned and very few improved.

Instead of a Saturday morning tryout in August to determine which team she should play on, the league could have allowed friends to register in groups as large as sixteen. If four friends wanted to play together, for example, they would all register to be on the same team. This would inevitably make life easier on the parents since they could most likely carpool to each practice. Unlike in football, the size of the soccer player is not a major factor.

The second change I'd make would be to restructure the league so that on one afternoon each weekend all teams in each particular age group meet at adjoining fields. (If you have access to only one soccer field, schedule four teams for the one field.)

Start the session with every team learning the same fundamental skill, such as passing. Each team occupies one quadrant of the field, with four groups of four in each quadrant. After forty-five minutes of drills specifically designed to emphasize passing, play four mini-games. A total of sixty-four players can play on one soccer field, everyone plays equally, and the game emphasizes the skill that was just taught.

Another way to divide the teams is to give every team reversible jerseys, one side a dark color and the other side white. This way you can mix up the players, providing kids a wide variety of experiences in interacting and executing drills with different teammates. Breaking up the teams also takes away the competitive edge, and allows everyone to focus on the skill to be executed.

The forty-five-minute mini-games should involve two squads of eight per team per field. One squad should play while the other prepares to come in as a group every five minutes (a five-minute halftime allows teams to readjust lineups and the field for competitions). The object of each competition would involve a passing theme.

For the first twenty minutes set up each field with a circle of cones at each end and place three other circles of cones a fair distance apart from each other around the field. The object is to pass the ball successfully to a teammate inside one of the circles to receive a point. You can't return to that same circle until you successfully complete a pass to a teammate in another circle.

For the second twenty minutes place two small goals at each end of the field. The object of the game is to set up to score on each goal. Surround each goal with a marked-off crease or circle with a perimeter of approximately ten feet so a defender cannot enter. Since the goals are small, a precise shot or pass through the cones is needed to score. The competition requires players to apply the fundamental skills they have learned in the session.

A STRESS-FREE DRAFT

If you are a parent who already has a child in a traditional organized sport league, let me suggest a solution that several Little League baseball organizations already use.

A North Andover, Massachusetts, Little League program adopted a new method to draft players. In the past, two hundred kids were gathered in a gym, and one player at a time was asked to field five ground balls in front of the parents and the other players. This type of evaluation was judged by the league to be intimidating and unfair.

Instead of having the regular coaches judge Little League players, the league brought in neutral evaluators, such as high school and college coaches, to run the tryout and assess the players. Each of the two hundred players was given a number, so no one was alarmed or embarrassed by having his name announced or mentioned during the entire process.

Meanwhile, the other players worked their way through six to eight different skill stations set up to allow for simultaneous evaluations. This eliminated any single solo performance from taking place in front of a large group and took the pressure and attention off any one player during the entire tryout. The kids got three opportunities to perform at each skill station, giving them many more chances to prove their skills than in a traditional draft.

The evaluators gave each player a score from one to five, one representing a beginner player and five an advanced player. Then coaches from each team received the numerical evaluation scores of all candidates, including their returning players. Prior to the draft, coaches made a list of their returning players as well as their "impact" players (identified as pitchers, catchers, shortstops, and second basemen). If a team had three returning impact players, the team did not participate in the first three rounds of the draft. By the end of the draft, all teams had a similar cumulative player evaluation score. The system allowed for more parity throughout the league and prevented the top teams from distancing themselves significantly from last-place teams.

Though I don't condone any type of draft system, this is at least a better alternative if you must continue to participate in a traditional system.

FAIR PLAYING TIME

Let's address the subject of playing time. If you have children involved in a traditional league, they most likely were selected through a tryout, draft, or other similar selection process. This immediately placed a hammerlock on their ability to improve their skills because they didn't get the advantage of prior (or proper) instruction. Simply because they went through a draft, they may not receive equal playing time during the season.

There is a simple solution to this problem. An easy Web-based tracking system has been created to ensure that everyone gets the same amount of playing time during the season. MyTeam.com offers a system called "Play Time Reporting," an effective tool that coaches can use to track and communicate everyone's playing time to all players and parents. Coaches use the system to track the total amount of time each player spends in a game. In baseball, for example, the system would track the total number of innings played by the team and by each player. The coach can then print out a report on the percentage of playing time received by each player and distribute the player-by-player breakdown to the team and the parents.

Of course, this can all be avoided if you incorporate the Fair Play philosophy and structure into your league. In a Fair Play structure the playing time for everyone participating is 100 percent. And there's no paperwork involved.

This is the Fair Play way:

- No drafts

- Teams arranged so everyone is happy and there is a sense of unity

- Everyone plays equally

- More time spent playing than in any traditional game

- Applied learning in gamelike situations

The results will include:

- A season of improved skills

- Themed sessions with clear objectives

- Full participation of every player

There are not too many youth leagues that accomplish these objectives.

6

KEEPING A CHILD'S INTEREST:
Proven Ways to Maintain Youth Involvement in Sports

Three-quarters of all kids drop out of organized sports by the age of twelve. Some of these children move on to music or other art-related activities. Some find alternative physical activities, such as skateboarding or BMX biking, to take the place of organized sports. But many become physically inactive, no longer building their bodies along with their minds.

There is an alarming fact that parents need to know: Children today make up their minds about organized sports, consciously or unconsciously, well before they reach the age of twelve. And far too many decide to get out.

Kids drop out of organized sports because they find no satisfaction or enjoyment. Many kids begin to get turned off from sports early on, and it often happens without you realizing it. Meanwhile, with well-meaning intent, you continue to sign them up and drive them to practices and games. You continue to encourage them, even if they start to show signs of disinterest. Then suddenly, one day, they just plain don't want to go.

To a certain extent I believe you should encourage your kids to participate in sports. However, in light of what happens every day on youth athletic fields, you must pay close attention to your child and monitor her reactions and emotions throughout the program.

But don't be surprised or, worse, feel guilty if you see signs that all is not well. Without a doubt I can guarantee you that your child will at some point find organized sports an unfulfilling experience. The timing varies from child to child. A naturally athletic child probably will receive more attention and feel better about herself a majority of the time. But even the most talented eventually find organized sports boring.

SOME THINGS NEVER CHANGE

Sports have been taught and played the same way for decades. Yes, the technology has improved, and so the games have evolved slightly. But the structure by which children learn and play has not changed. Baseball, basketball, and football practices are the same today as they were fifty years ago. In baseball, as when you were a kid, a team holds batting practice and everyone stands around while the coach attempts to throw a ball across the plate. At basketball practice two lines form with six kids on each line alternating, one taking layups and the other rebounding. Whatever happened to you as a child, it's likely the same thing is happening today.

The problem is today's generation is different from those that preceded it. If not continuously engaged, a kid's mind begins to wander. If that kid performs the same drill every practice, he gets bored. In contrast, there are plenty of other exciting things the child can do. He can go home and multitask on the computer, exchanging instant messages with a dozen friends and downloading information from numerous Web sites.

Perhaps this child hits the slopes with his friends on winter weekends and snowboards. On the mountain there's constant action. Everyone participates. There is no need to stand around and watch others. Each run becomes a new adventure and provides the freedom to learn new tricks at whatever pace feels comfortable. Come spring, the kid is back in line at baseball practice, performing the never-changing routine of shagging fly balls and hitting the cutoff man.

Do you get the point? Your kids hope so, because organized youth sports have missed the most vital point of all: They're not the only game in town.

If we don't give kids a contemporary experience in organized sports, they will find one and leave the traditional sports behind. I don't mean to say that this is all bad. It's great that kids participate in alternative sports. But because most alternative sports are unsupervised, kids don't get a chance to try them until they are older. Some kids have been so scarred by earlier childhood sports experiences they avoid sports altogether.

A SKATEBOARDER'S TALE

There is a lot we can learn from alternative action sports such as skateboarding and BMX riding. What is so appealing to kids that they'd rather be doing something like this than play baseball, basketball, or football? The answer tells us a lot about what's wrong with organized sports today and can be a blueprint for shaping a more contemporary experience in your community programs and prevent kids from dropping out.

To find out about the appeal of action sports, I spoke with Andy MacDonald, one of the top-ranked skateboarders in the country and a professional skater for the past fifteen years. Andy is as popular for his devotion to his fans and his sport as he is for his spectacular tricks. He regularly spends hours after events signing autographs and talking to young enthusiasts.

Andy left team sports to pursue his interest in skateboarding. As he explained, "Before I found skateboarding or skateboarding found me, I had participated in pretty much every team sport out there, with the exception of football, which my mom thought was too dangerous. For nine years, through junior high, I was in wrestling, gymnastics, soccer, basketball, and swimming. I did them all.

"I found skateboarding when I was twelve, and as I got into it, probably within two years, I had quit all the other sports. I'd be skateboarding, and soccer practice would start. I didn't want to put on my cleats and have someone tell me to run laps or tell me the right or wrong way to kick a ball.

"There's a whole lifestyle and a culture that goes with skateboarding. You *play* football or you *play* soccer, but you *are* a skateboarder. Basically you just become addicted to wanting to learn how to do it, to wanting to better yourself. But unlike all the other sports I was doing, it was up to me to figure it out. There was no right or wrong way to do it, and I had to motivate myself to become a better skateboarder. There was no coach telling me I had to do it a certain number of hours per day or that I had to do something one specific way. Soccer just wasn't fun for me anymore.

"It's better to learn by your own sweat, blood, and tears, not by having some guy tell you, 'You're going to have to sit out, because this kid is better at your position. He's a better halfback, and here we are in the critical game. You're going to have to make a sacrifice.' Sure, it teaches you that element, but where did the fun go? It's all about winning.

"In skateboarding there is no right or wrong way to do a trick. You can watch five kids do the same trick, and each has his own style for that particular move. One way is not any better than the other. I think that's probably what attracted me and what attracts most kids to the sport.

"One of the fundamental tricks in skateboarding is called the ollie—learning to hold your skateboard on your feet as you jump into the air. It's the starting point for every other trick. You need to learn how to ollie to be able to jump off a curb, for instance. It took me probably a year to learn how to jump off a curb, but in doing that I had so much fun. My friends and I used to lay little sticks in the road. Even when we couldn't get off the curb, we could say, 'Hey, we got over the little stick.'

"Kids will work on tricks for years. There are certain tricks I do now—which I still can't do consistently—that took me six years of practice before I could do my first. Six years of trying over and over, a little bit every day. The satisfaction in finally making that trick after trying it for six years can't compare to any other sport. You get a stab at winning the Super Bowl or something like that maybe once in a lifetime, if that. In skateboarding there's that feeling with every new trick you learn—especially when you start to get into more advanced tricks. They are so difficult that they can take years to learn.

"When it comes to competition, you can mess up, make it look good, and get extra points. If you watch gymnastics on television, someone might be up on the high bar looking great, and they say, 'No, his left toe wasn't flexed there. He's going to lose points for that.' Whereas in skateboarding it would be like, 'Wow, that was great. He missed with one hand, but he grabbed it with the other hand and he's still hanging on the bar.' He gets extra points.

"I was at the Y the other day watching some six-, seven-, and eight-year-olds play basketball. There was no dribbling going on, just grabbing the ball and running up the court. These kids looked like they were having such a great time. The two organizers weren't calling fouls or telling kids, 'No, that's traveling. You have to dribble.' They were just letting those kids go at it. Sure, eventually you'll teach those kids the rules of the game and that they're not allowed to run up the court with the ball. But for right now those kids are having a great time, and maybe that's going to instill a love of basketball. The kids just looked like they were having the best time. They couldn't even stay on their feet, they were falling down so much, and I was laughing out loud just watching them.

"The lessons that you attribute to a coach teaching his kids—teamwork, discipline, and motivation—are lessons that I learned myself in wanting to be a better skateboarder, without even knowing it. And those lessons stuck because I learned them myself, not by someone else telling me 'This is the way it is.'

"My main suggestion for organized youth sports would be to just put the fun back in it. People need to talk about how to do that. There are a million different ways."

ANOTHER REFUGEE FROM ORGANIZED SPORTS

Brett Downs has been a pioneer in BMX biking, a sport that includes racing, tricks, and jumping, for three decades. Like Andy MacDonald, Brett left organized sports because they failed to keep his interest. Brett caught my attention a few years ago when he performed back flips on his bike on the fifty-yard line of an Eagles versus Giants football game at halftime. We can learn a lot from what he has to say about youth sports. As Brett explained:

"I grew up in a football family, the second of three boys. I played midget football for one year and football in high school for my freshman, sophomore, and junior years. I was always primarily interested in jumping my bike, but my father never took it seriously and wasn't supportive at all. I actually went to the first football practice of my senior year and spent the whole time wishing I was on my bike. I realized that for the past three years, as soon as I got home from football, I hopped on my bike. The logical thing seemed to be to ride rather than play ball.

"When I was five, I lived on a street with big oak trees that pushed up the sidewalk sections. I noticed that if I went fast enough, the front wheel of my bike would pop up, and eventually I could jump. As I became aware of Evel Knievel, I wanted to progress in my riding. This kept me busy for about a decade before I found out about organized BMX racing and the sport of BMX itself. I just had fun stretching the limits and the adventure every time I pedaled down the street. I still do. I guess it's the daredevil factor combined with its just being fun.

"In my experience there was no instruction until I was about fourteen. Then I met some friends who rode, and one gave me all of his old BMX magazines. The magazines explained the whole paradigm of BMX. I saw tricks, bikes, ramps, jumps, riders, and every aspect. After that I met new friends with whom I would ride, and we would push each other to try harder and improve. Now with videos, television coverage, and camps such as Woodward in Pennsylvania, kids can see BMX riding and try it under the guidance of seasoned riders.

"Personally, I teach every kid in my neighborhood who shows an interest. It is almost a duty to me to pass on the knowledge and fun. I introduce kids to this little esoteric activity and show them what has been my passion for almost thirty years. Coaching is offered as authoritative guidance, not authoritarian yelling from the sidelines.

"Action sports are not team sports. Kids learn self-reliance and independence that team sports don't offer. Although being a team member is a gift I got from football, the reward of individual success surpasses my team's undefeated championship season. Even more important is that success in action sports is measured by individual improvement and achievement.

"Team sports are often evaluated on the ability to defeat another player or team. Being the best is what counts. With action sports, improvement is the benchmark. 'Was I better today than I was yesterday?' becomes the goal. Perhaps swimming or running, where you compete against a clock, is similar. Action sports are also lifestyle sports, which appeals to adolescents. This brings about a camaraderie among participants. As a high school teacher I saw that for many students it was often better to be a punk-rock skateboarder than a dumb jock.

"Organized sports need to become more stimulating. No one is a benchwarmer in BMX or skating. We all participate. The amount of structure in teenagers' lives today overwhelms them, but on their bikes, boards, and blades they are able to be released from life's confinements. Organized sports are great for kids, but sometimes kids need to be free to create and progress without supervision or specific goals. In action sports the goal is the practice, not the competition."

Brett's words really speak to the essence of why kids leave organized sports. He also explains perfectly what organized sports should learn from alternative sports—the passing of the torch through instruction when participants or peers act as coaches. I love Brett's comment about success being totally about something else such as self-improvement rather than about winning. He also destroys the myth that team sports are the only place to find camaraderie. And he's absolutely right that sitting on the bench in team sports is never stimulating.

THE DROPOUT FACTOR

Traditionalists who believe sports should remain constant in all regards are not concerned about the large dropout rate of kids at the age of twelve, because at thirteen, the elite athlete emerges and forces out the broader masses of hopeful players. In other words, traditionalists believe there is no room for casual or recreational participants in organized sports at this age and beyond. The hierarchy of sports allows for and even encourages this type of mind-set. No one takes into consideration or thinks about late bloomers. Therefore, many young athletes with latent talent in an organized sport have been told there is no room for them to play. A would-be star becomes an instant failure.

Interestingly, people are beginning to take notice. The shrinking pool of athletes after the age of twelve has started to alarm high school coaches. The large dropout rate coupled with the variety of other sports now available in high school is leaving coaches hard put to field full rosters in traditional sports such as football. How can you prevent your children from quitting sports at an early age? First ask yourself what your motivation is to seeing your kids participate in organized sports. If you believe they should play because of the possibility of receiving a college scholarship or becoming a professional athlete, you should realize how unrealistic this hope really is. The percentage of kids who actually achieve this goal is very small: Less than 1 percent of all kids participating in organized sports today will receive any sort of college athletic scholarship. You would be better off placing the money you spend on sports in a college savings account for your child.

Nevertheless, parents continue to spend a great deal of money on the best and latest equipment, team and club dues, summer skill camps, year-round clinics, tournament fees, and travel to and from tournaments. These figures can amount to thousands of dollars each year for just one sport. As a result, parents are a large factor in sports becoming too serious for their children. The greater the investment by the parents, the greater the pressure on the child.

FUTURE STARS

Childhood is lost soon enough in today's fast-paced society. Youth sports have contributed to the loss of innocence. They have broken the hearts and spirits of young athletes. For example, it may seem that if a child has not made the travel soccer team by the age of ten, she might as well pack it in and look for another sport. By this age not only are youth soccer organizations selecting the most talented, but they are registering them into year-round leagues, clinics, camps, and tournaments.

Youth basketball goes even further. Street agents prowl the playgrounds searching for eight-year-olds who show some promise. Soon the prospect is registered in a local church or youth organization league. Even more surprising, he may be committed to an agent who pays the parents for the rights for future representation. Of course this dream-maker often hides behind the veil of a youth coach or family friend.

Between those deemed unworthy at an early age to move into the elite level and those who do move on but never measure up to false expectations, we end up with millions of disillusioned kids giving up on sports altogether. With these high dropout rates, we can almost be certain that many children will eventually fall into the category of "former athletes."

As a parent you must not despair. Rather, you should rally to change what is wrong with organized sports today. Youth sports deliver too many lifetime benefits for kids to just give in—benefits such as learning how to act and cooperate in group situations, how to overcome adversity, and how important it is to take responsibility, to name just a few.

The contemporary and innovative methods used in Fair Play provide the structure that gives children the positive experience they want and deserve.

LEARNING TO CHANGE

As a parent you do not have to sit idly by and not participate in your child's youth sports experience. Gather together a group of other parents and begin restructuring youth sports in your community today. If you organize yourselves properly, it will not take much of your time, and you will be rewarded with happier kids.

To stress the importance of acting today, keep in mind what makes kids unhappy and drives them to drop out:

- They experience little or no improvement.

- They get limited opportunity to play.

- They get no choice in what they learn.

■ They spend more time doing nothing than doing something.

■ They get bored.

Earlier in the book I discussed how to revitalize your child's sports experience by following a nontraditional approach to learning and playing. In Chapter 3, I used the Junior Player Development model to explain how to break an entire season into sessions that involve both instruction and competitions. Traditional games are never played. I recommend that you use that model and apply it to any sport in which your children are involved.

In this chapter, I focus on the need to change traditional sports structures that are already in place by changing a sport's approach to practices. Meaningful, enjoyable practices will prevent kids from quitting. Unfortunately, most youth sports leagues and coaches place all their emphasis on the games.

PRACTICES MADE PERFECT

Designing a practice is the most important part of any coach's job at any level of sport. This is where the real learning takes place. This is where coaches have the opportunity to spend time with everyone and provide hands-on teaching and encouragement in a controlled environment. This is also where most coaches fail because too often they are not prepared to make this the most important part of an athlete's experience.

Paul Pasqualoni, the head football coach at Syracuse University, learned these skills prior to coaching. He said, "My best preparation to become a coach was my experience as an elementary school teacher. I had to go to class every day with every minute of the day planned out and organized. It was the only way to provide a quality learning experience for every student, and it helped me control the class and hold their attention. I apply those same methods today with my teams."

Here are five guidelines to follow in order to conduct practices that are both instructional and enjoyable:

1. Plan every practice.

Too many coaches waste their time strategizing at the chalkboard when they could be out on the field teaching the fundamentals. Most of them consider the game plan the glamorous side of the sport. But at the youth level it's a waste of time. No matter how innovative your game plans may be, you will accomplish little if your players are unable to execute the basics. Teaching the fundamentals of the game is the most essential part of youth sports.

Unfortunately, fundamentals have fallen by the wayside; they are either ignored or considered too boring to hold a child's interest. Ignoring instruction in the fundamentals is a disservice to every athlete you coach. But instruction in the fundamentals must be approached in a creative manner that holds a team's attention and is also effective in the development of everyone's skill execution.

Proper preparation for each practice should produce fast-paced sessions in which everyone is engaged in the drill and constantly moving. Learning is continuous and downtime is limited. To achieve this, pair everyone off with a partner or series of partners at the beginning of the season. The pairings should reflect approximate skill levels and/or similar size. These pairs will be constant throughout the season at every practice. Pairing kids off in the beginning of the season with a series of several alternative matchups will save you time when someone is absent from practice. The assigned pairs will work on all skills as a group, assisting each other in the learning process.

Every season should begin with several fundamental team objectives. Practices then become the building blocks to achieve those objectives. In ice or roller hockey, for example, your first season objective may be to become a good forechecking team. Forechecking is an offensive fundamental that keeps the puck in your scoring zone and causes the opposing team difficulty in clearing the puck from their defensive zone. Good forechecking teams score more goals and create more turnovers of the puck. Your second season objective may be to increase your percentage of scoring when your opponent is shorthanded or serving a penalty.

If you had eight practices throughout the season, each practice would focus on building the fundamentals to accomplish the seasonal goals. In each practice the team would split into groups of twos and threes, which works especially well for hockey since there are so many three-on-two situations. The groups would then be instructed in a series of skills such as passing, stick handling, stick checking, and puck pursuit (chasing to arrive first at the puck in designated parts of the ice). Each practice would review the prior practice and build on the skill development in each of these areas.

2. Break every practice into timed segments.

After planning a specific objective for the practice, break down the time minute by minute. This can easily be done by deciding what fundamental skill you would like to work on during that practice and then breaking down each element of that skill into ten-minute segments (fifteen minutes would be the maximum for teaching a more detailed aspect of a skill). Practices should be no more than ninety minutes in length. Remember, you want to keep everyone's interest at a maximum and also save the coaches' time. Many professional coaches approach each practice in this same organized fashion.

It is also helpful to recruit other parents to assist the team. An instructor-to-player ratio of one to six creates a perfect learning environment and limits the time that the players spend standing around. Each player gets plenty of attention.

For our hypothetical hockey team eighteen players can play for ninety minutes with three instructors stationed at different parts of the rink. At each of the stations the players can focus on learning and applying a skill in drills. Every ten minutes a time-keeper blows a whistle or sounds the scoreboard horn to alert the players to move on to the next skill. Fundamentals are more easily digested this way and are ultimately easier to teach. Each instructor should keep the players lined up and in pairs to demonstrate the skill and then have the players execute it at the same time. At this point the instructor can easily see what all three groups of twos are doing and make immediate hands-on corrections.

3. Use competitions to emphasize skills learned.

A series of group skill competitions should take place during the practice. Hold two fifteen-minute competitions, one in the middle of practice and another at the end. In our hockey example, half of the team can work on puck pursuit skills (which involve a series of skating and stick checking fundamentals) in their offensive zone. The other half of the team can work on how to defend against this pursuit (skating, stick handling, and passing fundamentals).

The competitions break up the practice and allow everyone to apply the skills just learned in a low-key yet competitive environment. They also force everyone to pay attention during practice in order to perform well in the competitions. In each competition segment, use a point system and award points to individuals and/or groups who execute successfully. Keep a tally of scores throughout the year as a friendly competitive element. This will also allow everyone to gauge his progress during the season.

4. Teach every position to every participant.

Teaching every position has been the cornerstone of NFL Junior Player Development's success. Football has many positions on both offense and defense that require several different types of skill sets. It is critical to allow everyone the opportunity to learn every position in order for all players to become comfortable and naturally pick the position that best suits them.

Since we are using hockey as our example, I should point out that there are fewer positions on a hockey team. There are two forward wings, one center, two defensemen, and one goalkeeper. It is crucial at the youth level that all players learn all four positions.

5. Be creative when designing drills and competitions.

In order to keep things fresh and contemporary for kids, you must think with an open mind and create fun drills and competitions that reinforce what you've just taught.

This is the area in which I make my living. I constantly come up with different ways for kids to play and learn the game of football. I create new programs for kids in order to develop fans for life. One program I created incorporates a skill development game as well as a means of further developing fans for a sport. I did this with NFL Youth Football programs, but the idea can be applied to any sport.

Parents often complain that their kids either watch too much television or spend too much time on the Internet. This next skill development tool takes some of the things that kids enjoy the most (televised sports, professional athletes, and the Internet) and integrates them with their performances in practices and games.

Let's say your hockey season objectives are to become a better passing team and be more aggressive in your offensive zone in order to score more goals. As a benchmark ask each player to select two National Hockey League players, one defensive and one offensive, after practice each week. Over the next seven days they will track their NHL players' statistics by watching games and surfing the Web. They will count assists (the number of times the player sets up a goal with a pass) and plus-minus ratio (a hockey statistic that gives one positive point when the player is on the ice when his team scores and one negative point when on the ice and the opponent scores). These scores are then combined with the youth player's individual statistics from practice and/or a game to give each player an NHL team score.

A point is given for each assist, and the total plus-minus scores are combined for a composite individual score. The child's score is then added to his two NHL players' scores for the week. For example, if a child has two assists for the week in games and designated drills during practice and is on the ice when his team scores five times and is scored against two times (plus five and minus two for a total score of three), his total weekly individual score would be five. He would then add his score to the scores of his two NHL players for a combined team total. This game places a focus on learning specific skills while still having fun.

When your team attends practice the next week, you can announce the scores for each of the players. This little activity accomplishes several things for a coach and a team, including the following:

- Less talented players can compete on an equal footing.

- Kids watch, focus, and learn from professional players who execute the same skills that the kids are learning.

- It's a fun and different slant on achieving your objectives as a team.

- It holds everyone's attention and excitement while emphasizing important fundamental skills.

You continue this each week by selecting different NHL players and recording the statistical and skill competition scores.

As a result of these structural changes, players will retain more information and be better equipped to apply the skills they are taught. Every practice will have an aura of excitement, and players will have added incentive to attend. By giving attention to your entire team, you will be able to teach more effectively and serve all players equally.

7

MAKING STRIDES:
Guaranteed Improvement for All— from Beginners to "Naturals"

Do you notice significant improvement in your child's athletic ability in any one season? Probably not. It's rare for parents to see consistent improvement in their children's performance when they participate in youth sports.

Improvement can be measured in many ways. Some parents may measure it by increased playing time, a reduction of mistakes, or more successful execution of plays during games. Others simply measure it by the number of wins. The problem with all these measures is that they are often relative.

Your child may receive more playing time by default, such as when others don't show up or the coach begins to distribute time equally. Or your child may begin to perform at a higher rate of success as she becomes more comfortable executing certain plays. This doesn't necessarily mean she is performing correctly or using the proper fundamental skills. Without the right kind of training, your child ultimately can form bad habits and become fundamentally unsound as she advances to future levels.

Fundamentals are the single most overlooked element in youth sports and the root cause of why kids drop out. When a child performs poorly but does not have a clue as to why, he gets discouraged and quickly loses interest. This is a huge disservice to your child. Without a fundamental foundation to fall back on, no child can expect to see any realistic improvement in his athletic capabilities. Yet all too often parents and coaches expect to see children in organized sports perform flawlessly, making plays that take pros years to perfect. This is unfair and unrealistic. And given the fact that fundamentals are all but ignored, it would be impossible for any child to live up to these expectations.

DO YOU BELIEVE IN MIRACLES?

A case that best illustrates this point occurred in October 2001 in the first round of the American League playoffs. Derek Jeter of the New York Yankees cut off a ball thrown by outfielder Paul O'Neill to home plate. Without hesitation and without fully turning his body, Jeter backhanded the ball to his catcher and teammate Jorge Posada to throw out Jeremy Giambi of the Oakland Athletics. The play was considered the turning point of the playoff series. The Yankees had already lost the first two games, but this play ignited them to win the pivotal third game and go on to take the series, three games to two.

So how did the play work? By pure instinct, Jeter did not turn the natural way to pivot and throw to home plate. Instead, he transferred the ball from his glove to his right throwing hand and backhanded the throw, which only required a half turn of his body. This saved precious time and allowed him to throw out the runner. Many people, the media included, have glamorized this play since it was executed in a pressure-packed situation, and at that very millisecond Jeter did exactly what was needed to execute a virtually impossible play. They consider the play so unique as to be practically a miracle, but that is simply not the case. The only way Jeter or anyone else of his ability could perform such a fantastic play was to have executed it hundreds of times before in practice.

Jeter spent thousands of hours in his lifetime working on the fundamental skills that prepared him to make such a play. At every practice he worked on fielding throws and experimenting with how to get the ball as quickly and as accurately as possible to his intended target. So when the time came, he was prepared. Fundamentals allow you to perform in pressure situations and thereby make the game enjoyable for a lifetime.

On that same play, Jeremy Giambi was tagged out primarily because he did not slide; instead, he attempted to avoid the tag by staying on his feet and running through home plate. One of the fundamental principles of baserunning is that you slide if there is even a chance of being tagged out. Giambi demonstrated another important lesson here: Even professionals who have been drilled endlessly in the fundamentals make mistakes. But by training in the basics and fundamentals of the game, you avoid such mistakes most of the time.

TEACHING THE FUNDAMENTALS PROPERLY

There are always pitfalls when teaching kids the fundamentals of any sport. Being taught incorrectly can be a greater disservice than not learning at all. Nothing disturbs me more than observing a child receiving poor instruction in the basics of a sport. At such impressionable ages, incorrect fundamental instruction will lead to bad habits that inhibit development. That can all be easily avoided.

Let's say you're a coach who has not properly prepared your-self to teach a fundamental skill. My advice is don't teach it. Work on something you do know until you learn how to teach the new skill correctly. Also, if you yourself cannot properly demonstrate a fundamental skill, let someone else show it while you explain the skill and make corrections. You will immediately lose credibility with your team if you attempt to perform a skill and do it incor-rectly.

A good instructor doesn't necessarily need to demonstrate. Instead, he must have the ability to communicate and articulate what he is attempting to accomplish. He should break down the skill into parts that are easy to understand and execute. Breaking down the fundamentals into a progression of steps is the key to success in improving skill development. Here are four strategic steps:

1. Master the mechanics.

Let's take the golf swing as an example. Golf is one of the most technical games to learn. The mechanics of the swing must be mas-tered in order to play at a high level of competency. To develop those vital mechanics the fundamentals of the swing must be bro-ken down and learned. Without learning how to swing a club prop-erly, you cannot even begin to play the game. The swing has four essential components: the grip, the stance and posture, the back-swing, and the downswing. These components have additional smaller parts that make up the fundamentals of the golf swing. Golfers seek to develop a swing that they can continue to replicate. Consistency in executing the fundamentals is the key to success in golf and any other sport. The basics of the game should become as familiar to athletes as walking.

Now let's take your child's current sports experience. Is she being taught all the fundamentals of the game? If so, are they broken down into easy-to-understand parts that can be pieced together to perform specific skills? Are these fundamentals repeated and reviewed thoroughly during the season? And, most important, is she having fun learning these fundamentals?

If the answer to these questions is no, then your child is getting cheated. If no one takes the time and effort to teach the basics, she will not have the foundation necessary to move to the next level or obtain a real appreciation for the sport. If the basic fundamentals are taught in the proper progression and are reinforced by competitions that emphasize the skills learned, your child will improve at any age.

2. Break down the skills for each position.

As a coach you must identify all the fundamental skills of every position and establish a breakdown of each position's skill components. Remember to make all components easy to describe and teach. As mentioned earlier, you should plan a practice that teaches one particular position. In football, for example, one practice can be spent teaching the defensive back position. (This is the player who defends against the pass by covering the receiver on the other team.)

Here is how we teach the defensive back position at NFL Junior Player Development. First we identify each of the components. There are six basic fundamentals that make up the position: stance, start, and alignment; form tackling; catching; backpedal and close; backpedal and break on receiver; and ball drills. Each participant has already received basic training in form tackling (the technique of proper tackling) and catching. Therefore, these components are reviewed. In actuality, form tackling is reviewed every time we teach a defensive position. For each component we devote a specific amount of time to describe, teach and demonstrate, execute and repeat, and correct the players.

The key to this structure is that everyone executes equally and with a substantial number of repetitions. This is accomplished with individuals paired off by size (in the case of football) and ability, as well as by breaking the team into groups of no more than six players to one instructor.

3. Teach in timed segments.

Components should be planned and assigned specific timed periods. Periods should last no more than fifteen minutes because you begin to lose a young person's attention after that. We challenge our instructors to know exactly what they want to accomplish each period. Our JPD defensive back session, for example, would include the following:

10 minutes	Agilities and stretching
10 minutes	Stance, start, and alignment
10 minutes	Form tackling
10 minutes	Catching
10 minutes	Backpedal and close
5 minutes	Review
15 minutes	Individual competition with receivers
10 minutes	Backpedal and break on receiver
10 minutes	Ball drills
10 minutes	Competition with receivers

You don't have to know football to understand how this structure works in teaching a particular position. The same concept works for any position in any sport.

4. Provide hands-on instruction.

The instructor must describe what is being taught and why it is important. If you are the instructor, place a group of six in a semicircle facing you. After describing the skill, break down its components and demonstrate the correct way to execute it. If you cannot demonstrate accurately, assign someone else to do it. Make sure you mention common mistakes that are made and how to avoid them. Then separate the group into their assigned pairs and instruct each pair to set up and execute the skill.

Remember to go to each pair and give hands-on attention and incorporate corrections. During this stage of teaching it is also important to identify and provide positive reinforcement to every participant. This is the best time to begin to take advantage of teaching moments. The players will make many mistakes, but each mistake presents a great opportunity for you to give positive reinforcement.

In this system you can be successful in introducing and teaching important fundamental skills by holding your group's attention at a maximum level. After several teaching segments similar to this one, the groups move to individual competitions in which all the players have the opportunity to apply what they've just learned. You keep score in the competitions by awarding points for proper execution of the fundamental skills just taught.

When you adopt the Fair Play structure and teach every position by the methods described, your entire team will experience improvement. When fundamentals are broken down into easy-to-understand and executable parts, kids can learn at their own pace, appropriately matched up with a partner at the same level. They focus entirely on the task at hand and reinforce what they've just learned in the competitions.

BETTER BASEBALL BY THE BASICS

One of the benefits of my job and my career is that I've had the opportunity to meet special people like David Bentencourt. Dave, a former head baseball coach at the University of New Hampshire, is today a high school baseball coach in a community in need (Lawrence, Massachusetts). He doesn't make a lot of money, yet he spends all his free time working with kids. When he's not instructing his high school players, he's working at the grassroots level in other struggling communities. In his programs he takes kids as young as six and helps them develop their skills in a fun and creative environment. When I visited with him recently, I witnessed his innovations in teaching youth baseball.

During a sixty-minute practice, Dave took twelve players from one team of eight- and nine-year-olds and instructed them simultaneously in three different skills of the game. As with JPD, all twelve kids were constantly learning and engaged, and there was limited standing around. Three groups of four were placed at three designated stations around the field, with one instructor assigned to each group. The instructors conducted twenty-minute segments, and the groups rotated from one station to the next. The stations focused on infield, outfield, and batting skills.

At the infield skill station an instructor hit a progression of ground balls to the four players. Each of the players had wooden paddles (similar to Ping-Pong paddles) attached to their hands. The kids fielded ground balls with the paddles through a series of drills. The paddles accentuated the use of two hands when fielding a ball and also the proper setup to throw the ball correctly.

The outfield station consisted of one instructor hitting tennis balls with a racket to the four players over a series of drills. By using a racket and tennis balls the instructors alleviated the fear

factor of catching a ball. When the fear was taken out, the eight-
and nine-year-olds were able to fully concentrate on their skills.

At the hitting station four players stood in a semicircle holding bats. The instructor threw plastic golf balls to each participant
from fifteen feet away. Since the plastic ball is much smaller than a
baseball and moves around when thrown, it is more challenging to
hit. The players were able to improve their hand-eye coordination
by working with the smaller ball. Again, the fact that it wasn't a
baseball removed the fear factor. This is also a great drill to use in-
doors on a rainy day.

I spoke with Dave about his philosophy of teaching youth
sports. I hope you'll find his remarks as interesting as I did.

"When I first started coaching baseball at the high school level,
I assumed that all the kids understood the fundamentals of the
game. But when I approached some of the pitchers on my team, I
realized they had never learned how to grip the ball properly—the
most basic element of pitching. From that point on I decided that
teaching the fundamentals of every position was critical, and I emphasize it to this day. Each season I assume it's the first time my
players have ever seen a baseball, and we take it from there.

"I played high school ball with a guy named John Tudor who
didn't make our freshman team and got cut as a junior. Later he became a professional athlete and pitched in the major leagues, mostly with the Red Sox and the Cardinals. Today he's wearing a World
Series ring and two division championship rings. My philosophy
when it comes to skill development is that I never want to tell
someone he can't play and find out later that he gained the ability.
Every youngster is worth working with and developing.

"When I played, I was a small guy, an underdog and a late
bloomer. It meant I had to spend a lot of time practicing. I had my

success, but I had to work to get it. I think all those things were a blessing to me as a coach, and I take them into account now in dealing with kids of different abilities.

"We set small goals for each player. For some youngsters it's just the ability to catch a ball properly. For others it might be to hit the ball over the fence because they're a little more advanced.

"From a coaching standpoint I keep my practices moving and supply a ton of repetitions. At the end of practice we have what's called 'championship' time. That's when each player assesses his weakest area and works on it for the last ten minutes.

"As far as practice time, practice shouldn't last longer than an hour and a half. In that hour and a half every youngster on our team—which could be fourteen to sixteen players—takes between eighty and one hundred ground balls, fly balls, and swings.

"I believe a coach should not be judged by how he deals with his number one player because that's easy. If I want to know about a coach, I ask him how his number fourteen or number sixteen player feels about his skill advancement.

"Baseball has lost too many kids because we have fourteen players standing around the field and one taking batting practice, and it's become a tedious experience. You have to come up with creative ways to engage kids all the time, or they will continue to leave the game.

"Take time during stretching to talk to kids you don't get to spend as much time with during a game. How often in a game do you get to talk to your right fielder? During warm-ups, go over to him and just ask him how he's doing.

"I try to deemphasize winning and losing. I always ask a child, 'Did you understand the material?' If it was a classroom and he got an eighty-nine or ninety-five on a test, I would ask the same question. That's more important than what the final score was. We ask kids to compete much too early—before we give them any training, before they even have the mental or physical skills.

"I tell our high school kids, 'I want all of you to become coaches.' I'm trying to teach fifteen future coaches. I tell them, 'Be patient. Don't get hung up on the scoreboard.' Our gauge is not wins and losses, it's achievements such as contacts with the bat, number of strikes, or first pitch strikes. Our measure of success is a little different.

"My greatest personal success as a coach came when I took a group of kids who at the beginning of the season couldn't make contact with the ball and by the end had learned to just barely connect with it. That was a win for them, and those are the rewards and the real wins in coaching.

"I wish more coaches could see that smile on every one of their players' faces. Better yet, have every one of their players return the next season. If more coaches could experience that, I think we'd solve a lot of problems in youth sports."

———

If you overlook the fundamentals and skip directly to playing games, you have accomplished very little. Search for the proper methods to teach all the fundamentals of the game. Remember, this should be the core of a child's sports experience. If you do not provide preparation in the fundamentals, you cannot call yourself a legitimate coach.

8

WOMEN WANTED:
Making the Leap from the Stands to the Sidelines

Women are the greatest untapped resource in youth sports. In the countless hours I have spent at youth games, practices, and tournaments, I have always been puzzled by the absence of women coaches. The sidelines seem to be reserved exclusively for men, while women are relegated to bringing the snack, driving the carpool, and sitting in the stands rooting for their kids.

To me this is clearly one of the most backward traditions in sports today. There is no reason why a woman cannot coach as effectively as a man. This is especially true when you consider that the new generation of moms probably played as many organized sports when growing up as their male counterparts.

Even if you didn't play sports at all as a child, you can still coach at the youth level. Do you really think all the men you see on the sidelines actually played or were ever any good? As a mom you have as much right to be coaching the kids as the dads. I'm not just talking about coaching girls' sports, either. Women are as qualified to coach boys as girls. If you enjoy teaching, are halfway organized, and have passion and dedication, I guarantee you will be one of the most successful coaches in your child's program.

As the Fair Play philosophy stresses, anyone—woman or man—can learn how to teach the basics of any sport. Just as we have allowed outdated tradition to ruin the experience of our children in organized sports, we have also failed to include women as coaches. Of course this trespasses on one of the last of the male bastions, but to women I say: We could use your help. If you want to make a difference in your children's sports experience, do yourself a favor and bury this men-only tradition.

I always hear or read about how dads have such limited time available to dedicate to coaching youth sports. I should know because I'm a busy dad myself. But many men use their limited time as an excuse to skip over most of the important elements of teaching and devote their time instead just to the games. This results in many of the problems we've already discussed. The world has changed, and so should youth sports. Man or woman, if you have the time, patience, passion, and ability to teach and can keep everything positive and in perspective, you should be coaching our kids today.

This applies to any sport. Let's take that most traditional of sports, football, as an example. Nothing seems more masculine than a tackle football game. Yet when we at the NFL offered to train women to become youth tackle football coaches, they signed up enthusiastically.

THE MOMS OF SOMERS

Just this past year we recruited thirty mothers from Somers, New York, a town in Westchester County, to run and instruct an NFL

Junior Player Development program. Some of these moms have sons who are either playing or have played football at the high school level. Others have sons who played in the youth town league or did not play at all. Their experiences with the game of football were varied.

One of the moms, Joey Scorrano, has two boys who played high school football several years ago, one of whom went on to play at Hofstra University. She wanted to give something back to the game and learn more about what her boys experienced.

As Ms. Scorrano explained, "Women can add a lot to coaching anyone. We look at things differently than men; there is no win-at-all-costs attitude. We add a different dimension that can attract more kids to a sport by eliminating the intimidation factor. Women tend to provide a softer approach and yet still have a foundation of discipline that encourages maximum learning."

Another of the Somers moms, Maureen Abdelnour, explained why she was so interested in learning how to coach the game: "As a cheerleader all my high school years, my back was always to the playing field—and no one *ever* explained football to me. Even though I dated football players, we never discussed the game.

"I have two boys, ten and twelve, who will be good athletes in the coming years. They want to play football; therefore, I need to understand the game. I *want* to understand the game and would love to be a proactive element in showing women, men, boys, and girls that women can be a vital asset to the game of football."

Yes, there were many critics and skeptics who did not believe the women could become football coaches. Somers High School football coach Tony DeMatteo best addressed this when he spoke to the moms one evening after a training session.

"You should be proud of what you're accomplishing here," DeMatteo said. "And you should not get discouraged no matter what people may think or say. Not many men couple replicate what you have learned so far about the fundamentals of teaching football. Go home tonight and ask your husband how he would teach your son to tackle or block. I guarantee you he doesn't know or understand more than you do about the fundamentals of teaching those skills. You now know and understand how the game should be properly taught and played."

Any sport can benefit from this encouraging example. As men we have to clear our minds of the notion that women have no place in the sports we've deemed to be ours. Women are a tremendous resource for youth sports that we must begin to utilize. Women, too, need to rid themselves of the mind-set that they cannot teach youth sports. If organized sports are to become a contemporary experience for kids, women need to play a greater role.

WOMAN IN CHARGE

Mary DeCesare became the first female head football coach in New York history when she took over the varsity program at John F. Kennedy High School in the Bronx in 2001. Prior to becoming the head coach Mary had been on the JFK staff for twenty years, received over sixty hours of NFL Junior Player Development training, and managed the Bronx JPD site.

"When I became the head football coach, it was not that big of a leap for me," she says. "I had been an assistant coach for twenty years, and the head coach before me always treated me as an equal. I contributed as much as the next coach on the team. I would break down film, film the games, and help out at practices.

And for two years prior to becoming the head coach I had trained and instructed in the Junior Player Development program. After JPD, I felt more confident and secure in my knowledge of football in terms of how to teach and respond to kids firsthand on the football field.

"I think women are natural teachers. They may be a little more patient because they understand how difficult it is to try something for the first or second time and not be good at it. One of the things that benefited me was the fact that the community in the Bronx in which I coach is primarily matriarchal. The community is made up of Hispanic and African-American kids who often have had only women around growing up. That certainly worked in my favor.

"When I spoke and made presentations in junior high schools with a gentlemen who had played college ball, the kids still tended to direct their questions to me. While he had the experience and had played the game, and obviously I hadn't, I was less of a threat. Maybe that's the way they see coaches in general: A coach should not be yelling and screaming but guiding and teaching. Women should not underestimate the rapport they have with kids. And, hey, if men can do it, we can, too."

Mary did not face resistance from her team even though they were the first high school football players in New York to be coached by a woman. Adam Gaddie, Mary's starting quarterback, described the experience this way: "She had a great impact on me. No matter what was in front of her, she always did whatever she could. She always thought about her players first, and that gave us a lot of trust in her. I trusted her in everything, as if she were my own parent. There aren't any real differences between a male or female coach, but a female may be a little more understanding and a bit more organized. We did not get off any easier with her. Mary was even a little tougher as a coach than the men we had. She didn't let anyone slack off."

When Mary served as site manager for the JPD program, she went out of her way to recruit moms to help her run the practices. She said, "Women feel that no one wants them to coach. But once people saw a woman coaching, they didn't feel so funny asking questions about the sport or about what the kids were doing that might make them look stupid. If I can understand it, they can, and it takes away the myth or mystery of football as an all-male bastion.

"The first night of the JPD program I told some of the moms that we were going to have a training session for volunteers, and they were welcome to come. They were a little reluctant in the beginning. One mother came every single night to be with her son, and at the end of the program she said, 'Next year I want to do this. I want to volunteer.' If other women tell them they can be involved, they may be more likely to do it. It is very important to ask the women directly and not just look at the men when calling for volunteers.

"When I said the women were welcome that first night, they didn't believe me, but a few weeks later they saw that they could have been doing it, too. Any program can include a component where the mothers who come to stay with the kids have something to do. They can check that the kids' hands are in the right place in the three-point stance—the standard football position. The key is seeing that other women are involved even if there are only one or two in the beginning.

"The women began to show up and get involved. Rather than just drop off their kids, they stuck around. I think they felt they could walk up to me and ask what the kids were working on that day or why they were playing different positions each day. It was easier coming from me than from a man. It was interesting to me how many mothers came back and said they had discussed the practice with their sons on the ride home. It opened up a whole new line of communication between mother and son. What could be better than that?

"One of the best things I did with my father was watch football games with him on Sundays. That started my interest in the sport. It's nice to see that it has come almost full circle for me. My father is always in the back of my mind when I'm on the football field, and I hope I gave those boys a chance to have similar experiences with their mothers. To be able to share that with a parent, to have something to talk about, argue about, a way to connect, is truly special."

WOMEN ARE NATURAL INSTRUCTORS

One thing that fascinated me when we launched the tackle football training program for women coaches in Somers was their lack of inhibition about asking questions. As I sat and listened to their questions, I thought about the hundreds of training sessions we'd held in which men had refused to ask anything. Women, on the other hand, had asked questions until they fully understood a concept or instructional method. Most men at our other JPD sessions had no prior coaching experience but still seemed to feel that this basic training was beneath them. The only problem was that when they stepped onto the field to teach these fundamentals, they often provided incorrect instruction. That forced one of the trainers to step in and run the drill correctly.

In any instructional situation it is wrong for the instructor to show up unprepared to teach skills correctly to kids. A coach should not be learning as he goes along at practice. I discovered that the women we trained would never step onto a field to instruct without knowing precisely what they were doing.

When coaches show up unprepared to a youth sports program, it leads to the root of one of the largest obstacles in youth sports. An unprepared youth coach—of whom there are far too many—will commit three major errors that ultimately damage youth sports:

1. Incorrect demonstration of skills

2. Disorganized practices

3. Unequal experiences for every child involved

Through fourteen years of professional experience in youth sports I've found that women generally have a better overall capacity to be organized and prepared to provide a quality experience to all kids involved. This is not to say there are no male youth coaches out there who possess these skills or could acquire them. The concern is that too many women have decided not to venture into coaching youth sports. This untapped group could ignite a Fair Play revolution and change the landscape of youth sports for the better. We must involve as many of the best people who possess the passion and ability to effect positive change.

I see Mary DeCesare and the thirty moms from Somers as an inspiration, and I hope they will pave the way for other women across the country to get involved in youth sports. While historically football never provided women the opportunity to play the game, these women learned how to teach the most important fundamentals of every position of the sport. They had never experienced what they eventually were fully prepared to teach.

GETTING STARTED

Someone who has never played a particular sport or who has no knowledge of it can become a coach by taking the following steps:

1. Study the basic history of the sport.

This is the logical starting point because a basic knowledge of the history will provide a perspective of what you are about to teach as well as some added confidence prior to getting started. A sport's history offers information on how the game began and evolved over time, and the early stages best illustrate what the specific fundamentals of the game are and why they were developed.

2. Learn and understand the basic terminology and rules of the game.

In order to maintain credibility with the kids, you must know and understand the terminology that is used. In basketball, for example, these terms would include fast break, outlet pass, setting a pick, posting up, zone defense, and man-to-man defense. Knowledge of the rules of the game is also vital. As a teacher you would be remiss if you did not explain the rules in their entirety.

3. Find and explore the tools that will help you teach the fundamentals of every position.

Books and videos are a great resource, but not all of them are complete or provide comprehensive explanations of all fundamental aspects. You may have to search around to find other sources that have the information you need. Then you can combine various approaches to fit your teaching style.

4. Use the Fair Play structures detailed in this book.

There are many ways to obtain the knowledge to teach the fundamentals of any sport, but if you don't present them in the proper stages, using a creative and enthusiastic approach, you will fall into the same negative patterns that currently plague youth sports.

Even when you are teaching a particular skill for the thirtieth time, it might be the first time that a player has had it explained to him properly. Your presentation of skills must always be exuberant and fresh. Remember, this is your chance to change youth sports for the better.

Use the Fair Play platform of nontraditional seasons of instruction and applied competitions in which everyone learns and plays equally. Not only will you be effecting positive change for children, but you will produce a larger group of eager athletes who are better prepared for the future.

5. Attend clinics and workshops for coaches whenever available.

Most youth sports have national governing bodies that provide schedules of such events. It is important for you to continue to gather information and watch how others present and teach skills. Borrow from what other coaches have found helpful in teaching fundamentals. There are limitless ways to introduce and teach particular skills. Some are effective, and some are not. The only way to acquire additional knowledge and have the opportunity to ask questions is by attending these clinics and workshops.

6. Watch a college team practice.

If you ever have the opportunity, visit a college campus and observe how college coaches and their staffs teach, especially in the preseason. It will be an invaluable experience.

Note how the specific fundamentals of each position are taught. Watch how the college coaches structure and organize their drills. Pay close attention to the pace of a practice session. Most college coaches will teach in a fast-paced environment in order to get as much out of a specific time period as possible. But you will also notice how the structure of the entire process allows for everyone to receive a full understanding and an opportunity to learn.

7. Take a class in CPR and first aid.

It seems like a logical thing to do, but would you believe that many youth coaches don't even have basic training in first aid? Do not overlook this important step. Remember, you are responsible for other people's children when they are in your care.

TEACHING THE OPPOSITE SEX

One element that persists in the case of female youth coaches is the fear of not being taken seriously by boys. Unfortunately, many boys take their cues from their dads and society in general. But attention to the details of teaching the game using Fair Play provides instant credibility and the confidence to face any challenge a coach may receive from a parent or child.

Terry Liskevych coached the United States Women's Volleyball Team for twelve years, and his team won a bronze medal at the 1992 Olympics in Barcelona. Terry spent a good portion of his career coaching women and feels the reverse—women coaching boys or even men—could certainly benefit any level of sport. He said, "There are what I believe to be gender differences, and this is very evident to me because I've coached men and women. Women are more team oriented in anything they do. Those who have read *Men Are from Mars, Women Are from Venus* know we are different. I applaud all efforts to get more women involved in coaching. It's the same as having women in high positions in business: They bring in a whole new perspective. They can be more nurturing, they make sure the group needs are met, and winning is not the only thing that matters to them.

"For most of the last two centuries sports have been coached and taught utilizing a traditional male sport model. What moms bring is a different and positive perspective about what's right and wrong in the area of a child's development. And I think it's a perspective that should be shared. A lot of boys are brought up in a very mother- or female-dominated structure anyway. Even if the mom is working full-time, she is still usually the primary caretaker in the family. Look at all the professional athletes who still do whatever their mom tells them.

"When comparing male and female coaches, there are different degrees of sensitivity. Women are more sensitive to everyone's feelings, which is especially important at the younger ages for both males and females. Women bring a sense of family to a team, which is needed at the youth level of sports. I frequently hear guys say it doesn't matter if we get along as long as we are winning. Well, it does matter if you are a family, and that's a good thing for any young athlete to learn."

If you're a woman and you have the will, passion, and desire to coach, why wait? There is certainly a need, and your contributions will be welcomed. Make a difference in youth sports today.

9

WHAT YOUR DAUGHTER NEEDS:
Experts Discuss the Facts on Girls in Sports

It may seem like old news that women's sports have experienced enormous growth in the last few decades. But many believe, myself included, that the women's revolution in sports has just begun.

As a parent, your daughters are no doubt just as active in organized sports as your sons. Coaches work with both girls and boys, often on the same team, in a variety of sports. As I've stressed throughout this book, the elements of the Fair Play program apply equally to boys and girls, but I felt it necessary to include a chapter specifically geared to the experiences of girls in organized sports. Where better to start than with one of the most heralded female athletes of our time.

MIA HAMM ON GIRLS' SPORTS

Back in the early 1990s I had the opportunity to work with the U.S. Women's National Soccer Team. These eighteen young women, ranging in age from their late teens to late twenties, were the pioneers of women's soccer in this country. As the team advanced toward the 1996 Olympics, it became increasingly apparent that they were catalyzing a national movement of girls in sports. They were also terrific role models. Despite bearing the responsibility of being shepherds of the game for millions of young girls, they never allowed negative elements to penetrate their love for their sport.

Much of this book has focused on how to repair all the negative elements that persist in youth sports. Now that a few years have passed since women's soccer first charged onto the national scene, have these same issues seeped into girls' sports as well? I asked Olympic gold medal winner Mia Hamm, a member of the U.S. Women's National Soccer Team and 2001 Women's World Wide Player of the Year, to give her perspective on the state of girls' youth sports today. Mia said, "Do I see women's and girls' sports going down that road? Absolutely. I mean the parents don't change even when we create so many opportunities. With all these wonderful and great and exciting opportunities come a lot of responsibilities and downsides as well.

"I was working at a camp a few years ago. The camp did not allow any parents to be there until the last day. They could only drop the girls off and pick them up; they were not allowed to stand around or observe. They were told that their kids did not need that type of pressure placed on them, that the camp was supposed to be fun.

"On the last day of camp the parents were allowed to be there. The girls played, and we walked around the different fields and watched them. I was watching the youngest group, the five- to seven-year-olds. One team had a five- and a six-year-old. You could tell because they were definitely the smallest kids on the field.

Their team lost. I looked over at the parents; they were standing there with disappointed looks on their faces, their arms crossed and their hands on their hips. I couldn't believe it. The kids were just having fun.

"I walked over to talk to the two parents who seemed the most disappointed. I asked them, 'What was the worst thing your parents could have said to you when you were growing up?' After they hesitated, I explained, 'For me it was "I'm so disappointed." That was the worst thing. But you don't necessarily have to say it verbally. There are a lot of different forms of communication, and nonverbal is a big one. If you don't think your kids out on that field can see that you're disappointed in them, you're wrong, because I see it.

"'Kids are very perceptive, insightful, and intelligent, even at a young age. What you're communicating to them right now is that their performance was not good enough. And besides, neither of you is their coach. All your kids want from you is your love, and that should be unconditional. It doesn't matter whether they're winning three to zero or losing three to zero.'

"When I was growing up, my parents, and especially my dad, were colorful on the sidelines and animated. But I sometimes went up to him and said something like 'Dad, I don't appreciate when you say this. I don't appreciate when you act this way. Because whether it's directed toward my teammates, me, or the other team, it affects me; it affects my friendships with those people. So if you're going to be here, I want it to be nothing but positive.'

"A lot of the times when I give speeches, parents hang on every word. They ask, 'When did you start playing?' I get that all the time. 'Well, I started at five.' Then they'll say to their child, 'She started at five, too. See, I told you that you can be as good as

Mia Hamm.' And it's like, whoa, hold on a second. 'What did you do, Mia, growing up?' I just played. I played with my friends. Whenever they played, I played. I went to practice, and I played."

HAVING FUN, WIN OR LOSE

Mia joined the U.S. Women's National Soccer Team at the unprecedented age of fifteen. She played her entire collegiate career at the University of North Carolina without losing a single game. I first met Mia in 1991 after the United States had just won its first World Championship.

Through the years I have witnessed not only Mia's numerous accomplishments but also a few disappointments—the 1995 bronze medal finish at the second World Championships and her professional team, the Washington Freedom, not qualifying for the Women's United Soccer Association (WUSA) playoffs during the 2001 season. But despite all Mia's experiences at the highest levels of competition, she always keeps things in perspective. I asked her what advice she would give a young girl playing on a losing team. She replied:

"Sometimes we get too caught up in wins and losses. Soccer is such a humbling game in that way because you can dominate, you can play really well, and still lose. It's the nature of the game we play, and we have all been part of a game like that. I know I have. You look at the stats: We had five corner kicks, and they had none. We outshot them twenty-four to three. They scored one goal, and we didn't. But you know what? Despite my disappointment, I get to do it. I get to be out there and be with my friends. Sometimes we lose sight of that, and I think that is so important. It's got to be fun for these young girls. If it's not fun and if it's not their decision to do it, then they shouldn't be doing it.

"Ever since I was little I played because I loved it. Sports was what I did well. It was where I felt comfortable, and I could express myself—I was a real emotional kid. I just loved doing it. But the other reason was that my friends played. It's what my friends did, and I still do it for the exact same reason.

"For me, regardless of win or lose, the relationships I have with these people are far more important than the scores. I can look back at an unbelievable, wonderful national team career. But when all is said and done, these players are my best friends, and that's priceless. That to me is what it means to be successful. These people have enriched, changed, and improved my life.

"If I were to go through this entire process and just worry about winning and not remember all the steps it took, all the lessons I learned, all the people I met, then I'd have lost the essence of what I get to do.

"Our sports psychologist always talks about focusing on the things you can control. I know as an athlete when I'm playing poorly, it's everything. When we're losing, I start to think that we can't do anything right. But my advice to kids would be to enjoy the little things even if it's just the oranges at halftime or the sodas at the end of the game. Just focus on small goals instead of winning the game. Set a goal that for the next ten minutes you will play as hard as you can."

VIEW FROM A COACH

Michele Uhlfelder is considered one of the best female lacrosse players in the world. Michele has played on three consecutive World Championship teams and is presently the head lacrosse coach at Stanford University in California. Michele sees a few negatives in female youth sports today and attributes the problems to the culture we are brought up in. She said:

"We as a society have become solely focused on winning and have disregarded the parts of the game that don't show up on the scoreboard. We've talked about that with our team here at Stanford. It's about how they play. We use words such as 'fearless'—how fearless they are when they play. And you need to start to measure yourself by things that the scoreboard doesn't measure. The winning and losing is a by-product of what you do. But if we get kids to measure themselves only by wins and losses early on, there's really no motivation, and that's why so many of them drop out.

"Kids begin to lose that passion—the way they were feeling, dreaming, and romanticizing at an earlier, more innocent age—because we fill their heads with much more outcome-oriented things, a lot of which they can't control. You can't always control the outcome. You can control the process. You can control what you commit to every day. You can certainly control your attitude and how you feel about what you do and what others do, but you can't control the outcome."

LEARNING THE FUNDAMENTALS

After Mia Hamm joined the women's national team, she found she had to focus on her fundamentals to excel at the highest level. As she recalled, "In terms of skill development, I played around, I kicked around, but I didn't start really focusing on things when I was young. When I made the national team at fifteen, it was kind of based on just raw talent. My athleticism carried me everywhere. And then all of a sudden I was on a team with eighteen great athletes. What would set me apart?

"It was then, at that age, that I started working on my own, going out and doing extra work, because I knew what I wanted. It was my decision. My dad wasn't saying, 'It's three-thirty, Mia. Have you gone out yet and kicked a soccer ball around for an hour?' It was never like that. I went out and made the decision by myself that this was what I wanted to do. I saw the highest level and thought it was awesome. I wanted to be a part of it, and I wanted to be a member of the team for as long as I could. And that's when I started doing it. I wasn't going to camps every summer. I didn't have a personal trainer when I was ten. I played a lot. I played a lot of different sports.

"When we played small-sided games in the neighborhood, I always wanted to see how many people I could beat, how many nutmegs [passing or dribbling the ball through your opponent's legs] I could get, or how many goals I could score. That was a great opportunity to try to do things that you wouldn't normally do in a structured game. You didn't have someone saying, 'Maybe you should have passed that ball. You had four people on you.' Well, in the backyard I could do that. It was all right."

As you can see, Mia stresses two important messages here, applicable to both girls and boys in sports: Fundamentals are critical, and the higher you go in sports, the more important they become. And have fun when you're learning to play a sport. Try a few different things and take a few chances. This combination of learning the fundamental skills properly and having fun is at the very heart of the Fair Play program.

DOLLARS AND SCHOLARS

Many girls still find themselves in the role of pioneers. Their parents are delighted at the possibility of college athletic scholarships, but they often misinterpret the likelihood of attaining one. Sports such as women's lacrosse and ice hockey are now experiencing growth nationwide, and more and more Division One colleges are incorporating them into their interscholastic menu. These sports offer scholarships, but, unfortunately, that is where the purity of these games can be lost. Often when parents get an inkling of a scholarship opportunity, they can end up destroying the purity in the game. This has become an area of perhaps even more concern for girls in sports than for boys.

Parents Can Ruin Kids' Chances

Michele Uhlfelder of Stanford University believes that overzealous parents can actually get in the way of their child's chances for a scholarship. "A pushy parent," she says, "can have an adverse effect on a coach, and as a result the athlete can get overlooked or even intentionally rejected. Most coaches feel that when they recruit an athlete, they recruit the family as well. You recognize that for the next four years this is going to be part of your team's family. And that's the way I look at it: Our program extends to the parents, and I want it to be that way.

"Sometimes when you're in the stands at an event, there is someone there who behaves so badly that it seems incurable. No coach really needs that headache. Someone is screaming his head off, and you'll say, 'Who's that?' 'Oh, that's so-and-so's father.' 'She's off the list.' That has definitely happened.

"You can also get the situation where a parent is over the top at a game and you'll notice the kid's performance change for the worse. It becomes obvious that the athlete feels the parent's presence and her performance really suffers. I've seen that on many occasions. In those cases, as a coach you think to yourself, 'I'm not going to get myself into that difficult situation. That's not what I want to do for four years.' You surmise that the athlete has limited potential because of the parent's negative influence."

New Opportunities, New Headaches

Coach Uhlfelder sees the rapid growth of her sport as a good thing for girls, but it has also given rise to some new problems. She said, "For lacrosse, it's worrisome. So many parents see lacrosse as an opportunity, and we're growing as a result. We're getting more kids interested and intrigued by the game. But also because of that opportunity I think we're seeing more expectations put on these kids. For us it's a double-edged sword because of our growth right now. I definitely see it having an effect. It has an effect on coaches who get a little frustrated with certain areas of the country that are producing very good players. It's getting very cutthroat and sort of inbred. The thinking is 'My kid's going to get a scholarship.' And as a result kids get pitted against one another a little bit in that regard.

"Certain places have started to get a reputation for having pushy parents because they're all after the same thing and want to one-up one another. The first question out of their mouth is always about scholarships. It seems to breed in certain areas. The result of those stories is that coaches would rather recruit a kid from an area that doesn't have that reputation, a kid they know is going to work and hasn't grown up marinating in this experience. They know these kids are going to work for them, that they're not motivated by all these external factors. That I know has definitely happened in our sport."

Get the Kids Involved

Another problem that Michele Uhlfelder identifies in this rapidly developing world of girls playing college sports is that the parents don't allow their daughters to participate in the process. "The parents are making most of the phone calls. They're the ones who are calling the coaches more than the coaches are having a relationship with the players. The parents make the first call rather than the athlete. You see parents trying to position their kids to get their foot in the door.

"Ultimately, this hurts the relationship of the coach and the athlete. The recruiting process is tough because it's so grinding on the kids and very arduous. They get calls all the time; they get letters all the time. They're taking visits all the time; they may even be playing another sport at the same time. They're really stressed. And I think some parents honestly believe that they are taking the pressure off the athlete.

"However, from a coach's standpoint, you want to get to know the kid. It's not that there's no place for talking to the parents—there's definitely a place for that—and the parents certainly have questions that are separate from the kids' questions. But a lot of times the first question is 'Do you have scholarships?' People don't hide it. They really want to know. They think they're acting in their daughter's best interest. In all fairness maybe they don't want their child to get too excited or get her expectations too high.

"If you had a kid who wanted to go to Stanford, you might want to soften the blow in case it doesn't work out. That's a parental instinct. But I think there's also a way to have your child drive the boat and still be there to support her.

"Overall it makes for a better relationship for your daughter with that coach right from the start. There won't be as many unknowns, and you will feel proud that there is a sense of accomplishment for that kid who made her own way. And that's usually the beginning of their four years. Many kids arrive at the college level with a lot of confidence, believing it is the beginning of their independence, the next step, and they had a big role in that."

CHOOSE A COLLEGE WISELY

Mia Hamm's four years at the University of North Carolina were rewarding both on and off the playing field. Mia feels an athlete should closely examine all aspects of a potential university prior to making a decision. She said, "There are so many more scholarships out there for girls, and the availability of scholarships has increased. I know a lot of parents who want their kids to get a full ride, whether it's because of financial strain or just an issue of ego. What I would say to the kids is that first of all you need to determine at what level you want to compete.

"There are a lot of really good Division One, high-level, competitive programs as well as Division Two and Division Three. Say, for example, you're going to Santa Clara, North Carolina, or Notre Dame to play soccer; the expectations are that they're going to compete for a national championship every year. And they work extremely hard to achieve that goal, just as every other team does. A girl who is going in there thinking, 'It's going to be fine. I'll play college soccer, and it will be something to do,' probably should take the time to reevaluate the situation and be sure of what she really wants.

"I'll never forget when someone said to me, 'Wherever you decide to go, Mia, make sure it feels like home.' The college you choose needs to be where you want to be regardless of soccer. If you get hurt or just don't feel like playing anymore, you should still love it. You should get the education that you want. That is first and foremost the most important thing. Without your sport, how do you feel about the academics, the structure of the school, and its support staff? How do you feel about it socially?

"We grow so much in those four years. That's why recruiting trips are so important; you get more than just a feel for the university and the team. Most of the girls do their homework about the schools to which they apply. They understand the soccer history, but do they understand the history of the institution they're looking at?"

COACHING QUALITIES

Mia and Michele are both world-class athletes and have been exposed to many different kinds of coaches. I asked them both what the qualities were that they found most important in a coach.

Mia Hamm said, "My best coaches created an environment for me and other players to be our best. They never made me feel that I was alone or by myself in doing it, and that was so important. It was never like 'Okay, Mia, we're going to help you set standards for yourself, but when things get tough, you're just going to have to deal with it.' That was never the case. It was always 'It's going to get hard, whether it's us deciding that we think you can score a goal each game or our asking you to be a team leader.' I never felt that I was by myself in trying to become better. That made all my decisions a lot easier. They were there to push me and help guide me, but also to support me."

Michele Uhlfelder said, "The people I thought were influential were always people I considered teachers of the game. They always had a good presence. They didn't treat the star differently. The team was the team, and no one player had that star mentality and dictated what the team did. There was this level of respect, and I remember that as a positive thing. The coaches who were patient, who could turn it up and turn it down, had a way of communicating with players without yelling. There's a way for you to get your point across without anybody taking it personally. And I definitely remember a few people who could be patient and explain things and put it in a way you could understand. I've also seen coaches who constantly barked and yelled, and I think you have to have ranges. A lot of times you just tune out people who are always at the same pitch.

"I was always a student of the game. I don't know how or why that is. Maybe as a kid you kind of are a little bit more open to that. I had a really patient brother, so as I grew up, I looked for a patient teacher.

"I find that I've been influenced by this and attempt to apply the same methods. You have to be dynamic. I don't think you can always be in the background. My biggest challenge is putting things in such a way that players can hear me and learn from me. Creativity is huge. There is a lot of respect for being able to do what you teach. As a player that's really a great asset. It's not necessary, but it helps me a lot to be able to relate. Sometimes coaches are speaking Greek to their players, coaching jargon, while the players are out there physically doing it, and the two don't mesh. They don't hear it the same way as the coach is saying it. If you can be attuned to what they're hearing, whether because of experience or because you're a player, I think that goes a long way."

BOYS AND GIRLS PLAYING TOGETHER

Former NFL quarterback Boomer Esiason coached boys and girls together on his flag football team. It turned out to be an extremely positive experience for all the kids. Boomer recalled, "We had a lot of players on the team who were playing flag football for the first time, and many of them were girls. There were some who didn't want to play at first because they were afraid they wouldn't understand the game. My point to them was that it didn't matter. Football is a very simple game to understand if you just keep in mind that you're trying to score and the other team is trying to keep you from scoring.

"After a few minutes the girls took right to it. I found that the ones who had never played before got the most out of it, played the hardest, and were the first ones there when we had games. They just couldn't wait until the next week."

As more girls get involved in sports, there is plenty of analysis being done on the differences in training girls and boys. Mia Hamm has had the benefit of training with both.

"Competing with guys when I was growing up helped me. At a practice guys are much more independent. I remember it was all about the tricks you could do. 'How long can you juggle the ball?' Whereas when girls practice, they listen and follow instructions well. Guys always seem to push that envelope: 'I kind of want to do it my own way. I'll do it somewhat the way you want me to, but I'll do it my own way.' Sometimes I think girls are the opposite; 'No. The coach said we should do it this way.' And we do it—because that's what they've asked of us."

APPROACH GIRLS AND BOYS DIFFERENTLY

If you had any doubt that boys and girls are different on the athletic field or should be approached differently, I hope these last two chapters have cleared up the matter for you. If not, I will leave you with these thoughts from Terry Liskevych. Terry learned many of the differences that exist between males and females in sports in his twelve years as the U.S. Women's Volleyball head coach and fourteen years as coach of men and women at the collegiate level. He believes the following:

■ Men are hierarchical (top to bottom), while women rely on a network (web) and connectedness. In women's organizations everyone is connected to the leader; they tend to be more decentralized. The leaders are more likely to bring the group together.

■ Women on a team must have a personal connection to the coach, and it has to be unique for each player.

■ Males have learned to be led by the powerful presence and will of a leader; they are used to intimidation by the coach or leader.

■ Females—as a coach, you must show your players that you care about them as people over and above their capabilities. "Nobody cares about how much you know until they know how much you care."

- Women do not view athletic success as a defining element of female development. Men see athletic success as a test of manhood.

- Women do not like bearing down and competing against their teammates. It is hard for them to be competitive against each other in one-on-one drills.

- Men can be disgusted with their teammates but still function just fine within the team structure. Women need group support; they want to be liked by their teammates. Good team chemistry is critical to the success of women's teams.

- Do not single out a female player—positive or negative—in front of the group. It is better to talk to her one-on-one.

- Women's teams need additional incentives beyond winning.

- Challenge women to help their teammate(s); for example, tell them that all-out effort in a drill equals commitment to the team.

- Women have a hard time saying publicly, "I am the best," while men thrive on saying it.

- Female athletes may actually "disable their performance" by personalizing corrective behavior. They may be more concerned with the tone of the message than the content of the message.

All these experts agree that the rapid growth of girls' sports in this country has both positive and negative aspects. Their words and experience should help guide you as a parent or coach of girls starting out in organized sports as well as those reaching for higher levels of success.

10

SKILLS FOR LIFE:
Teaching Important Lessons Beyond the Playing Field

Conventional wisdom tells us that sports programs teach kids important life messages. Unfortunately, this optimistic dream does not hold true for a majority of kids involved in organized sports today. Many teaching opportunities are missed or are entirely ruined when bad behavior and negative elements become more the norm than the exception.

Despite the many experts who claim that sports increase confidence, self-esteem, and scholastic performance, we as a society continue to prevent a great number of our children from reaping these desired benefits. Today's youth sports programs do more to belittle a child's confidence and self-esteem than they do to improve or benefit the child's overall welfare.

I don't mean to say that sports are an inappropriate setting in which to teach life skills. Quite the opposite: Sports by their very nature can teach essential life skills. For example, team sports teach athletes to work together in order to be successful, but this lesson isn't conveyed automatically. The coach or instructor working with kids needs to capitalize on and reinforce the natural lessons that present themselves in sports. When coaches do this, they produce positive results.

Bronx high school football coach Jerry Horowitz explained it this way: "In order for you to be successful as a coach, you have to create an environment in which learning can take place. Coaching is nothing more than teaching. You can do that through the life skills you present to these kids.

"Life skills certainly make a kid a better athlete. In both life and sports you need to be organized, disciplined, a team person, regimented. A basketball player might say, 'Why should I go out and practice foul shots? Last time I was out there I was ten for ten.' Well, if you don't keep practicing, you're not going to be ten for ten next time. You have to do it continuously to make it automatic. Life skills are not something you turn on or off each session. They have to be an ongoing part of your life.

"Great coordination may help make you a great athlete. There are many great athletes out there, but why are some better than others? It's because they've disciplined their minds and matured themselves through these life skills to become superior athletes. In golf, why does one guy make ninety-seven out of one hundred putts and the other guy only ninety-four? Why do some guys make their putts under great pressure and others fall apart when everything is on the line? It's how you train your mind. That's what life skills are all about. And you have to start teaching them to your kids when they are young."

INCORPORATE LIFE SKILLS INTO SPORTS TRAINING

The Fair Play structure calls for the inclusion of life skill lessons every time the team meets on the playing field. We provide JPD coaches with easy-to-use reference tools that assist them in capturing these teaching moments. The key to the success of this method is that teaching is intertwined with on-field skill training. It never interrupts the flow of an instructional or competitive segment, but it is designed to complement whatever the training situation is at that time.

For example, in JPD when we move to the competition phase to test a participant's progress, a coach encourages, instructs, and corrects mistakes, but he also monitors each athlete's behavior. If an athlete becomes dejected because an opponent outscores him or beats him on a play, the coach addresses that player immediately. He explains that the player executed the skills properly, improved, and was prepared, and that these are the more important results.

The JPD coach also addresses an athlete who is showboating or gloating about his achievements. The coach explains to the athlete that it's okay to take pleasure in success, but he must keep things in perspective, maintain his self-control, and always respect his opponent. And the coach reminds the player that even a good performance or victory should not stop him from continuing to prepare by reflecting on what he did correctly and how he can build upon that to improve further.

These JPD scenarios touch upon two critical life skill messages: preparation and self-control. Over the length of the JPD program we devote specific days to eight key life messages. The message of the day remains the focus for the entire ninety-minute session. Not many youth sports programs pay that much attention to life skill training.

The absence of life skill training in traditional programs was the primary reason I incorporated it into JPD. In order to truly create a Fair Play environment, life skill structures and methods are a crucial part of coaching responsibilities.

You may be wondering how you can possibly have the time to spend preparing and teaching life skills at each practice session. It's actually fairly easy. In the NFL's youth programs we use wristbands that have plastic pockets attached. You've probably seen these wristbands on the arms of college and NFL quarterbacks. Normally a quarterback will hold his plays in the pocket of the wristband as a quick reminder of what he can call. Instead of plays, customized life skill messages are inserted into each JPD participant's wristband each week with key reminders that reinforce the messages. Over the span of the eight-week program we emphasize eight life skills. The skills are also hung on banners around the field to make it clear how important they are to the instruction. The banners read:

Self-control

Responsibility

Goal Setting

Sportsmanship

Smart Moves

Teamwork

Leadership

Perseverance

Reminders or key points accompany each life skill message on each participant's wristband. The players receive a new card each week. The cards read:

SELF-CONTROL
On-field and Off-field

Key points:
- Think before you react.
- Keep a clear head.
- Control your emotions.

RESPONSIBILITY
On-field

Key points:
- Be on time.
- Learn your position.
- Be prepared.

Off-field

Key points:
- Complete your homework.
- Pay attention in class.
- Finish chores at home.

GOAL SETTING
On-field and Off-field

Key points:
- Make the most of your abilities.
- Be prepared.
- Don't quit.

SPORTSMANSHIP
On-field and Off-field

Key points:
- Play fair.
- Have respect for your opponent.
- Never cheat.

SMART MOVES
On-field and Off-field

Key points:
- Think before you react.
- Be proud of your decision.
- Accept the outcome.

TEAMWORK
On-field and Off-field

Key points:
- Together everyone achieves more.
- Think of others.
- Sacrifice for the welfare of all.

LEADERSHIP
On-field and Off-field

Key points:
- Work together.
- Lead by example.
- Generate enthusiasm.
- Teach and motivate.

PERSEVERANCE
On-field and Off-field

Key points:
- Be persistent.
- Be determined.
- Learn from your losses.

These life lessons are integrated into every single instructional session at JPD. We remind the instructors to begin each session by introducing the life skill focus of the day along with the fundamentals that will be taught. They give their players a short explanation of the life skill and how it applies to their sport, school, family, and friends. For example, if the life skill is "responsibility," a coach explains that the players must be responsible by paying attention when the fundamentals are taught. As a result they will be able to perform well, score points in competitions, and not let themselves or their teammates down. The coach also explains that when players are responsible at school by paying attention and doing their homework, they will reap the same benefits in the classroom. They must be equally responsible at home by helping out with chores and listening to their parents.

Throughout the session the coach gives brief reminders of the day's life skill. During the ebb and flow of athletic instruction and competition, examples of life lessons are used constantly. A young player who does not pay attention during an instructional period provides an ideal opportunity to speak to him about responsibility and explain what he missed and how that can affect the entire team.

A LIFE MESSAGE IN ACTION

At our JPD site in the Bronx, New York, instructor Charles Packowski gathered his team of twenty-five kids after a competition in which they had not played particularly well. What he told them is a great example of how to apply life messages. He said, "Remember that we learned the fundamentals of the linebacker position today, but we also learned about perseverance. Some of you may have made mistakes today, but is that any reason to get discouraged and lose your focus on what you should learn? No. The reason they put erasers on pencils is so that you can wipe out your mistakes and start over. When you make a mistake on your homework, you have the opportunity to erase it and correct it. Tomorrow is a new day. I want you to remember and feel good about what you did right today because everybody made progress and improved. But I also want you to think about what you might have done better, and come back tomorrow ready to improve. This is perseverance."

Unfortunately, many youth coaches allow these teaching moments to escape, missing the opportunities to reinforce and demonstrate how a life skill is applied in multiple situations on and off the playing field. This particular coach took a precious teaching moment of discouragement and dejection and turned it into a positive opportunity to learn and improve.

Athletes experience real-life scenarios at every level of their sport. One of the most common of these is overcoming a poor performance. No one is perfect, obviously, and sports give you the opportunity to test how you handle, learn, and recover from adversity. This acquired skill of not dwelling on a mistake but instead learning from it and moving forward can be invaluable throughout life. Once a young athlete understands how to recover from mistakes or poor performances, his future rate of success improves on and off the playing field.

COACHING THE COACH

Teaching moments and life skills can also be applied when dealing with negative coaches. During one JPD program in Brooklyn, a coach got out of hand during the competition portion of the program. As I explained in Chapter 3, our program is designed to be a positive experience, with competitions conducted in conjunction with what was learned on that particular day. Scores are primarily used to track progress of learning, not to be posted as a matter of comparison. However, in this situation the adult coach took the point evaluation system too seriously and began to argue with other coaches and place extra pressure on the kids.

When a situation like this occurs, we ask the designated site manager to take that coach aside. The site manager explains that the program does not tolerate this behavior and describes again the JPD objective of proper positive learning in which winning is not the emphasis. If bad coaching behavior persists, our program states that you must ask the adult to leave the program. In this particular case, Kevin Fountaine, a New York City policeman and our JPD site manager, took advantage of a teaching moment and turned this recurring problem into a positive experience. Rather than banish the coach from the program, he took extra time to work with him.

Kevin explained his action this way: "If you allow this guy to leave the program and not continue to work on his behavior and how he works with children, he will only go somewhere else and act the same way. Why not keep him on and closely supervise and guide him through a program that specifically addresses the problem rather then send him off to destroy the sports experience of another group of kids?"

That particular coach stayed on and continues to contribute in a positive manner within JPD. Not only was Kevin absolutely correct in sticking with the Fair Play philosophy, but he also used a teaching moment to save many kids from a misguided youth coach.

THE TEENAGE YEARS

Teaching life lessons through sports takes on added significance when you are involved with a team of adolescents. While this is a difficult age group both to parent and to coach, there is no more important time to reach out and communicate than during the critical years of twelve to seventeen. As a coach you have a tremendous advantage and opportunity to affect a young athlete's life when working with teenagers.

Paul Pasqualoni, the head football coach at Syracuse University, exemplified this perfectly one day when he addressed a group of teens from the Bronx during one of our NFL programs. These kids had just begun the program and were starting to show up late and demonstrate some cockiness. Coach Pasqualoni told them, "What you're learning here in this program—the personality characteristics that these coaches are trying to get you to develop—is what you need to succeed in life. Companions, friends, and buddies in many ways are like buttons on an elevator. Some friends will take you up, and some friends will take you down. The people that are here working with you are giving you an opportunity. Now maximize the opportunity!"

His simple but emotional address to these impressionable youngsters turned the program around. Kids no longer were absent or showed up late, and the overall spirit of the group picked up a notch. The point here is that a coach should continue to be alert and look for what we have referred to throughout this book as teaching moments to drive home important life lessons.

I also know that life skills work because I've asked the kids themselves. Remember Seyit Tabaru, the big kid we couldn't find a helmet for in Chapter 3? He spoke to me enthusiastically about the life skills he had learned. "I'm doing really well in school now," he said. "Before JPD, I stayed outside and didn't focus. Now I have responsibilities—to go to practice, to go home and do my homework. Now I keep myself on track. Life skills showed me how people on a team support one another, and that meant a lot to me. I also learned a lot about self-control because before JPD I had a real temper, but now every time I feel that way, I just release my emotions on the field. Before JPD, I could not keep up with my responsibilities. Now I really do like homework, keeping my promises, and setting goals."

A TWO-WAY STREET

Life skill development through youth sports should not be a one-way experience, with coaches teaching and kids listening. Instead, make the process interactive. Let kids provide active feedback throughout the program. For example, ask kids to describe a situation where they could and did apply the life skill of the day. Or ask them how they would apply the life skill beyond the playing field.

In response kids have said that their teammates demonstrated "sportsmanship" when they helped an opponent to get up off the ground after knocking him down during a competition. Explaining how they had learned that "smart moves" were important off the field, several young boys told how they realized it was not a smart move to stay up late and be tired for school and practice.

Mary DeCesare, the first female head football coach in New York, believes life skills can play a critical role in educating scholar-athletes. "As a head coach in the Bronx I've realized how important those life skills are," she said. "I've spent twenty years at Kennedy High School trying to get kids to carry their success from the football field into the classroom. Life skills can be the bridge we build from the football field 'across the cement' to the school. Skills such as responsibility, teamwork, leadership, and goal setting are the elements required to be a football player on the champion level. Why not make that commitment in the classroom?

"When kids learn to put their hand out, to reach down and pick up their friend, and the coach says, 'This is teamwork, this is sportsmanship,' he points it out to them and makes them aware of it. Life skills are the heart and soul of our program because if we don't put them in, it's just football. When we add life skills, we're giving kids the tools along with the football skills that put them head and shoulders above everyone else as they move ahead in sports and life."

RESPONSIBILITIES OF TEAM CAPTAINS

Many youth teams assign one or more kids the position of team captain. These individuals usually serve as representatives for the team during ceremonial moments in a game. For example, a team captain may be involved in the coin flip before a football or soccer game. In some sports team captains are the only players allowed to talk to an official during a game.

Rarely are team captains in youth sports trained to lead with correct life skills, however, even though this should be their responsibility. The point is that many youth teams do not provide the guidelines or structure by which team captains can perform those responsibilities. In addition, singling out specific individuals to perform such roles keeps other teammates from learning those same skills and responsibilities. In JPD we feel strongly that everyone should have the opportunity to represent their team as a captain. We then provide each captain with the information and direction necessary to make this a valuable experience.

Out of a team of twenty-four players in our eight-week program, we name three co-captains per week and assign them specific responsibilities. Each captain is responsible for assisting the four or five coaches with the life skill message for the week. They might be asked to lead the life skill by example. If, for instance, goal setting is the life skill, a team captain might wear in his wristband reminders of what he wants to accomplish during each practice as an individual and as a team. A coach would also call upon the captains during the week to provide examples of the particular life skill.

During competitions, team captains encourage their teammates vocally using references to the life skill they were assigned.

———————

The consistent yet unobtrusive presentation of key life skill messages has had a lasting effect on the thousands of kids across the country who have participated in Junior Player Development. Incorporate them into your own sports program, and you will provide a tremendous service to kids.

Epilogue

HEAD START:
A Vision for the Future

The Fair Play philosophy and model have proven to be successful around the country. As a result, more kids have had the opportunity to have fun and improve their skills through sports programs that promote an innovative learning experience.

There is no secret formula to Fair Play. It is simply the accumulation of years spent watching youth sports and listening to what kids want from their sports experience. For too long, adults have determined the nature of the youth sports experience, but kids often reveal their true feelings by taking action. Despite the large number of children playing organized sports, more and more young people leave these adult dictatorships for the freedom they find at skate parks and ski slopes. With Fair Play, all children have an equal opportunity to learn at their own pace while benefiting from accelerated results.

Personally, I have been split between my desire to see kids set their own path for athletic fun and accomplishment through action sports and my belief that organized youth sports can be improved in order to provide children with quality recreational choices. The key difference between these two alternatives is that action-sport athletes participate because they *want* to, while too many kids in organized sports are playing because they *have* to. Just go to a youth league game (the sport doesn't matter) where you don't know anyone involved. You will actually feel the tension of children attempting to perform to the expectations of adults. You won't find this at a skate park.

A skateboarder, BMX rider, or snowboarder enjoys and learns from every moment of the experience. It's an integral part of these sports. This doesn't mean that action-sports athletes are not competitive—they certainly are. But along with the competition, these athletes prosper from the journey. Whether it's mastering a difficult part of a trick or suffering a spill onto the snow or concrete, they know how to appreciate and put into perspective both accomplishments and setbacks. Positive or negative experiences are considered equally important when attempting to achieve the overall objectives of having fun and, as a by-product, improving skills.

Action sports were created by a younger and irreverent generation that sought out the freedom to get what they wanted from sports. Fair Play has borrowed from their innovative spirit and applied it to organized youth sports.

THE FAIR PLAY FUTURE

Don't allow your "comfort zone" with traditional structures such as tryouts, league play, and travel teams prevent you from incorporating portions or all of the Fair Play model.

You will find that some other parents use their children as excuses for maintaining the status quo. They will claim that kids want to play adult-like games and that winning really is their main focus. I have had youth coaches approach me after listening to the Fair Play philosophy and say, "What you talked about makes a lot of sense, but every kid out there wants to win—that's how they have fun." My response: Young kids will outwardly mimic what a parent or coach wants, but it's not necessarily what they truly desire. Kids look up to their coaches and are most influenced by their parents. When the importance of winning is being drilled into them daily, kids find it difficult to express themselves in any other way.

Coaches and parents have a responsibility to provide a full menu of experiences and alternatives for children in organized sports. Our culture places an overwhelming emphasis on watching and following the example of professional sports. If children are only exposed to one way of doing things, they have no other option but to buy into the adult version. Yet in countless surveys, children have explained that they care more about playing and improving than winning. And when they fail to have a positive experience, they simply quit.

In a society that strives for better health, equal rights, and individual freedoms, it astounds me that we have allowed ourselves to fail our most valuable future resource—our children. We should make every effort to provide children the experience of building a sound body and mind. Instead, we turn them off to the experience and drive them away. A majority of kids leave sports before their teen years. We are witnessing the creation of a future generation of complacent individuals who find their recreational satisfaction sitting in front of televisions and computers unaware of their own bodies and their development as healthy adults.

If we celebrated the art of learning the fundamentals of any sport at the youth level and glamorized it the way we do traditional victories and championships, we could effect positive change for our children. We would not only improve the quality of sports, but our children would continue to participate longer, and at the very least become less sedentary in their adult years. Coaches would improve the learning environment for everyone, and all kids would truly advance at their proper rate and to their maximum capability. In addition, many of the negative parental issues would be eliminated from youth sports if the focus were shifted to the finer points of the game.

Fair Play widens the window of learning for all kids. It provides a fair environment for anyone of any ability to thrive through a proven and—most importantly—positive learning experience. Under the current system, we begin to judge performances too early in a young person's life. We tend to obstruct natural growth by immediately judging a child's performance and capabilities. Most often these judgments are based on wins and losses, followed by the second most-asked question after a game—either "Did you get a hit?" or "Did you score?" We precondition our children to value only final results. Instead, we should be asking:

- "What did you learn today?"

- "Did you enjoy yourself?"

- "Do you feel like you improved?"

By asking these questions you will open a line of communication with your child and attain a better understanding of whether he or she is benefiting from the experience or not. When you only focus on final results, there will always be a downside to the child's experience. Once a parent or coach creates an environment of self-doubt for a child, the capability to learn becomes limited.

No tryouts or drafts. No traditional games, league play, or travel teams. No more championships won or lost. Fair Play is not about any of these long-accepted elements. At the same time, the Fair Play model is extremely competitive. Under Fair Play, no child is overlooked (no one sits on the bench or is designated to the third team) or provided any more special treatment than the next child (everyone receives equal instruction). And everyone improves at a more rapid rate and to a higher level than could be accomplished through traditional sports leagues and structures.

If you enjoy watching your son or daughter be the star of a youth game or league, that's fine. But the majority of kids and parents don't get that opportunity because of the existing system under which they are forced to participate. Even your star child is not receiving the maximum amount of time to learn effectively when participating in traditional adult-game settings.

In Fair Play we use effective child and athletic development methods to rid ourselves of the "end result" mind-set in order to allow for a more natural growth and learning experience.

Now you can avoid the gut-wrenching parental experience of watching your child sit on the bench, not make the travel squad, become disappointed at his lack of improvement, and finally decide to quit. The next time you witness adults yelling at kids and officials, or coaches acting poorly and unfairly, remember that a viable sports model does exist for your child. It is Fair Play. Talk about it, share it, and—most important for your kids—start it.

CELEBRATE THE JOURNEY

I have been blessed in so many different ways. In my career I've had the opportunity and honor to work with some of the best coaches of all time. That includes individuals at all levels of sport from youth leagues to the pros. The insights and friendships that I have established with these people have provided me with the foundation on which to develop the Fair Play philosophy.

All of these people have one thing in common: They appreciate and enjoy the journey of every day and every aspect of their careers and life. They celebrate and learn from the smallest details, while trusting and understanding that the end results will take care of themselves.

Maybe as parents we would be best served to do the same. We spend so much time stressing over what will become of our children in the future that we miss the importance of the present. We don't enjoy the journey of life with our children, the celebration of their small accomplishments, and even the appreciation and opportunity that come from their mistakes. Our preoccupation with what school our children will get into or what they will be when they grow up spills onto their athletic fields and has now ruined what should be the purest part of childhood—play.

None of us can control the future, but we can enjoy and learn from the present. The next time you attend a game or practice with your son or daughter, appreciate that moment and celebrate the journey, and the future will be a better place.

INDEX

"Scott Lancaster has ignited a much-needed revolution in youth sports that will set it in the right direction for generations to come. Fair Play gives everybody the opportunity to play, to learn the fundamentals and, above all, to have fun."
—Boomer Esiason

"Fair Play is a proven model that gets your kids off the couch and sidelines and onto a lifelong journey of constructive learning and playing. It's a must-read for parents with kids involved in sports."
—Pete Carroll, head football coach, University of Southern California

"If you really want to know what your kids want and need to improve and truly enjoy organized sports . . . Fair Play is your guide."
—Gary Williams, head men's basketball coach, University of Maryland

"Fair Play has carefully found solutions to many of the issues plaguing youth sports, and illustrates easy methods for all parents to use."
—Bob Brenly, manager, Arizona Diamondbacks

"The Fair Play model has allowed us to provide thousands of New York City kids an opportunity to benefit from a contemporary learning approach. We teach them crucial life skills that go beyond the playing field and will help them for the rest of their lives. As a result, our athletes are enthusiastic, have a great attitude, and return year after year."
—John J. Ryan, Ed.D., executive director,
New York City Police Athletic League

"My soccer team once lost 10-0, and one of my kids asked me after the game if we had won. I told him yes because we had played as hard as we could and had fun. He walked away feeling like a winner and so did I. That is what this very important book is all about: redefining winning in youth sports."
—Cris Collinsworth, FOX Football TV Analyst/former NFL player

"The Fair Play philosophy and the NFL's Junior Player Development program have benefited more than 3,500 junior high school players in the Houston Independent School District area. By adopting this model, we have improved the quality of our coaching and the experience of our kids."
—Ellis Douglas, director of athletics, Houston Independent School District

empires and racially defined "nations," as it exemplifies some ideas of the day that were not unique to the writer, and help account for his influence.

Most documents tell us something about both their topics and their creators, so that readers must get used to looking at them with more than one goal in mind. For example, Robert Walsh's description of a Brazilian slave market (in the casebook on coerced labor) provides a physical description of the market conditions, but it also lets readers make inferences about how Walsh understood the extent of shared humanity (through his sympathy for the wretchedness of the slaves) and about European expectations of elite women's behavior.

The documents' genres also vary; they include letters, diaries, public proclamations, advertisements, paintings, photos, poems, scientific reports, statistical graphs, and so on. We did not aim for a particular balance among types of sources, but for diversity and a distribution of visual materials. Historians try to relate different aspects of an era to each other, showing how economics, religion, technology, literature, and family life fit together in ways that specialists in these fields might not recognize. Students need experience in seeing how historians extract both factual information and points of view from a wide variety of materials and relate them to each other. They will get that here.

We include four casebooks that combine documents that are thematically related to each other but come from different places and belong to different genres. The casebooks address women and rulership in ancient times, mobilizing for war in the age of the Mongols, coerced labor in the early modern world, and rubber and commodity chains. Historians often emphasize that they read documents in context. While philosophers might care only about whether the arguments in a text are logical, historians also want to know the circumstances in which it was written. They also ask how a text's insights, errors, habitual references, and so on tell us about that document's world, and how knowing that world helps us in turn understand the document. But we do not receive the context in which to read a document ready-made; we have to build it by reading other documents. Moreover, and this is especially important in the study of *world* history, a document often yields new insights when it is placed in different contexts. An account of seventeenth-century Caribbean slavery (coerced labor casebook) can be read in a strictly Caribbean context, or in the context of an Atlantic world that included Africa, Europe, and the Americas. But it yields other insights when juxtaposed with an account of forced labor in eighteenth-century Siberia. Similarly, knowing that William Dampier, who wrote about "slavery" in Aceh (in present-day Indonesia), was familiar with Atlantic slavery can help us understand why he viewed Acehnese bound labor in certain ways.

We hope that these documents will help readers learn to do for themselves some of what we do in our headnotes and questions: provide context for thinking about these sources as evidence for world historical questions, and suggest some ways to begin exploring what they can tell us. Interpreting in context is, after all, how people navigate both the past and the present.

Acknowledgments

We would like to thank our colleagues in Irvine and elsewhere whose conversations, suggestions, and replies to our questions have improved this book. We are grateful to Maura Cunningham, whose unflagging research and organizational skills helped the project stay on track, and to Jennifer Liu, whose administrative help got us started. The team at W. W. Norton was a pleasure to work with. Jon Durbin provided valuable guidance on the project, while Jason Spears and Becky Homiski contributed research and legwork to track down elusive original sources and secure permission to reprint the documents we selected.

WORLDS TOGETHER, WORLDS APART

A Companion Reader

Chapter 1

BECOMING HUMAN

Laetoli Footprints (3.6 million years ago)

Around 3.6 million years ago the Sadiman volcano in what is now
Tanzania erupted. It deposited a layer of fine ash at the site known as
Laetoli. A rain turned this into mud. Various animals made tracks across
this. A subsequent eruption deposited another layer of ash, thus preserving the tracks. They were discovered in 1976. Among the tracks found at
the site are those belonging to members of what most archaeologists
believe is the hominin species known as *Australopithecus afarensis*. Two
individuals can be seen walking side by side. The larger one was probably
between 4 feet 4¾ inches and 5 feet 1½ inches (1.34 and 1.56 meters)
tall, the other between 3 feet 9¼ inches and 4 feet 4¾ inches (1.15 and
1.34 meters). Some archaeologists think a third individual followed these
two, walking in the prints of the larger individual. The tracks are clear
evidence of bipedalism. Some analysts think the smaller tracks were
made by someone carrying a burden on one side.

The footprints at Laetoli.

Questions

1. Most scholars think that upright walking, which allowed hominins to range farther in the same amount of time, long predated the growth of bigger brains. How might these developments be related? (For more on brain development and physiological changes, see Rachael Moeller Gorman, "Cooking Up Bigger Brains," in this chapter.)

2. What explanation or explanations can be given for the difference in size between the two individuals?

3. What might the smaller individual have been carrying?

Roger Lewin, Peopling the Earth: Genetic and Linguistic Evidence (1993)

There have been two major interpretations of the origins of *homo sapiens sapiens*, our species. One, the "Out of Africa" scenario, posits that fully anatomically modern humans first evolved in Africa, and from there migrated over the globe. The other, the "Multiregional Evolution," posits that humans evolved independently in several different areas of the Old World and eventually merged. Use the figure on the next page to evaluate these hypotheses. The figure on the left represents interrelationships among human groups as determined by "classic" genetic markers: blood groups and variants of immunological and other proteins. Population groups near each other on the chart share more genetic markers with each other than they do with groups further away on the chart. The figure on the right lays out the interrelationships between language groups. Closely related languages cluster together, indicating languages that developed from a shared mother language. Notice that all groups are connected genetically, but not linguistically. Both data sets come from population groups that were resident there before modern migrations.

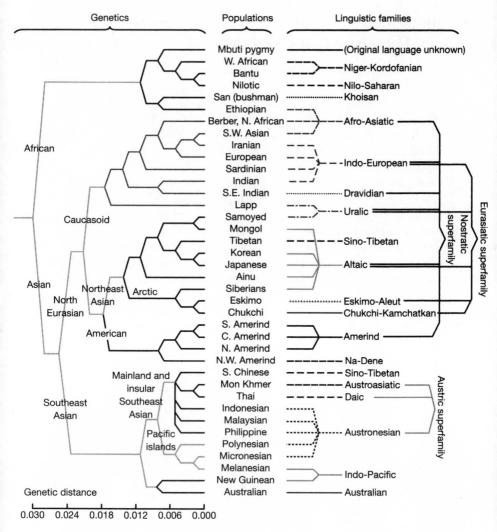

Genetic and linguistic chart

SOURCE: Redrawn from Roger Lewin, *The Origins of Modern Humans* (New York: Scientific American Library, 1993), p. 107.

Questions

1. To what extent do groups with related genetic markers also speak related languages?

2. Which of the two hypotheses given above better explains the data in this figure?

3. Would figures representing twenty-first century genetic markers and language distribution look similar to the pattern seen in this diagram?

African Language Map (2010)

The great diversity of languages in contemporary Africa is one indication of the very long history of human habitation on the continent and the degree of population movements and social change over time. With limited sources for early history, historians have turned to language for clues about the peopling of Africa and to assert long-term continuities. Languages change fairly slowly; frequently new languages emerge as a result of migrations, when a group moves away from its natal community and without ongoing contact adapts its language to new interactions or material circumstances. The presence of four major language families that developed on the continent—Afro-Asiatic, Khoisan, Niger-Congo, and Nilo-Saharan—is evidence of social and cultural diversity, showing at least three major shifts in patterns of human interaction. The number of languages within each family reflects migration; the wide geographic spread of each family suggests sustained interactions among language communities. The presence of two exogenous language families— Austronesian on Madagascar (Malagasy) and Indo-European in South Africa (Afrikaans)—is evidence of later migrations to Africa.

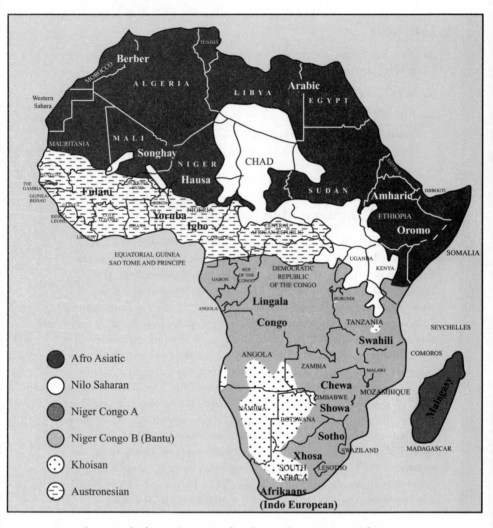

Distribution of African language families and some major African languages

SOURCE: Based on map by Mark Dingemanse (www.nationsonline.org/oneworld/map/african-language-map.htm), http://creativecommons.org/licenses/by/2.5.

Questions

1. The Niger-Congo language family has 1,532 languages, compared to Indo-European, which stretches from Britain (e.g., English) to India (e.g., Sanskrit) and has only 439. What can you infer from the denser distribution of different languages in Africa compared to Eurasia?

2. The Afro-Asiatic family includes Semitic languages such as Arabic and Hebrew. Given its geographic distribution, can you make any assumptions about early human connections between Africa and the Middle East?

3. How would you account for the relatively contained distribution of Khoisan languages in southwestern Africa, and isolated regions of Nilo-Saharan languages in West Africa?

Rachael Moeller Gorman, Cooking Up Bigger Brains (2008)

Reconstructing human evolution is very difficult. For one thing, because only a tiny percentage of people become fossils that we later find, dating the first appearance of any change is always provisional; statistical analysis of genetic divergence can sometimes yield more precise dates, but only sometimes. And without an established chronology, explaining change becomes very difficult.

We know that humans' powerful brains—though obviously a huge evolutionary advantage—also posed problems that required additional evolutionary adaptations in order to make bigger brains sustainable. For instance, female anatomy had to change so that such large-headed creatures could be born safely; an organ easily damaged by overheating required a better cooling system (which is why humans have lots of skin not covered by hair and unusually efficient sweat glands); and an organ requiring lots of calories necessitated more efficient gathering and digesting of food. In each case, the relationships among changes are hard to pinpoint. Did A come first and make B possible? Did B come first, and then create a problem solved by A, allowing B to be selected for more strongly than when it first appeared? Did the two somehow emerge together?

In the case of the brain-nutrition link, another complication appears: the adjustment to increased nutritional demands may well have been learning new behavior, rather than a change encoded in our genes. In her January 2008 article in *Scientific American*, Rachael Moeller Gorman introduces us to Richard Wrangham's suggestion that learning to cook, presumably made possible by a more powerful brain, may have been the key to further increases in brain power.

———

Richard Wrangham has tasted chimp food, and he doesn't like it. "The typical fruit is very unpleasant," the Harvard University biological anthropologist says of the hard, strangely shaped fruits endemic to the chimp diet, some of which look like cherries, others like cocktail sausages. "Fibrous, quite bitter. Not a tremendous amount of sugar. Some make your stomach heave." After a few tastings in western Uganda, where he works part of the year on his 20-year-old project studying wild chimpanzees, Wrangham came to the conclusion that no human could survive long on such a diet. Besides the unpalatable taste, our weak jaws, tiny teeth and small guts would never be able to chomp and process enough calories from the fruits to support our large bodies.

Then, one cool fall evening in 1997, while gazing into his fireplace in Cambridge, Mass., and contemplating a completely different question—"What stimulated human evolution?"—he remembered the chimp food. "I realized what a ridiculously large difference cooking would make," Wrangham says. Cooking could have made the fibrous fruits, along with the tubers and tough, raw meat that chimps also eat, much more easily digestible, he thought—they could be consumed quickly and digested with less energy. This innovation could have enabled our chimp-like ancestors' gut size to shrink over evolutionary time; the energy that would have gone to support a larger gut might have instead sparked the evolution of our bigger-brained, larger-bodied, humanlike forebears.

———

SOURCE: Rachael Moeller Gorman, "Cooking Up Bigger Brains," *Scientific American*, January 2008, pp. 102–105.

In the 10 years since coming on his theory, Wrangham has stacked up considerable evidence to support it, yet many archaeologists, paleontologists and anthropologists argue that he is just plain wrong. Wrangham is a chimp researcher, the skeptics point out, not a specialist in human evolution. He is out of his league. Furthermore, archaeological data does not support the use of controlled fire during the period Wrangham's theory requires it to.

Wrangham, who first encountered chimps as a student of Jane Goodall's in 1970, began his career looking at the way ecological pressures, especially food distribution, affect chimp society. He famously conducted research into chimp violence, leading to his 1996 book *Demonic Males*. But ever since staring into that fire 10 years ago, he has been plagued with thoughts of how humans evolved. "I tend to think about human evolution through the lens of chimps," he remarks. "What would it take to convert a chimpanzee-like ancestor into a human?" Fire to cook food, he reasoned, which led to bigger bodies and brains.

And that is exactly what he found in *Homo erectus*, our ancestor that first appeared 1.6 million to 1.9 million years ago. *H. erectus*'s brain was 50 percent larger than that of its predecessor, *H. habilis*, and it experienced the biggest drop in tooth size in human evolution. "There's no other time that satisfies expectations that we would have for changes in the body that would be accompanied by cooking," Wrangham says.

The problem with his idea: proof is slim that any human could control fire that far back. Other researchers believe cooking did not occur until perhaps only 500,000 years ago. Consistent signs of cooking came even later, when Neandertals were coping with an ice age. "They developed earth oven cookery," says C. Loring Brace, an anthropologist at the University of Michigan at Ann Arbor. "And that only goes back a couple hundred thousand years." He and others postulate that the introduction of energy-rich, softer animal products, not cooking, was what led to *H. erectus*'s bigger brain and smaller teeth.

So Wrangham did more research. He examined groups of modern hunter-gatherers all over the world and found that no human group currently eats all their food raw. Humans seem to be well adapted to eating cooked food: modern humans need a lot of high-quality calories (brain tissue requires 22 times the energy of skeletal muscle); tough, fibrous fruits and tubers cannot provide enough. Wrangham and his colleagues calculated that *H. erectus* (which was in *H. sapiens*'s size range) would have to eat roughly 12 pounds of raw plant food a day, or six pounds of raw plants plus raw meat, to get enough calories to survive. Studies on modern women show that those on a raw vegetarian diet often miss their menstrual periods because of lack of energy. Adding high-energy raw meat does not help much, either—Wrangham found data showing that even at chimps' chewing rate, which can deliver them 400 food calories per hour, *H. erectus* would have needed to chew raw meat for 5.7 to 6.2 hours a day to fulfill its daily energy needs. When it was not gathering food, it would literally be chewing that food for the rest of the day.

To prove that cooking actually does save energy, Wrangham partnered with Stephen Secor, a University of Alabama biologist who studies the evolutionary design of the digestive system. They found that the python—an animal model with easily studied gut responses—expends less effort breaking down cooked food than raw. Heat alters the physical structure of proteins and starches, thereby making enzymatic breakdown easier.

Wrangham's theory would fit together nicely if not for that pesky problem of controlled fire. Wrangham points to some data of early fires that may indicate that *H. erectus* did indeed tame fire. At Koobi Fora in Kenya, anthropologist Ralph Rowlett of the University of Missouri–Columbia has found evidence of scorched earth from 1.6 million years ago that contains a mixture of burned wood types, indicating purposely made fire and no signs of roots having burned underground (a tree struck by lightning would show only one wood type and burned roots). The discoveries are consistent with human-controlled fire. Rowlett plans next to study the starch granules found in the area to see if food could have been cooked there.

Still, most researchers state that unless evidence of controlled fire can be regularly confirmed at most *H. erectus* sites, they will remain skeptical of Wrangham's theory. Moreover, other food-based theories can explain the body and brain expansion without flames. One is the expensive tissue hypothesis, proposed in 1995 by Leslie C. Aiello, professor emeritus of biological anthropology at University College London, and physiologist Peter Wheeler of Liverpool John Moores University in England. The main idea of the hypothesis—that smaller guts correlate with bigger brains in primates—fits with Wrangham's theory, but Aiello and Wheeler think that energy-dense animal-derived foods, such as soft bone marrow and brain matter, were the reason humans developed these characteristics, not cooking.

Lacking the proof for widespread fire use by *H. erectus*, Wrangham hopes that DNA data may one day help his cause. "It would be very interesting to compare the human and *Homo erectus* genetics data to see when certain characteristics arose, such as, When did humans evolve improved defenses against Maillard reaction products?" he says, referring to the chemical products of cooking certain foods that can lead to carcinogens.

Even without such evidence yet, some think Wrangham's theory is just the thing to shake up the field of human evolution. "It doesn't matter who develops these ideas," says Aiello, who is also president of the Wenner-Gren Foundation, which supports anthropological research. "You have to listen to what Richard is saying because he has some very interesting, original data. Sometimes the most creative ideas come from unexpected places." She points to Goodall, who surprised the world by proving that humans were not the only toolmakers. "It's one of the best illustrations I know of the value of primate research informing our knowledge of human evolution and adaptation," Aiello says.

If Wrangham's strange ideas turn out to be true, we can thank an early hominid Emeril Lagasse who picked a charred tuber out of a campfire and swallowed it. Without that person, we might never have been able to examine our origins—or enjoy a good grilled steak—in the first place.

Questions

1. How does Wrangham use evidence gathered from contemporary humans and chimpanzees to support his hypothesis?

2. Why is the roughly simultaneous increase in brain size and decline in tooth size of *Homo erectus* significant for this hypothesis?

3. What are the objections raised against Wrangham's hypothesis? Who do you find most convincing, and why?

Temple Grandin, Dogs Make Us Human (2005)

Like "Cooking Up Bigger Brains," this document summarizes a controversial argument about how culturally learned behaviors may have given humans important advantages that also shaped subsequent biological evolution. In this case, however, the hypothesis involves more than one species. It claims that when humans domesticated wolves, creating dogs, both species were able to specialize, and to stop wasting precious resources on tasks that the other species could help with. At the same time, it suggests that when humans changed their environment by bringing in wolves/dogs, they positioned themselves to observe and then learn a series of very advantageous behaviors for which they (like other primates) were not hard-wired.

The thesis is controversial for many reasons. Among others, the dates at which dogs began diverging from wolves as estimated by DNA differ dramatically from the earliest dates at which we find unambiguous evidence of domestication by humans; and while this might simply reflect gaps in the fossil record, there are also some technical reasons to worry about the dating of DNA divergence in this case.

The summary of the research here comes from Temple Grandin, an expert on animal behavior (especially cattle) who was diagnosed in early childhood with autism, and has argued that mental differences reflected in that diagnosis actually make it easier for her than for most humans to understand the way many animals think.

Source: Temple Grandin and Catherine Johnson, *Animals in Translation* (New York: Scribner, 2005), pp. 304–306.

[A] study by Robert K. Wayne and his colleagues at UCLA of DNA variability in dogs found that dogs had to have diverged from wolves as a separate population 135,000 years ago. The reason the fossil record doesn't show any dogs with humans before 14,000 years ago is probably that before then people were partnered with wolves, or with wolves that were evolving into dogs. Sure enough, fossil records do show lots of wolf bones close to human bones before 100,000 years ago.

If Dr. Wayne is right, wolves and people were together at the point when *homo sapiens* had just barely evolved from *homo erectus*. When wolves and humans first joined together people only had a few rough tools to their name, and they lived in very small nomadic bands that probably weren't any more socially complicated than a band of chimpanzees. Some researchers think these early humans may not even have had language.

This means that when wolves and people first started keeping company they were on a lot more equal footing than dogs and people are today. Basically, two different species with complementary skills teamed up together, something that had never happened before and has really never happened since.

Going over all the evidence, a group of Australian anthropologists believes that during all those years when early humans were associating with wolves *they learned to act and think like wolves.* Wolves hunted in groups; humans didn't. Wolves had complex social structures; humans didn't. Wolves had loyal same-sex and nonkin friendships; humans probably didn't, judging by the lack of same-sex and nonkin friendships in every other primate species today. (The main relationship for chimpanzees is parent-child.) Wolves were highly territorial; humans probably weren't—again, judging by how nonterritorial all other primates are today.

By the time these early people became truly modern, they had learned to do all these wolfie things. When you think about how different we are from other primates, you see how doglike we are. A lot of the things we do that the other primates don't are dog things. The Australian group thinks it was the dogs who showed us how.

They take their line of reasoning even further. Wolves, and then dogs, gave early humans a huge survival advantage, they say, by serving as lookouts and guards, and by making it possible for humans to hunt big game in groups instead of hunting small prey as individuals. Given everything wolves did for early man, dogs were probably a big reason why early man survived and Neanderthals didn't. Neanderthals didn't have dogs.

But dogs didn't just help people stay alive long enough to reproduce. Dogs probably also made it possible for humans to pull ahead of all their primate cousins. Paul Tacon, principal research scientist at the Australian Museum, says that the development of human friendship "was a tremendous survival advantage because that speeds up the exchange of ideas between groups of people." All cultural evolution is based on cooperation, and humans learned from dogs how to cooperate with people they aren't related to.

Maybe the most amazing new finding is that wolves didn't just teach us a lot of useful new behaviors. Wolves probably also changed the structure of our brains. Fossil records show that whenever a species becomes domesticated its brain gets smaller. The horse's brain shrank by 16 percent; the pig's brain shrank as much as 34 percent; and the dog's brain shrank 10 to 30 percent. This probably happened because once humans started to take care of these animals, they no longer needed various brain functions in order to survive. I don't know what functions they lost, but I do know all domestic animals have reduced fear and anxiety compared to wild animals.

Now archaeologists have discovered that 10,000 years ago, just at the point when humans began to give their dogs formal burials, the human brain began to shrink, too. It shrank by 10 percent, just like the dog's brain. And what's interesting is what *part* of the human brain shrank. In all of the domestic animals the *forebrain,* which holds the frontal lobes, and the *corpus callosum,* which is the connecting tissue between the two sides of the brain, shrank. But in humans it was the *midbrain,* which handles emotions and sensory data, and the *olfactory bulbs,* which handle smell, that got smaller while the corpus callosum and the forebrain stayed pretty much the same. Dog brains and human brains specialized: humans took over the planning and organizing tasks, and dogs took over the sensory tasks. Dogs and people coevolved and became even better partners, allies, and friends.

Questions

1. What are the changes in human behavior that some scholars think might have come about as a result of the domestication of wolves/dogs? What are the changes in human and animal physiology?

2. What evidence is presented for those changes?

3. If true, what implications would this have for our understanding of human evolution? What if we don't have enough evidence to either accept or reject these hypotheses for certain?

Clive Gamble, Human Tool Use and the "Pioneer Phase" of Technological and Behavioral Development (1993)

What sets humans apart from other primates: brain size, complex language, bipedalism, domestication of dogs, or the sophistication of our tools? From these basic characteristics, other markers of human society followed: permanent hearths, burial sites, body ornaments, long-distance trade, and settlement in a broad range of ecosystems, including mountains, deserts, and rainforests.

Many of the elements associated with distinctively human behavior have left reliable archaeological traces only in the last 40,000 years—though there were significant precursors. Archaeologist Clive Gamble describes a "Pioneer phase" of human behavioral change that happened in the period between 60,000 and 40,000 years ago. He designed the following chart to compare when people began to demonstrate "modern" practices. Dates for many of these achievements have been established even earlier; ongoing research will no doubt provide continued revisions.

Gamble further supports this periodization by grouping tools representative of Ancients, Pioneers, and Moderns. The oldest tools show the simplest design. The three spearheads in the right-hand box are flint tools from Middle Paleolithic; the style goes back at least as far as

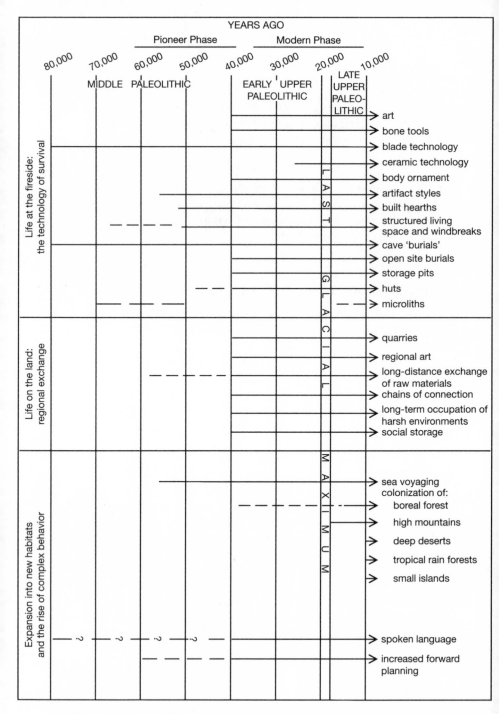

The change in behavior between the Ancients and Moderns, as captured in the archaeological record

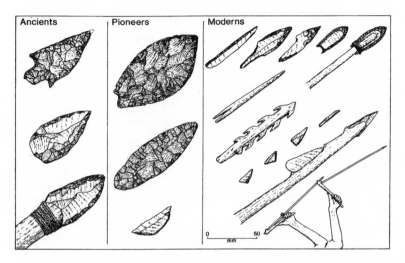

Technological changes in hunting weapons

300,000 BCE. The second group includes bifacial (two-sided) points found across much of Europe as well as a microlith from southern Africa, which shows that the Pioneer phase had wide geographic distribution. The third group, from the Upper Paleolithic, shows even more changes in size, shape, and materials, including bone and antler.

Questions

1. Which behaviors have the oldest archaeological record? Which emerge in the "Pioneer phase"?

2. Which behaviors appear in the Upper Paleolithic (after 40,000 BCE)? Do you see a relationship between tools and behavior in this period? Why?

SOURCE: Redrawn from Clive Gamble, *Timewalkers: The Prehistory of Global Colonization* (New York: Penguin Books, 1994).

3. Note that behaviors important for "life at the fireside" generally tend to have older archaeological traces, while many of the behaviors associated with expanding into new habitats are relatively recent—the last 10,000 years. Which behaviors do not fit into this generalization? Can you suggest any reasons why?

Chapter 2

RIVERS, CITIES, AND FIRST STATES, 4000–2000 BCE

Domesticated Corn (c. 4000 BCE)

Today, corn is one of the world's biggest crops; but its domestication was later (probably beginning over 6,000 years ago in what is now Mexico, versus 10,000 years ago for some Eurasian crops) and slower than those of major Afro-Eurasian cereals: wheat, rice, barley, and sorghum. It also resembles its wild ancestor, teosinte, much less than those crops resemble theirs. Teosinte had a number of features that made it less immediately useful to people than wild wheat or barley; those features changed gradually during this slow domestication. In fact, had barley or wheat been available in the Americas, one wonders whether teosinte would have seemed worth bothering with. One major change—larger cobs and seeds—is obvious here. Some very early cultivated cobs reached one-half inch; around 1500 BCE, some were six inches; today some are eighteen inches. These changes have made corn more useful to humans—and more dependent on us.

Evolution of corn. Domesticated corn gradually
increased in size.

SOURCE: Photo courtesy of John Doebley; www.plosbiology.org/article/
info:doi/10.1371/journal/pbio.0000008.

Questions

1. How might domestication and changes in corn cob size be related?

2. Teosinte ears would fall to the ground and scatter their seeds (covered by a tough skin) as soon as they ripened. How might this have suited a wild plant, but not a domesticated one?

3. Corn was probably pre-Columbian America's most important crop. How might its particular characteristics matter?

AGRICULTURE IN EARLY EGYPT

The centrality of agriculture in ancient societies is evident in many surviving sources, an emphasis which highlights daily human interaction with the environment and may suggest ways in which societies valued human mastery of natural resources. For example, the control of water through irrigation was crucial to the success of settled farming, which explains the attention irrigation receives in a wide variety of ancient texts and images.

The available evidence for most ancient societies is limited. Consequently, scholars exploit fragments of text, images, and material culture remains to piece together plausible interpretations of Egyptian political, social, and religious life, but still confront many gaps in their knowledge. A wall-painting clearly depicting domesticated animals and a three-dimensional, ceremonial object depicting a king creating irrigation show different facets of Egyptian agriculture. The mace-head relief is believed to celebrate the unification of Upper and Lower Egypt. It is significant that the image uses agricultural metaphors to symbolize peace and political reorganization.

In both images notice that the people appear to be at work, actively engaging with the natural world. Also pay attention to the range of plants and animals represented. Consider how these representations of different facets of agriculture compare to the references to farming in Ptah-hotep's instructions (see Ptah-hotep, *Precepts,* in this chapter).

Egyptian Domesticated Animals

Egyptian hieroglyphic painting showing domesticated animals

Questions

1. What conclusions can you draw from the range of animals depicted in this image?

2. Egyptians revered some animals, assigning them religious significance. What evidence from this image suggests Egyptian society also valued animals for material reasons?

3. Given the range of possible subjects for artwork, what is the significance of ordinary scenes such as this one?

Early Egyptian King Cutting an Irrigation Ditch, Drawn from Mace-Head Carving (3100 BCE)

Questions

1. What tools can you identify in this image? What can you infer about available technology from this depiction of men at work?

2. How is the king visually differentiated from other figures in this image? Can you use these visual cues to make any conclusions about social stratification in ancient Egypt?

3. What is significant about the king being depicted as involved in basic labor necessary for agriculture?

SOURCE: Walter B. Emery, *Archaic Egypt* (Baltimore: Penguin Books, 1961), p. 43.

Ptah-Hotep, Precepts (2300 BCE)

Ptah-hotep was an Egyptian official of the Fifth dynasty who served as a first minister to Pharaoh Djedkare Isesi. He compiled a set of maxims as advice for young people. Although the document reads as counsel from a father to his son, this format is most likely a rhetorical strategy rather than a specific letter of instruction. The genre—rules for behavior appropriate to social position and gender—is widespread. This text repeatedly emphasizes the importance of learning, humility, and stratified social relationships, exhorting readers to defer to superiors, extend kindness to dependents, and observe proper relationships between husbands and wives. Papyrus copies of Ptah-hotep's instructions exist today in the French Bibliothèque Nationale and the British Museum. The most notable is the Prisse Papyrus from the Twelfth Dynasty, at least five centuries after Ptah-hotep's life, so this idealized representation of good behavior must have remained relevant.

Precepts of the prefect the feudal lord Ptah-hotep, under the Majesty of the King of the South and North, Assa, living eternally forever.

* * *

The prefect, the feudal lord Ptah-hotep, says: * * * Who will cause me to have authority to speak, that I may declare to him the words of those who have heard the counsels of former days? And the counsels heard of the gods, who will give me authority to declare them? Cause that it be so and that evil be removed from those that are enlightened.

* * *

Be not arrogant because of that which thou knowest; deal with the ignorant as with the learned; for the barriers of art are not

SOURCE: Charles F. Horne, ed., *The Sacred Books and Early Literature of the East* (New York: Parke, Austin, and Lipscomb, Inc., 1917), pp. 62–66, 68–71, 74–76.

closed. * * * But good words are more difficult to find than the emerald, for it is by slaves that that is discovered among the rocks of pegmatite.

* * *

Let no one inspire men with fear; this is the will of [Ptah]. Let one provide sustenance for them in the lap of peace; it will then be that they will freely give what has been torn from them by terror.

* * *

If thou art an agriculturist, gather the crops in the field which the great [Ptah] has given thee, fill not thy mouth in the house of thy neighbors; it is better to make oneself dreaded by the possessor. As for him who, master of his own way of acting, being all-powerful, seizes the goods of others like a crocodile in the midst even of watchmen, his children are an object of malediction, of scorn, and of hatred on account of it, while his father is grievously distressed, and as for the mother who has borne him, happy is another rather than herself. But a man becomes a god when he is chief of a tribe which has confidence in following him.

* * *

Be active during the time of thy existence, doing more than is commanded. Do not spoil the time of thy activity; he is a blameworthy person who makes a bad use of his moments. Do not lose the daily opportunity of increasing that which thy house possesses. Activity produces riches, and riches do not endure when it slackens.

* * *

If thou desirest to excite respect within the house thou enterest, for example the house of a superior, a friend, or any person of consideration, in short everywhere where thou enterest, keep thyself from making advances to a woman, for there is nothing good in so doing. There is no prudence in taking part in it, and thousands of men destroy themselves in order to enjoy a moment, brief as a dream, while they gain death, so as to know it. It is a villainous intention, that of a man who thus excites himself; if he goes on to carry it out, his mind abandons him. For as for him who is without repugnance for such an act, there is no good sense at all in him.

If thou desirest that thy conduct should be good and preserved from all evil, keep thyself from every attack of bad humor. It is a fatal malady which leads to discord, and there is no longer any existence for him who gives way to it. For it introduces discord between fathers and mothers, as well as between brothers and sisters; it causes the wife and the husband to hate each other; it contains all kinds of wickedness, it embodies all kinds of wrong. When a man has established his just equilibrium and walks in this path, there where he makes his dwelling, there is no room for bad humor.

* * *

If thou art wise, look after thy house; love thy wife without alloy. Fill her stomach, clothe her back; these are the cares to be bestowed on her person. Caress her, fulfil her desires during the time of her existence; it is a kindness which does honor to its possessor. Be not brutal; tact will influence her better than violence; * * *

Treat thy dependents well, in so far as it belongs to thee to do so; and it belongs to those whom [Ptah] has favored. When there comes the necessity of showing zeal, it will then be the dependents themselves who say: "Come on, come on," if good treatment has not quitted the place; if it has quitted it, the dependents are defaulters.

* * *

If thou art a son of the guardians deputed to watch over the public tranquillity, execute thy commission without knowing its meaning, and speak with firmness. Substitute not for that which the instructor has said what thou believest to be his intention; the great use words as it suits them. Thy part is to transmit rather than to comment upon.

* * *

If thou takest a wife, * * * Let her be more contented than any of her fellow-citizens. She will be attached to thee doubly, if her chain is pleasant. Do not repel her; grant that which pleases her; it is to her contentment that she appreciates thy direction.

If thou hearest those things which I have said to thee, thy wisdom will be fully advanced.

In attending to instruction, a man loves what he attends to, and to do that which is prescribed is pleasant. When a son attends to his father, it is a twofold joy for both; when wise things are prescribed to him, the son is gentle toward his master. Attending to him who has attended when such things have been prescribed to him, he engraves upon his heart that which is approved by his father; and the recollection of it is preserved in the month of the living who exist upon this earth.

When a son receives the instruction of his father there is no error in all his plans. Train thy son to be a teachable man whose wisdom is agreeable to the great. Let him direct his mouth according to that which has been said to him; in the docility of a son is discovered his wisdom. His conduct is perfect, while error carries away the unteachable. To-morrow knowledge will support him, while the ignorant will be destroyed.

As for the man without experience who listens not, he effects nothing whatsoever. He sees knowledge in ignorance, profit in loss; he commits all kinds of error, always accordingly choosing the contrary of what is praiseworthy.

Questions

1. Why is it important for Ptah-hotep to instruct readers to be kind and fair to their dependents? What can you infer from his instructions for husbands?

2. Consider the instructions for farmers, just a small segment of the text. What are a farmer's duties? How would you characterize Ptah-hotep's attitude toward agricultural resources? How would you compare this attitude to the depiction of agriculture in the two previous images in this chapter?

3. Given the intended audience of this document, do you think the tidy division of class and gender roles accurately depicts ancient Egyptian life?

Royal Standard of Ur (c. 2600–2400 BCE)

A wooden box 8 ½ inches high and 19½ inches long, decorated with shell, red limestone, and lapis lazuli, and dating from c. 2600–2400 BCE, was found in the 1920s in the section of the city of Ur known as the Royal Graves. Its function is unknown. Sir Leonard Woolley, who discovered it, thought it was carried on a pole as a standard. It has also been hypothesized to be the sound box of a musical instrument. One of the two main panels, known as "War" (*Worlds Together, Worlds Apart,* pp. 42–43), shows war chariots, infantry, enemy soldiers being trampled underneath the chariots and killed with axes, and naked prisoners being presented to the king. The other main panel, known as "Peace" (illustrated here), shows a banquet; and various animals and other goods being brought to it.

Questions

1. What does this object tell us about Sumerian conceptions of royal power?

2. What do these panels tell us about Sumerian ideas about war and peace?

3. Do you think this was or was not used as a standard? Why? What would be the significance of the box if it was a standard as compared to a sound box for a musical instrument?

Mencius, On the Legendary Sage Kings (c. 2200–2400 BCE)

Mencius (c. 371–289 BCE), eventually recognized as the most important follower of Confucius, spent much of his life lecturing various rulers of Chinese states, trying to persuade them that following a Confucian philosophy would benefit both their subjects and themselves. Here he describes the labors of Yao, Shun, and Yü, legendary civilizers who paved the way for China's first dynasty, the Xia—though they chose their successors based on merit, not heredity. (Very little about the Xia is verifiable, but its founding is commonly dated between 2200 and 2000 BCE.) Note the connections made between agriculture, land and water management, and human struggles to "rise above" nature. Mencius also hoped that the contemporary rulers would take these men as their role models. (For an example of Mencius trying to improve rulers' behavior, see Mencius, "Humane Government," in Chapter 5.)

In the time of Yao, the Empire was not yet settled. The Flood still raged unchecked, inundating the Empire; plants grew thickly; birds and beasts multiplied; the five grains did not ripen; birds and beasts encroached upon men, and their trail criss-crossed even the Central Kingdoms. The lot fell on Yao to worry about this situation. He raised Shun to a position of authority to deal with it. Shun put Yi in charge of fire. Yi set the mountains and valleys alight and burnt them, and the birds and beasts went into hiding. Yü dredged the Nine Rivers, cleared the courses of the [Ji] and the [Ta] to

---

SOURCE: *Mencius*, translated by D. C. Lau (Harmondsworth: Penguin Books, 1970), pp. 102–103.

channel the water into the Sea, deepened the beds of the Ju and the Han, and raised the dykes of the Huai and the [Si] to empty them into the River. Only then were the people of the Central Kingdoms able to find food for themselves. During this time Yü spent eight years abroad and passed the door of his own house three times without entering. Even if he had wished to plough the fields, could he have done it?

Hou [Ji] taught the people how to cultivate land and the five kinds of grain. When these ripened, the people multiplied. This is the way of the common people: once they have a full belly and warm clothes on their back they degenerate to the level of animals if they are allowed to lead idle lives, without education and discipline. This gave the sage King further cause for concern, and so he appointed [Xie] as the Minister of Education whose duty was to teach the people human relationships: love between father and son, duty between ruler and subject, distinction between husband and wife, precedence of the old over the young, and faith between friends. Fang [Xun] said,

Encourage them in their toil,
Put them on the right path,
Aid them and help them,
Make them happy in their station,
And by bountiful acts further relieve them of hardship.

The Sage worried to this extent about the affairs of the people. How could he have leisure to plough the fields? Yao's only worry was that he should fail to find someone like Shun, and Shun's only worry was that he should fail to find someone like Yü and [Gao] Yao. He who worries about his plot of a hundred *mu* not being well cultivated is a mere farmer.

* * *

Confucius said, "Great indeed was Yao as a ruler! Heaven alone is great, and it was Yao who modelled himself on Heaven. So great was he that the people could not find a name for him. What a ruler Shun was! He was so lofty that while in possession of the Empire he held aloof from it."

It is not true that Yao and Shun did not have to use their minds to rule the Empire. Only they did not use their minds to plough the fields.

Questions

1. How do the great rulers benefit the people? What marks them as not only capable, but virtuous?

2. How are agriculture, state interests and popular interests connected in this document?

3. What constitutes civilization in Mencius' view? How is this account of its origins similar to and different from others you have encountered in this course?

Sargon of Assyria, Record of His Deeds for Posterity (ruled 722–705 BCE)

Sargon II (his name, Šarru-kên in Akkadian, means "legitimate king") was king of Assyria from 722 to 705 BCE. In the eighth and early seventh century BCE the Assyrian empire dominated the Near East. Sargon II was almost continuously involved in wars with his neighbors, campaigning in Asia Minor, Iran, to the borders of Egypt, and conquering much of Mesopotamia. He also deported the population of Israel to Babylonia. He was killed fighting a nomadic people in what is today Turkey. The following passage describes his campaign against Marduk-apal-iddina II, the king of Babylon, and the building of a new capital at Dûr-Sharrukin ("the house of Sargon") north of Nineveh. The place referred to as Dûr-Iakin in the passage is in southern Iraq.

———————

66. Merodach-baladan, son of Iakin, king of Chaldea, seed of a murderer (*lit.*, murder), prop of a wicked devil, who did not fear the

SOURCE: Daniel David Luckenbill, *Ancient Records of Assyria and Babylonia* (New York: Greenwood Press, 1968), vol. 2, pp. 33–35, 62–64.

name of the lord of lords, put his trust in the Bitter Sea, (with its) tossing waves, violated the oath of the great gods and withheld his gifts. Humbanigash, the Elamite, he brought to (his) aid and all of the Sutû, desert folk, he caused to revolt against me; he prepared for battle and made straight for Sumer and Akkad. Twelve years he ruled and governed Babylon, the city of the lord of the gods, against the will of the gods. At the command of Assur, father of the gods, and the great lord Marduk I made ready my span (i.e., battle chariot), set my camp in order and gave the word to advance against the Chaldean, the treacherous enemy. And that Merodach-baladan heard of the approach of my expedition, he was seized with anxiety for his own (safety) and fled from Babylon to the city of Ikbi-Bêl, like a *sudinnu*-bird (a bat?), at night. The inhabitants of his cities (*lit.*, his inhabited cities) and the gods who dwelt therein he gathered together into one (body) and brought them into Dûr-Iakin, whose defenses he strengthened.

67. The (tribes of) Gambulu, Pukudu, Damunu, Ru'ua (and) Hindaru, he invited and brought into it. He raised the battle cry. (Ground) by the chain, he removed from the front of its great wall and made the moat 200 cubits wide. 1½ GAR (9 cubits) he made it deep and reached the nether waters. He cut a channel (leading) from the Euphrates, and carried it up to its (the city's) plain. The city's meadows, where battles (are fought), he filled with water and cut the bridges (dykes). That one, with his allies and his warriors, pitched the royal tent in the midst of the ditches (canals), like a pelican(?), and set his camp in order. I caused my fighters to fly across his ditches like eagles(?). They defeated him. The waters of his ditches they dyed with the blood of his warriors, like wool. The Sutû, his allies, who had turned aside to rescue him and had come to his aid, together with the Marshanians, I slaughtered like lambs and bespattered with the venom of death the rest of the rebellious people. And that one left his royal tent (with its) couch of gold, the golden throne, golden footstool(?), golden scepter, silver chariot, golden palanquin, and the chain about his neck, in the midst of his camp and fled alone. Like a rat(?) he crept along the side of the city wall and entered his city.

68. Dûr-Iakin I besieged, I captured. Himself, together with his wife, his sons, his daughters, the gold, silver, property, goods and

treasures of his palace, all that there was, and the rich spoil of his city, the rest of his rebellious people as well, who had fled from before my weapons,—I gathered them all together and counted them as spoil. Dûr-Iakin, the royal city, I burned with fire; its high battlements I destroyed, I devastated; its foundation platform I tore up, like a mound (left by) a flood, I made it. The citizens of Sippar, Nippur, Babylon and Borsippa, who were imprisoned therein for no crime (*or*, detained against their will) I set free and let them see the light (of day). I restored to them their fields which the Sutû had seized long since, during the disturbances in the land. The Sutû, desert folk, I cut down with the sword; their abandoned (*lit.*, forgotten) districts (ranges, stamping-grounds) which had been given up during the anarchy in the land, I put at their disposal.

69. The freedom of Ur, Uruk, Eridu, Larsa, Kullab, Kisik (and) Nimid-Laguda I (re-)established and returned their captured gods to their shrines (places). Bît-Iakin, north and south, as far as the cities of Sam'una, Bâb-Telitum, Bubê, (and) Til-Humba which are on the Elamite border, I brought completely under my sway and settled therein people of Kummuhu, which is in the Hittite-land, whom my hand had captured with the aid of the great gods, my lords; I had them inhabit its devastated areas. On the Elamite border, at Sagbat, I had Nabû-dumuk-ilâni build a fortress to hinder any advance (*lit.*, the feet) of the Elamite. That land I divided totally and turned it over to (*lit.*, counted it into the hands of) my official, the governor of Babylon, and my official, the governor of Gambulu.

* * *

119. The sagacious king, full of kindness (words of grace), who gave his thought to the restoration of (towns) that had fallen to ruins, to bringing fields under cultivation, to the planting of orchards, who set his mind on raising crops on steep (high) slopes whereon no vegetation had flourished since the days of old; whose heart moved him to set out plants in waste areas where a plow was unknown in (all the days) of former kings, to make (these regions) ring with (the sound) of jubilation, to cause the springs of the plain to gush forth, to open ditches, to cause the waters of abundance to rise high,

north and south, like the waves of the sea. The king endowed with
clear understanding, sharp (*lit.*, strong) of eye, in all matters the
equal of the Master (Adapa), who waxed great in wisdom and insight
and grew old in understanding:—(in my time) for the wide land of
Assyria, the choicest food, to repletion and revival of spirit (*lit.*,
heart), as was befitting my reign, their (the gods') rains made plentiful; (there were) the choicest things to save from want and hunger
and (even) the beggar was not forced, through the spoiling of the
wine, (to drink) what he did not want (what was not to his liking);
there was no lack (*lit.*, cessation) of grain of the heart's desire, that
the oil of abundance which eases the muscles of men should not be
too costly in my land, sesame was sold at the (same) price as (other)
grain; that the feasts be richly provided with covers and vessels,
befitting the table of god and king, the price of every article had its
limit(s) fixed. Day and night I planned (how) to build that city. I
ordered a sanctuary to be built therein for Shamash, the great judge
of the gods, who made me attain unto victory. The town of Magga-
nubba, which lay at the foot of Mount Musri, a mountain (standing)
above the watercourses and cultivable area of Nineveh like a pillar,
whose site none among the 350 ancient princes who lived before
me, who exercised dominion over Assyria and ruled the subjects of
Enlil, had thought of (*lit.*, remembered), nor knew they how to
make it habitable, whose canal none thought to dig,—(but I), in my
all-embracing wisdom, which at the bidding of the god Ea (*lit.*,
Shar-apsi, the king of the nether waters), lord of profundity, was
made rich in understanding and filled with craftiness, and by the
fertile planning of my brain, which thinking had been made to surpass that of the kings, my fathers, by Nin-men-anna, ("Lady of the
Heavenly Disk"), mother (creatress) of the gods, planned day and
night to settle that town, to raise aloft a noble shrine, a dwelling of
the great gods, and palaces for my royal abode. I gave the order and
I commanded that it be built.

120. In accordance with the name which the great gods have
given me,—to maintain justice and right, to give guidance to those
who are not strong, not to injure the weak,—the price (*lit.*, silver)
of the fields of that town I paid back to their owners according to
the record of the purchase documents, in silver and copper, and to

avoid wrong (or, ill feeling), I gave to those who did not want to (take) silver for their fields, field for field, in locations over against (facing) the old. The "way" of its (the city's) building I lifted up(?) with fervor, opposite————, to the gods Damku and Sharilâni, the judges of men, the full brothers, and that, in future days, entrance thereinto might be in joy of heart and gladness, I raised my hands in prayer, in the chamber of the "masterbuilder of the land," to Shaushka, the powerful goddess of Nineveh. The pious word of my mouth, which she made pleasing(?), was exceedingly pleasing to the great gods(?), my lords, and they commanded that the town be built and the canal dug. I trusted in their word which cannot be brought to naught, mustered my masses of (work)men and made (them) carry the basket and headpad(?). At the beginning of the month of the son of Dara-gal, the god who renders decisions, who reveals snares, Nannar of heaven and earth, the strong one among the gods, Sin, whose name, by decree of Anu, Enlil and Ea, was called "Month of the Brick-God," (because of) the making of bricks, the building of cities and houses (undertaken therein), on the feast day of the son of Bêl, the exceedingly wise Nabû, recorder (scribe, of all things, leader of all of the gods), I had its bricks made; to the brick-god, lord of foundation (and) brickwork, and chief architect of Bêl, I offered sacrifices, I poured out libations, and raised my hand in prayer.

Questions

1. What techniques did Sargon use to conquer and rule other people?

2. What is Sargon's conception of the duties of kingship?

3. How did Sargon think of himself in relation to the gods?

The Curse of Agade (c. 2150–2000 BCE)

This epic describes events in the reign of Naram Sin (c. 2190–2154 BCE), grandson of Sargon I, during a period when the Akkadian empire built by Sargon encountered numerous setbacks, including a catastrophic drought (since confirmed by analysis of wind-blown sand deposited as sediment in the Persian Gulf) and an invasion by Gutians from the Zagros Mountains. In the epic's account (written sometime between 2150 and 2000 BCE), the problems begin when Naram Sin conquers Nippur and plunders its temple to the god Enlil. Enlil wants to destroy all of Mesopotamia in revenge; other gods intervene to limit the devastation to Agade (Akkad).

––––––––––

It sunk low as the foundation of the land,
He set axes against its branches, and
The temple, like a dead soldier, fell prostrate—
All the foreign lands fell prostrate—
He ripped out its drain pipes, and
The heavens' rains came down into it,
He removed its door frames, and the land's vigor was subverted.
At its "Gate from Which Grain Is Never Diverted," he diverted
    grain(-offerings), and
Grain was thereby diverted from the "hand" of the (home)land,
At its "Gate of Well-Being," the pickax struck, and
Well-being was subverted in all the foreign lands,

* * *

The people saw the bedchamber, its room which knows no
    daylight,
Akkad saw the holy vessels of the gods,
Naramsin cast down into the fire
Its *lahama*-figures, standing in the great gateway at the temple,
Though they had committed no sacrilege.

* * *

He put its gold in containers,

He put its silver in leather bags,

––––––––––

SOURCE: Jerrold S. Cooper, *The Curse of Agade* (Baltimore: The Johns Hopkins University Press, 1983), pp. 57, 59, 61, 63.

He filled the docks with its copper, as if he were delivering huge
    ears of grain.
Metalsmiths were to work its precious metals,
Lapidaries were to work its precious stones,
Smiths were to beat its copper.
Though they were not the goods of a plundered city,

* * *

Large ships were docked at Enlil's temple, and
The goods were removed from the city.
As the goods were removed from the city,
So was the good sense of Agade removed,

* * *

IV. *Enlil and Gutium*

* * *

Enlil, because his beloved Ekur was destroyed, what should he
    destroy (in revenge) for it?
He looked toward the Gubin mountains,
He *scoured* all of the broad mountain ranges—
Not classed among people, not reckoned as part of the land,
Gutium, a people who know no inhibitions,
With human instincts, but canine intelligence, and monkeys'
    features—
Enlil brought them out of the mountains.
Like hordes of locusts they lie over the land,
Their arms are stretched over the plain for him (Enlil) like a snare
    for animals,
Nothing leaves their arms,
No one escapes their arms.
Messengers no longer travel the highways,
The courier's boat no longer takes to the rivers.
They (the Guti) drive the trusty goats of Enlil from the fold, and
    make their herdsmen follow,
They drive the cows from the pens, and make their cowherds follow.

The *criminal* manned the watch,
The brigand occupied the highways,
The doors of all the city-gates of the land lay dislodged in the dirt, and
All the foreign lands uttered bitter cries from the walls of their cities.
In the cities' midst, though not the widespread exterior plains, they planted gardens,
(For the first time) since cities were built and founded,
The great agricultural tracts produced no grain,
The inundated tracts produced no fish,
The irrigated orchards produced neither syrup nor wine,
The gathered clouds did not rain, the *mašgurum* did not grow.
At that time, one shekel's worth of oil was only one-half quart,
One shekel's worth of grain was only one-half quart,
One shekel's worth of wool was only one-half mina,
One shekel's worth of fish filled only one *ban*-measure—
These sold at such (prices) in the markets of all the cities!
He who slept on the roof, died on the roof,
He who slept in the house, had no burial,
People were flailing at themselves from hunger.
In the *ki'ur*, Enlil's great place,
Dogs were gathered together in the silent streets,

* * *

Three men would come, and be eaten together,

* * *

Honest people were confounded with liars,
Young men lay upon young men,
The blood of liars ran upon the blood of honest men.
At that time, Enlil remodeled
His great sanctuaries into tiny reed sanctuaries, and
From east to west he reduced their stores.

* * *

V. The Gods Curse Agade

At that time, Sin, Enki, Inanna, Ninurta, Iškur, Utu, Nusku, and
    Nisaba, the great gods,
Cooled Enlil's (angry) heart with cool water, and prayed to him:
"Enlil, may the city that destroyed your city, be done to as your city,
"That defiled your *giguna*, be done to as Nippur!
"(Because of) your city, may heads fill its wells!
"May no one find his acquaintance there,
"May brother not recognize brother!
"May its young woman be cruelly killed in her woman's domain,
"May its old man cry bitterly for his slain wife!
"May its pigeons moan in their holes,
"May its birds be smitten in their nooks,
"May they, like frightened pigeons, become immobilized!"
Once again, Sin, Enki, Inanna, Ninurta, Iškur, Utu, Nusku, and
    Nisaba—all the gods whosoever—
Turned their attention to the city, and
Cursed Agade severely:
"City that attacked Ekur—it was Enlil!
"Agade that attacked Ekur—it was Enlil!
"May your holy walls, to their highest point, resound with mourning!

* * *

"May your grain be returned to its furrow,
"May it be grain cursed by Ezinu!
"May your timber be returned to its forest,
"May it be timber cursed by Ninildum!
"May the cattle slaughterer slaughter his wife,
"May your sheep butcher butcher his child,
"May your pauper drown the child who seeks money for him!
"May your prostitute hang herself at the entrance to her brothel,
"May your cult prostitutes and hierodules, who are mothers, kill
    their children!
"May your gold be bought for the price of silver,
"May your silver be bought for the price of *pyrite*,
"May your copper be bought for the price of lead!

"Agade, may your athlete be deprived of his strength,
"May he be unable to lift his gear bag *onto its stand*!
"May your *niskum*-ass not enjoy its strength, but lie about all day,
"May that city thereby die of hunger!
"May your aristocrats, who eat fine food, lie (hungry) in the
    grass,
"May your upstanding nobleman
"Eat the *thatching* on his roof,
"The leather hinges on the main door of his father's house—
"May he *gnaw* at those hinges!
"May depression descend upon your palace, constructed in joy!
"May the 'evil one' of the silent plains scream out!
"In your fattening pens, established for purification ceremonies,
"May foxes that frequent ruined mounds sweep with their tails!
"In your city-gate, established for the land,
"May the 'sleep bird,' the bird of depression, establish its nest!
"In your city that couldn't sleep because of the *tigi*-drum music,
"That couldn't rest because of its rejoicing,
"The cattle of Nanna, that fill the pens—
"May they shriek like the 'wandering one' of the silent plains!
"May long grass grow on your canal bank tow-paths,
"May 'mourning grass' grow on your highways laid for coaches!
"Moreover, on your tow-paths, places (built up) with canal
    sediment,
"May *recurved* mountain sheep and mountain *ul*-snakes allow no
    one to pass!
"On your plains, where fine grass grows, may 'lamentation reeds'
    grow!
"Agade, may your flowing sweet water flow as brackish water!

*   *   *

And with the *rising* of the sun, so it was!

*   *   *

Agade is destroyed—hail Inanna!

Questions

1. What can you tell about the economy and society of Agade from the account of its devastation?

2. Why are the Gutians chosen as the instrument of Enlil's wrath?

3. What kinds of relationships seem to exist between gods and human affairs? (Note: Though it is not mentioned here, Naram Sin, unlike his predecessors, claimed to be a divinity himself.)

Chapter 3

Nomads, Territorial States, and Microsocieties, 2000–1200 bce

Egyptian Funerary Texts (c. 2000 bce)

The Pyramid Texts are among the oldest known religious texts. They date from the Old Kingdom in the third millennium bce, and were reserved for royal use. The spells and chants were intended to protect the pharaoh's remains. The first text excerpted below was for Teti, the first pharaoh of the Sixth dynasty.

The Coffin Texts date from the First Intermediate Period, an era of contraction after the Old Kingdom. Derived from older Pyramid Texts, they have more to do with everyday life. The diffusion of the Coffin Texts beyond the royal circle suggests that some wealthy, non-royal people also had access to the afterlife. In a speech the sun-god Re takes credit for participating in creation. "The Negative Confession" is a promise that the dead will enter heaven.

Elements of the Pyramid Texts and the Coffin Texts eventually were brought together in *The Book of Coming Forth by Day and Night*, also called the *Book of the Dead*. When Karl Richard Lepsius first published selections taken from papyri scrolls in 1842, scholars compared the religious writings to the Bible. Although the hymns and spells offer instructions for passing into the afterlife, the texts do not codify religious tenets, nor do they claim divine revelation.

These three texts illuminate Ancient Egyptian apprehensions about death and fears of the supernatural, the distance between royals and commoners, the distance between the living and the dead, and appropriate behavior in various contexts.

A PYRAMID TEXT

The king is raised from his tomb

Oho! Oho! Rise up, O Teti!
Take your head,
Collect your bones,
Gather your limbs,
Shake the earth from your flesh!
Take your bread that rots not,
Your beer that sours not,
Stand at the gates that bar the common people!
The gatekeeper comes out to you,
He grasps your hand,
Takes you into heaven, to your father Geb.
He rejoices at your coming,
Gives you his hands,
Kisses you, caresses you,
Sets you before the spirits, the imperishable stars.
The hidden ones worship you,
The great ones surround you,
The watchers wait on you.
Barley is threshed for you,
Emmer is reaped for you,
Your monthly feasts are made with it,
Your half-month feasts are made with it,
As ordered done for you by Geb, your father,
Rise up, O Teti, you shall not die!

SOURCE: Miriam Lichtheim, *Ancient Egyptian Literature: A Book of Readings* (Berkeley: University of California Press, 1975), vol. 1, pp. 41–42, 131–33, and vol. 2, pp. 124–26.

A Spell from the Coffin Texts

Words spoken by Him-whose-names-are-hidden, the All-Lord, as he speaks before those who silence the storm, in the sailing of the court:

Hail in peace! I repeat to you the good deeds which my own heart did for me from within the serpent-coil, in order to silence strife. I did four good deeds within the portal of lightland:

I made the four winds, that every man might breathe in his time. This is one of the deeds.

I made the great inundation, that the humble might benefit by it like the great. This is one of the deeds.

I made every man like his fellow; and I did not command that they do wrong. It is their hearts that disobey what I have said. This is one of the deeds.

I made that their hearts are not disposed to forget the West, in order that sacred offerings be made to the gods of the nomes. This is one of the deeds.

I have created the gods from my sweat, and the people from the tears of my eye.

The dead speaks

I shall shine and be seen every day as a dignitary of the All-Lord, having given satisfaction to the Weary-hearted.

I shall sail rightly in my bark, I am lord of eternity in the crossing of the sky.

I am not afraid in my limbs, for Hu and Hike overthrow for me that evil being.

I shall see lightland, I shall dwell in it. I shall judge the poor and the wealthy.

I shall do the same for the evil-doers; for mine is life, I am its lord, and the scepter will not be taken from me.

I have spent a million years with the Weary-hearted, the son of Geb, dwelling with him in one place; while hills became towns and towns hills, for dwelling destroys dwelling.

I am lord of the flame who lives on truth; lord of eternity maker of joy, against whom that worm shall not rebel.

I am he who is in his shrine, master of action who destroys the storm; who drives off the serpents of many names when he goes from his shrine.

Lord of the winds who announces the northwind, rich in names in the mouth of the Ennead.

Lord of lightland, maker of light, who lights the sky with his beauty.

I am he in his name! Make way for me, that I may see Nun and Amun! For I am that equipped spirit who passes by the guards. They do not speak for fear of Him-whose-name-is-hidden, who is in my body. I know him, I do not ignore him! I am equipped and effective in opening his portal!

As for any person who knows this spell, he will be like Re in the eastern sky, like Osiris in the netherworld. He will go down to the circle of fire, without the flame touching him ever!

THE NEGATIVE CONFESSION

Hail to you, great God, Lord of the Two Truths!
I have come to you, my Lord,
I was brought to see your beauty.
I know you, I know the names of the forty-two gods,
Who are with you in the Hall of the Two Truths.
Who live by warding off evildoers,
Who drink of their blood,
On that day of judging characters before Wennofer.
Lo, your name is "He-of-Two-Daughters,"
(And) "He-of-Maat's-Two-Eyes."
Lo, I come before you,
Bringing Maat to you,
Having repelled evil for you.

I have not done crimes against people,
I have not mistreated cattle,

I have not sinned in the Place of Truth.
I have not known what should not be known,
I have not done any harm.
I did not begin a day by exacting more than my due,
My name did not reach the bark of the mighty ruler.
I have not blasphemed a god,
I have not robbed the poor.
I have not done what the god abhors,
I have not maligned a servant to his master.
I have not caused pain,
I have not caused tears.
I have not killed,
I have not ordered to kill,
I have not made anyone suffer.
I have not damaged the offerings in the temples,
I have not depleted the loaves of the gods,
I have not stolen the cakes of the dead.
I have not copulated nor defiled myself.
I have not increased nor reduced the measure,

* * *

I have not cheated in the fields.
I have not added to the weight of the balance,
I have not falsified the plummet of the scales.
I have not taken milk from the mouth of children,
I have not deprived cattle of their pasture.
I have not snared birds in the reeds of the gods,
I have not caught fish in their ponds.
I have not held back water in its season,
I have not dammed a flowing stream,
I have not quenched a needed fire.
I have not neglected the days of meat offerings,
I have not detained cattle belonging to the god,
I have not stopped a god in his procession.
I am pure, I am pure, I am pure, I am pure!

* * *

No evil shall befall me in this land,
In this Hall of the Two Truths;
For I know the names of the gods in it,
The followers of the great God!

Questions

1. How do the realms of the dead compare in the Pyramid Text and the Coffin Text? Can you identify specific similarities or differences? Is one vision of the afterlife more appealing than the other?

2. The Coffin Text, the Negative Confession, and the *Precepts* of Ptah-Hotep (Chapter 2) all describe appropriate relationships between people of different status, yet in the Coffin Text Re also claims to have made "man like his fellow." Can you account for evidence of social differentiation alongside claims of equality?

3. What do these texts say about relationships between people, animals, and crops?

Guanzi, How to Rule (completed c. 122 BCE)

Guan Zhong or Guanzi (725–645 BCE) could not have written the *Guanzi*, an extended set of instructions for rulers. It was probably written by many authors over four or five centuries, and perhaps not completed until 122 BCE. But Guan Zhong—a very successful prime minister of the North Chinese state of Qi (in modern Shandong)—did pursue policies like those described in the *Guanzi*: bypassing the aristocracy to tax and rule peasants directly, creating state monopolies of strategic goods, aiding agriculture, and so on. In this selection, he emphasizes limiting luxuries, and giving priority to food production and military power.

[III]

On entering the capital (*guo*) and towns (*vi*), examine the residences and observe the chariots, horses, and clothing to ascertain whether a state is wasteful or frugal. * * *

Therefore it is said: "If the ruler on high has no stockpiles of provisions but his residences are splendid, if the households of the common people [also] have no stockpiles but their clothing is highly ornate, if those who ride in chariots make an elaborate display and those walking about are dressed in variegated colors, if basic commodities are scarce but nonessential items are plentiful—these are the practices of a wasteful state."

When the state is wasteful, it exhausts its resources. When its resources are exhausted, its people are impoverished. When the people are impoverished, wicked ideas arise. When wicked ideas arise, there are evil and cunning acts. Thus the origin of wickedness and evil lies in scarcity and insufficiency. The origin of scarcity and insufficiency lies in wastefulness. The origin of wastefulness lies in not setting proper limits.

Therefore it is said: "It is vital for the state to be judicious in setting limits, frugal in dress, economical in the use of resources, and to prohibit extravagance."

* * *

[IV]

Take note of extensive hunger, calculate the amount of military and labor service, observe [the number of] pleasure pavilions, and measure the state's expenditures to ascertain whether a state rests on a solid basis or not. In general, it takes an area of land fifty *li* square to feed ten thousand households. If the number is less than ten thousand, the people may spread [freely] into the mountains and marshlands. If it is more, they may [be required to] leave them. If the fields are fully developed yet the people have no stockpiles of provisions, it is because the area of the state is too small and food-producing land is spread too thin. If the fields are only half cultivated yet the people have surplus food and grain is plentiful, it is because the area of the state is large and food-producing land is

SOURCE: *Guanzi: Political, Economic, and Philosophical Essays from Early China: A Study*, translated by W. Allyn Rickett (Princeton, N.J.: Princeton University Press, 1985), vol. 1, pp. 228–30.

ample. If the area is large yet the fields are not developed, it is because the prince likes possessions and his ministers like profit. If the developed land covers a wide area yet the people do not have enough, it is because levies exacted by the sovereign are heavy and the reserves [of the people] are drained away.

Therefore it is said: "If one-tenth [of the people] become soldiers and three-tenths do not engage in productive work, one-third of the crop will be lost. If one-third of the crop is lost and no reserves have been previously set aside, the roads will be filled with the corpses of displaced persons. If one-tenth [of the people] become soldiers and are not released within three years, and if there was no excess food [to begin with], the people will sell their children."

Even though the mountains and forests be near at hand and the grass and trees lush, proper limits must be set on residences and the proper times set for the closing and opening [of mountains and forests]. Why is this? The answer is that large trees cannot be felled, lifted, or transported by an individual acting alone, nor can they be used for the thin walls [of small houses].

Therefore it is said: "Even though the mountains and forests be extensive and the grass and trees lush, proper times must be set for the closing and opening [of the mountains and forests]."

Even though the state be overflowing [with riches] and possess an abundance of gold and jade, there must be proper limits set on residences. Even though rivers and lakes be extensive, pools and marshes widespread, and fish and turtles plentiful, there must be regulations on the use of nets and lines. Boats and nets cannot be the only resources for there to be success. It is wrong to be partial toward grass and trees or favor fish and turtles, and it is inadmissible to subvert people from the production of grain.

Therefore it is said: "When the former kings prohibited work in the mountains and marshlands, it was to expand [the efforts of] the people in the production of grain."

Unless the people have grain, they will have nothing to eat. Unless there is land, [grain] will not be produced. Unless there are people, [the land] will not be worked. Unless people have the energy to work, there will be no way to acquire the resources [required by the state]. What the world produces emanates from the expenditure of energy. Such energy emanates from hard physical labor. For this reason, if the ruler on high is unrestrained in the use of resources, it means the people will have no rest in their expenditure of energy.

Therefore it is said: "If pleasure pavilions are [so numerous that they stand] in sight of each other, those above and below will harbor resentments against each other."

If the people have no surplus stores, prohibitions will certainly not be obeyed. If the masses become refugees and die of starvation, battles will certainly not be won * * * danger and destruction will follow.

Questions

1. What reasons does Guanzi give for the ruler to focus on grain supplies?

2. Guanzi says repeatedly that rulers should limit people's use of forests, ponds, and other nonagricultural lands. Why? What do these reasons suggest about his views of what elites will do if they are not controlled? Peasants? People in general?

3. Compare Guanzi's attitude toward farming, civilization and state interests with that of Mencius (Mencius, On the Legendary Sage Kings, in Chapter 2). What are the differences and how might you account for them?

The Code of Hammurapi (c. 1792 BCE)

Hammurapi (also spelled Hammurabi) became king of the Mesopotamian city-state of Babylon in 1792 BCE. His career as a conqueror began when the Elamite state, which controlled the trade routes through the Zagros mountains, tried to expand its influence into the Mesopotamian plain. Allying with other Mesopotamian rulers, Hammurapi defeated the Elamites. He then turned on his former allies and conquered the lands to his south and, later, those to his north. The empire he ruled over contained virtually all of Mesopotamia. To facilitate the rule of such a large state, Hammurapi issued one of the earliest known codes of law. Carved on a stone stele, it was displayed in a public place. In the twelfth century BCE it was acquired as war booty by the Elamites, who took it to Susa, their capital, which is located in modern Iran. French archaeologists discovered it in 1901. Spelling has been updated in the following excerpt to reflect modern orthography.

When the lofty Anu, King of the Anunnaki, and Ellil, lord of heaven and earth, he who determines the destiny of the land, committed the rule of all mankind to Marduk, the chief son of Ea; when they made him great among the Igigi; when they pronounced the lofty name of Babylon; when they made it famous among the quarters of the world and in its midst established an everlasting kingdom whose foundations were firm as heaven and earth—at that time, Anu and Enlil called me, Hammurapi the exalted prince, the worshipper of the gods, to cause justice to prevail in the land, to destroy the wicked and the evil, to prevent the strong from oppressing the weak, to go forth like the Sun over the Black Head Race, to enlighten the land, and to further the welfare of the people.

* * *

15. If a man aid a male or female slave of the palace, or a male or female slave of a freeman [former slave], to escape from the city gate, he shall be put to death.

16. If a man harbour in his house a male or female slave who has fled from the palace or from a freeman, and do not bring him (the slave) forth at the call of the commandant, the owner of that house shall be put to death.

17. If a man seize a male or female slave, a fugitive, in the field, and bring that (slave) back to his owner, the owner of the slave shall pay him two shekels of silver.

* * *

128. If a man take a wife and do not arrange with her the (proper) contracts, that woman is not a (legal) wife.

SOURCE: Percy Handcock, *The Code of Hammurabi* (New York: Macmillan, 1920), pp. 6, 11, 22–24, 27, 33–34.

129. If the wife of a man be taken in lying with another man, they shall bind them and throw them into the water. If the husband of the woman would save his wife, or if the king would save his male servant (he may).

130. If a man force the (betrothed) wife of another who has not known a male and is living in her father's house, and he lie in her bosom and they take him, that man shall be put to death and that woman shall go free.

131. If a man accuse his wife and she has not been taken in lying with another man, she shall take an oath in the name of the god and she shall return to her house.

132. If the finger have been pointed at the wife of a man because of another man, and she have not been taken in lying with another man, for her husband's sake she shall throw herself into the river.

*　*　*

137. If a man set his face to put away a concubine who has borne him children, or a wife who has presented him with children, he shall return to that woman her dowry and shall give to her the income of field, garden, and goods, and she shall bring up her children; from the time that her children are grown up, from whatever is given to her children, they shall give to her a portion corresponding to that of a son, and the man of her choice may marry her.

138. If a man would put away his wife who has not borne him children, he shall give her money to the amount of her marriage settlement, and he shall make good to her the dowry which she brought from her father's house and then he may put her away.

*　*　*

141. If the wife of a man who is living in his house set her face to go out and play the part of a fool, neglect her house, belittle her husband, they shall call her to account; if her husband say: "I have put her away," he shall let her go. On her departure nothing shall be given to her for her divorce. If her husband say: "I have not put her away," her husband may take another woman. The first woman shall dwell in the house of her husband as a maid-servant.

142. If a woman hate her husband, and say: "Thou shalt not have me," they shall inquire into her antecedents for her defects, and if she have been a careful mistress and be without reproach, and her husband have been going about and greatly belittling her, that woman has no blame. She shall receive her dowry and shall go to her father's house.

* * *

167. If a man take a wife and she bear him children, and that woman die, and after her (death) he take another wife and she bear him children, and later the father die, the children of the mothers shall not divide (the estate). They shall receive the dowries of their respective mothers and they shall divide equally the goods of the house of the father.

* * *

195. If a son strike his father, they shall cut off his fingers.

196. If a man destroy the eye of a man (gentleman), they shall destroy his eye.

198. If one destroy the eye of a freeman or break the bone of a freeman, he shall pay 1 mana of silver.

199. If one destroy the eye of a man's slave, or break a bone of a man's slave, he shall pay one-half his price.

* * *

209. If a man strike a man's daughter and bring about a miscarriage, he shall pay 10 shekels of silver for her miscarriage.

Questions

1. Hammurapi's code contains several decrees concerning slaves. What seems to be the importance of slavery in Babylonia? Are offenses involving slaves punished more severely than other types of offenses?

2. What can we deduce from the code about the nature of the Babylonian family?

3. Why would Hammurapi put his laws on public display at a time when almost everyone was illiterate?

Relief of Assyrians Crossing the Euphrates (c. 701 BCE)

This relief, now in the British Museum, originally decorated the Nineveh palace of the Assyrian king Sennacherib (in modern Iraq). It shows the Assyrian army crossing a river during the siege of Lachish, a fortress town near Jerusalem, probably in 701 BCE. The Assyrians won the battle, though accounts of how the war ended vary. Biblical accounts suggest that the Assyrian army was destroyed outside of Jerusalem (possibly by cholera), miraculously saving the state of Judah. An Assyrian account says instead that Jerusalem surrendered.

Stone panel from Sennacherib's palace

SOURCE: Photographs by Kenneth L. Pomeranz.

Stone panel from Sennacherib's palace

Questions

1. What are the various techniques used to get soldiers and equipment across the river?

2. It would seem advantageous to send everyone across on rafts like the ones that transport the charioteers in the picture above, rather than some soldiers making tiring and risky crossings (such as those who are swimming using inflated animal intestines for flotation). Why might the Assyrians have done things the way we see here?

3. Can you formulate any hypotheses about class divisions in the army? What about technology and logistical capabilities?

Egyptian Account of the Battle of Qadesh (c. 1274 BCE)

The battle of Qadesh, fought c. 1274 BCE, was possibly the largest chariot battle in history. The Egyptians had been expanding their power into Canaan and Syria, gaining control of Qadesh in what is now Syria under the reign of the Pharaoh Seti I. However, the Hittite kingdom, based in what is now Turkey, was expanding its influence southward into Syria. Seti I handed Qadesh over to the Hittite ruler, Muwatalli I. Seti's successor, Ramses II, attempted to recover control of the city, which led to the battle. Egyptian records, excerpted below, indicate that the Egyptians won. Hittite sources, however, suggest that the Hittites won. In any case, Ramses had to abandon Qadesh. Spelling has been updated in the following excerpt to reflect modern orthography.

---

307. Behold, his majesty prepared his infantry and his chariotry, the Sherden of the captivity of his majesty from the victories of his sword * * * they gave the plan of battle. His majesty proceeded northward, his infantry and his chariotry being with him. * * * Every country trembled before him, [fear] was in their hearts; all the rebels came bowing down for fear of the fame of his majesty, when his [army] came upon the narrow road, being like one who is upon the highway. * * *

308. * * * His majesty proceeded northward, and he then arrived at the high-land of Qadesh. Then his majesty * * * marched before, like his father, Montu lord of Thebes, and crossed over the channel of the Orontes there being with him the first division of Amon (named): "Victory-of-King-Usermare-Setepnere. * * *"

309. When his majesty * * * reached the city, behold, the wretched, vanquished chief of Kheta had come, having gathered together all countries from the ends of the sea to the land of Kheta,

---

SOURCE: James Henry Breasted, ed. and trans., *Ancient Records of Egypt: Historical Documents from the Earliest Times to the Persian Conquest* (Chicago: University of Chicago Press, 1906), Vol. 3, pp. 136–41, 143–47.

which came entire: the Naharin likewise, and Arvad, Mesa, Kesh-kesh, Kelekesh, Luka, Kezweden, Carchemish, Ekereth, Kode, the entire land of Nuges, Mesheneth, and Qadesh. He left not a country which was not brought, to[gether with] their chiefs who were with him, every man bringing his chariotry, an exceeding great multitude, without its like. They covered the mountains and the valleys; they were like grasshoppers with their multitudes. He left not silver nor gold in his land (but) he plundered it of all its possessions and gave to every country, in order to bring them with him to battle.

310. Behold, the wretched, vanquished chief of Kheta, together with the numerous allied countries, were stationed in battle array, concealed on the northwest of the city of Qadesh, while his majesty was alone by himself, [with] his bodyguard, and the division of Amon was marching behind him. The division of Re crossed over the river-bed on the south side of the town of Shabtuna, at the distance of an iter from the [division of Amon]; the division of Ptah was on the south of the city of Aranami; and the division of Sutekh was marching upon the road. His majesty had formed the first rank of all the leaders of his army, while they were on the shore in the land of the Amor. Behold, the wretched vanquished chief of Kheta was stationed in the midst of the infantry which was with him, and he came not out to fight, for fear of his majesty. Then he made to go the people of the chariotry, an exceedingly numerous multitude like the sand, being three people to each span. Now, they had made their combinations (thus): among every three youths was one man of the vanquished of Kheta, equipped with all the weapons of battle. Lo, they had stationed them in battle array, concealed on the northwest the city of Qadesh.

311. They came forth from the southern side of Qadesh, and they cut through the division of Re in its middle, while they were marching without knowing and without being drawn up for battle. The infantry and chariotry of his majesty retreated before them. Now, his majesty had halted on the north of the city of Qadesh, on the western side of the Orontes. Then came one to tell it to his majesty. * * *

312. His majesty * * * shone like his father Montu, when he took the adornments of war; as he seized his coat of mail, he was like

Baal in his hour. The great span which bore his majesty * * * called: "Victory-in-Thebes," from the great stables of Ramses (II), was in the midst of the leaders. His majesty halted in the rout; then he charged into the foe, the vanquished of Kheta, being alone by himself and none other with him. When his majesty went to look behind him, he found 2,500 chariotry surrounding him, in his way out, being all the youth of the wretched Kheta, together with its numerous allied countries: from Arvad, from Mesa, from Pedes, from Keshkesh, from Erwenet, from Kezweden, from Aleppo, Eketeri, Qadesh, and Luka, being three men to a span, acting in unison.

* * *

319. When his majesty appeared like the rising of Re, he assumed the adornments of his father, Montu. When the king proceeded northward, and his majesty had arrived at the locality south of the town of Shabtuna, there came two Shasu, to speak to his majesty as follows: "Our brethren, who belong to the greatest of the families with the vanquished chief of Kheta, have made us come to his majesty, to say: 'We will be subjects of Pharaoh * * * and we will flee from the vanquished chief of Kheta; for the vanquished chief of Kheta sits in the land of Aleppo, on the north of Tunip. He fears because of Pharaoh * * * to come southward.'" Now, these Shasu spake these words, which they spake to his majesty, falsely, (for) the vanquished chief of Kheta made them come to spy where his majesty was, in order to cause the army of his majesty not to draw up for fighting him, to battle with the vanquished chief of Kheta.

320. Lo, the vanquished chief of Kheta came with every chief of every country, their infantry and their chariotry, which he had brought with him by force, and stood, equipped, drawn up in line of battle behind Qadesh the Deceitful, while his majesty knew it not. Then his majesty proceeded northward and arrived on the northwest of Qadesh; and the army of his majesty [made camp] there.

321. Then, as his majesty sat upon a throne of gold, there arrived a scout who was in the following of his majesty, and he brought two scouts of the vanquished chief of Kheta. They were conducted into the presence, and his majesty said to them: "What

are ye?" They said: "As for us, the vanquished chief of the Kheta has caused that we should come to spy out where his majesty is." Said his majesty to them: "He! Where is he, the vanquished chief of Kheta? Behold, I have heard, saying: 'He is in the land of Aleppo.'" Said they: "See, the vanquished chief of Kheta is stationed, together with many countries, which he has brought with him by force, being every country which is in the districts of the land of Kheta, the land of Naharin, and all Kode. They are equipped with infantry and chariotry, bearing their weapons; more numerous are they than the sand of the shore. See, they are standing, drawn up for battle, behind Qadesh the Deceitful."

322. Then his majesty had the princes called into the presence, and had them hear every word which the two scouts of the vanquished chief of Kheta, who were in the presence, had spoken. Said his majesty to them: "See ye the manner wherewith the chiefs of the peasantry and the officials under whom is the land of Pharaoh * * * have stood, daily, saying to the Pharaoh: 'The vanquished chief of Kheta is in the land of Aleppo, he has fled before his majesty, since hearing that, behold, he came.' So spake they to his majesty daily. But see, I have held a hearing in this very hour, with the two scouts of the vanquished chief of Kheta, to the effect that the vanquished chief of Kheta is coming, together with the numerous countries [that are with] him, being people and horses, like the multitudes of the sand. They are stationed behind Qadesh the Deceitful. But the governors of the countries and the officials under whose authority is the land of Pharaoh * * * were not able to tell it to us."

* * *

324. Then the vizier was ordered to hasten the army of his majesty, while they were marching on the south of Shabtuna, in order to bring them to the place where his majesty was.

325. Lo, while his majesty sat talking with the princes, the vanquished chief of Kheta came, and the numerous countries, which were with him. They crossed over the channel on the south of Qadesh, and charged into the army of his majesty while they were marching, and not expecting it. Then the infantry and chariotry of his majesty retreated before them, northward to the place where his majesty

was. Lo, the foes of the vanquished chief of Kheta surrounded the bodyguard of his majesty, who were by his side.

326. When his majesty saw them, he was enraged against them, like his father, Montu, lord of Thebes. He seized the adornments of battle, and arrayed himself in his coat of mail. He was like Baal in his hour. Then he betook himself to his horses, and led quickly on, being alone by himself. He charged into the foes of the vanquished chief of Kheta, and the numerous countries which were with him. His majesty was like Sutekh, the great in strength, smiting and slaying among them; his majesty hurled them headlong, one upon another into the water of the Orontes.

Questions

1. How does Ramses II represent his role in the battle?

2. What does this document tell us about the "community of major powers" (*Worlds Together, Worlds Apart*, pp. 100–101) that was taking shape in the Near East?

3. What military tactics were employed during the battle?

Casebook

WOMEN AND POLITICAL POWER IN THE ANCIENT WORLD

Most human societies have created cultural meanings and structured social roles that differentiate between men and women; some have recognized third-gender or transgender social roles, too. That a fundamental species commonality—sexual difference—has such a wide variety of cultural instantiations poses a compelling challenge to world historians: when can we discern widespread patterns, and when do locally specific details turn such generalizations into oversimplifications?

The study of gender—understood as the cultural meaning ascribed to male and female bodies and the socially constructed relationship between them—illuminates significant dimensions of political authority in ancient times. In many societies, access to political power for both men and women was linked to family connections. Birth order, marriage, and bonds of affection shaped opportunities to claim power or exert influence. For women, the ability to exercise power beyond their household often was directly related to their role in that household as mother, wife, sister, or daughter. Women could also manipulate their positions through the assertion or denial of their sexuality, a position that generally constrained women's behavior more than it enabled their exercise of power. As you analyze the following representations of Hatshepsut, Livia, Wu Jiang, Vashti, and Esther, pay attention to how these sources portray chastity, reproduction, and sexual availability—and whether those elements were part of a woman's claim to power.

Family structure frequently served as a metaphor for social order and political authority; expectations about appropriate behavior were tied firmly to both gender and generation, age being an important

61

determinant. In societies with strict generational and/or class hierarchies, rank could be more significant than gender, meaning that even when men dominated family and political structures, elite or older women had more authority than subordinate men. In other cases, women who wielded authority had to make specific claims about transcending gender norms, acting or appearing "like a man." In reading these and other sources, note instances when women were able to exercise power by appropriating male symbols or appearance, and instances when their claim to power stemmed from asserting idealized feminine attributes, such as motherhood or sexuality.

Images of Hatshepsut of Egypt (ruled c. 1479–1458 BCE)

Hatshepsut (ruled c. 1479–1458 BCE) was one of the few female pharaohs of Ancient Egypt. The sister and wife of Tuthmosis II, she acted as regent for his heir, Tuthmosis III, her husband's son by a different wife. Ultimately, however, she ruled as a pharaoh together with Tuthmosis III. She justified her retention of power by claiming both to be the designated heir of her father Tuthmosis I, and the daughter of Amun-Re, king of the gods. When Tuthmosis III became the sole pharaoh, he erased many of Hatshepsut's inscriptions and reliefs. Her name was also omitted from ceremonial lists of royal ancestors. One of the images below, a wall decoration from her mortuary tomb, portrays her as male, complete with beard and kilt, making an offering to the god Horus. The other, a funerary statue now displayed at Boston's Museum of Fine Arts, depicts her as a woman.

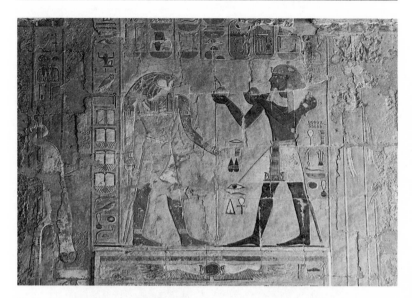

Wall decorations inside the Temple of Hatshepsut, Luxor, Egypt

Questions

1. What do these pictures reveal about the way in which ancient Egyptians thought about royal power?

2. How does the image from Hatshepsut's tomb make a claim that she was a legitimate ruler?

3. What are the differences between her depiction as a man or a woman? What do these differences say about Egyptian gender norms?

SOURCES: *Wall decoration inside Temple.* Photo: Przemyslaw "Blueshade" Idzkiewicz. October 2004. http://creativecommons.org/licenses/by-sa/2.5/deed.en. *Statue of Hatshepsut.* Photo: Keith Schengili-Roberts March 2007. http://creativecommons.org/licenses/by-sa/2.5/deed.en.

Hatshepsut statue

Dio Cassius, Livia (early third century CE)

Dio Cassius (c. 150 or 164–235 CE) was a Roman senator who served as consul and governor of Dalmatia. Born in Byzantium, he wrote his celebrated eighty-volume history of Rome in Greek. His political position gave him personal access to major figures of the Roman Empire in his lifetime. His intellectual reach was extensive; his *History* spanned 1,400 years and took twenty-two years to write. His appraisal of Livia, who lived over a century before Dio, was not from personal experience, but rather reflects Dio's understanding of the relatively recent past.

Livia was a noble woman described as beautiful and wise. She gained prominence as the wife of Julius Caesar Octavian (known as Augustus after 27 BCE). She was still married to her first husband and pregnant with their second child when she agreed to marry Octavian. Both Livia and her first husband agreed to this arrangement for political gain. Scholars continue to speculate about the emotional bonds of Livia and Octavian's marriage, which lasted over fifty years, until his death in 14 CE. Tiberius was Livia's first son from her first marriage.

Dio's discussion of prominent individuals and political structures also reveals information about elite Roman gender roles, generational expectations, property law in public and familial contexts, and a differentiation between public and private life.

[H]is [Augustus'] will Drusus took from the Vestal Virgins, with whom it had been deposited, and carried it into the senate. Those who had witnessed the document examined the seals, and then it was read in the hearing of the senate.

* * * It showed that two-thirds of the inheritance had been left to Tiberius and the remainder to Livia; at least this is one report. For, in order that she, too, should have some enjoyment of his estate, he had asked the senate for permission to leave her so much, which was more than the amount allowed by law. * * * [H]e did not restore his own daughter from exile, though he did hold her

SOURCE: *Dio Cassius: Roman History Books LVI–LX*, translated by Earnest Cary (Cambridge: Harvard University Press, 2000), pp. 71, 73, 141, 187, 189.

worthy to receive gifts; and he commanded that she should not be buried in his own tomb. So much was made clear by the will.

* * *

For [Livia] occupied a very exalted station, far above all women of former days, so that she could at any time receive the senate and such of the people as wished to greet her in her house; and this fact was entered in the public records. The letters of Tiberius bore for a time her name, also, and communications were addressed to both alike. Except that she never ventured to enter the senate-chamber or the camps or the public assemblies, she undertook to manage everything as if she were sole ruler. For in the time of Augustus she had possessed the greatest influence and she always declared that it was she who had made Tiberius emperor; consequently she was not satisfied to rule on equal terms with him, but wished to take precedence over him. As a result, various extraordinary measures were proposed, many persons expressing the opinion that she should be called Mother of her Country, and many that she should be called Parent. Still others proposed that Tiberius should be named after her, so that, just as the Greeks were called by their father's name, he should be called by that of his mother. All this vexed him, and he would neither sanction the honours voted her, with a very few exceptions, nor otherwise allow her any extravagance of conduct. For instance, she had once dedicated in her house an image to Augustus, and in honour of the event wished to give a banquet to the senate and the knights together with their wives, but he would not permit her to carry out any part of this programme.

* * *

* * * Livia passed away at the age of eighty-six. Tiberius neither paid her any visits during her illness nor did he himself lay out her body. * * * The senate, however, did not content itself with voting merely the measures that he had commanded, but ordered mourning for her during the whole year on the part of the women. * * * They furthermore voted an arch in her honour—a distinction conferred upon no other woman—because she had saved the lives of not a few of them, had reared the children of many, and had helped many to pay their daughters' dowries, in consequence of all which some were calling her Mother of her Country. She was buried in the mausoleum of Augustus.

Tiberius did not pay to anybody a single one of her bequests.

Among the many excellent utterances of hers that are reported are the following. * * * When someone asked her how and by what course of action she had obtained such a commanding influence over Augustus, she answered that it was by being scrupulously chaste herself, doing gladly whatever pleased him, not meddling with any of his affairs, and, in particular, by pretending neither to hear of nor to notice the favourites that were the objects of his passion. Such was the character of Livia.

Questions

1. Though she did not have an official position in the Roman government, Livia exercised effective power. Why would Tiberius oppose popular opinion that Livia should be given a formal title?

2. As emperor, what avenues were open to Tiberius to limit his mother's influence?

3. How did Livia use expected gender roles, including her sexuality, as a means of exercising power?

The Zuo Zhuan, Mother and Son: Alienation and Reconciliation (c. 463–389 BCE)

The *Zuo Zhuan* was written sometime between 463 BCE and 389 BCE, though the text we now have was probably altered at a later date. It is an extension of and commentary on the *Chun Qiu* (Spring and Autumn Annals), a rather cryptic listing of events involving the small state of Lu (in modern-day Shandong Province) from 722 BCE to 481 BCE during China's Warring States period. Later scholars often claimed that the *Chun Qiu* was written by Confucius (who came from Lu), and some claimed that he hid prophecies and other deep meanings in it; however, the *Zuo Zhuan*, which sticks to fairly matter-of-fact interpretations, was the most influential commentary for most of the next two millennia. Anyone claiming to be well educated had to read it.

Here the *Zuo Zhuan* deals with a recurrent problem at Chinese rulers' courts (and in some other institutions, such as family firms). Political decisions, including the appointment of officials and of heirs to the realm, were supposed to be made by male office holders, and based on the public interest. However, the loyalty and affection owed by sons to their mothers often gave these women considerable influence, and it was considered unsurprising, though unfortunate, that they often used this influence to advance more personal and emotional agendas. (Wives and concubines also had influence, although this was usually considered much more improper.) Note that even though the duke's mother (and younger brother) had acted very badly, the commentary ends by praising Ying Kao Shu for getting Duke Zhuang to reconcile with her; it thus emphasizes filial piety even more than concern for society's interests.

––––––––––––––

Duke Wu of Zheng married a woman of the house of Shen, called Wu Jiang, who bore duke Zhuang and his brother Duan of Gong. Duke Zhuang was born as she was waking from sleep, which frightened the lady so that she named him Wu Sheng [born in waking]. She hated him, while she loved Duan and wished him to be declared his father's heir. Often did she ask this of duke Wu, but he refused it.

When duke Zhuang came to the earldom, she begged him to confer on Duan the city of Zhi. "It is too dangerous a place," was the reply. "The younger of Guo died there, but in regard to any other place, you may command me." She then requested Jing, and there Duan took up his residence and came to be styled Tai Shu [the Great Younger] of Jing city.

Zhong of Ji [one of duke Zhuang's officials] said to the duke, "Any metropolitan city, whose wall is more than 3,000 cubits round, is

––––––––––––––

SOURCE: *The Chinese Classics: With a Translation, Critical Exegetical Notes, Prolegomena, and Copies Indexes in Seven Volumes,* translated by James Legge (Hong Kong: London Missionary Society's Publishing Office, 1893–95), vol. 5, pp. 5–6.

dangerous to the state. According to the regulations of the former kings, such a city of the first order can have its wall only a third as long as that of the capital; one of the second order, only a fifth as long; and one of the least order, only a ninth. Now Jing is not in accordance with these measures and regulations. As ruler, you will not be able to endure Duan in such a place." The duke replied, "It was our mother's wish. How could I avoid the danger?" "The lady Jiang," returned the officer, "is not to be satisfied. You had better take the necessary precautions and not allow the danger to grow so great that it will be difficult to deal with it. Even grass, when it has grown and spread all about, cannot be removed. How much less the brother of yourself, and the favored brother as well!" The duke said, "By his many deeds of unrighteousness he will bring destruction on himself. Just wait a while."

After this Tai Shu ordered the places on the western and northern borders of the state to render to himself the same allegiance as they did to the earl. Then Gong Zi Lü [another official at the Duke's court] said to the duke, "A state cannot sustain the burden of two services. What will you do now? If you wish to give [the whole realm of] Zheng to Tai Shu, allow me to serve him as a subject. If you do not mean to give it to him, allow me to put him out of the way, so that the minds of the people be not perplexed." "There is no need," the duke replied, "for such a step. His calamity will come of itself."

Tai Shu went on to take as his own the places from which he had required their divided contributions, as far as Lin Yan. Zi Feng [i.e., Gong Zi Lü] said, "Now is the time. With these enlarged resources, he will draw all the people to himself." The duke replied, "They will not cleave to him, so unrighteous as he is. Through his prosperity he will fall the more."

Tai Shu worked at his defences, gathered the people about him, put in order buff-coats and weapons, prepared footmen and chariots, intending to surprise Zheng, while his mother was to open to him from within. The duke heard the time agreed on between them and said, "Now we can act." So he ordered [his subordinate] Zi Feng, with 200 chariots to attack Jing. Jing revolted from Tai Shu, who then entered Yan, which the duke himself proceeded to attack. In the fifth month, on the day Xin Chou, Tai Shu fled from it to Gong. * * *

Immediately after these events, Duke Zhuang placed his mother Jiang in [internal exile in the the town of] Xing Ying and swore an oath, saying, "I will not see you again, till I have reached the yellow spring [i.e., till I am dead, and under the yellow earth]." But he repented of this. Some time later Ying Kao Shu, the border-warden of the valley of Ying, heard of it and presented an offering to the duke, who caused food to be placed before him. Kao Shu put a piece of meat on one side, and when the duke asked the reason, he said, "I have a mother who always shares in what I eat. But she has not eaten of this meat which you, my ruler, have given, and I beg to be allowed to leave this piece for her." The duke said, "You have a mother to give it to. Alas! I alone have none." Kao Shu asked what the duke meant, who then told him all the circumstances, and how he repented of his oath. "Why should you be distressed about that?" said the officer. "If you dig into the earth to the yellow springs and then make a subterranean passage where you can meet each other, who can say that your oath is not fulfilled?" The duke followed this suggestion, and as he entered the passage, he sang:

This great tunnel, within,
With joy doth run.

When his mother came out, she sang:

This great tunnel, without,
The joy flies about.

After this they were mother and son as before.

A superior man may say, "Ying Kao Shu was filial indeed. His love for his mother passed over to and affected Duke Zhuang. Was there not here an illustration of what is said in the Book of Poetry:

A filial son of piety unfailing
There shall for ever be conferred blessing on you.

Questions

1. Why do you think Duke Zhuang waits so long to rein in his brother and mother? How does the author seem to feel about this?

2. How does Ying Kao Shu—who ranks well below the Duke—get him to reverse the ostracism of his mother without directly challenging his superior?

3. What does the story seem to say about how public and familial duties should interact in the family of a ruler? About how they actually do interact?

Royal Women at the Court of Xerxes (fourth century BCE)

The biblical book of Esther relates events at the court of Xerxes (called Ahasuerus in Hebrew) who ruled from 486 to 465 BCE. The text was written many years afterward. It describes the opulence and hierarchy of the Persian court, which was ruled with absolute power by the king. The story opens when Xerxes banishes Queen Vashti because she refused an order to appear before him and display her beauty to his guests (scholars debate whether this appearance was intended to be in the nude). Esther, a Jewish orphan who was raised by her cousin Mordecai, answered the call for virgins to enter the royal harem so that Xerxes could search for a new queen. After a year of beauty treatments, Esther was called before Xerxes. Smitten, he made her queen. When Xerxes' principal adviser ordered all Jews in the empire to be killed, Mordecai persuaded Esther to ask Xerxes for clemency. Even though no one was allowed to approach the king without an invitation, and he had not sent for her in over thirty days, Xerxes granted Esther an audience. Memucan was a high government official.

ESTHER 1

Queen Vashti Disobeys King Xerxes

* * *

16 Then Memucan told the king and the officials:

Your Majesty, Queen Vashti has not only embarrassed you, but she has insulted your officials and everyone else in all the provinces.

17 The women in the kingdom will hear about this, and they will refuse to respect their husbands. They will say, "If Queen Vashti doesn't obey her husband, why should we?" 18 Before this day is over, the wives of the officials of Persia and Media will find out what Queen Vashti has done, and they will refuse to obey their husbands. They won't respect their husbands, and their husbands will be angry with them.

19 Your Majesty, if you agree, you should write for the Medes and Persians a law that can never be changed. This law would keep Queen Vashti from ever seeing you again. Then you could let someone who respects you be queen in her place.

20 When the women in your great kingdom hear about this new law, they will respect their husbands, no matter if they are rich or poor.

21 King Xerxes and his officials liked what Memucan had said, 22 and he sent letters to all of his provinces. Each letter was written in the language of the province to which it was sent, and it said that husbands should have complete control over their wives and children.

* * *

SOURCE: Esther 1.16–22, Esther 5.1–8, Esther 7.1–10, Contemporary English Version, American Bible Society.

ESTHER 5

Esther's Request to the King

1 On the third day Esther put on her royal robes and stood in the inner court of the palace, in front of the king's hall. The king was sitting on his royal throne in the hall, facing the entrance. 2 When he saw Queen Esther standing in the court, he was pleased with her and held out to her the gold scepter that was in his hand. So Esther approached and touched the tip of the scepter.

3 Then the king asked, "What is it, Queen Esther? What is your request? Even up to half the kingdom, it will be given you."

4 "If it pleases the king," replied Esther, "let the king, together with Haman, come today to a banquet I have prepared for him."

5 "Bring Haman at once," the king said, "so that we may do what Esther asks."

So the king and Haman went to the banquet Esther had prepared. 6 As they were drinking wine, the king again asked Esther, "Now what is your petition? It will be given you. And what is your request? Even up to half the kingdom, it will be granted."

7 Esther replied, "My petition and my request is this: 8 If the king regards me with favor and if it pleases the king to grant my petition and fulfill my request, let the king and Haman come tomorrow to the banquet I will prepare for them. Then I will answer the king's question."

* * *

ESTHER 7

Haman Hanged

1 So the king and Haman went to dine with Queen Esther, 2 and as they were drinking wine on that second day, the king again asked, "Queen Esther, what is your petition? It will be given you. What is your request? Even up to half the kingdom, it will be granted."

3 Then Queen Esther answered, "If I have found favor with you, O king, and if it pleases your majesty, grant me my life—this

is my petition. And spare my people—this is my request. 4 For I and my people have been sold for destruction and slaughter and annihilation. If we had merely been sold as male and female slaves, I would have kept quiet, because no such distress would justify disturbing the king."

5 King Xerxes asked Queen Esther, "Who is he? Where is the man who has dared to do such a thing?"

6 Esther said, "The adversary and enemy is this vile Haman."

Then Haman was terrified before the king and queen. 7 The king got up in a rage, left his wine and went out into the palace garden. But Haman, realizing that the king had already decided his fate, stayed behind to beg Queen Esther for his life.

8 Just as the king returned from the palace garden to the banquet hall, Haman was falling on the couch where Esther was reclining.

The king exclaimed, "Will he even molest the queen while she is with me in the house?"

As soon as the word left the king's mouth, they covered Haman's face. 9 Then Harbona, one of the eunuchs attending the king, said, "A gallows seventy-five feet high stands by Haman's house. He had it made for Mordecai, who spoke up to help the king."

The king said, "Hang him on it!" 10 So they hanged Haman on the gallows he had prepared for Mordecai. Then the king's fury subsided.

Questions

1. Why might the actions of one woman have prompted Xerxes to issue a decree reinforcing patriarchal power relationships in all the languages and scripts of the empire?

2. How does Esther use her sexuality and other gendered expectations of her behavior to influence Xerxes?

3. What commonalities in the portrayals of aristocratic women can you identify in these sources from Egypt, Rome, China, and Persia? In what ways do culturally specific differences appear in these sources?

Chapter 4

First Empires and Common Cultures in Afro-Eurasia, 1200–350 bce

Rig-Veda (c. 1700–1100 BCE)

The Rig-Veda is a collection of sacred hymns; it is among the oldest examples of Sanskrit literature and of Hindu religious texts. The name comes from the Sanskrit words *rg* (praise) and *veda* (knowledge). The Rig-Veda is one of four canonical Hindu texts, each of which has a specific religious and social function. Sections of these Vedas are still recited as prayers, an indication of long cultural continuities that survived processes of political change. The text originated between 1700 and 1100 BCE in the ancient kingdoms of northwestern India—and so coincides with the period of Vedic migrations (*Worlds Together, Worlds Apart*, pp. 147–49).

For at least a millennium, the Vedas survived only orally, with specific formulas, performance, and mnemonic markers serving to maintain remarkable continuity. The Rig-Veda is organized into 10 *mandalas* (books) of varying lengths and purposes: religious ritual, prayers, hymns, sacrifices, and commentary on everyday life. The following selection, from Hymn 90 in Book 10, tells a story of creation through sacrifice.

Thousand-headed Purusha, thousand-eyed, thousand-footed—
he, having pervaded the earth on all sides, still extends ten fingers
beyond it.

Purusha alone is all this—whatever has been and whatever is
going to be. Further, he is the lord of immortality and also of what
grows on account of food.

Such is his greatness; greater, indeed, than this is Purusha. All
creatures constitute but one-quarter of him, his three-quarters are
the immortal in the heaven.

With his three-quarters did Purusha rise up; one-quarter of
him again remains here. With it did he variously spread out on all
sides over what eats and what eats not.

From him was Virāj born, from Virāj the evolved Purusha. He,
being born, projected himself behind the earth as also before it.

When the gods performed the sacrifice with Purusha as the
oblation, then the spring was its clarified butter, the summer the
sacrificial fuel, and the autumn the oblation.

The sacrificial victim, namely, Purusha, born at the very beginning, they sprinkled with sacred water upon the sacrificial grass.
With him as oblation, the gods performed the sacrifice, and also
the Sādhyas [a class of semidivine beings] and the rishis [ancient
seers].

From that wholly offered sacrificial oblation were born the
verses [ṛc] and the sacred chants; from it were born the meters
[chandas]; the sacrificial formula was born from it.

From it horses were born and also those animals who have
double rows [i.e., upper and lower] of teeth; cows were born from
it, from it were born goats and sheep.

When they divided Purusha, in how many different portions
did they arrange him? What became of his mouth, what of his two
arms? What were his two thighs and his two feet called?

His mouth became the brāhman; his two arms were made into
the rājanya; his two thighs the vaishyas; from his two feet the shū-
dra was born.

SOURCE: *Sources of Indian Tradition*, edited by Ainslee T. Embree (New
York: Columbia University Press, 1988), vol. 1, pp. 18–19.

The moon was born from the mind, from the eye the sun was born; from the mouth Indra and Agni, from the breath [*prāṇa*] the wind [vāyu] was born.

From the navel was the atmosphere created, from the head the heaven issued forth; from the two feet was born the earth and the quarters (the cardinal directions) from the ear. Thus did they fashion the worlds.

Seven were the enclosing sticks in this sacrifice, thrice seven were the fire-sticks made when the gods, performing the sacrifice, bound down Purusha, the sacrificial victim.

With this sacrificial oblation did the gods offer the sacrifice. These were the first norms [*dharma*] of sacrifice. These greatnesses reached to the sky wherein live the ancient Sādhyas and gods.

Questions

1. Paragraph 11 is an explicit discussion of castes. How does this hymn describe or justify the hierarchical relationships among Brahmin (priests and nobles), Rājanya (warriors and administrators), Vaiśya (merchants, cattle herders, artisans), and Śūdra (servants and unfree peasants) castes?

2. How does this hymn characterize the relationships between humans and the natural world?

3. On one level, this hymn is a creation story—the birth of the cosmos, people, and animals from various parts of Puruṣa. How is sacrifice related to creation here? Why might such a tale be appealing in a society with strong memories of recent conflict?

Upanishads (first millennium BCE)

The *Upanishads*, a collection of Indian sacred texts, have grown over centuries; some have even been added in modern times. The earliest ones, however, date to the middle of the first millennium BCE, and include many of the fundamental principles of Hinduism. They also influenced the development of Buddhism and other faiths. The excerpt here lays out some of the basic ideas of *karma* and reincarnation, linking people's conduct and desires in their current life to the fate of their soul in the future.

———————————

According as one acts, according as one conducts himself, so does he become. The doer of good becomes good. The doer of evil becomes evil. One becomes virtuous by virtuous action, bad by bad action.

But people say: "A person is made [not of acts, but] of desires only." [In reply to this I say:] As is his desire, such is his resolve; as is his resolve, such the action he performs; what action (*karma*) he performs, that he procures for himself.

On this point there is this verse:—

Where one's mind is attached—the inner self
Goes thereto with action, being attached to it alone.

> Obtaining the end of his action,
> Whatever he does in this world,
> He comes again from that world
> To this world of action.

—So the man who desires.

*   *   *

Now the man who does not desire.—He who is without desire, who is freed from desire, whose desire is satisfied, whose desire is the Soul—his breaths do not depart. Being very Brahma, he goes to Brahma.

*   *   *

Accordingly, those who are of pleasant conduct here—the prospect is, indeed, that they will enter a pleasant womb, either the womb of a Brahman, or the womb of a Kshatriya, or the womb of a Vaiśya. But those who are of stinking conduct here—the prospect is, indeed, that they will enter a stinking womb, either the womb of a dog, or the womb of a swine, or the womb of an outcast (*caṇḍāla*).

———————————

SOURCE: Robert Ernst Hume, *The Thirteen Principal Upanishads* (Oxford: Oxford University Press, 1931), pp. 140–41, 233.

Questions

1. What happens to the person who is free of earthly desires?

2. For those who are reborn in this world, what determines what kind of body they are reborn in?

3. What are the possible outcomes for those who have not behaved well in their current life? What does this suggest about social hierarchy in this world?

The Near-Sacrifice of Isaac (c. 722–c. 586 BCE)

The date of this text—perhaps written as early as 722 BCE, or perhaps not until after the Israelites were exiled to Babylon in 586 BCE—is unclear; its meanings are also contested. It may be claiming moral superiority for Judaism over other religions based on rejecting human sacrifice; however, it also singles Abraham out as worthy of being chosen by God because he was willing to sacrifice Isaac. However it is understood, it remains one of the most frequently dramatized and discussed biblical passages.

1 Some years later God decided to test Abraham, so he spoke to him. Abraham answered, "Here I am, Lord."

2 The Lord said, "Go get Isaac, your only son, the one you dearly love! Take him to the land of Moriah, and I will show you a mountain where you must sacrifice him to me on the fires of an altar." 3 So Abraham got up early the next morning and chopped wood for the fire. He put a saddle on his donkey and left with Isaac and two servants for the place where God had told him to go.

4 Three days later Abraham looked off in the distance and saw the place. 5 He told his servants, "Stay here with the donkey, while my son and I go over there to worship. We will come back."

6 Abraham put the wood on Isaac's shoulder, but he carried the hot coals and the knife. As the two of them walked along, 7–8 Isaac said, "Father, we have the coals and the wood, but where is the lamb for the sacrifice?"

"My son," Abraham answered, "God will provide the lamb."

The two of them walked on, and 9 when they reached the place that God had told him about, Abraham built an altar and placed the wood on it. Next, he tied up his son and put him on the wood. 10 He then took the knife and got ready to kill his son. 11 But the Lord's angel shouted from heaven, "Abraham! Abraham!"

"Here I am!" he answered.

12 "Don't hurt the boy or harm him in any way!" the angel said. "Now I know that you truly obey God, because you were willing to offer him your only son."

13 Abraham looked up and saw a ram caught by its horns in the bushes. So he took the ram and sacrificed it in place of his son.

14 Abraham named that place "The Lord Will Provide." And even now people say, "On the mountain of the Lord it will be provided." 15 The Lord's angel called out from heaven a second time:

16 You were willing to offer the Lord your only son, and so he makes you this solemn promise, 17 "I will bless you and give you such a large family, that someday your descendants will be more numerous than the stars in the sky or the grains of sand along the beach. They will defeat their enemies and take over the cities where their enemies live. 18 You have obeyed me, and so you and your descendants will be a blessing to all nations on earth."

19 Abraham and Isaac went back to the servants who had come with him, and they returned to Abraham's home in Beersheba.

Questions

1. What are we told about the motives of the characters involved? What is left unstated?

2. What does God promise Abraham at the end of this passage? Why does this happen at this moment?

3. The passage barely mentions either the physical or social setting, focusing exclusively on the relationship between god and believer. How is this different from the *Iliad* (see Homer, *Iliad*, in Chapter 5), the Rig-

SOURCE: Genesis 22.1–19, Contemporary English Version, American Bible Society.

Veda (see Rig-Veda, in this chapter), or the Coffin Text (see Egyptian Funerary Texts, in Chapter 3), which also deal with the foundation of religions and/or communities? Does monotheism fundamentally change the demands placed on believers?

Cyrus the Great, The Decree for the Return of the Jews (c. 538 BCE)

The following documents give two perspectives on the return of the Jews to the land of Israel after their exile in Babylon. Cyrus "the Great" was the founder of the Achaeminid dynasty of the Persian Empire. From 550 BCE he conquered most of the Near East, as well as much of central Asia, creating the largest empire that had yet existed. The ancient sources present him as a ruler who was religiously tolerant and welcomed by the peoples he conquered. The biblical book of Ezra describes the return of the Jews to Jerusalem and their rebuilding of the temple. It was probably compiled in the fourth century BCE by an unknown author.

I am Cyrus, King of the world, the great King, the mighty King, King of Babylon, King of Sumer and Akkad, King of the four quarters of the world, son of Cambyses, the great King, King of Anshan, grandson of Cyrus, the great King, King of Anshan, great-grandson of Teispes, the great King, King of Anshan; an everlasting seed of royalty, whose government Bel and Nabu love, whose reign in the goodness of their hearts they desire. When I entered in peace into Babylon, with joy and rejoicing I took up my lordly dwelling in the royal palace, Marduk, the great lord, moved the understanding heart of the people of Babylon to me, while I daily sought his worship. * * *

[As to the region from as far as] Ashur and Susa, Agade, Eshnunak, Zamban, Meturnu, Deri, to the border of Gutium, the cities beyond the Tigris, whose sites had been founded of old—the gods who dwelt in them I returned to their places, and caused them to settle in their eternal shrines. All their people I assembled and returned them to their dwellings. And the gods of Sumer and Akkad, whom Nabuna'id, to the anger of the lord of the gods, had brought into Babylon, at the command of Marduk, the great lord, I caused in peace to dwell in their abodes, the dwellings in which their hearts delighted.

EZRA I

1 * * * Then in the first year that Cyrus was king of Persia, the Lord kept his promise by having Cyrus send this official message to all parts of his kingdom: 2–3 I am King Cyrus of Persia.

The Lord God of heaven, who is also the God of Israel, has made me the ruler of all nations on earth. And he has chosen me to build a temple for him in Jerusalem, which is in Judah. The Lord God will watch over and encourage any of his people who want to go back to Jerusalem and help build the temple.

4 Everyone else must provide what is needed. They must give money, supplies, and animals, as well as gifts for rebuilding God's temple.

5 Many people felt that the Lord God wanted them to help rebuild his temple, and they made plans to go to Jerusalem. Among them were priests, Levites, and leaders of the tribes of Judah and Benjamin. 6 The others helped by giving silver articles, gold, personal possessions, cattle, and other valuable gifts, as well as offerings for the temple.

7 King Cyrus gave back the things that Nebuchadnezzar had taken from the Lord's temple in Jerusalem and had put in the temple of his own gods. 8 Cyrus placed Mithredath, his chief treasurer, in charge of these things. Mithredath counted them and gave a list to Sheshbazzar, the governor of Judah.

SOURCE: *The Sacred Books and Early Literature of the East,* edited by Charles F. Horne (New York: Parke, Austin and Lipscomb, 1917), pp. 461–62, and Ezra 1.1–8, Contemporary English Version, American Bible Society.

Questions

1. What does Cyrus see as the basis of his legitimacy?

2. What is Cyrus' strategy for dealing with his conquered peoples?

3. How does the author of Ezra interpret Cyrus' decision to let the Jews return to the land of Israel?

Herodotus, Persians Debate Governance (c. 522 BCE)

Herodotus (c. 484–c. 425 BCE) is regarded in the West as the father of history and of anthropology. His curiosity about the origins of the Greco-Persian wars (490, 480–479 BCE) resulted in *The Histories*, a researched, documented, structured account of the past. Although he calls some of his informants "liars" and scholars today believe that Herodotus himself elaborated his material, the work nevertheless remains an important source for an otherwise poorly documented period, and particularly valuable for understanding how Greeks understood other cultures.

The Histories is roughly structured by the reigns of four Persian kings: Cyrus, Cambyses, Darius, and Xerxes. Although it purports to explain a period of Persian conquest and consolidation followed by imperial downfall, much of the book is "digressions," stories and descriptions of other peoples that Herodotus gathered by traveling around the Mediterranean.

In this passage Herodotus portrays a debate about appropriate forms of governance. In the preceding passage (not shown), seven Persian conspirators had unseated a usurper. In the wake of their victory, they made a conscious decision about how to rule.

---

80. And now when five days were gone, and the hubbub had settled down, the conspirators met together to consult about the

SOURCE: George Rawlinson, *The History of Herodotus* (New York: D. Appleton & Company, 1866), vol. 2, pp. 393–95.

situation of affairs. At this meeting speeches were made, to which many of the Greeks give no credence, but they were made nevertheless. Otanes [who led the fight against the Magian usurper Gaumâta] recommended that the management of public affairs should be entrusted to the whole nation. "To me," he said, "it seems advisable, that we should no longer have a single man to rule over us—the rule of one is neither good nor pleasant. Ye cannot have forgotten to what lengths Cambyses went in his haughty tyranny, and the haughtiness of the Magi ye have yourselves experienced. How indeed is it possible that monarchy should be a well-adjusted thing, when it allows a man to do as he likes without being answerable? Such licence is enough to stir strange and unwonted thoughts in the heart of the worthiest of men. Give a person this power, and straightway his manifold good things puff him up with pride, while envy is so natural to human kind that it cannot but arise in him. But pride and envy together include all wickedness; both leading on to deeds of savage violence. True it is that kings, possessing as they do all that heart can desire, ought to be void of envy, but the contrary is seen in their conduct towards the citizens. They are jealous of the most virtuous among their subjects, and wish their death; while they take delight in the meanest and basest, being ever ready to listen to the tales of slanderers. A king, besides, is beyond all other men inconsistent with himself. Pay him court in moderation, and he is angry because you do not show him more profound respect— show him profound respect, and he is offended again, because (as he says) you fawn on him. But the worst of all is, that he sets aside the laws of the land, puts men to death without trial, and subjects women to violence. The rule of the many, on the other hand, has, in the first place, the fairest of names, to wit, *isonomy*; and further it is free from all those outrages which a king is wont to commit. There, places are given by lot, the magistrate is answerable for what he does, and measures rest with the commonalty. I vote, therefore, that we do away with monarchy, and raise the people to power. For the people are all in all."

81. Such were the sentiments of Otanes. Megabyzus [an important military commander and one of the conspirators] spoke next, and advised the setting up of an oligarchy:—"In all that Otanes has

said to persuade you to put down monarchy," he observed, "I fully concur; but his recommendation that we should call the people to power seems to me not the best advice. For there is nothing so void of understanding, nothing so full of wantonness as the unwieldy rabble. It were folly not to be borne for men, while seeking to escape the wantonness of a tyrant, to give themselves up to the wantonness of a rude unbridled mob. The tyrant, in all his doings, at least knows what he is about, but a mob is altogether devoid of knowledge; for how should there be any knowledge in a rabble, untaught, and with no natural sense of what is right and fit? It rushes wildly into state affairs with all the fury of a stream swollen in the winter, and confuses everything. Let the enemies of the Persians be ruled by democracies; but let us choose out from the citizens a certain number of the worthiest, and put the government into their hands. For thus both we ourselves shall be among the governors, and power being entrusted to the best men, it is likely that the best counsels will prevail in the state."

82. This was the advice which Megabyzus gave, and after him Darius came forward, and spoke as follows:—"All that Megabyzus said against democracy was well said, I think; but about oligarchy he did not speak advisedly; for take these three forms of government, democracy, oligarchy, and monarchy, and let them each be at their best, I maintain that monarchy far surpasses the other two. What government can possibly be better than that of the very best man in the whole state? The counsels of such a man are like himself, and so he governs the mass of the people to their heart's content; while at the same time his measures against evil-doers are kept more secret than in other states. Contrariwise, in oligarchies, where men vie with each other in the service of the commonwealth, fierce enmities are apt to arise between man and man, each wishing to be leader, and to carry his own measures; whence violent quarrels come, which lead to open strife, often ending in bloodshed. Then monarchy is sure to follow; and this too shows how far that rule surpasses all others. Again, in a democracy, it is impossible but that there will be malpractices: these malpractices, however, do not lead to enmities, but to close friendships, which are formed among those engaged in them, who must hold well

together to carry on their villanies. And so things go on until a man stands forth as champion of the commonalty, and puts down the evil-doers. Straightway the author of so great a service is admired by all, and from being admired soon comes to be appointed king; so that here too it is plain that monarchy is the best government. Lastly, to sum up all in a word, whence, I ask, was it that we got the freedom which we enjoy?—did democracy give it us, or oligarchy, or a monarch? As a single man recovered our freedom for us, [Cyrus the Great, r. 559–529] my sentence is that we keep to the rule of one. Even apart from this, we ought not to change the laws of our forefathers when they work fairly; for to do so, is not well."

83. Such were the three opinions brought forward at this meeting; the four other Persians voted in favour of the last.

Questions

1. What are the benefits and drawbacks of each of the three forms of governance debated by Persian leaders in the period immediately before the reign of Darius I?

2. How would the Persians taking part in this debate have known about these various forms of government?

3. Darius claims that a monarchy is best able to provide stability and put down "evil doers." Years later, he erected the Beisitun inscription (*World's Together Worlds Apart*, p. 138) to commemorate his accomplishments and remind people of royal power. Does the inscription bear out the views on monarchy attributed to him by Herodotus? Why or why not?

Thucydides, The Plague (c. 430 BCE)

One of the consequences of increasing contacts between the agricultural societies of Afro-Eurasia was the outbreak of epidemic diseases. Mortality among populations exposed to a disease for the first time, and therefore with no immunity to it, could be catastrophic. One of the earliest descriptions of a major epidemic is that of the plague outbreak in Athens contained in *The History of the Peloponnesian War* by the Greek historian Thucydides (c. 460 BCE–c. 395 BCE). Like Herodotus, Thucydides thought that history had to be more than a chronicle. Unlike Herodotus, Thucydides was interested in discerning patterns of human behavior, including the breakdown of social norms in the face of disaster—both natural and man-made. This passage gives us the unique perspective of an individual who contracted the plague and survived.

XLVII. Such were the funeral ceremonies that took place during this winter, the close of which brought the first year of this war to an end. At the very beginning of summer the Peloponnesians and their allies, with two-thirds of their forces as before, invaded Attica, under the command of Archidamus, son of Zeuxidamus, king of the Lacedaemonians, and establishing themselves proceeded to ravage the country. And before they had been many days in Attica the plague began for the first time to show itself among the Athenians. It is said, indeed, to have broken out before in many places, both in Lemnos and elsewhere, though no pestilence of such extent nor any scourge so destructive of human lives is on record anywhere. For neither were physicians able to cope with the disease, since they at first had to treat it without knowing its nature, the mortality among them being greatest because they were most exposed to it, nor did any other human art avail. And the supplications made at sanctuaries, or appeals to oracles and the like, were all futile, and at last men desisted from them, overcome by the calamity.

XLVIII. The disease began, it is said, in Ethiopia beyond Egypt, and then descended into Egypt and Libya and spread over the greater part of the King's territory. Then it suddenly fell upon the city of Athens, and attacked first the inhabitants of the Peiraeus, so that the people there even said that the Peloponnesians had put poison in their cisterns; for there were as yet no public fountains there. But afterwards it reached the upper city also, and from that time the mortality became much greater. Now any one, whether physician or

SOURCE: *Thucydides*, translated by Charles Foster Smith (Cambridge: Harvard University Press, 1919), vol. 1, pp. 341–57.

layman, may, each according to his personal opinion, speak about its probable origin and state the causes which, in his view, were sufficient to have produced so great a departure from normal conditions; but I shall describe its actual course, explaining the symptoms, from the study of which a person should be best able, having knowledge of it beforehand, to recognize it if it should ever break out again. For I had the disease myself and saw others sick of it.

XLIX. That year, as was agreed by all, happened to be unusually free from disease so far as regards the other maladies; but if anyone was already ill of any disease all terminated in this. In other cases from no obvious cause, but suddenly and while in good health, men were seized first with intense heat of the head, and redness and inflammation of the eyes, and the parts inside the mouth, both the throat and the tongue, immediately became blood-red and exhaled an unnatural and fetid breath. In the next stage sneezing and hoarseness came on, and in a short time the disorder descended to the chest, attended by severe coughing. And when it settled in the stomach, that was upset, and vomits of bile of every kind named by physicians ensued, these also attended by great distress; and in most cases ineffectual retching followed producing violent convulsions, which sometimes abated directly, sometimes not until long afterwards. Externally, the body was not so very warm to the touch; it was not pale, but reddish, livid, and breaking out in small blisters and ulcers. But internally it was consumed by such a heat that the patients could not bear to have on them the lightest coverings or linen sheets, but wanted to be quite uncovered and would have liked best to throw themselves into cold water—indeed many of those who were not looked after did throw themselves into cisterns—so tormented were they by thirst which could not be quenched; and it was all the same whether they drank much or little. They were also beset by restlessness and sleeplessness which never abated. And the body was not wasted while the disease was at its height, but resisted surprisingly the ravages of the disease, so that when the patients died, as most of them did on the seventh or ninth day from the internal heat, they still had some strength left; or, if they passed the crisis, the disease went down into the bowels, producing there a violent ulceration, and at the same time an acute diarrhoea set in, so that in this later stage most of them perished through weakness caused by it. For the malady, starting from the head where it was first seated, passed down until it spread through the whole body, and if one got over the worst, it seized upon the extremities at least and left its marks there; for it attacked the privates and fingers and toes, and many escaped with the loss of these, though some lost their eyes also. In some cases the sufferer was attacked immediately after recovery by loss of memory, which extended to every object alike, so that they failed to recognize either themselves or their friends.

L. Indeed the character of the disease proved such that it baffles description, the violence of the attack being in each case too great for human nature to endure, while in one way in particular it showed plainly that it was different from any of the familiar diseases: the birds, namely, and the four-footed animals, which usually feed upon human bodies, either would not now come near them, though many lay unburied, or died if they tasted of them. The evidence for this is that birds of this kind became noticeably scarce, and they were no longer to be seen either about the bodies or anywhere else; while the dogs gave a still better opportunity to observe what happened, because they live with man.

LI. Such, then, was the general nature of the disease; for I pass over many of the unusual symptoms, since it chanced to affect one man differently as compared with another. And while the plague lasted there were none of the usual complaints, though if any did occur it ended in this. Sometimes death was due to neglect, but sometimes it occurred in spite of careful nursing. And no one remedy was found, I may say, which was sure to bring relief to those applying it—for what helped one man hurt another—and no constitution, as it proved, was of itself sufficient against it, whether as regards physical strength or weakness, but it carried off all without distinction, even those tended with all medical care. And the most dreadful thing about the whole malady was not only the despondency of the victims, when they once became aware that they were sick, for their minds straightway yielded to despair and they gave themselves up for lost instead of resisting, but also the fact that they became infected by nursing one another and died like sheep. And this caused the heaviest mortality; for if, on the one hand, they were restrained by fear from visiting one another, the sick perished uncared for, so that many houses were left empty through lack of anyone to do the nursing; or if, on the other hand, they visited the sick, they perished, especially those who made any pretensions to goodness. For these made it a point of honour to visit their friends without sparing themselves at a time when the very relatives of the dying, overwhelmed by the magnitude of the calamity, were growing weary even of making their lamentations. But still it was more often those who had recovered who had pity for the dying and the sick, because they had learnt what it meant and were themselves by this time confident of immunity; for the disease never attacked the same man a second time, at least not with fatal results. And they were not only congratulated by everybody else, but themselves, in the excess of their joy at the moment, cherished also a fond fancy with regard to the rest of their lives that they would never be carried off by any other disease.

LII. But in addition to the trouble under which they already laboured, the Athenians suffered further hardship owing to the crowding into the city of the people from the country districts; and this affected the new arrivals especially. For since no houses were available for them and they had to live in huts that were stifling in the hot season, they perished in wild disorder. Bodies of dying men lay one upon another, and half-dead people rolled about in the streets and, in their longing for water, near all the fountains. The temples, too, in which they had quartered themselves were full of the corpses of those who had died in them; for the calamity which weighed upon them was so overpowering that men, not knowing what was to become of them, became careless of all law, sacred as well as profane. And the customs which they had hitherto observed regarding burial were all thrown into confusion, and they buried their dead each one as he could. And many resorted to shameless modes of burial because so many members of their households had already died that they lacked the proper funeral materials. Resorting to other people's pyres, some, anticipating those who had raised them, would put on their own dead and kindle the fire; others would throw the body they were carrying upon one which was already burning and go away.

LIII. In other respects also the plague first introduced into the city a greater lawlessness. For where men hitherto practised concealment, that they were not acting purely after their pleasure, they now showed a more careless daring. They saw how sudden was the change of fortune in the case both of those who were prosperous and suddenly died, and of those who before had nothing but in a moment were in possession of the property of the others. And so they resolved to get out of life the pleasures which could be had speedily and would satisfy their lusts, regarding their bodies and their wealth alike as transitory. And no one was eager to practise self-denial in prospect of what was esteemed honour, because everyone thought that it was doubtful whether he would live to attain it, but the pleasure of the moment and whatever was in any way conducive to it came to be regarded as at once honourable and expedient. No fear of gods or law of men restrained; for, on the one hand, seeing that all men were perishing alike, they judged that piety and impiety came to the same thing, and, on the other, no one expected that he would live to be called to account and pay the penalty of his misdeeds. On the contrary, they believed that the penalty already decreed against them, and now hanging over their heads, was a far heavier one, and that before this fell it was only reasonable to get some enjoyment out of life.

LIV. Such then was the calamity that had befallen them by which the Athenians were sore pressed, their people dying within the walls and their land being ravaged without. And in their distress they recalled, as was natural, the following verse which their older men said had long ago been uttered:

A Dorian war shall come and pestilence with it.

A dispute arose, however, among the people, some contending that the word used in the verse by the ancients was not λοιμός, "pestilence," but λιμός, "famine," and the view prevailed at the time that "pestilence" was the original word; and quite naturally, for men's recollections conformed to their sufferings. But if ever another Dorian war should visit them after the present war and a famine happen to come with it, they would probably, I fancy, recite the verse in that way. Those, too, who were familiar with it, recalled that other oracle given to the Lacedaemonians, when, in answer to their inquiry whether they should go to war, the god responded that if they "warred with all their might victory would be theirs," adding that he himself would assist them. Now so far as the oracle is concerned, they surmised that what was then happening was its fulfilment, for the plague broke out immediately after the Peloponnesians had invaded Attica; and though it did not enter the Peloponnesus to any extent, it devastated Athens most of all, and next to Athens the places which had the densest population. So much for the history of the plague.

LV. The Peloponnesians, after ravaging the plain, advanced into the district called Paralus as far as Laurium, where are the silver mines of the Athenians. And first they ravaged that part of this district which looked towards the Peloponnesus, and afterwards the part facing Euboea and Andros. But Pericles, who was general, still held to the same policy as during the earlier invasion, insisting that the Athenians should not take the field against them.

Questions

1. What are the symptoms of the plague?

2. How do the Athenians react to the plague? What is its impact on social customs?

3. How do the Athenians try to explain the outbreak of this epidemic?

Chapter 5

WORLDS TURNED INSIDE OUT, 1000–350 BCE

Homer, Shield of Achilles (c. 750 BCE)

The *Iliad* is an epic Greek poem traditionally attributed to a poet named Homer. It was probably composed about 750 BCE and describes the Trojan War, which the ancient Greeks believed had taken place in the thirteenth or twelfth century BCE. The action of the poem turns on the tragic consequences of the wrath of Achilles, the son of a human father and a sea nymph, Thetis, who was insulted by Agamemnon, the leader of the Greek army besieging Troy. The passage below describes the shield that Thetis asked the Greek god of fire, Hephaestos, to forge for her son. Spelling has been updated in the following excerpt to reflect modern orthography.

He [Hephaestos] cast on the fire bronze which is weariless, and tin with it and valuable gold, and silver, and thereafter set forth upon its standard the great anvil, and gripped in one hand the ponderous hammer, while in the other he grasped the pincers.

First of all he forged a shield that was huge and heavy, elaborating it about, and threw around it a shining triple rim that glittered, and the shield strap was cast of silver. There were five folds composing the shield itself, and upon it he elaborated many things in his skill and craftsmanship.

SOURCE: *The Iliad of Homer*, translated by Richmond Lattimore (Chicago: University of Chicago Press, 1951), pp. 388–91.

He made the earth upon it, and the sky, and the sea's water, and the tireless sun, and the moon waxing into her fullness, and on it all the constellations that festoon the heavens, the Pleiades and the Hyades and the strength of Orion and the Bear, whom men give also the name of the Wagon, who turns about in a fixed place and looks at Orion and she alone is never plunged in the wash of the Ocean.

On it he wrought in all their beauty two cities of mortal men. And there were marriages in one, and festivals. They were leading the brides along the city from their maiden chamber under the flaring of torches, and the loud bride song was arising. The young men followed the circles of the dance, and among them the flutes and lyres kept up their clamour as in the meantime the women standing each at the door of her court admired them. The people were assembled in the market place, where a quarrel had arisen, and two men were disputing over the blood price for a man who had been killed. One man promised full restitution in a public statement, but the other refused and would accept nothing. Both then made for an arbitrator, to have a decision; and people were speaking up on either side, to help both men. But the heralds kept the people in hand, as meanwhile the elders were in session on benches of polished stone in the sacred circle and held in their hands the staves of the heralds who lift their voices. The two men rushed before these, and took turns speaking their cases, and between them lay on the ground two talents of gold, to be given to that judge who in this case spoke the straightest opinion.

But around the other city were lying two forces of armed men shining in their war gear. For one side counsel was divided whether to storm and sack, or share between both sides the property and all the possessions the lovely citadel held hard within it. But the city's people were not giving way, and armed for an ambush. Their beloved wives and their little children stood on the rampart to hold it, and with them the men with age upon them, but meanwhile the others went out. And Ares led them, and Pallas Athene. These were gold, both, and golden raiment upon them, and they were beautiful and huge in their armour, being divinities, and conspicuous from afar, but the people around them were smaller. These, when they were come to the place that was set for their ambush, in a river, where there was a watering place for all animals, there they sat down in place shrouding themselves in the bright bronze. But apart from these were sitting two men to watch for the rest of them and waiting until they could see the sheep and the shambling cattle, who appeared presently, and two herdsmen went along with them playing happily on pipes, and took no thought of the treachery. Those others saw them, and made a rush, and quickly thereafter cut off on both sides the herds of cattle and the beautiful flocks of shining sheep, and killed the shepherds upon them. But the other army, as soon as they heard the uproar arising from the cattle, as they sat in their councils, suddenly mounted behind their light-foot horses, and went after, and soon overtook them. These stood their ground and fought a battle by the banks of the river, and they were making casts at each other with their spears bronze-headed; and Hate was there with Confusion among them, and Death the destructive; she was holding a live man with a new wound, and another one unhurt, and dragged a dead man by the feet through the carnage. The clothing upon her shoulders showed strong red with the men's blood. All closed together like living men and fought with each other and dragged away from each other the corpses of those who had fallen.

He made upon it a soft field, the pride of the tilled land, wide and triple-ploughed, with many ploughmen upon it who wheeled their teams at the turn and drove them in either direction. And as these making their turn would reach the end-strip of the field, a man would come up to them at this point and hand them a flagon of honey-sweet wine, and they would turn again to the furrows in their haste to come again to the end-strip of the deep field. The earth darkened behind them and looked like earth that has been ploughed though it was gold. Such was the wonder of the shield's forging.

He made on it the precinct of a king, where the labourers were reaping, with the sharp reaping hooks in their hands. Of the cut swathes some fell along the lines of reaping, one after another, while the sheaf-binders caught up others and tied them with bind-rope. There were three sheaf-binders who stood by, and behind them were children picking up the cut swathes, and filled their arms with them and carried and gave them always; and by them the king in silence and holding his staff stood near the line of the reapers, happily. And apart and under a tree the heralds made a feast ready and trimmed a great ox they had slaughtered. Meanwhile the women scattered, for the workmen to eat, abundant white barley.

He made on it a great vineyard heavy with clusters, lovely and in gold, but the grapes upon it were darkened and the vines themselves stood out through poles of silver. About them he made a field-ditch of dark metal, and drove all around this a fence of tin; and there was only one path to the vineyard, and along it ran the grape-bearers for the vineyard's stripping. Young girls and young men, in all their light-hearted innocence, carried the kind, sweet fruit away in their woven baskets, and in their midst a youth with a singing lyre played charmingly upon it for them, and sang the beautiful song for Linos in a light voice, and they followed him, and with singing and whistling and light dance-steps of their feet kept time to the music.

He made upon it a herd of horn-straight oxen. The cattle were wrought of gold and of tin, and thronged in speed and with lowings out of the dung of the farmyard to a pasturing place by a sounding river, and beside the moving field of a reed bed. The herdsmen were of gold who went along with the cattle, four of them, and nine dogs shifting their feet followed them. But among the foremost of the cattle two formidable lions had caught hold of a bellowing bull, and he with loud lowings was dragged away, as the dogs and the young men went in pursuit of him. But the two lions, breaking open the hide of the great ox, gulped the black blood and the inward guts, as meanwhile the herdsmen were in the act of setting and urging the quick dogs on them. But they, before they could get their teeth in, turned back from the lions, but would come and take their stand very close, and bayed, and kept clear.

And the renowned smith of the strong arms made on it a meadow large and in a lovely valley for the glimmering sheepflocks, with dwelling places upon it, and covered shelters, and sheepfolds.

And the renowned smith of the strong arms made elaborate on it a dancing floor, like that which once in the wide spaces of Knosos Daidalos built for Ariadne of the lovely tresses. And there were young men on it and young girls, sought for their beauty with gifts of oxen, dancing, and holding hands at the wrist. These wore, the maidens long light robes, but the men wore tunics of finespun work and shining softly, touched with olive oil. And the girls wore fair garlands on their heads, while the young men carried golden knives that hung from sword-belts of silver. At whiles on their under-standing feet they would run very lightly, as when a potter crouch-ing makes trial of his wheel, holding it close in his hands, to see if it will run smooth. At another time they would form rows, and run, rows crossing each other. And around the lovely chorus of dancers stood a great multitude happily watching, while among the dancers two acrobats led the measures of song and dance revolving among them.

He made on it the great strength of the Ocean River which ran around the uttermost rim of the shield's strong structure.

Then after he had wrought this shield, which was huge and heavy, he wrought for him a corselet brighter than fire in its shin-ing, and wrought him a helmet, massive and fitting close to his temples, lovely and intricate work, and laid a gold top-ridge along it, and out of pliable tin wrought him leg-armour. Thereafter when the renowned smith of the strong arms had finished the armour he lifted it and laid it before the mother of Achilles. And she like a hawk came sweeping down from the snows of Olympos and carried with her the shining armour, the gift of Hephaestos.

Questions

1. Why do you think scenes of daily life are depicted on Achilles' shield?

2. What makes for the good life in the city at peace? What threatens it? How are disputes handled in the city at peace?

3. What can we learn about the agrarian economy of the ancient Greeks from the shield?

Confucius, Analects (fifth century BCE)

Confucius (551–479 BCE) was a minor aristocrat in one of the small states struggling for survival in China's Warring States period, brought on by the decline of the Zhou dynasty. Concerned about what he perceived as a decline in social order and ethical conduct, he offered advice to rulers and instruction to young men on both public and private behavior.

The *Analects* were assembled by his students some time after his death, and are thought to contain the basics of his philosophical teachings. In these selections, Confucius deals with the virtues of reciprocity, humaneness, and filial piety, which he saw as the essential bases for both a proper personal life and an ordered society. Spelling has been updated in the following excerpt to reflect modern orthography.

THE UNITARY PRINCIPLE: RECIPROCITY OR HUMANITY

* * *

39. Confucius said: "Shen! My teaching contains one principle that runs through it all." "Yes," replied Zeng Zi. When Confucius had left the room the disciples asked: "What did he mean?" Zeng Zi replied: "Our Master's teaching is simply this: loyalty and reciprocity."

40. Zi Gong asked: "Is there any one word that can serve as a principle for the conduct of life?" Confucius said: "Perhaps the word 'reciprocity': Do not do to others what you would not want others to do to you."

41. Confucius said: "Perfect indeed is the virtue which is according to the Mean. For long people have seldom had the capacity for it."

* * *

SOURCE: *Sources of Chinese Tradition*, compiled by Wm. Theodore de Bary et al. (New York: Columbia University Press, 1960), vol. 1, pp. 25–28.

43. Zhonggong asked about humanity. Confucius said: "Behave when away from home as though you were in the presence of an important guest. Deal with the common people as though you were officiating at an important sacrifice. Do not do to others what you would not want others to do to you. Then there will be no dissatisfaction either in the state or at home."

44. Confucius said: * * * "The humane man, desiring to be established himself, seeks to establish others; desiring himself to succeed, he helps others to succeed. To judge others by what one knows of oneself is the method of achieving humanity."

45. Fan Chi asked about humanity. Confucius said: "Love men."

46. Zi Zhang asked Confucius about humanity. Confucius said: "To be able to practice five virtues everywhere in the world constitutes humanity." Zi Zhang begged to know what these were. Confucius said: "Courtesy, magnanimity, good faith, diligence, and kindness. He who is courteous is not humiliated, he who is magnanimous wins the multitude, he who is of good faith is trusted by the people, he who is diligent attains his objective, and he who is kind can get service from the people."

47. Confucius said: "Without humanity a man cannot long endure adversity, nor can he long enjoy prosperity. The humane rest in humanity; the wise find it beneficial."

48. Confucius said: "Only the humane man can love men and can hate men."

49. Someone inquired: "What do you think of 'requiting injury with kindness'?" Confucius said: "How will you then requite kindness? Requite injury with justice, and kindness with kindness."

* * *

FILIAL PIETY

56. Zi You asked about filial piety. Confucius said: "Nowadays a filial son is just a man who keeps his parents in food. But even dogs or horses are given food. If there is no feeling of reverence, wherein lies the difference?"

* * *

58. Confucius said: "In serving his parents, a son may gently remonstrate with them. If he sees that they are not inclined to follow his suggestion, he should resume his reverential attitude but not abandon his purpose. If he is belabored, he will not complain."

59. The Duke of She observed to Confucius: "Among us there was an upright man called Gong who was so upright that when his father appropriated a sheep, he bore witness against him." Confucius said: "The upright men among us are not like that. A father will screen his son and a son his father—yet uprightness is to be found in that."

60. Zai Wo questioned the three years' mourning and thought one year was long enough: "If the gentlemen for three years abstain from the practice of ritual, ritual will decay; if for three years they make no music, music will go to ruin. In one year the old crops are exhausted and the new crops have come up, the friction-sticks have made the several seasonal fires—one year should be enough." Confucius said: "Would you then feel at ease in eating polished rice and wearing fineries?" "Quite at ease," was the reply. Confucius continued: "If you would really feel at ease, then do so. When a gentleman is in mourning, he does not relish good food if he eats it, does not enjoy music if he hears it, and does not feel at ease in a comfortable dwelling. Hence he abstains from these things. But now since you would feel at ease, then you can have them." When Zai Wo had gone out, Confucius said: "What lack of humanity in Yu Zai Wo! Only when a child is three years old does it leave its parents' arms. The three years' mourning is the universal observance in the world. And Yu—did he not enjoy the loving care of his parents for three years?"

Questions

1. What is reciprocity, and how does it differ from treating everyone equally? What is humaneness (humanity), and how does it differ from selflessness?

2. What is the point of the anecdote about the Duke of She? Why does Confucius want to base social order on putting family loyalty above obedience to the law?

3. In the last anecdote, Confucius clearly thinks Zai Wo's values are fundamentally wrong. Why, then, doesn't he argue with him?

Mencius, Humane Government (c. 371–289 BCE)

Mencius (c. 371–289 BCE) was recognized in his lifetime as a very important Confucian thinker, though it took over 1,000 years before his interpretation was accepted as *the* orthodox repository of the Confucian Way, marginalizing Xunzi's (c. 312–c. 230 BCE) more hard-nosed views. These passages portray Mencius at his usual occupation: visiting kings and nobles, and trying to persuade them that attending to the welfare of commoners was not only a moral duty, but the most practical way to succeed as a ruler amid intense, often violent competition.

————————

Mencius went to see King Hui of Liang. The king said: "You have not considered a thousand *li* too far to come, and must therefore have something of profit to offer my kingdom?" Mencius replied: "Why must you speak of profit? What I have to offer is humanity and righteousness, nothing more. If a king says, 'What will profit my kingdom?' the high officials will say, 'What will profit our families?' and the lower officials and commoners will say, 'What will profit ourselves?' Superiors and inferiors will try to seize profit one from another, and the state will be endangered. * * * Let your Majesty speak only of humanity and righteousness. Why must you speak of profit?"

Mencius said: "It was by virtue of humanity that the Three Dynasties won the empire, and by virtue of the want of humanity that they lost it. States rise and fall for the same reason. Devoid of humanity, the emperor would be unable to safeguard the four seas, a feudal lord would be unable to safeguard the altars of land and grain [i.e., his state], a minister would be unable to safeguard the ancestral temple [i.e., his clan-family], and the individual would be

SOURCE: *Sources of Chinese Tradition,* compiled by Wm. Theodore de Bary et al. (New York: Columbia University Press, 1960), vol. 1, pp. 92–94.

unable to safeguard his four limbs. Now people hate destruction and yet indulge in want of humanity—this is as if one hates to get drunk and yet forces oneself to drink wine."

Mencius said: "An overlord is he who employs force under a cloak of humanity. To be an overlord one has to be in possession of a large state. A king, on the other hand, is he who gives expression to his humanity through virtuous conduct. To be a true king, one does not have to have a large state. Tang [founder of the Shang dynasty] had only a territory of seventy *li* and King Wen [founder of the Zhou] only a hundred. When men are subdued by force, it is not that they submit from their hearts but only that their strength is unavailing. When men are won by virtue, then their hearts are gladdened and their submission is sincere, as the seventy disciples were won by the Master, Confucius.

* * *

Mencius said: "It was because Jie and Zhou lost the people that they lost the empire, and it was because they lost the hearts of the people that they lost the people. Here is the way to win the empire: win the people and you win the empire. Here is the way to win the people: win their hearts and you win the people. Here is the way to win their hearts: give them and share with them what they like, and do not do to them what they do not like. The people turn to a humane ruler as water flows downward or beasts take to wilderness."

* * *

Mencius said to King Xuan of Qi: * * * "Only the true scholar is capable of maintaining, without certain means of livelihood, a steadfast heart. As for the multitude, if they have no certain means of livelihood, they surely cannot maintain a steadfast heart. Without a steadfast heart, they are likely to abandon themselves to any and all manner of depravity. If you wait till they have lapsed into crime and then mete out punishment, it is like placing traps for the people. If a humane ruler is on the throne how can he permit such a thing as placing traps for the people? Therefore, when an intelligent ruler regulates the livelihood of the people, he makes sure that they will have enough to serve their parents on the one hand

and to support their wives and children on the other, so that in good years all may eat their fill and in bad years no one need die of starvation. Thus only will he urge them to walk the path of virtue, and the people will follow him effortlessly. But as the people's livelihood is ordered at present, they do not have enough to serve their parents on the one hand or to support their wives and children on the other. * * * Such being the case, they are only anxiously trying to stay alive. What leisure have they for cultivating decorum and righteousness?

"If your Majesty wishes to practice humane government, would it not be well to go back to the root of the matter?

"Let the five *mu* of land surrounding the farmer's cottage be planted with mulberry trees, and persons over fifty may all be clothed in silk. Let poultry, dogs, and swine be kept and bred in season, and those over seventy may all be provided with meat. Let the cultivation of the hundred-*mu* farm not be interfered with, and a family of eight mouths need not go hungry. Let attention be paid to teaching in schools and let the people be taught the principles of filial piety and brotherly respect, and white-headed old men will not be seen carrying loads on the road. When the aged wear silk and eat meat and the common people are free from hunger and cold, never has the lord of such a people failed to become king."

Questions

1. Why does Mencius claim that it is self-defeating for a ruler (or anyone else) to focus on his own self-interest?

2. How does Mencius expect people to respond to humane government? What does this assume about human nature?

3. What relationships does Mencius see between popular material welfare, personal virtue, and political loyalty? What economic policies does he favor?

Aristotle, Politica (384–322 BCE)

Aristotle (384–322 BCE), a pupil of Plato and tutor of Alexander the Great, is one of the foremost philosophers in the western tradition. His ideas greatly influenced Islamic philosophy, Latin Christian theology, and science throughout Southwest Asia, North Africa, and Europe. He wrote over 400 works on a great variety of topics, including philosophy, natural history, poetics, rhetoric, ethics and politics. The following selection is from his *Politica*, a treatise on the science of politics. For Aristotle man was by nature a social animal, one who had to live in a community in order to live the good life.

I.2 He who thus considers things in their first growth and origin, whether a state or anything else, will obtain the clearest view of them. In the first place there must be a union of those who cannot exist without each other; for example, of male and female, that the race may continue; and this is a union which is formed, not of deliberate purpose, but because, in common with other animals and with plants, mankind have a natural desire to leave behind them an image of themselves. And there must be a union of natural ruler and subject, that both may be preserved. For he who can foresee with his mind is by nature intended to be lord and master, and he who can work with his body is a subject, and by nature a slave; hence master and slave have the same interest. Nature, however, has distinguished between the female and the slave. For she is not niggardly, like the smith who fashions the Delphian knife for many uses; she makes each thing for a single use, and every instrument is best made when intended for one and not for many uses. But among barbarians no distinction is made between women and slaves, because there is no natural ruler among them: they are a community of slaves, male and female. Wherefore the poets say,—

"It is meet that Hellenes should rule over barbarians;"

SOURCE: *The Politics of Aristotle*, translated by B. Jowett (Oxford: Clarendon Press, 1885), vol. 1, pp. 2–3, 6–10.

as if they thought that the barbarian and the slave were by nature one.

Out of these two relationships between man and woman, master and slave, the family first arises, and Hesiod is right when he says,—

"First house and wife and an ox for the plough,"

for the ox is the poor man's slave. The family is the association established by nature for the supply of men's everyday wants, and the members of it are called by Charondas "companions of the cupboard" and by Epimenides the Cretan, "companions of the manger." But when several families are united, and the association aims at something more than the supply of daily needs, then comes into existence the village. And the most natural form of the village appears to be that of a colony from the family, composed of the children and grandchildren, who are said to be "suckled with the same milk." And this is the reason why Hellenic states were originally governed by kings; because the Hellenes were under royal rule before they came together, as the barbarians still are. Every family is ruled by the eldest, and therefore in the colonies of the family the kingly form of government prevailed because they were of the same blood. As Homer says

"Each one gives law to his children and to his wives"

For they lived dispersedly, as was the manner in ancient times. Wherefore men say that the Gods have a king, because they themselves either are or were in ancient times under the rule of a king. For they imagine, not only the forms of the Gods, but their ways of life to be like their own.

* * *

I.4 Property is a part of the household, and therefore the art of acquiring property is a part of the art of managing the household; for no man can live well, or indeed live at all, unless he be provided with necessaries. And as in the arts which have a definite sphere the workers must have their own proper instruments for the accomplishment of their work, so it is in the management of a household. Now, instruments are of various sorts; some are living, others lifeless; in the rudder, the pilot of a ship has a lifeless, in the look-out man, a living instrument; for in the arts the servant is a kind of instrument. Thus, too, a possession is an instrument for maintaining life. And so, in the arrangement of the family, a slave is a living possession, and property a number of such instruments; and the servant is himself an instrument, which takes precedence of all other instruments. For if every instrument could accomplish its own work, obeying or anticipating the will of others, like the statues of Daedalus, or the tripods of Hephaestus, which, says the poet,

"of their own accord entered the assembly of the Gods;"

if, in like manner, the shuttle would weave and the plectrum touch the lyre without a hand to guide them, chief workmen would not want servants, nor masters slaves. * * *

I.5 But is there any one thus intended by nature to be a slave, and for whom such a condition is expedient and right, or rather is not all slavery a violation of nature?

There is no difficulty in answering this question, on grounds both of reason and of fact. For that some should rule, and others be ruled is a thing, not only necessary, but expedient; from the hour of their birth, some are marked out for subjection, others for rule.

* * * And it is clear that the rule of the soul over the body, and of the mind and the rational element over the passionate is natural and expedient; whereas the equality of the two or the rule of the inferior is always hurtful. The same holds good of animals as well as of men; for tame animals have a better nature than wild, and all tame animals are better off when they are ruled by man; for then they are preserved. Again, the male is by nature superior, and the female inferior; and the one rules, and the other is ruled; this principle, of necessity, extends to all mankind. Where then there is such a difference as that between soul and body, or between men and animals (as in the case of those whose business is to use their body, and who can do nothing better), the lower sort are by nature slaves, and it is better for them as for all inferiors that they should be under the rule of a master. For he who can be, and therefore is another's, and he who participates in reason enough to apprehend,

but not to have, reason, is a slave by nature. Whereas the lower animals cannot even apprehend reason; they obey their instincts. And indeed the use made of slaves and of tame animals is not very different; for both with their bodies minister to the needs of life. Nature would like to distinguish between the bodies of freemen and slaves, making the one strong for servile labour, the other upright, and although useless for such services, useful for political life in the arts both of war and peace. But this does not hold universally: for some slaves have the souls and others have the bodies of freemen. And doubtless if men differed from one another in the mere forms of their bodies as much as the statues of the Gods do from men, all would acknowledge that the inferior class should be slaves of the superior. And if there is a difference in the body, how much more in the soul? [B]ut the beauty of the body is seen, whereas the beauty of the soul is not seen. It is clear, then, that some men are by nature free, and others slaves, and that for these latter slavery is both expedient and right.

I.6 But that those who take the opposite view have in a certain way right on their side, may be easily seen. For the words slavery and slave are used in two senses. There is a slave or slavery by law as well as by nature. The law of which I speak is a sort of convention, according to which whatever is taken in war is supposed to belong to the victors. But this right many jurists impeach, as they would an orator who brought forward an unconstitutional measure: they detest the notion that, because one man has the power of doing violence and is superior in brute strength, another shall be his slave and subject. Even among philosophers there is a difference of opinion. The origin of the dispute, and the reason why the arguments cross, is as follows: Virtue, when furnished with means, may be deemed to have the greatest power of doing violence: and as superior power is only found where there is superior excellence of some kind, power is thought to imply virtue. But does it likewise imply justice?—that is the question. And, in order to make a distinction between them, some assert that justice is benevolence: to which others reply that justice is nothing more than the rule of a superior. If the two views are regarded as antagonistic and exclusive [i.e., if the notion that justice is benevolence excludes the idea of a just rule of a superior], the alternative [viz. that no one should rule over others] has no force or plausibility, because it implies that not even the superior in virtue ought to rule, or be master. Some, clinging, as they think, to a principle of justice (for law and custom are a sort of justice), assume that slavery in war is justified by law, but they are not consistent. For what if the cause of the war be unjust? No one would ever say that he is a slave who is unworthy to be a slave. Were this the case, men of the highest rank would be slaves and the children of slaves if they or their parents chance to have been taken captive and sold. Wherefore Hellenes do not like to call themselves slaves, but confine the term to barbarians. Yet, in using this language, they really mean the natural slave of whom we spoke at first; for it must be admitted that some are slaves everywhere, others nowhere.

Questions

1. For Aristotle, what is the basis of political authority?

2. How does Aristotle understand the development of political society?

3. How does Aristotle justify slavery?

Aristotle, On the Constitution of Carthage (384–322 BCE)

Aristotle (384–322 BCE), like Herodotus (see Herodotus, Persians Debate Governance, in Chapter 4), displayed a deep interest in understanding his own society and engagement with Greece's neighbors, trading partners, and political rivals. In a quest for more harmonious social and political organization, Aristotle collected evidence about institutional structures from Greek city-states and beyond. One of the places that interested Aristotle was Carthage. Originally a Phoenician colony, it became a major trading port and leading power in the Mediterranean. Aristotle found much to admire in the civic administration of Carthage, as well cautionary lessons about policies to be avoided.

The Carthaginian constitution resembles the Spartan and Cretan: all three are like one another, but unlike any others. The Carthaginian, though containing an element of democracy, has lasted well, and has never degenerated into a tyranny. At Carthage there are clubs which have common tables: these answer to the Spartan pheiditia. There is also a magistracy of 104, which answers to the Ephoralty, but unlike the Ephors, the Carthaginian magistrates are elected for merit. Like the Spartans they have Kings and a Council of Elders, but, unlike the Spartan, their Kings are elected for merit, and are not always of the same family.

The deviations of Carthage from the perfect state are the same as in most other states. The deviations from aristocracy and polity incline both to democracy and to oligarchy. For instance, the people discuss and determine any matter which has been brought before them by the Kings and Elders (this is not the case at Sparta and Crete); and when the Kings and Elders are not unanimous, the people may decide whether the matter shall be brought forward or not. These are democratical features. But the election of the magistrates by co-optation and their great power after they have ceased to hold office are oligarchical features. The inclination to oligarchy is further shown in the regard which is paid in all elections, to wealth. (On this point however the majority of mankind would agree with the Carthaginians.) Once more, the appointment to offices without salary, the election by vote and not by lot, and the practice of having all suits tried by certain magistrates, and not some by one and some by another, are characteristic of aristocracy. The constitution of Carthage therefore is neither a pure aristocracy nor an oligarchy, but a third form which includes both, and has regard both to merit and wealth. (1) The over-estimation of wealth leads to the sale of offices, which is a great evil. True, the rulers must have the leisure which wealth alone can supply, but office should be the reward of merit, and therefore the legislator should find some other way of making a

SOURCE: *The Politics of Aristotle*, translated by B. Jowett (Oxford: Clarendon Press, 1885), vol. 1, pp. xlvi–xlvii.

provision for the ruling class. The sale of offices is a gross abuse, and is a bad example to the people, who always imitate their rulers. (2) It is not a good principle that one man should hold several offices. In a large state they should be distributed as much as possible. (3) The Carthaginians remedy the evils of their government by sending out colonies. The accident of their wealth and position enables them to avail themselves of this outlet; but the safety of the state should not depend upon accidents.

Questions

1. What elements of Carthaginian government does Aristotle admire? Why?

2. In Aristotle's view, what is significant about the connection between wealth and leadership roles?

3. What could explain Aristotle's interest in comparative politics?

Aśoka, Three Edicts (ruled 269–231 BCE)

Aśoka (ruled 269–231 BCE) was the third king of the Mauryan dynasty; he ruled the empire at its height and his territories extended across most of South Asia. Aśoka ruled an ethnically, linguistically, and religiously diverse population. Although he was a devoted follower of the Buddha, his rule was effective in part because of the tolerance he showed to other religions. He had inscriptions carved onto pillars, boulders, and cave walls, written in various local languages. More than thirty-three remain, distributed throughout modern day India, Pakistan, and Nepal. They are the first concrete evidence of Buddhism. Many of the inscriptions address recurrent themes of Aśoka's conversion to Buddhism, his efforts to spread the religion, his religious and moral ideas, and his ideas of social and animal welfare.

Excerpts from three different edicts show Aśoka's concerns with just governance, social welfare, and the connection between material and moral well-being. The selection from the Kalinga edict adds to the passage reprinted in *Worlds Together Worlds Apart*, p. 219; in addition to acknowledging the diversity of people under his rule, Aśoka makes clear his standards of fair administration. He also explicitly asks for obedience in return for tolerance and justice.

———————

From the Kalinga Edict

By order of the Beloved of the Gods. Addressed to the officers in charge of Tosali. * * * Let us win the affection of all men. All men are my children, and as I wish all welfare and happiness in this world and the next for my own children, so do I wish it for all men. But you do not realize what this entails—here and there an officer may understand in part, but not entirely.

Often a man is imprisoned and tortured unjustly, and then he is liberated for no [apparent] reason. Many other people suffer also [as a result of this injustice]. Therefore it is desirable that you should practice impartiality, but it cannot be attained if you are inclined to habits of jealousy, irritability, harshness, hastiness, obstinacy, laziness, or lassitude. I desire you not to have these habits. The basis of all this is the constant avoidance of irritability and hastiness in your business. * * *

This inscription has been engraved in order that the officials of the city should always see to it that no one is ever imprisoned or tortured without good cause. To ensure this I shall send out every five years on a tour of inspection officers who are not fierce or harsh. * * * The prince at Ujjain shall do the same not more than every three years, and likewise at Taxila.

From the Fourth Pillar Edict

My governors are placed in charge of hundreds of thousands of people. Under my authority they have power to judge and to punish, that they calmly and fearlessly carry out their duties, and that they may bring welfare and happiness to the people of the provinces and

———————

Source: *Sources of Indian Tradition*, edited by Ainslee T. Embree (New York: Columbia University Press, 1988), vol. 1, p. 145–46, 148–49.

be of help to them. They will know what brings joy and what brings sorrow, and, conformably to righteousness, they will instruct the people of the provinces that they may be happy in this world and the next. * * * And as when one entrusts a child to a skilled nurse one is confident that * * * she will care for it well, so have I appointed my governors for the welfare and happiness of the people. That they may fearlessly carry out their duties I have given them power to judge and to inflict punishment on their own initiative. I wish that there should be uniformity of justice and punishment.

FROM THE SEVENTH PILLAR EDICT

In the past, kings sought to make the people progress in righteousness, but they did not progress. * * * And I asked myself how I might uplift them through progress in righteousness. * * * Thus I decided to have them instructed in righteousness, and to issue ordinances of righteousness, so that by hearing them the people might conform, advance in the progress of righteousness, and themselves make great progress. * * * For that purpose many officials are employed among the people to instruct them in righteousness and to explain it to them. * * *

Moreover I have had banyan trees planted on the roads to give shade to man and beast; I have planted mango groves, and I have had ponds dug and shelters erected along the roads at every eight kos. Everywhere I have had wells dug for the benefit of man and beast. But his benefit is but small, for in many ways the kings of olden time have worked for the welfare of the world; but what I have done has been done that men may conform to righteousness.

All the good deeds that I have done have been accepted and followed by the people. And so obedience to mother and father, obedience to teachers, respect for the aged, kindliness to brāhmans and ascetics, to the poor and weak, and to slaves and servants, have increased and will continue to increase. * * * And this progress of righteousness among men has taken place in two manners, by enforcing conformity to righteousness, and by exhortation. I have enforced the law against killing certain animals and many others, but the greatest progress of righteousness among men comes from exhortation in favor of noninjury to life and abstention from killing living beings.

I have done this that it may endure * * * as long as the moon and sun and that my sons and my great-grandsons may support it; for by supporting it they will gain both this world and the next.

Questions

1. Both the Kalinga and the Fourth Pillar edicts emphasize ideas of uniform rather than arbitrary punishments. Why would this idea be important to Aśoka?

2. The exercise of state power in the Fourth Pillar and Seventh Pillar edicts is described in familial terms, using metaphors of child care and parental obedience. Do you think such descriptions of obedience have particular relevance in a multicultural empire?

3. Does Aśoka appeal to moral or religious values in his discussions of governance? Why or why not?

Chapter 6

SHRINKING THE AFRO-EURASIAN WORLD, 350 BCE–300 CE

The Buddha, Sermons and Teachings (fourth century BCE to first century BCE)

Siddhartha Gautama (c. 563–c. 483 BCE), sometimes called Shakyamnuni Buddha or simply "the Buddha," was the son of the king of a small North Indian state. Accordingly, he grew up in luxury, but at age twenty-nine a series of encounters with suffering people changed his life. Escaping his father's palace (leaving his wife and newborn son), Siddhartha spent six years mastering the teachings of holy ascetics, who insisted that only those who made themselves suffer physically could attain spiritual truth. Ultimately, he rejected this idea. After forty-nine days of meditation, he came to understand the truth (*dharma*). While he initially doubted that humans could understand this truth, he decided that some could. He then spent the rest of his life traveling and preaching, attracting many followers.

The material world, according to the Buddha, is an illusion, and misery results from attachment to the things of this world: thus not only hatred and greed, but even such seemingly positive emotions as love for one's family, are traps that bind a person to this hopeless world. Yet, as this sermon emphasizes, going to the opposite extreme by mortifying the flesh is still relying on the physical world for enlightenment rather than transcending that world.

The records of the Buddha's life and teachings were first transmitted orally, and written down much later, some time before the end of the first century BCE. Still most scholars' believe that accounts of his teachings, such as this sermon, are reasonably accurate. There is, of course, much greater disagreement over the miraculous events included in his life story.

The five bhikshus saw their old teacher approach and agreed among themselves not to salute him, nor to address him as a master, but by his name only. "For," so they said, "he has broken his vow and has abandoned holiness. He is no bhikshu but Gautama, and Gautama has become a man who lives in abundance and indulges in the pleasures of worldliness."

But when the Blessed One approached in a dignified manner, they involuntarily rose from their seats and greeted him in spite of their resolution. Still they called him by his name and addressed him as "friend."

When they had thus received the Blessed One, he said: "Do not call the Tathâgata by his name nor address him 'friend,' for he is Buddha, the Holy One. Buddha looks equally with a kind heart on all living beings and they therefore call him 'Father.' To disrespect a father is wrong; to despise him, is sin.

"The Tathâgata," Buddha continued, "does not seek salvation in austerities, but for that reason you must not think that he indulges in worldly pleasures, nor does he live in abundance. The Tathâgata has found the middle path.

"Neither abstinence from fish or flesh, nor going naked, nor shaving the head, nor wearing matted hair, nor dressing in a rough garment, nor covering oneself with dirt, nor sacrificing to Agni, will cleanse a man who is not free from delusions.

"Reading the Vêdas, making offerings to priests, or sacrifices to the gods, self-mortification by heat or cold, and many such penances performed for the sake of immortality, these do not cleanse the man who is not free from delusions.

"Anger, drunkenness, obstinacy, bigotry, deception, envy, self-praise, disparaging others, superciliousness, and evil intentions constitute uncleanness; not verily the eating of flesh.

SOURCE: Paul Carus, *The Gospel of Buddha: According to Old Records,* 5th ed. (Chicago: Open Court Publishing Company, 1897), pp. 38–42.

"Let me teach you, O bhikshus, the middle path, which keeps aloof from both extremes. By suffering, the emaciated devotee produces confusion and sickly thoughts in his mind. Mortification is not conducive even to worldly knowledge; how much less to a triumph over the senses!

"He who fills his lamp with water will not dispel the darkness, and he who tries to light a fire with rotten wood will fail.

"Mortifications are painful, vain, and profitless. And how can any one be free from self by leading a wretched life if he does not succeed in quenching the fires of lust.

"All mortification is vain so long as self remains, so long as self continues to lust after either worldly or heavenly pleasures. But he in whom self has become extinct is free from lust; he will desire neither worldly nor heavenly pleasures, and the satisfaction of his natural wants will not defile him. Let him eat and drink according to the needs of the body.

* * *

"On the other hand, sensuality of all kind is enervating. The sensual man is a slave of his passions, and pleasure-seeking is degrading and vulgar.

"But to satisfy the necessities of life is not evil. To keep the body in good health is a duty, for otherwise we shall not be able to trim the lamp of wisdom, and keep our mind strong and clear.

"This is the middle path, O bhikshus, that keeps aloof from both extremes."

And the Blessed One spoke kindly to his disciples, pitying them for their errors, and pointing out the uselessness of their endeavors, and the ice of ill-will that chilled their hearts melted away under the gentle warmth of the Master's persuasion.

* * *

"He who recognises the existence of suffering, its cause, its remedy, and its cessation has fathomed the four noble truths. He will walk in the right path.

"Right views will be the torch to light his way. Right aims will be his guide. Right words will be his dwelling-place on the road. His gait will be straight, for it is right behavior. His refreshments will be the right way of earning his livelihood. Right efforts will be his steps: right thoughts his breath; and peace will follow in his footprints."

And the Blessed One explained the instability of the ego.

"Whatsoever is originated will be dissolved again. All worry about the self is vain; the ego is like a mirage, and all the tribulations that touch it will pass away. They will vanish like a nightmare when the sleeper awakes.

"He who has awakened is freed from fear; he has become Buddha; he knows the vanity of all his cares, his ambitions, and also of his pains.

"It easily happens that a man, when taking a bath, steps upon a wet rope and imagines that it is a snake. Horror will overcome him, and he will shake from fear, anticipating in his mind all the agonies caused by the serpent's venomous bite. What a relief does this man experience when he sees that the rope is no snake. The cause of his fright lies in his error, his ignorance, his illusion. If the true nature of the rope is recognised, his tranquility of mind will come back to him; he will feel relieved; he will be joyful and happy.

"This is the state of mind of one who has recognised that there is no self, that the cause of all his troubles, cares, and vanities is a mirage, a shadow, a dream.

"Happy is he who has overcome all selfishness; happy is he who has attained peace; happy is he who has found the truth.

* * *

"Have confidence in the truth, although you may not be able to comprehend it, although you may suppose its sweetness to be bitter, although you may shrink from it at first. Trust in the truth.

"The truth is best as it is. No one can alter it; neither can any one improve it. Have faith in the truth and live it.

* * *

"Self is a fever; self is a transient vision, a dream; but truth is wholesome, truth is sublime, truth is everlasting. There is no immortality except in truth. For truth alone abideth forever."

Questions

1. Why do the bhikshus (monks) have doubts about greeting Gautama (Gotama)? How does he respond to their doubts about him?

2. What is the middle path? Why is it better than extreme self-denial?

3. What does the story about the rope mean? How should one live in the world after recognizing that the self is illusory?

Ketubot, Jewish Premarital Agreements (written c. 200 BCE)

Jewish oral traditions began to be written around 200 BCE, when Jews became concerned that their community would forget the history, customs, and legal practice from before the destruction of the Second Temple (536 BCE–70 CE). The Mishna was the first major written compilation. Divided into six sections, it deals with prayers, blessings, agricultural practice and tithing; festivals and the Sabbath; women—which includes marriage, divorce, and inheritance; civil and criminal law; rituals and dietary laws; and purity. Note that Nasheem, the third order, is named for women, though it addresses a whole range of social and cultural issues such as household structure, property ownership, and the transfer of wealth. The Ketubot falls within the Nasheem. It is comprised of thirteen chapters that describe the roles and responsibilities of married men and women. It is the basis of the Ketubah, or prenuptial agreement, which outlines a groom's responsibilities to provide for his wife, in particular her financial survival in case of divorce or his death. Note that these rules offer financial, social, and moral guidelines. Like other ancient sets of rules (see Ptah-hotep, *Precepts*, in Chapter 2; *The Code of Hammurapi*, in Chapter 3) and commentaries (see Dio Cassius, Livia, and the book of Esther in Casebook: Women and Political Power in the Ancient World, following Chapter 3), as well as Yuan Cai's reflections (see Yuan Cai, The Problems of Women, in Chapter 10), the Ketubot clearly differentiates between expectations for men and women.

3:4 A. The one who seduces a girl pays on three counts, and the one who rapes a girl pays on four:

B. the one who seduces a girl pays for (1) the shame, (2) the damage, and (3) a fine,

C. and the one who rapes a girl adds to these,

D. for he in addition pays for (4) the pain [which he has inflicted].

* * *

4:4 A. The father retains control of his daughter [younger than twelve and a half] as to effecting any of the tokens of betrothal: money, document, or sexual intercourse.

B. And he retains control of what she finds, of the fruit of her labor, and of abrogating her vows.

C. And he receives her writ of divorce [from a betrothal].

D. But he does not dispose of the return [on property received by the girl from her mother] during her lifetime.

E. [When] she is married, the husband exceeds the father, for he disposes of the return [on property received by the girl from her mother] during her lifetime.

F. But he is liable to maintain her, and to ransom her, and to bury her.

G. R. Judah says, "Even the poorest man in Israel should not hire fewer than two flutes and one professional wailing woman."

* * *

4:12 VI A. [If he did not write for her,] "You will dwell in my house and derive support from my property so long as you are a widow in my house,"

B. [his estate] nonetheless is liable [to support his widow].

* * *

5:5 A. These are the kinds of labor which a woman performs for her husband:

SOURCE: *The Mishnah*, translated by Jacob Neusner (New Haven: Yale University Press, 1988), pp. 383–403.

B. she (1) grinds flour, (2) bakes bread, (3) does laundry, (4) prepares meals, (5) feeds her child, (6) makes the bed, (7) works in wool.

C. [If] she brought with her a single slave girl, she does not (1) grind, (2) bake bread, or (3) do laundry.

D. [If she brought] two, she does not (4) prepare meals and does (5) not feed her child.

E. [If she brought] three, she does not (6) make the bed for him and does not (7) work in wool.

F. If she brought four, she sits on a throne.

G. R. Eliezer says, "Even if she brought him a hundred slave girls, he forces her to work in wool,

H. "for idleness leads to unchastity."

I. Rabban Simeon b. Gamaliel says, "Also: He who prohibits his wife by a vow from performing any labor puts her away and pays off her marriage contract.

J. "For idleness leads to boredom."

* * *

11:1 D. [A widow's] heirs who inherit her marriage contract are liable to bury her.

* * *

12:3 A. A widow who said, "I don't want to move from my husband's house"—

B. the heirs cannot say to her, "Go to your father's house and we'll take care of you [there]."

C. But they provide for her in her husband's house,

D. giving her a dwelling in accord with her station in life.

E. [If] she said, "I don't want to move from my father's house,"

F. the heirs can say to her, "If you are with us, you will have support. But you are not with us, you will not have support."

G. If she claimed that it is because she is a girl and they are boys, they do provide for her while she is in her father's house.

Questions

1. Why might the Ketubot need to explicitly discuss financial support for divorced or widowed women? What support could widowed women expect?

2. Why would the Ketubot differentiate between rape and seduction? Who is held responsible for these breaches of moral conduct?

3. What was the connection between women's labor and household maintenance? What about between women's labor and morality?

Pliny the Elder, The Seres (c. 77 CE)

Gaius Plinius Secundus (23 CE–79 CE), called Pliny the Elder since his nephew was a well-known lawyer and writer, was a military commander of the Roman Empire, equally well-remembered for his scholarship as for his military accomplishments and political connections. His major surviving work is *The Natural History*, an encyclopedia published c. 77 CE. It still serves as a model for the genre, achieving breadth and accuracy (in its day); validating the need for references; and providing an index. *The Natural History* investigates the diversity of human societies, plants, animals, and the physical world, making claims to encompass the entire field of ancient knowledge (Herodotus and Thucydides also made universalist claims to knowledge). Pliny's descriptions served as the basis for many subsequent European descriptions of Asia well into the modern era.

"The Seres" chapter of *The Natural History* refers to various groups of people of central, east, and south Asia, some of whom were, in fact, drawn from Greek mythology. Other groups were among those Pliny refers to elsewhere as the "fabulous Indian races." Pliny famously describes silk cultivation and production—and the reasons behind Rome's demand for silk.

After we have passed the Caspian Sea and the Scythian Ocean, our course takes an easterly direction, such being the turn here taken by the line of the coast. The first portion of these shores, after we pass the Scythian Promontory, is totally uninhabitable, owing to the snow, and the regions adjoining are uncultivated, in consequence of the savage state of the nations which dwell there. Here are the abodes of the Scythian Anthropophagi [described earlier by Herodotus], who feed on human flesh. Hence it is that all around them consists of vast deserts, inhabited by multitudes of wild beasts, which are continually lying in wait, ready to fall upon human beings just as savage as themselves. After leaving these, we again come to a nation of the Scythians, and then again to desert tracts tenanted by wild beasts, until we reach a chain of mountains which runs up to the sea, and bears the name of Tabis. It is not, however, before we have traversed very nearly one half of the coast that looks towards the north-east, that we find it occupied by inhabitants.

The first people that are known of here are the Seres, so famous for the wool that is found in their forests. After steeping it in water, they comb off a white down that adheres to the leaves; and then to the females of our part of the world they give the twofold task of unravelling their textures, and of weaving the threads afresh. So manifold is the labour, and so distant are the regions which are thus ransacked to supply a dress through which our ladies may in public display their charms. The Seres are of inoffensive manners, but, bearing a strong resemblance therein to all savage nations, they shun all intercourse with the rest of mankind, and await the approach of those who wish to traffic with them. The first river that is known in their territory is the Psitharas, next to that the Cambari, and the third the Laros; after which we come to the Promontory of Chryse, the Gulf of Cynaba, the river Atianos, and the nation of the Attacori on the gulf of that name, a people protected by their sunny hills from all noxious blasts, and living in a climate of the same temperature as that of the Hyperhorei. Amometus has written a work entirely devoted to the history of these people, just as Hecatæus has done in his treatise on the Hyperborei. After the Attacori, we find the nations of the Phruri and the Tochari, and, in the interior, the Casiri, a people of India, who look

SOURCE: "The Seres," in *The Natural History of Pliny*, translated by John Bostock and H. T. Riley (London: George Bell and Sons, 1855), vol. 2, pp. 35–38.

toward the Scythians, and feed on human flesh. Here are also numerous wandering Nomad tribes of India. There are some authors who state that in a north-easterly direction these nations touch upon the Cicones and the Brysari.

Questions

1. What was the role of silk in connecting Rome to Asia? What does Pliny think about Roman demand for silk?

2. Why might Pliny have described Anthropophagi as cannibals? Do you think this description is accurate or exaggerated? Why?

3. Pliny describes Seres, peoples who lived in the area that is now north-western China, as being disconnected from "the rest of mankind." If they had been entirely isolated, however, they could not have traded their silk. Why might Pliny have described them as so cut off from mankind?

Arthashastra, Duties of a King (c. fourth century BCE)

The Arthashastra (roughly translated as "the science of politics") has often been attributed to Chānaka (c. 350–283 BCE), a prime minister during the Mauryan Empire. At its greatest extent the empire covered most of contemporary India, Pakistan, and Bangladesh, plus bits of Afghanistan. Other scholars think it was probably not compiled until some time after 100 CE, but concede that it is based on earlier materials of some sort. It appears to have been heavily studied prior to the twelfth century CE, but it later became lost, and was not rediscovered until the early twentieth century. Today it has a new life, not only as an important guide to South Asian statecraft in earlier times, but also as an advice book for businessmen. (The same thing has happened to classic texts from other traditions, such as Sunzi's *Art of War.*)

The text is very broad-ranging, covering issues ranging from war making to law enforcement, the conservation of forests, economic policy, the use of spies, and the education of future leaders. Scholars often note the treatise's emphasis on unsentimental realism, both in dealing with other states and with the ruler's own people, including its support for the use of violence in many contexts. But as the excerpt below shows, it also insists that the ruler discipline himself strictly, and pay attention to the welfare of his subjects, providing support of various kinds when his people need it.

Only if a king is himself energetically active, do his officers follow him energetically. If he is sluggish, they too remain sluggish. And, besides, they eat up his works. He is thereby easily overpowered by his enemies. Therefore, he should ever dedicate himself energetically to activity.

He should divide the day as well as the night into eight parts. * * * During the first one-eighth part of the day, he should listen to reports pertaining to the organization of law and order and to income and expenditure. During the second, he should attend to the affairs of the urban and the rural population. During the third, he should take his bath and meal and devote himself to study. During the fourth, he should receive gold and the departmental heads. During the fifth, he should hold consultations with the council of ministers through correspondence and also keep himself informed of the secret reports brought by spies. During the sixth, he should devote himself freely to amusement or listen to the counsel of the ministers. During the seventh, he should inspect the military formations of elephants, cavalry, chariots, and infantry. During the eighth, he, together with the commander-in-chief of the army, should make plans for campaigns of conquest. When the day has come to an end he should offer the evening prayers.

During the first one-eighth part of the night, he should meet the officers of the secret service. During the second, he should take his bath and meals and also devote himself to study. During the third, at the sounding of the trumpets, he should enter the bed chamber and should sleep through the fourth and fifth. Waking up at the sound-

---

SOURCE: *Source of Indian Tradition*, edited by Ainslie T. Embree (New York: Columbia University Press, 1988), vol. 1, pp. 241–43, 248–49.

ing of the trumpets, he should, during the sixth part, ponder over the teachings of the sciences and his urgent duties for the day. During the seventh, he should hold consultations and send out the officers of the secret service for their operations. During the eighth, accompanied by sacrificial priests, preceptors, and the chaplain, he should receive benedictions; he should also have interviews with the physician, the kitchen-superintendent, and the astrologer. Thereafter, he should circumambulate by the right a cow with a calf and an ox and then proceed to the reception hall. Or he should divide the day and the night into parts in accordance with his own capacities and thereby attend to his duties.

When he has gone to the reception hall, he should not allow such persons, as have come for business, to remain sticking to the doors of the hall [i.e., waiting in vain]. For, a king, with whom it is difficult for the people to have an audience, is made to confuse between right action and wrong action by his close entourage. Thereby he suffers from the disaffection of his own subjects or falls prey to the enemy. Therefore he should attend to the affairs relating to gods, hermitages, heretics, learned brāhmans, cattle, and holy places as also those of minors, the aged, the sick, those in difficulty, the helpless, and women—in the order of their enumeration or in accordance with the importance or the urgency of the affairs.

A king should attend to all urgent business, he should not put it off. For what has been thus put off becomes either difficult or altogether impossible to accomplish.

* * *

In the happiness of the subjects lies the happiness of the king; in their welfare, his own welfare. The welfare of the king does not lie in the fulfillment of what is dear to him; whatever is dear to the subjects constitutes his welfare.

* * *

[In foreign affairs observe] the sixfold policy. The teacher says: "Peace, war, marking time, attack, seeking refuge, and duplicity. * * *" "There are only two forms of policy," says Vātavyādhi, "for the sixfold policy is actually accomplished through peace and war." Kautilya says: "The forms of policy are, verily, six in number, for conditions are different in different cases."

Of these six forms: binding through pledges means peace; offensive operation means war; apparent indifference means marking time; strengthening one's position means attack; giving oneself to another [as a subordinate ally or vassal] means seeking refuge; keeping oneself engaged simultaneously in peace and war with the same state means duplicity. These are the six forms of policy.

When one king [the would-be conqueror] is weaker than the other [i.e., his immediate neighbor, the enemy], he should make peace with him. When he is stronger than the other, he should make war with him. When he thinks: "The other is not capable of putting me down nor am I capable of putting him down," he should mark time. When he possesses an excess of the necessary means, he should attack. When he is devoid of strength, he should seek refuge with another. When his end can be achieved only through the help of an ally, he should practice duplicity.

Questions

1. What does this recommended schedule for a king suggest about his priorities? What sorts of things does a king need to know?

2. What are the possible failures of leadership that the author seems most concerned to prevent?

3. What are the things that the king is told to consider when making policy toward neighboring states? What does this suggest about the political environment of the time?

The Periplus of the Erythraean Sea
(first century CE)

A periplus consisted of sailing directions that listed ports and coastal landmarks, with the approximate distance between them, to help navigate along a shore line. These Greek documents were familiar to merchants and travelers in the ancient Mediterranean world; some passages in the histories of Herodotus and Thucydides appear to draw from such descriptions. *The Periplus of the Erythraean* [Red] *Sea* describes travel from the Egyptian port of Berenice to locations in the Red Sea, along the east coast of Africa (Azania in the text), into the Persian Gulf and across to India. The document was likely written by a resident of Alexandria sometime in the first century CE. Given the extent of the details provided, the author probably had firsthand knowledge of many of the ports. The text is an important source for understanding what the ancient Mediterranean societies knew about far-distant trading opportunities. While some of the locations described in the text can be correlated to present-day towns or archaeological sites (for example, Adulis, the port city of the Axum kingdom in present-day Eretria, or the Ganges River in India), other place names have several possible locations.

The text gives topographical descriptions, tides, detailed lists of trade goods imported and exported at specific ports, descriptions of local political relationships, and occasional commentary on the local inhabitants.

---

2. On the right-hand coast next below Berenice is the country of the Berbers. Along the shore are the Fish-Eaters, living in scattered caves in the narrow valleys. Further inland are the Berbers, and beyond them the Wild-flesh-Eaters and Calf-Eaters, each tribe governed by its chief; and behind them, further inland, in the country toward the west, there lies a city called Meroe.

3. Below the Calf-Eaters there is a little market-town on the shore after sailing about four thousand stadia from Berenice, called Ptolemais of the Hunts, from which the hunters started for the interior under the dynasty of the Ptolemies. This market-town has the true land-tortoise in small quantity; it is white and smaller in the shells. And here also is found a little ivory, like that of Adulis. But the place has no harbor and is reached only by small boats.

4. Below * * * is Adulis, a port established by law, lying at the inner end of a bay that runs in toward the south. Before the harbor

SOURCE: *The Periplus of the Erythraean Sea*, translated by Wilfred H. Schoff (London: Longmans, Green, and Co., 1912), pp. 22–23, 27–30, 34, 40–43.

lies the so-called Mountain Island, about two hundred stadia seaward from the very head of the bay, with the shores of the mainland close to it on both sides. Ships bound for this port now anchor here because of attacks from the land. They used formerly to anchor at the very head of the bay, by an island called Diodorus, close to the shore, which could be reached on foot from the land; by which means the barbarous natives attacked the island. Opposite Mountain Island, on the mainland twenty stadia from shore, lies Adulis, a fair-sized village, from which there is a three-days' journey to Coloe, an inland town and the first market for ivory. From that place to the city of the people called Auxumites there is a five days' journey more; to that place all the ivory is brought from the country beyond the Nile through the district called Cyeneum, and thence to Adulis. Practically the whole number of elephants and rhinoceros that are killed live in the places inland, although at rare intervals they are hunted on the seacoast even near Adulis. Before the harbor of that market-town, out at sea on the right hand, there lie a great many little sandy islands called Alalæi, yielding tortoise-shell, which is brought to market there by the Fish-Eaters.

5. And about eight hundred stadia beyond there is another very deep bay, with a great mound of sand piled up at the right of the entrance; at the bottom of which the opsian stone is found, and this is the only place where it is produced. These places, from the Calf-Eaters to the other Berber country, are governed by Zoscales; who is miserly in his ways and always striving for more, but otherwise upright, and acquainted with Greek literature.

6. There are imported into these places, undressed cloth made in Egypt for the Berbers; robes from Arsinoe; cloaks of poor quality dyed in colors; doubles-fringed linen mantles; many articles of flint glass, and others of murrhine, made in Diospolis; and brass, which is used for ornament and in cut pieces instead of coin; sheets of soft copper, used for cooking-utensils and cut up for bracelets and anklets for the women; iron, which is made into spears used against the elephants and other wild beasts, and in their wars. Besides these, small axes are imported, and adzes and swords; copper drinking-cups, round and large; a little coin for those coming to the market; wine of Laodicea and Italy, not much; olive oil, not much; for the

king, gold and silver plate made after the fashion of the country, and for clothing, military cloaks, and thin coats of skin, of no great value. Likewise from the district of Ariaca across this sea, there are imported Indian iron, and steel, and Indian cotton cloth; the broad cloth called *monachê* and that called *sagmatogênê*, and girdles, and coats of skin and mallow-colored cloth, and a few muslins, and colored lac. There are exported from these places ivory, and tortoise-shell and rhinoceros-horn.

* * *

15. Beyond Opone, the shore trending more toward the south, first there are the small and great bluffs of Azania; this coast is destitute of harbors, but there are places where ships can lie at anchor, the shore being abrupt; and this course is of six days, the direction being south-west. Then come the small and great beach for another six days' course * * * beyond which, a little to the south of southwest, after two courses of a day and night along the Ausanitic coast, is the island Menuthias, about three hundred stadia from the mainland, low and wooded, in which there are rivers and many kinds of birds and the mountain-tortoise. There are no wild beasts except the crocodiles; but there they do not attack men. In this place there are sewed boats, and canoes hollowed from single logs, which they use for fishing and catching tortoise. In this island they also catch them in a peculiar way, in wicker baskets, which they fasten across the channel-opening between the breakers.

16. Two days' sail beyond, there lies the very last market-town of the continent of Azania, which is called Rhapta [perhaps near the mouth of the Rufiji River, Tanzania]; which has its name from the sewed boats (*rhaptôn ploiariôn*) already mentioned; in which there is ivory in great quantity, and tortoise-shell. Along this coast live men of piratical habits, very great in stature, and under separate chiefs for each place. The Mapharitic chief governs it under some ancient right that subjects it to the sovereignty of the state that is become first in Arabia. And the people of Muza now hold it under his authority, and send thither many large ships; using Arab captains and agents, who are familiar with the natives and intermarry with them, and who know the whole coast and understand the language.

* * *

20. [In Arabia,] different tribes inhabit the country, differing in their speech, some partially, and some altogether. The land next the sea is similarly dotted here and there with caves of the Fish-Eaters, but the country inland is peopled by rascally men speaking two languages, who live in villages and nomadic camps, by whom those sailing off the middle course are plundered, and those surviving shipwrecks are taken for slaves. And so they too are continually taken prisoners by the chiefs and kings of Arabia; and they are called Carnaites. Navigation is dangerous along this whole coast of Arabia, which is without harbors, with bad anchorages, foul, inaccessible because of breakers and rocks, and terrible in every way. Therefore we hold our course down the middle of the gulf and pass on as fast as possible by the country of Arabia until we come to the Burnt Island; directly below which there are regions of peaceful people, nomadic, pasturers of cattle, sheep and camels.

* * *

31. It happens that just as Azania is subject to Charibael and the Chief of Mapharitis, this island is subject to the King of the Frankincense Country. Trade is also carried on there by some people from Muza and by those who chance to call there on the voyage from Damirica and Barygaza; they bring in rice and wheat and Indian cloth, and a few female slaves; and they take for their exchange cargoes, a great quantity of tortoise-shell. Now the island is farmed out under the Kings and is garrisoned.

* * *

45. Now the whole country of India has very many rivers, and very great ebb and flow of the tides; increasing at the new moon, and at the full moon for three days, and falling off during the intervening days of the moon. But about Barygaza it is much greater, so that the bottom is suddenly seen, and now parts of the dry land are sea, and now it is dry where ships were sailing just before; and the rivers, under the inrush of the flood tide, when the whole force of the sea is directed against them, are driven upwards more strongly against their natural current, for many stadia.

46. For this reason entrance and departure of vessels is very dangerous to those who are inexperienced or who come to this market-town for the first time. For the rush of waters at the incoming tide is irresistible, and the anchors cannot hold against it; so that large ships are caught up by the force of it, turned broadside on through the speed of the current, and so driven on the shoals and wrecked; and smaller boats are overturned; and those that have been turned aside among the channels by the receding waters at the ebb, are left on their sides, and if not held on an even keel by props, the flood tide comes upon them suddenly and under the first head of the current they are filled with water. For there is so great force in the rush of the sea at the new moon, especially during the flood tide at night, that if you begin the entrance at the moment when the waters are still, on the instant there is borne to you at the mouth of the river, a noise like the cries of an army heard from afar; and very soon the sea itself comes rushing in over the shoals with a hoarse roar.

* * *

49. There are imported into this market-town, wine, Italian preferred, also Laodicean and Arabian; copper, tin, and lead; coral and topaz; thin clothing and inferior sorts of all kinds; bright-colored girdles a cubit wide; storax, sweet clover, flint glass, realgar, antimony, gold and silver coin, on which there is a profit when exchanged for the money of the country; and ointment, but not very costly and not much. And for the King there are brought into those places very costly vessels of silver, singing boys, beautiful maidens for the harem, fine wines, thin clothing of the finest weaves, and the choicest ointments. There are exported from these places spikenard, costus, bdellium, ivory, agate and carnelian, lycium, cotton cloth of all kinds, silk cloth, mallow cloth, yarn, long pepper and such other things as are brought here from the various market-towns. Those bound for this market-town from Egypt make the voyage favorably about the month of July, that is Epiphi.

50. Beyond Barygaza the adjoining coast extends in a straight line from north to south; and so this region is called Dachinabades, for *dachanos* in the language of the natives means "south." The

inland country back from the coast toward the east comprises many desert regions and great mountains; and all kinds of wild beasts—leopards, tigers, elephants, enormous serpents, hyenas, and baboons of many sorts; and many populous nations, as far as the Ganges.

Questions

1. Based on these excerpts, what topics seem most important to the person who wrote this periplus? Why?

2. Scholars continue to debate whether this is a firsthand account of these voyages, or a collection of reports. Which passages in the text make you think the author visited these ports? Which passages support the notion that this document is secondhand reporting?

3. How do the descriptions of distant lands and people in the Periplus compare to such descriptions in other ancient texts?

The Questions of King Milinda (c. 100 BCE)

King Milinda (called Menander in Greek sources) ruled one of several kingdoms of Bactrian Greeks. These were kingdoms, at times unified into a single empire, founded by men who accompanied Alexander the Great and their descendants; they covered parts of today's Iran, Afghanistan, Uzbekistan, Tajikistan, Pakistan, and India. These kingdoms, adjacent to what later became known as the Silk Road and to many nomadic migration routes, included the homelands of the famous Sogdian and Bokharan merchants. They were important conduits for trade and cultural exchanges across much of Afro-Eurasia. Milinda's particular kingdom was in Punjab, and he reigned between about 160 and 130 BCE. This dialogue, in which he is converted to Buddhism, and then resigns his kingship, first appeared in written form (in Pali) around 100 BCE.

In the land of the Bactrian Greeks there was a city called Sagala, a great center of trade. * * * [I]t possessed many parks, gardens, woods, lakes and lotus-ponds. Its king was Milinda, a man who was learned, experienced, intelligent and competent, and who

at the proper times carefully observed all the appropriate Brah-
minic [Hindu] rites, with regard to things past, future and present.
As a disputant he was hard to assail, hard to overcome, and he was
recognized as a prominent sectarian teacher.

One day a numerous company of Arhats [Buddhists who had
reached Nirvana,] who lived in a well-protected spot in the Himala-
yas, sent a messenger to the Venerable Nagasena, * * * asking him
to come, as they wished to see him. Nagasena immediately com-
plied by vanishing from where he was and miraculously appearing
before them. And the Arhats said to him: "That king Milinda,
Nagasena, constantly harasses the order of monks with questions
and counter-questions, with arguments and counter-arguments.
Please go, Nagasena, and subdue him!" * * * And the Elders went
to Sagala, lighting up the city with their yellow robes which shone
like lamps, and bringing with them the fresh breeze of the holy
mountains.

The Venerable Nagasena stayed at the Sankheyya hermitage
together with 80,000 monks. King Milinda, accompanied by a retinue of 500 Greeks, went up to where he was, gave him a friendly
and courteous greeting, and sat on one side. Nagasena returned his
greetings.

* * *

And King Milinda asked him: "How is your Reverence known,
and what is your name, Sir?" "As Nagasena I am known, O great
king, and as Nagasena do my fellow religious habitually address me.
But although parents give such names as Nagasena, or Surasena, or
Virasena, or Sihasena, nevertheless this word 'Nagasena' is just a
denomination, a designation, a conceptual term, a current appellation, a mere name. For no real person can here be apprehended." But
King Milinda explained: "* * * [T]his Nagasena tells me that he is
not a real person! How can I be expected to agree with that?" And
to Nagasena he said: "If, most reverend Nagasena, no person can

SOURCE: *Buddhist Scriptures*, translated by Edward Conze
(Harmondsworth: Penguin Books, 1959), pp. 146–51, 155–56, 162.

be apprehended in reality, who then, I ask you, gives you what you require by way of robes, food, lodging, and medicines? Who is it that consumes them? Who is it that guards morality, practises meditation, and realizes the [four] Paths and their Fruits, and thereafter Nirvana? Who is it that kills living beings, takes what is not given, commits sexual misconduct, tells lies, drinks intoxicants? Who is it that commits the five Deadly Sins? For, if there were no person, there could be no merit and no demerit; no doer of meritorious or demeritorious deeds, and no agent behind them; no fruit of good and evil deeds, and no reward or punishment for them. * * * You just told me that your fellow religious habitually address you as 'Nagasena.' What then is this 'Nagasena'? Are perhaps the hairs of the head 'Nagasena'?"—"No, great king!" "Or perhaps the hairs of the body?"—"No, great king!" "Or perhaps the nails, teeth, skin, muscles, sinews, * * * snot, fluid of the joints, urine, or the brain in the skull—are they this 'Nagasena'?"—"No, great king!"—"Or is form this 'Nagasena,' or feeling, or perceptions, or impulses, or consciousness?"—"No, great king!"—"Then is it the combination of form, feelings, perceptions, impulses, and consciousness?"—"No, great king!"—"Then is it outside the combination of form, feelings, perceptions, impulses, and consciousness?"—"No, great king!"—"Then, ask as I may, I can discover no Nagasena at all. Just a mere sound is this 'Nagasena,' but who is the real Nagasena? Your Reverence has told a lie, has spoken a falsehood! There really is no Nagasena!"

Thereupon the Venerable Nagasena said to King Milinda: * * * "If you have come on a chariot, then please explain to me what a chariot is. Is the pole the chariot?"—"No, reverend Sir!"—"Is then the axle the chariot?"—"No, reverend Sir!"—"Is it then the wheels, or the framework, or the flag-staff, or the yoke, or the reins, or the goad-stick?"—"No, reverend Sir!"—"Then is it the combination of pole, axle, wheels, framework, flagstaff, yoke, reins, and goad which is the 'chariot'?"—"No, reverend Sir!"—"Then is this 'chariot' outside the combination of pole, axle, wheels, framework, flag-staff, yoke, reins, and goad?"—"No, reverend Sir!"—"Then, ask as I may, I can discover no chariot at all. Just a mere sound is this 'chariot.' But what is the real chariot? Your Majesty has told a lie, has spoken a falsehood! There really is no chariot! Your Majesty is the greatest king in the whole of India. Of whom then are you afraid, that you do not speak the truth?" * * *

The five hundred Greeks thereupon applauded the Venerable Nagasena and said to king Milinda: "Now let your Majesty get out of that if you can!"

But king Milinda said to Nagasena: "I have not, Nagasena, spoken a falsehood. For it is in dependence on the pole, the axle, the wheels, the framework, the flagstaff, etc., that there takes place this denomination 'chariot,' this designation, this conceptual term, a current appellation and a mere name."—"Your Majesty has spoken well about the chariot. It is just so with me. In dependence on the thirty-two parts of the body and the five Skandhas there takes place this denomination 'Nagasena,' this designation, this conceptual term, a current appellation and a mere name. In ultimate reality, however, this person cannot be apprehended. And this has been said by our Sister Vajira when she was face to face with the Lord [Buddha]:

'Where all constituent parts are present,
The word "a chariot" is applied.
So likewise where the skandhas are,
The term a "being" commonly is used.'"

"It is wonderful, Nagasena, it is astonishing, Nagasena! Most brilliantly have these questions been answered! Were the Buddha himself here, he would approve what you have said. Well spoken, Nagasena, well spoken!"

* * *

The king asked: "When someone is reborn, Venerable Nagasena, is he the same as the one who just died, or is he another?"—The Elder replied: "He is neither the same nor another."—"Give me an illustration!"—"What do you think, great king: when you were a tiny infant, newly born and quite soft, were you then the same as the one who is now grown up?"—"No, that infant was one, I, now grown up, am another."—"If that is so, then, great king, * * * [d]o we then take it that there is one mother for the embryo in the first stage, another for the second stage, another for the third, another for the fourth, another for the baby, another for the grown-up man? Is the schoolboy one person, and the one who has finished school another? Does one commit a crime, but the hands and feet of another are cut off?"— "Certainly not! But what would you say, Reverend Sir, to all that?"— The Elder replied: "I was neither the tiny infant, newly born and quite soft, nor am I now the grown-up man; but all these are comprised in one unit depending on this very body."—"Give me a simile!"—"If a man were to light a lamp, could it give light throughout the whole night?"—"Yes, it could."—"Is now the flame which bums in the first watch of the night the same as the one which burns in the second?"—"It is not the same."—"Or is the flame which burns in the second watch the same as the one which burns in the last one?"—"It is not the same."—"Do we then take it that there is one lamp in the first watch of the night, another in the second, and another again in the third?"—"No, it is because of just that one lamp that the light shines throughout the night."—"Even so must we understand the collocation of a series of successive dharmas. At rebirth one dharma arises, while another stops; but the two processes take place almost simultaneously (i.e., they are continuous). Therefore the first act of consciousness in the new existence is neither the same as the last act of consciousness in the previous existence, nor is it another."—"Give me another simile!"—"Milk, once the milking is done, turns after some time into curds; from curds it turns into fresh butter, and from fresh butter into ghee. Would it now be correct to say that the milk is the same thing as the curds, or the fresh butter, or the ghee?"—"No, it would not. But they have been produced because of it."—"Just so must be understood the collocation of a series of successive dharmas."

* * *

The king asked: "Is cessation Nirvana?"—"Yes, your majesty!"— "How is that, Nagasena?"—"All the foolish common people take delight in the senses and their objects, are impressed by them, are attached to them. In that way they are carried away by the flood, and are not set free from birth, old age, and death, from grief, lamentation, pain, sadness, and despair—they are, I say, not set free from suffering. But the well-informed holy disciples do not take delight in the senses and their objects, are not impressed by them, are not attached to them, and in consequence their craving ceases; the cessation of craving leads successively to that of grasping, of becoming, of birth, of old age and death, of grief, lamentation, pain, sadness, and despair—that is to say to the cessation of all this mass of ill. It is thus that cessation is Nirvana."—"Very good, Nagasena!"

The king asked: "Do all win Nirvana?"—"No, they do not. Only those win Nirvana who, progressing correctly, know by their superknowledge those dharmas which should be known by superknowledge, comprehend those dharmas which should be comprehended, forsake those dharmas which should be forsaken, develop those dharmas which should be developed, and realize those dharmas which should be realized."—"Very good, Nagasena!"

* * *

The king, as a result of his discussions with the Venerable Nagasena, was overjoyed and humbled; he saw the value in the Buddha's religion, * * * gained faith in the qualities of the Elder—in his observation of the monastic rules, his spiritual progress and his general demeanour—became trusting and resigned, free from conceit and arrogance. * * * [H]e said: "Well said. * * * May the Venerable Nagasena accept me as a lay-follower, as one who takes his refuge with the Triple Jewel, from today onwards, as long as I shall live!"

Questions

1. How does Nagasena explain why it makes sense to speak of a person—and hold him responsible for his actions—even if what we perceive to be the physical attributes of people (and things) are not really there? How does he deal with the problem of persistence of a person (or thing) through time in a world of continual flux?

2. What are the roles of intellect, intuition, and feeling in the attainment of Nirvana?

3. The author of this text could have written a treatise on the philosophical issues at stake, but instead chose to present these issues in the form of a drama with characters. Why do you think the text is written that way?

The Jataka or Stories of the Buddha's Former Births (c. 300 BCE)

The Jataka tales, written down around 300 BCE, tell stories involving Buddha in various incarnations. They were originally said to be a prose commentary that helped explain a series of difficult poems in the Buddhist canon, but many also draw on earlier Hindu legends. They are still immensely popular today among both Hindus and Buddhists, especially as a way of introducing various moral lessons for children.

Most of the tales have the same basic pattern seen in this No. 4 one. Buddha tells a story about a person or animal who accomplished something difficult through wisdom and/or virtue, sometimes contrasting this with the failure of someone less admirable. He then informs his audience that he was one of the characters in the tale, and that one of the people in attendance was one of the others, often likening that person's current striving for spiritual enlightenment to their earlier efforts to reach some earthly goal.

Once on a time when Brahmadatta was reigning in Benares in Kāsi, the Bodhisatta was born into the Treasurer's family, and growing up, was made Treasurer, being called Treasurer Little. A wise and clever man was he, with a keen eye for signs and omens. One day on his way to wait upon the king, he came on a dead mouse lying on the road; and, taking note of the position of the stars at that moment, he said, "Any decent young fellow with his wits about him has only to pick that mouse up, and he might start a business and keep a wife."

His words were overheard by a young man of good family but reduced circumstances, who said to himself, "That's a man who has always got a reason for what he says." And accordingly he picked up the mouse, which he sold for a farthing at a tavern for their cat.

SOURCE: *The Jataka or Stories of the Buddha's Former Births*, edited by E. B. Cowell, translated by Robert Chalmers (Cambridge: Cambridge University Press, 1855), vol. 1, pp. 19–20.

With the farthing he got molasses and took drinking water in a water-pot. Coming on flower-gatherers returning from the forest, he gave each a tiny quantity of the molasses and ladled the water out to them. Each of them gave him a handful of flowers, with the proceeds of which, next day, he came back again to the flower grounds provided with more molasses and a pot of water. That day the flower-gatherers, before they went, gave him flowering plants with half the flowers left on them; and thus in a little while he obtained eight pennies.

Later, one rainy and windy day, the wind blew down a quantity of rotten branches and boughs and leaves in the king's pleasaunce [pleasure garden], and the gardener did not see how to clear them away. Then up came the young man with an offer to remove the lot, if the wood and leaves might be his. The gardener closed with the offer on the spot. Then this apt pupil of Treasurer Little repaired to the children's playground and in a very little while had got them by bribes of molasses to collect every stick and leaf in the place into a heap at the entrance to the pleasaunce. Just then the king's potter was on the look out for fuel to fire bowls for the palace, and coming on this heap, took the lot off his hands. The sale of his wood brought in sixteen pennies to this pupil of Treasurer Little, as well as five bowls and other vessels. Having now twenty-four pennies in all, a plan occurred to him. He went to the vicinity of the city-gate with a jar full of water and supplied 500 mowers with water to drink. Said they, "You've done us a good turn, friend. What can we do for you?" "Oh, I'll tell you when I want your aid," said he; and as he went about, he struck up an intimacy with a land-trader and a sea-trader. Said the former to him, "To-morrow there will come to town a horse-dealer with 500 horses to sell." On hearing this piece of news, he said to the mowers, "I want each of you to-day to give me a bundle of grass and not to sell your own grass till mine is sold." "Certainly," said they, and delivered the 500 bundles of grass at his house. Unable to get grass for his horses elsewhere, the dealer purchased our friend's grass for a thousand pieces. Only a few days later his sea-trading friend brought him news of the arrival of a large ship in port; and another plan struck him. He hired for eight pence a well appointed carriage which plied for hire by the hour, and went in great style down to the port. Having bought the ship on credit and deposited his signet-ring as security, he had a pavilion pitched hard by and said to his people as he took his seat inside, "When merchants are being [shown] in, let them be passed on by three successive ushers into my presence." Hearing that a ship had arrived in port, about a hundred merchants came down to buy the cargo; only to be told that they could not have it as a great merchant had already made a payment on account. So away they all went to the young man; and the footmen duly announced them by three successive ushers, as had been arranged before-hand. Each man of the hundred severally gave him a thousand pieces to buy a share in the ship and then a further thousand each to buy him out altogether. So it was with 200,000 pieces that this pupil of Treasurer Little returned to Benares.

[Wanting to show] his gratitude, he went with one hundred thousand pieces to call on Treasurer Little. "How did you come by all this wealth?" asked the Treasurer. "In four short months, simply by following your advice," replied the young man; and he told him the whole story, starting with the dead mouse. Thought Lord High Treasurer Little, on hearing all this, "I must see that a young fellow of these parts does not fall into anybody else's hands." So he married him to his own grown-up daughter and settled all the family estates on the young man. And at the Treasurer's death, he became Treasurer in that city. And the Bodhisatta passed away to fare according to his deserts.

Questions

1. What are the different strategies that the young man uses to increase his wealth? What role does luck (or heavenly favor) play in his successes?

2. What character traits do these different episodes illustrate? Does the tale seem to regard some of them as more important or more admirable than others? Explain.

3. Why do you think that this tale revolves around a merchant hero's pursuit of wealth (this is also true of other Jataka tales)? Does this suggest anything to you about the religion?

Chapter 7

HAN DYNASTY CHINA AND IMPERIAL ROME, 300 BCE–300 CE

Polybius, The Roman Maniple versus the Macedonian Phalanx (c. 150 BCE)

Polybius (c. 203–118 BCE) was a Greek historian whose most notable work, *The Histories,* covers the period 220–146 BCE. His historical writing influenced the practice of later scholars such as the Roman Livy; his ideas about balanced power in government informed Enlightenment-era thinkers such as Montesquieu and Jefferson. You can see Polybius thinks like a historian: he pays attention to working from verifiable information (details about military formations, for example), he references earlier sources (Homer's *Iliad*), and he takes care to connect various sections of his book to produce a coherent whole (though not all the books of his *Histories* survived to modern times). In this passage Polybius is wrestling with what he sees as a vexing problem of historical interpretation: why were the Romans militarily more successful than the Macedonians, when the phalanx formation appeared to be a more formidable tactic?

The maniple was a tactical unit of the Roman Legion; a phalanx was a rectangular formation of heavy infantry armed with stabbing weapons such as spears, pikes, and *sarissae* (pikes between approximately 13 and 23 feet long) used by armies throughout the Hellenistic world, including Rome.

141

28. In my sixth book I made a promise, still unfulfilled, of taking a fitting opportunity of drawing a comparison between the arms of the Romans and Macedonians, and their respective system of tactics, and pointing out how they differ for better or worse from each other. I will now endeavour by a reference to actual facts to fulfil that promise. For since in former times the Macedonian tactics proved themselves by experience capable of conquering those of Asia and Greece; while the Roman tactics sufficed to conquer the nations of Africa and all those of Western Europe; and since in our own day there have been numerous opportunities of comparing the men as well as their tactics,—it will be, I think, a useful and worthy task to investigate their differences, and discover why it is that the Romans conquer and carry off the palm from their enemies in the operations of war: that we may not put it all down to Fortune, and congratulate them on their good luck, as the thoughtless of mankind do; but, from a knowledge of the true causes, may give their leaders the tribute of praise and admiration which they deserve.

Now as to the battles which the Romans fought with Hannibal [248–c. 183 BCE, general from Carthage], and the defeats which they sustained in them, I need say no more. It was not owing to their arms or their tactics, but to the skill and genius of Hannibal that they met with those defeats: and that I made quite clear in my account of the battles themselves. And my contention is supported by two facts. First, by the conclusion of the war: for as soon as the Romans got a general of ability comparable with that of Hannibal, victory was not long in following their banners. Secondly, Hannibal himself, being dissatisfied with the original arms of his men, and having immediately after his first victory furnished his troops with the arms of the Romans, continued to employ them thenceforth to the end. Pyrrhus [319–272 BCE, Greek general], again, availed himself not only of the arms, but also of the troops of Italy, placing a maniple of Italians and a company of his own phalanx alternately, in his

SOURCE: *The Histories of Polybius*, translated by Evelyn S. Shuckburgh (London: Macmillan, 1889), vol. 2, pp. 226–29.

battles against the Romans. Yet even this did not enable him to win; the battles were somehow or another always indecisive.

* * *

29. Many considerations may easily convince us that, if only the phalanx has its proper formation and strength, nothing can resist it face to face or withstand its charge. For as a man in close order of battle occupies a space of three feet; and as the length of the sarissae is sixteen cubits according to the original design, which has been reduced in practice to fourteen; and as of these fourteen four must be deducted, to allow for the distance between the two hands holding it, and to balance the weight in front; it follows clearly that each hoplite [citizen-soldier of a Greek city-state] will have ten cubits of his sarissa projecting beyond his body, when he lowers it with both hands, as he advances against the enemy: hence, too, though the men of the second, third, and fourth rank will have their sarissae projecting farther beyond the front rank than the men of the fifth, yet even these last will have two cubits of their sarissae beyond the front rank; if only the phalanx is properly formed and the men close up properly both flank and rear, like the description in Homer—

"So buckler pressed on buckler; helm on helm;
And man on man: and waving horse-hair plumes
In polished head-piece mingled, as they swayed
In order: in such serried rank they stood."
[*Iliad*, 13, 131].

And if my description is true and exact, it is clear that in front of each man of the front rank there will be five sarissae projecting to distances varying by a descending scale of two cubits.

30. With this point in our minds, it will not be difficult to imagine what the appearance and strength of the whole phalanx is likely to be, when, with lowered sarissae, it advances to the charge sixteen deep. Of these sixteen ranks, all above the fifth are unable to reach with their sarissae far enough to take actual part in the fighting. They, therefore, do not lower them, but hold them with the points inclined upwards over the shoulders of the ranks in front of them,

to shield the heads of the whole phalanx; for the sarissae are so closely serried, that they repel missiles which have carried over the front ranks and might fall upon the heads of those in the rear. These rear ranks, however, during an advance, press forward those in front by the weight of their bodies; and thus make the charge very forcible, and at the same time render it impossible for the front ranks to face about.

Such is the arrangement, general and detailed, of the phalanx. It remains now to compare with it the peculiarities and distinctive features of the Roman arms and tactics. Now, a Roman soldier in full armour also requires a space of three square feet. But as their method of fighting admits of individual motion for each man— because he defends his body with a shield, which he moves about to any point from which a blow is coming, and because he uses his sword both for cutting and stabbing,—it is evident that each man must have a clear space, and an interval of at least three feet both on flank and rear, if he is to do his duty with any effect. The result of this will be that each Roman soldier will face two of the front rank of a phalanx, so that he has to encounter and fight against ten spears, which one man cannot find time even to cut away, when once the two lines are engaged, nor force his way through easily— seeing that the Roman front ranks are not supported by the rear ranks, either by way of adding weight to their charge, or vigour to the use of their swords. Therefore it may readily be understood that, as I said before, it is impossible to confront a charge of the phalanx, so long as it retains its proper formation and strength.

31. Why is it then that the Romans conquer? And what is it that brings disaster on those who employ the phalanx? Why, just because war is full of uncertainties both as to time and place; whereas there is but one time and one kind of ground in which a phalanx can fully work. If, then, there were anything to compel the enemy to accommodate himself to the time and place of the phalanx, when about to fight a general engagement, it would be but natural to expect that those who employed the phalanx would always carry off the victory. But if the enemy finds it possible, and even easy, to avoid its attack, what becomes of its formidable character? Again, no one denies that for its employment it is indispensable to have a country flat, bare,

and without such impediments as ditches, cavities, depressions, steep banks, or beds of rivers: for all such obstacles are sufficient to hinder and dislocate this particular formation. And that it is, I may say, impossible, or at any rate exceedingly rare to find a piece of country of twenty stades, or sometimes of even greater extent, without any such obstacles, every one will also admit. However, let us suppose that such a district has been found. If the enemy decline to come down into it, but traverse the country sacking the towns and territories of the allies, what use will the phalanx be? For if it remains on the ground suited to itself, it will not only fail to benefit its friends, but will be incapable even of preserving itself; for the carriage of provisions will be easily stopped by the enemy, seeing that they are in undisputed possession of the country: while if it quits its proper ground, from the wish to strike a blow, it will be an easy prey to the enemy. Nay, if a general does descend into the plain, and yet does not risk his whole army upon one charge of the phalanx or upon one chance, but manoeuvres for a time to avoid coming to close quarters in the engagement, it is easy to learn what will be the result from what the Romans are now actually doing.

Questions

1. Describe the formations of the maniple and the phalanx in your own words. What were the tactical advantages and disadvantages of the phalanx?

2. Polybius claims that the Roman military was more successful than its enemies, but then proceeds to discuss Hannibal and Pyrrhus, two generals who defeated Roman armies. How does Polybius handle evidence that might undermine his arguments?

3. Do you think Polybius is over-representing Roman success? Why or why not?

Diodorus Siculus, On the Slave Revolt in Sicily (136–132 BCE)

The domination of the Mediterranean by Rome in the second century BCE transformed Roman society. Victorious Roman wars produced a massive flow of slaves into Italy. Small-scale farming was replaced by large aristocratic estates worked by slave labor. Between the 130s BCE and the 70s BCE three massive slave rebellions took place. The first of these occurred in Sicily between 136 and 132 BCE. Rebellious slaves under the leadership of Eunus from Apamea in Syria, their elected king, successfully resisted the Romans for several years. The following account of this "First Servile War" comes from the *Library* of Diodorus Siculus. Diodorus was a Greek-speaking inhabitant of Sicily who composed his work before 30 BCE.

The Sicilians, having shot up in prosperity and acquired great wealth, began to purchase a vast number of slaves, to whose bodies, as they were brought in droves from the slave markets, they at once applied marks and brands. The young men they used as cowherds, the others in such ways as they happened to be useful. But they treated them with a heavy hand in their service, and granted them the most meagre care, the bare minimum for food and clothing. As a result most of them made their livelihood by brigandage, and there was bloodshed everywhere, since the brigands were like scattered bands of soldiers.

* * *

There was a certain Syrian slave, belonging to Antigenes of Enna; he was an Apamean by birth and had an aptitude for magic and the working of wonders. He claimed to foretell the future, * * * he not only gave oracles by means of dreams, but even made a pretence of having waking visions of the gods and of hearing the future from their own lips. * * * [H]is reputation advanced apace. Finally, through some device, while in a state of divine possession,

---

SOURCE: *Diodorus of Sicily*, translated by Francis R. Walton (Cambridge: Harvard University Press, 1967), vol. 7, pp. 57–71.

he would produce fire and flame from his mouth, and thus rave oracularly about things to come. For he would place fire, and fuel to maintain it, in a nut—or something similar—that was pierced on both sides; then, placing it in his mouth and blowing on it, he kindled now sparks, and now a flame. Prior to the revolt he used to say that the Syrian goddess appeared to him, saying that he should be king, and he repeated this, not only to others, but even to his own master. Since his claims were treated as a joke, Antigenes, taken by his hocus-pocus, would introduce Eunus (for that was the wonder-worker's name) at his dinner parties, and cross-question him about his kingship and how he would treat each of the men present. And since he gave a full account of everything without hesitation, explaining with what moderation he would treat the masters and in sum making a colourful tale of his quackery, the guests were always stirred to laughter. * * * The beginning of the whole revolt took place as follows.

There was a certain Damophilus of Enna, a man of great wealth but insolent of manner; he had abused his slaves to excess, and his wife Megallis vied even with her husband in punishing the slaves and in her general inhumanity towards them. The slaves, reduced by this degrading treatment to the level of brutes, conspired to revolt and to murder their masters. Going to Eunus they asked him whether their resolve had the favour of the gods. He, resorting to his usual mummery, promised them the favour of the gods, and soon persuaded them to act at once. Immediately, therefore, they brought together four hundred of their fellow slaves and, having armed themselves in such ways as opportunity permitted, they fell upon the city of Enna, with Eunus at their head and working his miracle of the flames of fire for their benefit. When they found their way into the houses they shed much blood, sparing not even suckling babes. * * * By now a great multitude of slaves from the city had joined them, who, after first demonstrating against their own masters their utter ruthlessness, then turned to the slaughter of others. When Eunus and his men learned that Damophilus and his wife were in the garden that lay near the city, they sent some of their band and dragged them off. * * * Only in the case of the couple's daughter were the slaves seen to show consideration throughout, and this was because of her kindly nature, in that to the extent of her power she was always compassionate and ready to succour the slaves. Thereby it was demonstrated that the others were treated as they were, not because of some "natural savagery of slaves," but rather in revenge for wrongs previously received. The men appointed to the task, having dragged Damophilus and Megallis into the city * * * brought them to the theatre, where the crowd of rebels had assembled. But when Damophilus attempted to devise a plea to get them off safe and was winning over many of the crowd with his words, Hermeias and Zeuxis, men bitterly disposed towards him, denounced him as a cheat, and without waiting for a formal trial by the assembly the one ran him through the chest with a sword, the other chopped off his head with an axe. Thereupon Eunus was chosen king. * * *

* * * [H]e called an assembly and put to death all the citizenry of Enna except for those who were skilled in the manufacture of arms: these he put in chains and assigned them to this task. He gave Megallis to the maidservants to deal with as they might wish; they subjected her to torture and threw her over a precipice. * * * Having set a diadem upon his head, and arrayed himself in full royal style, he proclaimed his wife queen, * * * and appointed to the royal council such men as seemed to be gifted with superior intelligence, among them one Achaeus, * * * a man who excelled both at planning and in action. In three days Eunus had armed, as best he could, more than six thousand men, besides others in his train who had only axes and hatchets, or slings, or sickles, or fire-hardened stakes, or even kitchen spits; and he went about ravaging the countryside. Then, since he kept recruiting untold numbers of slaves, he ventured even to do battle with Roman generals, and on joining combat repeatedly overcame them with his superior numbers, for he now had more than ten thousand soldiers.

* * *

* * * Cities were captured with all their inhabitants, and many armies were cut to pieces by the rebels, until Rupilius, the Roman commander, recovered Tauromenium for the Romans by placing it under strict siege and confining the rebels under conditions of unspeakable duress and famine: conditions such that, beginning

by eating the children, they progressed to the women, and did not altogether abstain even from eating one another. * * * Finally, after Sarapion, a Syrian, had betrayed the citadel, the general laid hands on all the runaway slaves in the city, whom, after torture, he threw over a cliff. From there he advanced to Enna, which he put under siege in much the same manner, bringing the rebels into extreme straits and frustrating their hopes. * * * Rupilius captured this city also by betrayal, since its strength was impregnable to force of arms. Eunus, taking with him his bodyguards, a thousand strong, fled in unmanly fashion to a certain precipitous region. The men with him, however, aware that their dreaded fate was inevitable, * * * killed one another with the sword, by beheading. Eunus, the wonder-worker and king, who through cowardice had sought refuge in certain caves, was dragged out with four others, a cook, a baker, the man who massaged him at his bath, and a fourth, whose duty it had been to amuse him at drinking parties. Remanded to prison, where his flesh disintegrated into a mass of lice, he met such an end as befitted his knavery, and died at Morgantina.

Questions

1. How do the rebellious slaves organize themselves? What problems do they encounter in resisting the Roman forces?

2. What can we conclude about relationships between slaves and masters from Diodorus' description of the rebellion and its origins?

3. Does Diodorus believe that the slaves' rebellion is justified?

The Debate on Salt and Iron (81 BCE)

This excerpt is a famous example of a frequent practice in ancient China: debates on political, religious, or other policies held before a ruler. In the text below, two groups that we would call Confucian and Legalist debate economic policy. The Confucian literati advocate a state with low taxes and limited regulatory and military ambitions; the Legalist officials support much greater state activism. (The recently deceased Legalist emperor, Han Wudi, had expanded deep into central Asia—succeeding

militarily, but placing a considerable strain on the imperial finances.)
Iron, used for both weapons and plows, and salt—a necessity produced
in just a few places, and thus highly profitable—were hotly debated,
but so were other topics. Afterward, some of the monopolies were
abolished—even though, in this record of the debate, the Confucians
seem to wind up on the defensive.

In the sixth year of the era Shiyuan [81 BCE], an imperial edict
was issued directing the chancellor and the imperial secretaries to
confer with the worthies and literati who had been recommended
to the government and to inquire into the grievances and hardships
of the people.

The literati responded: We have heard that the way to govern
men is to prevent evil and error at their source, to broaden the begin-
nings of morality, to discourage secondary occupations, and open
the way for the exercise of humaneness and rightness. Never should
material profit appear as a motive of government. Only then can
moral instruction succeed and the customs of the people be reformed.
But now in the provinces the salt, iron, and liquor monopolies, and
the system of equitable marketing have been established to compete
with the people for profit, dispelling rustic generosity and teaching
the people greed. Therefore those who pursue primary occupations [farming] have grown few and those following secondary occupations [trading] numerous. As artifice increases, basic simplicity
declines; and as the secondary occupations flourish, those that are
primary suffer. When the secondary is practiced the people grow
decadent, but when the primary is practiced they are simple and sincere. When the people are sincere then there will be sufficient wealth
and goods, but when they become extravagant then famine and cold
will follow. We recommend that the salt, iron, and liquor monopolies
and the system of equitable marketing be abolished so that primary

---

SOURCE: *Sources of Chinese Tradition*, 2nd ed., compiled by Wm.
Theodore de Bary and Irene Bloom et al. (New York: Columbia
University Press, 1999), vol. 1, pp. 360–63.

pursuits may be advanced and secondary ones suppressed. This will have the advantage of increasing the profitableness of agriculture.

His Lordship [the Imperial Secretary Sang Hongyang] replied: The Xiongnu have frequently revolted against our sovereignty and pillaged our borders. If we are to defend ourselves, then it means the hardships of war for the soldiers of China, but if we do not defend ourselves properly, then their incursions cannot be stopped. The former emperor [Wu] took pity upon the people of the border areas who for so long had suffered disaster and hardship and had been carried off as captives. Therefore he set up defense stations, established a system of warning beacons, and garrisoned the outlying areas to ensure their protection. But the resources of these areas were insufficient, and so he established the salt, iron, and liquor monopolies and the system of equitable marketing in order to raise more funds for expenditures at the borders. Now our critics, who desire that these measures be abolished, would empty the treasuries and deplete the funds used for defense. They would have the men who are defending our passes and patrolling our walls suffer hunger and cold. How else can we provide for them? Abolition of these measures is not expedient!

His Lordship stated: In former times the peers residing in the provinces sent in their respective products as tribute, but there was much confusion and trouble in transporting them and the goods were often of such poor quality that they were not worth the cost of transportation. For this reason transportation offices have been set up in each district to handle delivery and shipping and to facilitate the presentation of tribute from outlying areas. Therefore the system is called "equitable marketing." Warehouses have been opened in the capital for the storing of goods, buying when prices are low and selling when they are high. Thereby the government suffers no loss and the merchants cannot speculate for profit. Therefore this is called the "balanced level" [stabilization]. With the balanced level the people are protected from unemployment, and with equitable marketing the burden of labor service is equalized. Thus these measures are designed to ensure an equal distribution of goods and to benefit the people and are not intended to open the way to profit or provide the people with a ladder to crime.

The literati replied: In ancient times taxes and levies took from the people what they were skilled in producing and did not demand what they were poor at. Thus the husbandmen sent in their harvests and the weaving women their goods. Nowadays the government disregards what people have and requires of them what they have not, so that they are forced to sell their goods at a cheap price in order to meet the demands from above. * * * The farmers suffer double hardships and the weaving women are taxed twice. We have not seen that this kind of marketing is "equitable." The government officials go about recklessly opening closed doors and buying everything at will so they can corner all the goods. With goods cornered prices soar, and when prices soar the merchants make their own deals for profit. The officials wink at powerful racketeers, and the rich merchants hoard commodities and wait for an emergency. With slick merchants and corrupt officials buying cheap and selling dear we have not seen that your level is "balanced." The system of equitable marketing of ancient times was designed to equalize the burden of labor upon the people and facilitate the transporting of tribute. It did not mean dealing in all kinds of commodities for the sake of profit.

The Literati Attack Legalist Philosophy

The literati spoke: He who is good with a chisel can shape a round hole without difficulty; he who is good at laying foundations can build to a great height without danger of collapse. The statesman Yi Yin made the ways of Yao and Shun the foundation of the Yin dynasty, and its heirs succeeded to the throne for a hundred generations without break. But Shang Yang made heavy penalties and harsh laws the foundation of the Qin state and with the Second Emperor it was destroyed. Not satisfied with the severity of the laws, he instituted the system of mutual responsibility, made it a crime to criticize the government, and increased corporal punishments until the people were so terrified they did not know where to put their hands and feet. Not content with the manifold taxes and levies, he prohibited the people from using the resources of forests and rivers and made a hundredfold profit on the storage of commodities, while the people were given no chance to voice the slightest objection. Such worship of profit and slight of what is right, such exaltation of power and achievement, lent, it is true, to expansion of land and acquisition of territory. Yet it was like pouring more water upon people who are already suffering from flood and only increasing their distress. You see how Shang Yang opened the way to imperial rule for the Qin, but you fail to see how he also opened for the Qin the road to ruin!

CONFUCIAN LITERATI RIDICULED

His Excellency spoke: * * * Now we have with us over sixty worthy men and literati who cherish the ways of the Six Confucian Arts, fleet in thought and exhaustive in argument. It is proper, gentlemen, that you should pour forth your light and dispel our ignorance. And yet you put all your faith in the past and turn your backs upon the present, tell us of antiquity and give no thought to the state of the times. Perhaps we are not capable of recognizing true scholars. Yet do you really presume with your fancy phrases and attacks upon men of ability to pervert the truth in this manner?

See them [the Confucians] now present us with nothingness and consider it substance, with emptiness and call it plenty! In their coarse gowns and worn shoes they walk gravely along, sunk in meditation as though they had lost something. These are not men who can do great deeds and win fame. They do not even rise above the vulgar masses.

Questions

1. What problems do the literati blame on state monopolies? What benefits do the officials attribute to them?

2. How does each side defend its policies?

3. Our passage ends with the officials criticizing the literati, not just their proposals. Why is this significant? Why might a pro-literati chronicler have included this?

The Legend of Meng Jiangnü (third century BCE)

Multiple versions of this legend have circulated for centuries; this one comes from a website for tourists. Some basic elements of the story do not vary, however: a couple is separated when he is forced to work on building the Great Wall, and his loyal wife's tears break the wall open, revealing her husband's bones and embarrassing the emperor. The original source of the story is obscure, but forced labor to supply armies and build fortifications on remote northern frontiers were a major grievance in Qin times (221–206 BCE), contributing to rebellions that brought down the dynasty.

This story happened during the Qin Dynasty (221 BCE–206 BCE). There was once an old man named Meng who lived in the southern part of the country with his wife. One spring, Meng sowed a seed of bottle gourd in his yard. The bottle gourd grew up bit by bit and its vines climbed over the wall and entered his neighbor Jiang's yard. Like Meng, Jiang had no children and so he became very fond of the plant. He watered and took care of the plant. With tender care of both men, the plant grew bigger and bigger and gave a beautiful bottle gourd in autumn. Jiang plucked it off the vine, and the two old men decided to cut the gourd and divide it by half. To their surprise when they cut the gourd a pretty and lovely girl was lying inside! They felt happy to have a child and both loved her very much, so they decided to bring the child up together. They named the girl Meng Jiangnü, which means Meng and Jiang's daughter.

As time went by, Meng Jiangnü grew up and became a beautiful young woman. She was very smart and industrious. She took care of old Meng and Jiang's families, washing the clothes and doing the house work. People knew that Meng Jiangnü was a good girl and liked her very much. One day while playing in the yard, Meng Jiangnü saw a young man hiding in the garden. She called out to her parents, and the young man came out.

SOURCE: "The Story of Meng Jiangnü," CRIEnglish.com, http://english .cri.cn/725/2006/03/28/202@67861.htm.

At that time, Emperor Qin Shihuang (the first emperor of Qin) announced plans to build the Great Wall. So lots of men were caught by the federal officials. Fan Qiliang was an intellectual man and very afraid of being caught, so he went to Meng's house to hide from the officials. Meng and Jiang liked this good-looking, honest, and good-mannered young man. They decided to wed their daughter to him. Both Fan Qiliang and Meng Jiangnü accepted happily, and the couple was married several days later. However, three days after their marriage, officials suddenly broke in and took Fan Qiliang away to build the Great Wall in the north of China.

It was a hard time for Meng Jiangnü after her husband was taken away—she missed her husband and cried nearly every day. She sewed warm clothes for her husband and decided to set off to look for him. Saying farewell to her parents, she packed her luggage and started her long journey. She climbed over mountains and went through the rivers. She walked day and night, slipping and falling many times, but finally she reached the foot of the Great Wall at the present Shanhaiguan Pass.

Upon her arrival, she was eager to ask about her husband. Bad news came to her, however, that Fan Qiliang had already died of exhaustion and was buried into the Great Wall! Meng Jiangnü could not help crying. She sat on the ground and cried and cried. Suddenly with a tremendous noise, a 400-kilometer-long (248-mile-long) section of the Great Wall collapsed over her bitter wail. The workmen and supervisors were astonished. Emperor Qin Shihuang happened to be touring the wall at that exact time, and he was enraged and ready to punish the woman.

However, at the first sight of Meng Jiangnü Emperor Qin Shihuang was attracted by her beauty. Instead of killing her, the Emperor asked Meng Jiangnü to marry him. Suppressing her feeling of anger, Meng Jiangnü agreed on the basis of three terms. The first was to find the body of Fan Qiliang, the second was to hold a state funeral for him, and the last one was to have Emperor Qin Shihuang wear black mourning for Fan Qiliang and attend the funeral in person. Emperor Qin Shihuang thought for a while and reluctantly agreed. After all the terms were met, Emperor Qin Shihuang was ready to take her to his palace. When the guards were not watching, she suddenly turned around and jumped into the nearby Bohai Sea.

This story tells of the hard work of Chinese commoners, as well as expos[ing] the cruel system of hard labor during the reign of Emperor [Qin] Shihuang. The Ten-Thousand-Li Great Wall embodied the power and wisdom of the Chinese nation. In memory of Meng Jiangnü, later generations built a temple, called the Jiangnü Temple, at the foot of the Great Wall in which a statue of Meng Jiangnü is located. Meng Jiangnü's story has been passed down from generation to generation.

Questions

1. How does this contemporary version of the tale, written for English-speaking tourists, mix together modern and ancient ideals of marriage and womanhood?

2. Why do you think Meng Jiangnü sets the three specific conditions for her remarriage listed here?

3. If you leave out the last paragraph (which is a contemporary gloss on the story), what attitude does the legend seem to have toward the Great Wall? How does the final paragraph add to or alter that?

Pliny the Younger and Trajan, Exchange on Prosecuting Christians (c. 98–117 CE)

The Romans were generally tolerant of the religions of their subject peoples, often assimilating their subjects' gods to their own. Judaism and Christianity, however, as monotheistic religions, appeared strange to them, indeed something little different from atheism. Judaism, however, was a long-established religion in Judea before the coming of the Romans and was therefore tolerated. Christianity, which arose during Roman rule, was a newcomer, and thus a different matter. The imperial authorities usually left Christians alone. However, Christians were occasionally persecuted because they refused to sacrifice to the old gods and to the imperial cult. (Many inhabitants of the empire also believed that Christians were guilty of sexual promiscuity, incest, and cannibalism.) Anyone who did not offer sacrifice to the gods and the emperor was legally liable to severe punishment, including death. The following excerpts, taken from the correspondence of Pliny the Younger (c. 61–c. 113 CE) with Trajan, emperor from 98 to 117 CE, show one Roman governor trying to grapple with the problem of what to do with recalcitrant Christians. Pliny was a wealthy Roman aristocrat, prominent in Roman government and literary circles. Around 110 CE he became governor of the province of Bithynia, which is in modern Turkey. Uncertain as to how he should deal with the Christians in his province, he wrote to consult the emperor.

PLINY THE YOUNGER TO TRAJAN

It is my rule, Sire, to refer to you in matters where I am uncertain. For who can better direct my hesitation or instruct my ignorance? I was never present at any trial of Christians; therefore I do not know what are the customary penalties or investigations, and what limits are observed. I have hesitated a great deal on the question whether there should be any distinction of ages; whether the weak should have the same treatment as the more robust; whether those who recant should be pardoned, or whether a man who has ever been a Christian should gain nothing by ceasing to be such; whether the name itself, even if innocent of crime, should be punished, or only the crimes attaching to that name.

Meanwhile, this is the course that I have adopted in the case of those brought before me as Christians. I ask them if they are Christians. If they admit it I repeat the question a second and a third time, threatening capital punishment; if they persist I sentence them to death. For I do not doubt that, whatever kind of crime it may be to which they have confessed, their pertinacity and inflexible obstinacy should certainly be punished. There were others who displayed a like madness and whom I reserved to be sent to Rome, since they were Roman citizens.

SOURCE: *Documents of the Christian Church*, ed. Henry Bettenson, 2nd ed. (London: Oxford University Press, 1963), pp. 3–6.

Thereupon the usual result followed; the very fact of my dealing with the question led to a wider spread of the charge, and a great variety of cases were brought before me. An anonymous pamphlet was issued, containing many names. All who denied that they were or had been Christians I considered should be discharged, because they called upon the gods at my dictation and did reverence, with incense and wine, to your image which I had ordered to be brought forward for this purpose, together with the statues of the deities; and especially because they cursed Christ, a thing which, it is said, genuine Christians cannot be induced to do. Others named by the informer first said that they were Christians and then denied it; declaring that they had been but were so no longer, some having recanted three years or more before and one or two as long ago as twenty years. They all worshipped your image and the statues of the gods and cursed Christ. But they declared that the sum of their guilt or error had amounted only to this, that on an appointed day they had been accustomed to meet before daybreak, and to recite a hymn antiphonally to Christ, as to a god, and to bind themselves by an oath, not for the commission of any crime but to abstain from theft, robbery, adultery and breach of faith, and not to deny a deposit when it was claimed. After the conclusion of this ceremony it was their custom to depart and meet again to take food; but it was ordinary and harmless food, and they had ceased this practice after my edict in which, in accordance with your orders, I had forbidden secret societies. I thought it the more necessary, therefore, to find out what truth there was in this by applying torture to two maid-servants, who were called deaconesses. But I found nothing but a depraved and extravagant superstition, and I therefore postponed my examination and had recourse to you for consultation.

The matter seemed to me to justify my consulting you, especially on account of the number of those imperilled; for many persons of all ages and classes and of both sexes are being put in peril by accusation, and this will go on. The contagion of this superstition has spread not only in the cities, but in the villages and rural districts as well; yet it seems capable of being checked and set right. There is no shadow of doubt that the temples, which have been almost deserted, are beginning to be frequented once more, that the sacred rites which have been long neglected are being renewed, and that sacrificial victims are for sale everywhere, whereas, till recently, a buyer was rarely to be found. From this it is easy to imagine what a host of men could be set right, were they given a chance of recantation.

TRAJAN TO PLINY

You have taken the right line, my dear Pliny, in examining the cases of those denounced to you as Christians, for no hard and fast rule can be laid down, of universal application. They are not to be sought out; if they are informed against, and the charge is proved, they are to be punished, with this reservation—that if any one denies that he is a Christian, and actually proves it, that is by worshipping our gods, he shall be pardoned as a result of his recantation, however suspect he may have been with respect to the past. Pamphlets published anonymously should carry no weight in any charge whatsoever. They constitute a very bad precedent, and are also out of keeping with this age.

Questions

1. What is Pliny's understanding of the religion practiced by the Christians? What does he portray them doing? Why does he feel it necessary to consult the emperor on their treatment?

2. What does Pliny's letter tell us about the religious climate in first-century Bithynia?

3. How would you characterize the attitudes of Pliny and Trajan toward the Christians? How concerned are they about the Christians' behavior?

Vindolanda Tablets (second century CE)

The following documents are from a body of artifacts known as the Vindolanda tablets. Vindolanda was a Roman fort just south of Hadrian's Wall. Construction of the 72½-mile-long barrier began around 122 CE. When completed, it ran from the North Sea to the Irish Sea. The wall itself was part of a complex of ditches, berms, glacis, and a military road which marked the frontier between the Roman province of Britannia and the independent peoples living to the north. It was not intended to be an impermeable barrier but instead a base for controlling the movements of local tribes and for regulating trade between Romans and barbarians. The tablets themselves are thin, flexible pieces of wood which preserve letters, accounts, and various lists. Discarded in a garbage dump, these delicate objects survived because unusual soil conditions at the site prevented their deterioration. They provide a host of details about military life on the Roman frontier. The first tablet below appears to be a report on the fighting characteristics of the local native people. The second is a report on the strength of one of the units guarding the wall, the first cohort of Tungrians, recruited among tribesmen living in what is today Belgium. They are an example of the "auxiliary" troops which made up a large part of the Roman military. In return for twenty-five years of service, they received Roman citizenship. The third appears to be the accounts of a family business. (The *modius* is a measure of grain.)

The Britons are unprotected by armour(?). There are very many cavalry. The cavalry do not use swords nor do the wretched Britons mount in order to throw javelins. (*Tab. Vindol.* II 164)

18 May, net number of the First Cohort of Tungrians, of which the commander is Julius Verecundus the prefect, 752, including 6 centurions.

Of whom there are absent:

guards of the governor		46
at the office of Ferox		
at Coria		337
	including (?) 2 centurions	
at London	(?) a centurion	

SOURCE: From *Life and Letters on the Roman Frontier* by Alan K. Bowman.

. . . outside the province	6
including 1 centurion	
set out (?) to Gaul	9
including 1 centurion	
at Eburacum (?) to collect	
pay	11
at (?) . . .	(?) 1
	45
total absentees	456
including 5 centurions	
remainder, present	296
including 1 centurion	
from these:	
sick	15
wounded	6
suffering from inflammation	
of the eyes	10
total of these	31
remainder, fit for active	
service	265
including 1 centurion	

(*Tab. Vindol.* II 154)

Account of wheat measured out from that which
I myself have put into the barrel:
to myself, for bread . . .
to Macrinus, *modii* 7
to Felicius Victor on the order of Spectatus provided as a loan (?),
    modii 26
in three sacks, to father, *modii* 19
to Macrinus, *modii* 13
to the oxherds at the wood, *modii* 8
likewise to Amabilis at the shrine, *modii* 3

. . . September . . , to Crescens
on the order of Firmus (?), *modii* 3
likewise . . . , *modii* ..
to Macr . . . . . . , *modii* (?) 15
likewise to Ma . . . (?), *modii* .3
to father . . . , *modii* 2
September 26
to Lu . . . the *beneficiarius, modii* 6
to Felicius Victor, *modii* 15
for twisted loaves (?), to you, *modii* 2
to Crescens, *modii* 9
to the legionary soldiers
on the order of Firmus, *modii* 11+
to Candidus, *modii* ..
to you, in a sack from Briga (?), . . .
to you, . . .
to Lucco, in charge of the pigs . . .
to Primus, slave (?) of Lucius . . .
to you . . .
to Lucco for his own use . . .
likewise that which I have sent . . . *modii*.. (?)
in the century of Voturius (?)
to father, in charge of the oxen . . .
likewise, within the measure . . . (?)
15 pounds yield 15+ pounds (?) . . .
total, *modii* . . .
likewise to myself, for bread, *modii* ..
total of wheat, *modii* 320½."

(*Tab. Vindol.* II 180)

Questions

1. What is the attitude of the Roman garrison toward the native people?

2. What can we learn about Roman military organization from these tablets?

3. How important was literacy to the functioning of the Roman military?

Chapter 8

THE RISE OF UNIVERSAL RELIGIONS, 300–600 CE

Priscus, The Court of Attila (449 CE)

For almost two thousand years the pastoral nomads of Inner Asia presented a major challenge to the settled peoples on whose frontiers they lived. The Huns, a federation of nomadic peoples, originating in central Asia, played a major role in the events that marked the disintegration of the Roman Empire. In the late 300s CE they entered the southern Russia steppe and drove the Goths over the Danube into the Roman Empire. They alternately raided the empire and served as mercenaries in its armies. Their political and military strength was at its peak during the reign of Attila (434–453 CE), who regularly raided the Roman Empire. He defeated the East Roman emperor and received tribute from him. In 451 CE he invaded Gaul; in 452 CE he devastated much of Italy. After his death, however, the Hunnic empire quickly disintegrated. Priscus, the author of the selection below, was an East Roman imperial servant and historian. In 449 CE he took part in an embassy sent from Constantinople to negotiate with Attila. He wrote in a classicizing style and therefore referred to the Huns as Scythians, a nomadic people described by Herodotus in the fifth century BCE.

The next morning, at dawn of day, Maximin sent me to Onegesius, with presents offered by himself as well as those which the

SOURCE: J. B. Bury, *History of the Later Roman Empire from the Death of Theodosius I to the Death of Justinian* (New York: Dover Publications, 1958), vol. 1, pp. 283–85.

Emperor had sent, and I was to find out whether he would have an interview with Maximin and at what time. When I arrived at the house, along with the attendants who carried the gifts, I found the doors closed, and had to wait until some one should come out and announce our arrival. As I waited and walked up and down in front of the enclosure which surrounded the house, a man, whom from his Scythian dress I took for a barbarian, came up and addressed me in Greek, with the word Χαῖρε, "Hail!" I was surprised at a Scythian speaking Greek. For the subjects of the Huns, swept together from various lands, speak, besides their own barbarous tongues, either Hunnic or Gothic, or—as many as have commercial dealings with the western Romans—Latin; but none of them easily speak Greek, except captives from the Thracian or Illyrian sea-coast; and these last are easily known to any stranger by their torn garments and the squalor of their heads, as men who have met with a reverse. This man, on the contrary, resembled a well-to-do Scythian, being well dressed, and having his hair cut in a circle after Scythian fashion. Having returned his salutation, I asked him who he was and whence he had come into a foreign land and adopted Scythian life. When he asked me why I wanted to know, I told him that his Hellenic speech had prompted my curiosity. Then he smiled and said that he was born a Greek and had gone as a merchant to Viminacium, on the Danube, where he had stayed a long time, and married a very rich wife. But the city fell a prey to the barbarians, and he was [stripped] of his prosperity, and on account of his riches was allotted to Onegesius in the division of the spoil, as it was the custom among the Scythians for the chiefs to reserve for themselves the rich prisoners. Having fought bravely against the Romans and the Acatiri, he had paid the spoils he won to his master, and so obtained freedom. He then married a barbarian wife and had children, and had the privilege of eating at the table of Onegesius.

He considered his new life among the Scythians better than his old life among the Romans, and the reasons he gave were as follows: "After war the Scythians live in inactivity, enjoying what they have got, and not at all, or very little, harassed. The Romans, on the other hand, are in the first place very liable to perish in war, as they have to rest their hopes of safety on others, and are not allowed, on account of their *tyrants,* to use arms. And those who use them are injured by the cowardice of their generals, who cannot support the conduct of war. But the condition of the subjects in time of peace is far more grievous than the evils of war, for the exaction of the taxes is very severe, and unprincipled men inflict injuries on others, because the laws are practically not valid against all classes. A transgressor who belongs to the wealthy classes is not punished for his injustice, while a poor man, who does not understand business, undergoes the legal penalty, that is if he does not depart this life before the trial, so long is the course of lawsuits protracted, and so much money is expended on them. The climax of the misery is to have to pay in order to obtain justice. For no one will give a court to the injured man unless he pay a sum of money to the judge and the judge's clerks."

In reply to this attack on the Empire, I asked him to be good enough to listen with patience to the other side of the question. "The creators of the Roman republic," I said, "who were wise and good men, in order to prevent things from being done at haphazard, made one class of men guardians of the laws, and appointed another class to the profession of arms, who were to have no other object than to be always ready for battle, and to go forth to war without dread, as though to their ordinary exercise, having by practice exhausted all their fear beforehand. Others again were assigned to attend to the cultivation of the ground, to support both themselves and those who fight in their defence, by contributing the military corn-supply. * * * To those who protect the interests of the litigants a sum of money is paid by the latter, just as a payment is made by the farmers to the soldiers. Is it not fair to support him who assists and requite him for his kindness? The support of the horse benefits the horseman. * * * Those who spend money on a suit and lose it in the end cannot fairly put it down to anything but the injustice of their case. And as to the long time spent on lawsuits, that is due to concern for justice, that judges may not fail in passing correct judgments, by having to give sentence offhand; it is better that they should reflect, and conclude the case more tardily, than that by judging in a hurry they should both injure man and transgress against the Deity, the institutor of justice. * * * The Romans treat their servants better than the king of the Scythians treats his subjects. They deal with them as fathers or teachers, admonishing them to abstain from evil and follow the lines of conduct which they have esteemed honourable; they reprove them for their errors like their own children. They are not allowed, like the Scythians, to inflict death on them. They have numerous ways of conferring freedom; they can manumit not only during life, but also by their wills, and the testamentary wishes of a Roman in regard to his property are law."

My interlocutor shed tears, and confessed that the laws and constitution of the Romans were fair, but deplored that the governors, not possessing the spirit of former generations, were ruining the State.

Questions

1. What can be inferred from this passage about the organization of the Huns under Attila?

2. How does the Greek-speaking man whom Priscus meets argue that life among the Huns is better than among the Romans?

3. How does Priscus counter this and argue for the superiority of Roman ways?

Salvian of Marseilles, On the Governance of God (fifth century CE)

The fifth century CE was a very difficult time for the peoples of the western half of the Roman Empire. Imperial governing institutions weakened, the economy went into decline, and various "barbarian" peoples, most speaking Germanic languages, crossed the Roman frontiers and created kingdoms within former Roman provinces, including in North Africa. Making sense of the empire's troubles posed a major challenge to its inhabitants. One of these was Salvian of Marseilles (c. 400–c. 480 CE). He was born in Trier in modern Germany, not far from the Roman frontier with the German barbarians. In the fourth century Trier had been a major administrative center and a frequent residence for Roman emperors. Salvian eventually moved to Marseilles, an ancient port city on the Mediterranean, where he served as priest. There he wrote *The Governance of God*, in which he argued that the disasters of the fifth century were God's punishment of the Romans for their sins.

CRIMES OF THE RICH AND POWERFUL

As regards people in high places, of what does their dignity consist but in confiscating the property of the cities? As regards some whose names I do not mention, what is a prefecture, but a kind of plunder? There is no greater pillaging of the poor than that done by those in power. For this, office is bought by the few to be paid for by ravaging the many. What can be more disgraceful and wicked than this? The poor pay the purchase price for positions which they themselves do not buy. They are ignorant of the bargain, but know the amount paid. The world is turned upside down that the light of a few may become illustrious. The elevation of one man is the downfall of all the others. The cities of Spain know all about this, for they have nothing left them but their name. The cities of Africa know it—and they no longer exist. The cities of Gaul know it, for they are laid waste, but not by all their officials. They still hold a tenuous existence in a very few corners of the land, because the honesty of a few has temporarily supported those provinces which the ravages of the many have made void.

UNJUST REMISSION OF TAXATION

Now who can speak eloquently about the following robbery and crime: because the Roman state, if not already dead or at least drawing its last breath where it still has a semblance of life, is dying, strangled by the chains of taxation as if by the hands of brigands, a great number of rich can be found whose taxes are borne by the poor; that is to say there is found a great number of rich whose taxes

SOURCE: *From Roman to Merovingian Gaul: A Reader*, edited and translated by Alexander Callander Murray (Peterborough: Broadview Press, 2000), pp. 113–17.

kill the poor. I say many can be found. I am afraid I should more truly say all. So few, if there are any at all, are free from this crime that we can find almost all the rich in the category in which I said there were many.

Consider the remedies recently given to some cities. What this accomplished was to make all the rich immune and pile more taxes on the wretched poor. The old taxes were remitted for the benefit of the rich and new taxes imposed on the poor. The cancellation of the least type of taxation enriched the wealthy; the increase of the heaviest has made the poor suffer. The rich have become richer by lessening the obligations which they bore lightly; the poor are dying from the multiplication of the burdens which they were already unable to bear. Thus, the great remedy most unjustly exalted the one and most unjustly killed the other; to one it was a most wicked reward, to the other a most wicked poison. Hence it is I make the observation that there is nothing more vicious than the rich who are destroying the poor by their remedies, and none more unfortunate than the poor whom those things kill which are given as a remedy to all.

ROMANS AND BARBARIANS COMPARED

[Those who assert nothing is seen by God] say that if God watches over human affairs, if He cares for and loves and rules, why does He permit us to be weaker and more wretched than all other peoples? Why does He allow us to be conquered by the barbarians? Why does He allow us to be subject to the law of the enemy? Very briefly, as I have said before, He allows us to bear these evils because we deserve to suffer them. * * *

Someone says, so be it! Certainly we are sinners and evil. What cannot be denied is that we are better than the barbarians. By this also it is clear that God does not watch over human affairs, because, although we are better, we are subject to those who are worse. We will now see whether we are better than the barbarians. Certainly, there is no doubt that we should be better. For this very reason we are worse, if we who should be better are not better. The more honorable the position, the more criminal the fault. If the person of the sinner is the more honorable, the odium of his sin is also greater. * * *

* * * Therefore, because some men think it is unbearable that we are judged worse, or not even much better than the barbarians, let us see how, and of which barbarians we are better. For there are two kinds of barbarians in every nation: heretics and pagans. I say we are incomparably better than all these, therefore, insofar as it pertains to divine Law. In what pertains to life and the acts of life, I sorrow and weep that we are worse * * *. It profits us nothing that the Law is good if our life and way of life are not good. That the Law is good is a gift of Christ, but that our life is bad is the product of our own sin. * * *

Having put aside the prerogative of the Law, which either helps us not at all or condemns us by a just condemnation, let us compare the pursuits, morals, and vices of the barbarians with ours. The barbarians are unjust, and so are we. The barbarians are avaricious, and so are we. The barbarians are unfaithful, and so are we. The barbarians are greedy, and so are we. The barbarians are lewd, and so are we. The barbarians have all manner of wickedness and impurities, and so do we. * * *

COMPARISON WITH PAGANS

And by this we understand, as I have said above, that we who have and spurn the Law of God are much more culpable than those who neither have it nor know it at all. Nobody despises things which are unknown to him. * * * But we are scorners as well as transgressors of the Law and, accordingly, are worse than the pagans, for they do not know the commandments of God and we do. They do not have them, but we do. They do not follow commands which are unknown to them, but we trample underfoot what we know. Therefore, ignorance among them is transgression among us, because it is being guilty of a lesser crime to be ignorant of the commandments of God than to spurn them. * * *

Questions

1. What does Salvian see as the chief problems in the late Roman Empire?

2. What is his explanation for these problems?

3. How does Salvian use his comments on the "barbarians" as a way to criticize his Roman contemporaries?

Eusebius, The Conversion of Constantine to Christianity (fourth century CE)

One of the pivotal moments in the history of Christianity was the conversion of the Roman Emperor Constantine (c. 274–337 CE) to Christianity. Christianity became, first, the empire's favored religion, then its official religion, and finally the only legal religion (apart from Judaism, which had a tolerated inferior status). This description of Constantine's final conversion comes from Eusebius of Caesarea's *Life of Constantine*. Eusebius (c. 260–339 CE) was bishop of Caesarea, a town north of the modern Jaffa and Tel Aviv in Israel. He was a prominent figure in the ecclesiastical politics of the eastern half of the Roman Empire, and a man who knew the Emperor Constantine personally. In the passage below, Eusebius depicts Constantine on the eve of a battle with a pagan rival for control of the western half of the Roman Empire. The text suggests that at this point Constantine was already beginning to think of himself as a Christian. Eusebius's *Life* is a mixture of eulogy and hagiography, and avoids discussing anything negative about the emperor. The reliability of the text, and even its authorship by Eusebius, have been questioned by some historians.

CHAPTER XXVII.

* * *

Being convinced, however, that he needed some more powerful aid than his military forces could afford him, on account of the wicked and magical enchantments which were so diligently practised by the tyrant, [Constantine] began to seek for Divine assistance; deeming the possession of arms and a numerous soldiery of secondary importance, but trusting that the co-operation of a Deity would be his security against defeat or misfortune. He considered, therefore, on what God he might rely for protection and assistance. While engaged in this inquiry, the thought occurred to him, that, of the many emperors who had preceded him, those who had rested their hopes in a multitude of gods, and served them with sacrifices and offerings, had in the first place been deceived by flattering predictions, and oracles which promised them all prosperity, and at last had met with an unhappy end, while not one of their gods had stood by to warn them of the impending wrath of Heaven. On the other hand he recollected that his father, who had pursued an entirely opposite course, who had condemned their error, and honoured the one Supreme God during his whole life, had found Him to be the Saviour and Protector of his empire, and the Giver of every good thing. Reflecting on this, and well weighing the fact that they who had trusted in many gods had also fallen by manifold forms of death, without leaving behind them either family or offspring, stock, name, or memorial among men: and considering further that those who had already taken arms against the tyrant, and had marched to the battle field under the protection of a multitude of gods, had met with a dishonourable end (for one of them had shamefully retreated from the contest without a blow, and the other, being slain in the midst of his own troops, had become as it were the mere sport of death); reviewing, I say, all these considerations, he judged it to be folly indeed to join in the idle worship of those

SOURCE: Eusebius Pamphilus, *The Life of the Blessed Emperor Constantine, in Four Books, from 306 to 337 A.D.* (London: Samuel Bagster and Sons, 1845), pp. 25–30.

who were no gods, and, after such convincing evidence, to wander from the truth; and therefore felt it incumbent on him to honour no other than the God of his father.

CHAPTER XXVIII.

* * *

Accordingly he called on Him with earnest prayer and supplications that He would reveal to him who He was, and stretch forth His right hand to help him in his present difficulties. And while he was thus praying with fervent entreaty, a most marvellous sign appeared to him from heaven, the account of which it might have been difficult to receive with credit, had it been related by any other person. But since the victorious emperor himself long afterwards declared it to the writer of this history, when he was honoured with his acquaintance and society, and confirmed his statement by an oath, who could hesitate to accredit the relation, especially since the testimony of after-time has established its truth? He said that about mid-day, when the sun was beginning to decline, he saw with his own eyes the trophy of a cross of light in the heavens, above the sun, and bearing the inscription, CONQUER BY THIS. At this sight he himself was struck with amazement, and his whole army also, which happened to be following him on some expedition, and witnessed the miracle.

CHAPTER XXIX.

* * *

He said, moreover, that he doubted within himself what the import of this apparition could be. And while he continued to ponder and reason on its meaning, night imperceptibly drew on; and in his sleep the Christ of God appeared to him with the same sign which he had seen in the heavens, and commanded him to procure a standard made in the likeness of that sign, and to use it as a safeguard in all engagements with his enemies.

CHAPTER XXX.

* * *

At dawn of day he arose, and communicated the secret to his friends: and then, calling together the workers in gold and precious stones, he sat in the midst of them, and described to them the figure of the sign he had seen, bidding them represent it in gold and precious stones. And this representation I myself have had an opportunity of seeing.

CHAPTER XXXI.

* * *

Now it was made in the following manner. A long spear, overlaid with gold, formed the figure of the cross by means of a piece transversely laid over it. On the top of the whole was fixed a crown, formed by the intertexture of gold and precious stones; and on this, two letters indicating the name of Christ, symbolized the Saviour's title by means of its first characters, the letter P being intersected by X [the first two letters of Christ in Greek] exactly in its centre: and these letters the emperor was in the habit of wearing on his helmet at a later period. From the transverse piece which crossed the spear was suspended a kind of streamer of purple cloth, covered with a profuse embroidery of most brilliant precious stones; and which, being also richly interlaced with gold, presented an indescribable degree of beauty to the beholder. This banner was of a square form, and the upright staff, which in its full extent was of great length, bore a golden half-length portrait of the pious emperor and his children on its upper part, beneath the trophy of the cross, and immediately above the embroidered streamer.

The emperor constantly made use of this salutary sign as a safeguard against every adverse and hostile power, and commanded that others similar to it should be carried at the head of all his armies.

CHAPTER XXXII.

These things were done shortly afterwards. But at the time above specified, being struck with amazement at the extraordinary vision, and resolving to worship no other God save Him who had appeared to him, he sent for those who were acquainted with the mysteries of His doctrines, and inquired who that God was, and what was intended by the sign of the vision he had seen.

They affirmed that He was God, the only begotten Son of the one and only God: that the sign which had appeared was the symbol of immortality, and the trophy of that victory over death which He had gained in time past when sojourning on earth. They taught him also the causes of His advent, and explained to him the true account of His incarnation. Thus he sought instruction in these matters, but was still impressed with wonder at the divine manifestation which had been presented to his sight. Comparing, therefore, the heavenly vision with the interpretation given, he found his judgment confirmed; and, in the persuasion that the knowledge of these things had been imparted to him by Divine teaching, he determined thenceforth to devote himself to the perusal of the Inspired writings.

Moreover, he made the priests of God his counsellors, and deemed it incumbent on him to honour the God who had appeared to him with all devotion. And after this, being fortified by well-grounded hopes in Him, he undertook to quench the fury of the fire of tyranny.

Questions

1. What is the process by which Constantine decided to convert? What roles did "reason" and revelation play in his decision?

2. How did Constantine conceive of religion? What effects does correct belief have in this world? How are politics related to religion in the emperor's mind?

3. What was the role of Christian believers in the emperor's conversion?

Gregory of Tours, On the Conversion of Clovis to Christianity (sixth century CE)

In many ways the most important legacy of the Roman Empire to medieval Europe was the Christian church, "the noblest Roman of them all." Indeed, in the centuries after the disintegration of the western half of the Roman Empire, Christianity made considerable progress in converting new peoples. Among these were the pagan Franks, a Germanic people who had lived on the northern frontier of the province of Gaul. In the fourth century CE imperial authorities allowed them to settle in what is today Belgium. In the fifth century one of their kings, Clovis (c. 466–511 CE), defeated rival Frankish kings and the last Romans exercising rule in northern Gaul. He fought a series of wars against other Germanic peoples, including the Alemanni, the Visigoths, the Thuringians and the Saxons. By the time of his death he had made the Franks the dominant political power in western Europe. He converted to Christianity some time in the last decade of the fifth century or the first decade of the sixth. This description of his baptism comes from Gregory (538–594 CE), Bishop of Tours. Gregory's *History of the Franks* is one of the most important sources for the history of the earlier middle ages. Note that he is writing almost a century after the events he describes.

———————

At this time [AD 486] the army of Clovis pillaged many churches, for he was still sunk in the errors of idolatry. The soldiers had borne away from a church, with all the other ornaments of the holy ministry, a vase of marvelous size and beauty. The bishop of this church sent messengers to the king, begging that if the church might not recover any other of the holy vessels, at least this one might be restored. The king, hearing these things, replied to the messenger: "Follow thou us to Soissons, for there all things that have been acquired are to be divided. If the lot shall give me this vase, I will do what the bishop desires."

———————

SOURCE: James Harvey Robinson, *Readings in European History* (Boston: Ginn, 1904), vol. 1, pp. 51–55.

When he had reached Soissons, and all the booty had been placed in the midst of the army, the king pointed to this vase, and said: "I ask you, O most valiant warriors, not to refuse to me the vase in addition to my rightful part." Those of discerning mind among his men answered, "O glorious king, all things which we see are thine, and we ourselves are subject to thy power; now do what seems pleasing to thee, for none is strong enough to resist thee." When they had thus spoken one of the soldiers, impetuous, envious, and vain, raised his battle-ax aloft and crushed the vase with it, crying, "Thou shalt receive nothing of this unless a just lot give it to thee." At this all were stupefied.

The king bore his injury with the calmness of patience, and when he had received the crushed vase he gave it to the bishop's messenger; but he cherished a hidden wound in his breast. When a year had passed he ordered the whole army to come fully equipped to the Campus Martius and show their arms in brilliant array. But when he had reviewed them all he came to the breaker of the vase, and said to him, "No one bears his arms so clumsily as thou; for neither thy spear, nor thy sword, nor thy ax is ready for use." And seizing his ax, he cast it on the ground. And when the soldier had bent a little to pick it up the king raised his hands and crushed his head with his own ax. "Thus," he said, "didst thou to the vase at Soissons."

[Clovis took to wife Clotilde, daughter of the king of the Burgundians. Now Clotilde was a Christian. When her first son was born] she wished to consecrate him by baptism, and begged her husband unceasingly, saying, "The gods whom thou honorest are nothing; they cannot help themselves nor others; for they are carved from stone, or from wood, or from some metal. The names which you have given them were of men, not of gods,—like Saturn, who is said to have escaped by flight, to avoid being deprived of his power by his son; and like Jupiter himself, foul perpetrator of all uncleanness. * * * What power have Mars and Mercury ever had? They are endowed with magical arts rather than divine power.

"The God who should be worshiped is he who by his word created from nothingness the heavens and the earth, the sea and all that in them is; he who made the sun to shine and adorned the sky with stars; who filled the waters with creeping things, the land with animals, the air with winged creatures; by whose bounty the earth is glad with crops, the trees with fruit, the vines with grapes; by whose hand the human race was created; whose bounty has ordained that all things should give homage and service to man, whom he created."

But when the queen had said these things, the mind of Clovis was not stirred to believe. He answered: "By the will of our gods all things are created and produced. Evidently your god can do nothing, and it is not even proved that he belongs to the race of gods."

Meantime the faithful queen presented her son for baptism. She had the church adorned with tapestry, seeking to attract by this splendor him whom her exhortations had not moved. But the child whom they called Ingomer, after he had been born again through baptism, died in his white baptismal robe. Then the king reproached the queen bitterly. "If the child had been consecrated in the name of my gods he would be alive still. But now, because he is baptized in the name of your god, he cannot live." * * *

After this another son was born to him, and called in baptism Clodomir. He fell very ill. Then the king said: "Because he, like his brother, was baptized in the name of Christ, he must soon die." But his mother prayed, and by God's will the child recovered.

The queen unceasingly urged the king to acknowledge the true God, and forsake idols. But he could not in any wise be brought to believe until a war broke out with the Alemanni. Then he was by necessity compelled to confess what he had before willfully denied.

It happened that the two armies were in battle, and there was great slaughter. Clovis' army was near to utter destruction. He saw the danger; his heart was stirred; he was moved to tears, and he raised his eyes to heaven, saying: "Jesus Christ, whom Clotilde declares to be the son of the living God, who it is said givest aid to the oppressed, and victory to those who put their hope in thee, I beseech the glory of thy aid. If thou shalt grant me victory over these enemies and I test that power which people consecrated to thy name say they have proved concerning thee, I will believe in thee and be baptized in thy name. For I have called upon my gods, but, as I have proved, they are far removed from my aid. So I believe that they have no power, for they do not succor those who serve them. Now I call upon thee, and I long to believe in thee—all the more that I may escape my enemies."

When he had said these things, the Alemanni turned their backs and began to flee. When they saw that their king was killed, they submitted to the sway of Clovis, saying: "We wish that no more people should perish. Now we are thine." When the king had forbidden further war, and praised his soldiers, he told the queen how he had won the victory by calling on the name of Christ.

Then the queen sent to the blessed Remigius, bishop of the city of Rheims, praying him to bring to the king the gospel of salvation. The priest, little by little and secretly, led him to believe in the true God, maker of heaven and earth, and to forsake idols, which could not help him nor anybody else.

But the king said: "Willingly will I hear thee, O father; but one thing is in the way—that the people who follow me are not content to leave their gods. I will go and speak to them according to thy word."

When he came among them, the power of God went before him, and before he had spoken all the people cried out together: "We cast off mortal gods, O righteous king, and we are ready to follow the God whom Remigius tells us is immortal."

These things were told to the bishop. He was filled with joy, and ordered the font to be prepared. The streets were shaded with embroidered hangings; the churches were adorned with white tapestries, the baptistery was set in order, the odor of balsam spread around, candles gleamed, and all the temple of the baptistery was filled with divine odor. * * * Then the king confessed the God omnipotent in the Trinity, and was baptized in the name of the Father, and of the Son, and of the Holy Ghost, and was anointed with the sacred chrism with the sign of the cross of Christ. Of his army there were baptized more than three thousand.

Questions

1. What is Clovis's conception of religion? What benefits does right belief bring; what evils result from wrong belief?

2. Who plays the principal role in converting Clovis to Christianity? What does this tell us about the conversion process in general?

3. Why do Clovis's followers decide to receive baptism?

Taming Frontier Deities in China (third–tenth centuries CE)

These tales are typical of a large body of local legends from roughly the third- to tenth-century China. (In some frontier areas, they appear later.) In all of them a powerful local deity faces off against a man of culture and virtue who comes in from outside, often an imperial official or candidate for office, but sometimes a Buddhist or Daoist clergyman. The local deity is sometimes represented as an aristocrat, sometimes as a monster, and sometimes as a dangerous natural force, such as a plague or a river subject to powerful floods. Sometimes he can assume all of these identities, and often, as in the second story here, he requires live sacrifices from the community. (In fact, human sacrifice was very rare, though not nonexistent, in imperial China.)

"The Magistrate and the Local Deity" is the older of these two tales, definitely already known in the period of disunion between the end of the Han (220 CE) and the beginning of the Sui (589 CE). "Yu guai lu" dates from some time during the Tang dynasty (618–907 CE). (There was a famous official named Guo Yuanzhen during the Tang, but his biography doesn't match up well with this tale.) In general, earlier tales, like the first one here, tend to end in the defeat of the outsider, and later ones in his victory. Many of the victorious heroes—though certainly not all of them—were later enshrined as local "city gods": deities specific to one county, with a temple in the county capital. They were generally represented as the supernatural counterpart of the imperial magistrate or other official based in that town. Spelling has been updated in the following excerpts to reflect modern orthography.

SOURCE: Hsien-i Yang, *The Man Who Sold a Ghost: Chinese Tales of the 3rd–6th Centuries* (Peking: Foreign Languages Press, 1958), pp. 100–101, and E. D. Edwards, *Chinese Prose Literature of the T'ang Period A.D. 618–906.* (London: Arthur Probsthain, 1938), vol. 2, pp. 248–52.

THE MAGISTRATE AND THE LOCAL DEITY

Zhen Chong, a native of Zhongshan, was appointed magistrate of Yuntu. On his way to his post he was informed that the son of the local deity wished to call on him. Soon a young, handsome god arrived and they exchanged the usual courtesies.

"I am here at my father's behest," announced the young god. "He longs to be allied to your noble house, and hopes you will take my younger sister in marriage. I have come to bring you this message."

"I am past my prime and have one wife already." Zhen was taken aback. "How can I do such a thing?"

"My sister is young and remarkably beautiful. We must find a good match for her. How can you refuse?"

"I am old and have a wife. It would not be right."

They argued back and forth several times, but Zhen remained adamant. The young god looked put out.

"Then my father will come himself," he said. "I doubt if you can refuse him."

He left, followed on both banks of the river by a large retinue of attendants with caps and whips.

Soon the local deity arrived in person with an equipage like a baron's. His carriage had a dark-green canopy and red reins and was escorted by several chariots. His daughter rode in an open carriage with several dozen silk pennants and eight maids before it, all of them dressed in embroidered gowns more splendid than mortal eye has ever seen. They pitched a tent on the bank near Zhen and spread a carpet. Then the deity alighted and sat by a low table on a white woollen rug. He had a jade spittoon, a hat-box of tortoise-shell and a white fly-whisk. His daughter remained on the east bank, with eunuchs carrying whisks at her side and maids in front. The local deity ordered his assistant officers, some sixty of them, to sit down before him, and called for music. The instruments they used seemed to be of glass.

"I have a humble daughter dear to my heart," said the deity. "Since you come of a renowned and virtuous family, we are eager to be connected with you by marriage. That is why I sent my son with this request."

"I am old and my health is failing," replied Zhen Chong. "I already have a wife and my son is quite big. Much as I am tempted by this proffered honour, I must beg to decline."

"My daughter is twenty," continued the deity. "She is beautiful and gentle, and possesses all the virtues. As she is now on the bank, there is no need for any preparations. The wedding can take place at once."

Still Zhen Chong stood out stubbornly, and even called the deity an evil spirit. He drew his sword and laid it on his knees, determined to resist to the death, and refused to discuss the matter any further. The local deity flew into a passion. He summoned three leopards and two tigers, which opened wide their crimson mouths and shook the earth with their roars as they leaped at Zhen. They attacked several dozen times, but Zhen held them at bay till dawn when the deity withdrew, thwarted. He left behind one carriage and several dozen men to wait for Zhen, however. Then Zhen moved into the Huihuai County office. The waiting carriage and men followed him in, and a man in plain clothes and cap bowed to him and advised him to stay there and not go any further.

Zhen Chong did not dare leave for another ten days. Even then he was followed home by a man in a cap with a whip. And he had not been back many days before his wife contracted an illness and died.

Yu guai lu

In the early part of the 8th century A.D. Guo Yuanzhen returning home after failing in the official examination, was on the road from Qin to Fên one night when he lost his way. After wandering about for a long time, he saw a light in the distance. Thinking it must indicate some sort of human habitation he hastened forward and found himself before a lofty and imposing mansion. The rooms were brightly lighted and he could see a wedding-feast spread, but all was silent and deserted. He tethered his horse, and approached the main hall.

As he hesitated at the door, wondering where he was, he heard sounds of sobbing from a room somewhere on the east side of the house.

"Is it a human or a demon there?" he cried. "Why do you weep so bitterly?"

"I am being offered as a sacrifice," replied a tearful voice. "General Wu, who holds the fortunes of this village in his hands, demands a new bride every year and the people are forced to give him a beautiful maiden. Though I am ugly and stupid, my father, being in debt, has been obliged to let them make me the victim. This evening the wedding-feast was prepared and I was beguiled into this room, locked in, and left to await the general. Now that my parents have cast me out what is left but death? I am so frightened! If you have the courage to save me I will serve you with the faithfulness of a wife as long as I live."

Deeply moved, Guo asked when the general would arrive.

"At the second watch," replied the girl.

"I will play the man and save you!" he cried. "I would rather die than allow you to fall into the hands of this licentious demon."

Gradually the sobbing ceased. Guo sat on the western steps and ordered a man to lead his horse to the back of the house, and another to stand in front as if on duty. Before long General Wu appeared with his attendants, and after a preliminary exchange of courtesies he and Guo sat down to table, wine and laughter flowing freely. Guo had a dagger in his wallet but lacked an excuse to use it, so presently he inquired:

"Are you fond of dried venison, General?"

"One can never get it in this district," replied the other.

"I have a small portion which came from the imperial kitchen," Guo returned. "May I cut you a piece?"

The general was delighted. Guo took out the venison and the dagger, and cut several slices. These he laid upon a small dish, and the general, invited to help himself and suspecting nothing, stretched out his hand to take a piece. Seizing the moment when he was off his guard, Guo threw down the venison, gripped his wrist, and cut off his hand.

The general fled with a yell, and his terrified followers scattered in all directions. Wrapping the hand in his cloak, Guo dispatched a man to look for the general and his party, but they had all vanished. He then knocked and called to the maiden to come out and have something to eat.

"I have the general's hand here," he called, "and judging by the blood-tracks, he will soon die and you will be safe."

The maiden came out and Guo saw a pretty girl of about seventeen.

"I pledge myself to be your handmaid and obey your orders," she said bowing low to her rescuer.

As soon as it was light they opened the cloak, but inside, instead of a hand they found a pig's foot! Soon the sound of wailing announced the approach of the girl's relatives and the village elders bringing a coffin for her corpse. Seeing her alive they demanded an explanation. When Guo told the story they were furious with him for injuring their patron spirit.

"General Wu was the guardian of the village," they cried. "We have always sacrificed to him, and so long as we give him a bride once a year we are safe, but if we fail he will send tempests to destroy us. Shall a chance wayfarer be allowed to wound our patron and injure our people? We will not submit to it! Let the stranger be sacrificed to General Wu!"

Quickly they bound Guo, and were about to hale him before the magistrate when he began to cry out on them for their folly in serving a spirit who preferred evil to good.

"If he were a good spirit, would he have a pig's foot? And if he is only a licentious brute, was I not right to slay him? How do you know that I was not sent expressly to rid you of this vile beast? Listen to my words and let me destroy for ever this incubus which you maintain."

Perceiving the truth of these arguments the elders gathered several hundred men armed with bows and arrows, swords, spears, spades and bill-hooks, and set out to pursue the general. Guided by the blood-tracks they came at length to a cave, and having enlarged the opening, they gathered quantities of brushwood and set fire to it outside. Peering in, Guo could see a great boar with its left forefoot cut off and blood soaking the ground round about it. Driven out by the smoke, the beast rushed forth and was quickly dispatched. The villagers then wished to reward Guo, but he would accept nothing, nor would he allow them to entertain him.

"I am a righter of wrongs," he said, preparing to depart, "not a hunter to be hired."

The rescued maiden bade farewell to her relatives.

"But for this man," she told them, "I should not be alive to-day. You sacrificed me to a loathsome beast, and left me to die. To you therefore I am dead henceforth, and from this moment I begin to live for Guo. My one desire is to go with him and never more remember my native place."

With tears streaming from her eyes, and deaf to the kindly words with which he tried to dissuade her, she followed Guo. Yielding at last, he took her with him and she became his concubine, bearing him many sons. In after years he rose to high rank, and occupied the most exalted posts in the administration.

It is apparent that that which is fore-ordained must befall a man, however remote he may live, and demons notwithstanding.

Questions

1. What different kinds of power does the deity in "The Magistrate and the Local Deity" possess? Why is it significant that he combines these attributes? How does the struggle between him and Zhen Chong end?

2. How is the general/demon in "Yu guai lu" like and unlike the local deity in the other story? How is Guo Yuanzhen like and unlike Zhen Chong?

3. In both stories, the deity wants to arrange a marriage with a human. Why? What does this suggest in each case?

4. What role do the community elders play in "Yu guai lu"? How do Guo and the maiden react to them?

5. What kinds of social, political, and cultural change might these tales (which were especially common in parts of China subordinated to the empire relatively recently) represent?

6. In some tales like this, the beast is not destroyed but tamed, and becomes a servant or bodyguard to the conqueror. What might that ending do to the meaning of a story like "Yu guai lu"?

Han Yu, Memorial on the Bone of the Buddha (819 CE)

Buddhism arrived in China (via central Asian merchants) during the first century CE, and initially spread slowly. But by the time that Sui Wendi (581–618 CE) reunified the Chinese Empire, Buddhism had become very popular, and the dynasty publicly supported Buddhist temples, clerics, and text-copying projects. The Tang dynasty (618–907 CE) extended this patronage; among other things, Buddhism provided a set of religious and cultural practices that the hybrid Chinese and central Asian elite of the Tang court could share. (By contrast, the practices we call "Confucian" and "Daoist" had little resonance for central Asian society.)

But the relative merits of different religious traditions were always controversial; so were the expensive gifts, tax exemptions and other privileges given to Buddhist and Daoist establishments. After the An Lushan Rebellion (755–763 CE), started by a general of Turkish origin, some elites turned against what they considered excessive foreign influence, seeking alternative models in the Chinese past.

Han Yu (768–824 CE), a high-ranking official and leading intellectual, was probably the most important advocate of this "back to the classics" movement, promoting ancient models for prose writing, ritual, and political institutions. This essay, written in 819 CE to protest imperial celebration of the arrival of a Buddhist relic, got him sentenced to exile on the empire's southern frontier. But in 845 CE, another emperor greatly reduced state support for Buddhism; the succeeding Song dynasty (960–1279) gave Confucianism the central place in official culture, which it retained until the twentieth century. Subsequent generations of Chinese scholars generally celebrated Han Yu as a pioneer of this Confucian (or, as Westerners later called it, Neo-Confucian) revival.

Your servant begs leave to say that Buddhism is no more than a cult of the barbarian peoples, which spread to China in the time of

SOURCE: *Sources of Chinese Tradition*, 2nd ed., compiled by Wm. Theodore de Bary and Irene Bloom et al. (New York: Columbia University Press, 1999), vol. 1, pp. 583–85.

the Latter Han. It did not exist here in ancient times. * * * When Emperor Gaozu [founder of the Tang] received the throne from the House of Sui, he deliberated upon the suppression of Buddhism. But at that time the various officials, being of small worth and knowledge, were unable fully to comprehend the ways of the ancient kings and the exigencies of past and present, and so could not implement the wisdom of the emperor and rescue the age from corruption. Thus the matter came to naught, to your servant's constant regret.

Now Your Majesty, wise in the arts of peace and war, unparalleled in divine glory from countless ages past, upon your accession prohibited men and women from taking Buddhist orders and forbade the erection of temples and monasteries, and your servant believed that at Your Majesty's hand the will of Gaozu would be carried out. Even if the suppression of Buddhism should be as yet impossible, your servant hardly thought that Your Majesty would encourage it and, on the contrary, cause it to spread. Yet now your servant hears that Your Majesty has ordered the community of monks to go to Fengxiang to greet the bone of Buddha, that Your Majesty will ascend a tower to watch as it is brought into the palace, and that the various temples have been commanded to welcome and worship it in turn. Though your servant is abundantly ignorant, he understands that Your Majesty is not so misled by Buddhism as to honor it thus in hopes of receiving some blessing or reward, but only that, the year being one of plenty and the people joyful, Your Majesty would accord with the hearts of the multitude in setting forth for the officials and citizens of the capital some curious show and toy for their amusement. * * * But the common people are ignorant and dull, easily misled and hard to enlighten, and should they see their emperor do these things they might say that Your Majesty was serving Buddhism with a true heart. "The Son of Heaven is a Great Sage," they would cry, "and yet he reverences and believes with all his heart! How should we, the common people, then begrudge our bodies and our lives?" Then would they set about singeing their heads and scorching their fingers, binding together in groups of ten and a hundred, doffing their common clothes and scattering their money, from morning to evening urging each other on lest one be slow, until old and young alike had abandoned their occupations to follow [Buddhism]. * * * Then will our old ways be corrupted, our customs violated, and the tale will spread to make us the mockery of the world. This is no trifling matter!

Now Buddha was a man of the barbarians who did not speak the language of China and wore clothes of a different fashion. His sayings did not concern the ways of our ancient kings, nor did his manner of dress conform to their laws. He understood neither the duties that bind sovereign and subject nor the affections of father and son. If he were still alive today and came to our court by order of his ruler, Your Majesty might condescend to receive him, but [it would amount to no more than one audience in the Xuancheng Hall, a banquet by the office for receiving guests, the presentation of a suit of clothes, and] he would then be escorted to the borders of the state, dismissed, and not allowed to delude the masses. How then, when he has long been dead, could his rotten bones, the foul and unlucky remains of his body, be rightly admitted to the palace? * * * Now without reason Your Majesty has caused this loathsome thing to be brought in and would personally go to view it. * * * The host of officials have not spoken out against this wrong, and the censors have failed to note its impropriety. Your servant is deeply shamed and begs that this bone be given to the proper authorities to be cast into fire and water, that this evil may be rooted out, the world freed from its error, and later generations spared this delusion. Then may all men know how the acts of their wise sovereign transcend the commonplace a thousandfold. Would this not be glorious? Would it not be joyful?

Should the Buddha indeed have supernatural power to send down curses and calamities, may they fall only upon the person of your servant, who calls upon high Heaven to witness that he does not regret his words. With all gratitude and sincerity your servant presents this memorial for consideration, being filled with respect and awe.

Questions

1. What does Han Yu say about the effects of welcoming the Buddha bone? About the Buddha himself?

2. What sorts of precedents does Han Yu try to get the emperor to heed?

3. Why do you think Han Yu became such a great hero to later generations of non-Buddhist Chinese intellectuals?

Chapter 9

New Empires and Common Cultures, 600–1000 CE

Quranic Comments on the Torah and the Gospels (early seventh century CE)

One of the chief issues that early Islam had to deal with was its relation to the preexisting monotheistic religions. Muhammad saw himself as the last in a line of prophets sent by God, which included the Jewish patriarchs and Jesus of Nazareth. This became particularly acute when Muslims began to rule over large populations of Jews, Christians, and Zoroastrians. In general, there have been two schools of thought in Islam about the other monotheistic religions. One line of interpretation held that Christians, Jews, and other "people of the book," despite having neglected and altered the messages they had received from their prophets, could achieve salvation in their own religions. Another held that Muhammad's revelation had superseded and abrogated previous revelations and that salvation was possible only in Islam. The source Muslims have for guidance on these issues is the Quran, which Muslims regard as the direct, unmediated word of God delivered to Muhammad. Islam holds that Alah revealed the Quran to Muhammad through the angel Jibrīl (Gabriel) starting around 610 CE and continuing until Muhammad's death in 632. The following passage is Sura (chapter) 5, verses 43–48.

43. But why should they make you a judge when the Torah is with them which contains the Law of God? Even then they turn away. They are those who will never believe.

[44.] We sent down the Torah which contains guidance and light, in accordance with which the prophets who were obedient (to God) gave instructions to the Jews, as did the rabbis and priests, for they were the custodians and witnesses of God's writ. So, therefore, do not fear men, fear Me, and barter not My messages away for a paltry gain. Those who do not judge by God's revelations are infidels indeed.

45. And there (in the Torah) We had ordained for them a life for a life, and an eye for an eye, and a nose for a nose, and an ear for an ear, and a tooth for a tooth, and for wounds retribution, though he who forgoes it out of charity, atones for his sins. And those who do not judge by God's revelations are unjust.

46. Later, in the train (of the prophets), We sent Jesus, son of Mary, confirming the Torah which had been (sent down) before him, and gave him the Gospel containing guidance and light, which corroborated the earlier Torah, a guidance and warning for those who preserve themselves from evil and follow the straight path.

47. Let the people of the Gospel judge by what has been revealed in it by God. And those who do not judge in accordance with what God has revealed are transgressors.

48. And to you We have revealed the Book containing the truth, confirming the earlier revelations, and preserving them (from change and corruption). So judge between them by what has been revealed by God, and do not follow their whims, side-stepping the truth that has reached you. To each of you We have given a law and a way and a pattern of life. If God had pleased He could surely have made you one people (professing one faith). But He wished to try and test you by that which He gave you. So try to excel in good deeds. To Him will you all return in the end, when He will tell you of what you were at variance.

SOURCE: *Al-Qur'ān: A Contemporary Translation*, translated by Ahmed Ali (Princeton: Princeton University Press, 1993), pp. 103–4.

Questions

1. What is the understanding of Christianity and Judaism that appears in this text?

2. How does this passage portray the relationship between Judaism and Christianity?

3. What is the relationship of Judaism and Christianity to Islam? Is it necessary for someone to become a Muslim to worship God correctly?

Ibn Ishaq, Biography of Messenger of God (eighth century CE)

After the death of the Prophet Muhammad in 632 CE, the members of the Muslim community maintained many traditions about his life. In the eighth century the Muslim scholar Muhammad ibn Ishaq ibn Yasār collected many of these and wrote the first biography of Muhammad, *The Life of God's Messenger*. The original of this work has been lost, but much of it is preserved in the abbreviated edition put together by Ibn Hisham (died 827 CE). The following passage describes how Muhammad, who had made a practice of retiring to a cave on Mount Hira near Mecca for reflection and contemplation, began receiving the divine revelation of the Quran.

When Muhammad the apostle of God reached the age of forty God sent him in compassion to mankind, "as an evangelist to all men." Now God had made a covenant with every prophet whom he had sent before him that he should believe in him, testify to his truth and help him against his adversaries, and he required of them that they should transmit that to everyone who believed in them, and they carried out their obligations in that respect. God

SOURCE: Ibn Ishaq, *The Life of Muhammad*, translated by A. Guillaume (Karachi: Oxford University Press, 1967), pp. 104–7.

said to Muhammad, "When God made a covenant with the prophets (He said) this is the scripture and wisdom which I have given you, afterwards an apostle will come confirming what you know that you may believe in him and help him." He said, "Do you accept this and take up my burden?" i.e. the burden of my agreement which I have laid upon you. They said, "We accept it." He answered, "Then bear witness and I am a witness with you." Thus God made a covenant with all the prophets that they should testify to his truth and help him against his adversaries and they transmitted that obligation to those who believed in them among the two monotheistic religions.

* * *

The apostle would pray in seclusion on Ḥirā' every year for a month to practise *taḥannuth* as was the custom of Quraysh in heathen days. *Taḥannuth* is religious devotion.

* * *

Wahb b. Kaisān told me that "Ubayd said to him: Every year during that month the apostle would pray in seclusion and give food to the poor that came to him. And when he completed the month and returned from his seclusion, first of all before entering his house he would go to the Ka'ba and walk round it seven times or as often as it pleased God; then he would go back to his house until in the year when God sent him, in the month of Ramaḍān in which God willed concerning him what He willed of His grace, the apostle set forth to Ḥirā" as was his wont, and his family with him. When it was the night on which God honoured him with his mission and showed mercy on His servants thereby, Gabriel brought him the command of God. "He came to me," said the apostle of God, "while I was asleep, with a coverlet of brocade whereon was some writing, and said, "Read!" I said 'What shall I read?' He pressed me with it so tightly that I thought it was death; then he let me go and said, 'Read!' I said, 'What shall I read?' He pressed me with it again so that I thought it was death; then he let me go and said 'Read!' I said, 'What shall I read?' He pressed me with it the third time so that I thought it was death and said 'Read!' I said, 'What then shall I read?'—and this I said only to deliver myself from him, lest he should do the same to me again. He said:

'Read in the name of thy Lord who created,
Who created man of blood coagulated.
Read! Thy Lord is the most beneficent,
Who taught by the pen,
Taught that which they knew not unto men.'

So I read it, and he departed from me. And I awoke from my sleep, and it was as though these words were written on my heart. (T. Now none of God's creatures was more hateful to me than an (ecstatic) poet or a man possessed: I could not even look at them. I thought, Woe is me poet or possessed—Never shall Quraysh say this of me! I will go to the top of the mountain and throw myself down that I may kill myself and gain rest. So I went forth to do so and then) when I was midway on the mountain, I heard a voice from heaven saying, 'O Muhammad! thou art the apostle of God and I am Gabriel.' I raised my head towards heaven to see (who was speaking), and lo, Gabriel in the form of a man with feet astride the horizon saying, 'O Muhammad! thou art the apostle of God and I am Gabriel.' I stood gazing at him, (T. and that turned me from my purpose) moving neither forward nor backward; then I began to turn my face away from him, but towards whatever region of the sky I looked, I saw him as before. And I continued standing there, neither advancing nor turning back until Khadīja sent her messengers in search of me and they gained the high ground above Mecca and returned to her while I was standing in the same place; then he parted from me and I from him, returning to my family. And I came to Khadīja and sat by her thigh and drew close to her. She said, 'O Abū'l-Qāsim, where hast thou been? By God, I sent my messengers in search of thee, and they reached the high ground above Mecca and returned to me.' (T. I said to her, 'Woe is me poet or possessed. She said, 'I take refuge in God from that O Abūl-Qāsim. God would not treat you thus since he knows your truthfulness, your great trustworthiness, your fine character, and your kindness. This cannot be, my dear. Perhaps you did see something.' 'Yes, I did,' I said.) Then I told her of what I had seen; and she said, 'Rejoice, O son of my uncle, and be of good heart. Verily, by Him in whose hand is Khadīja's soul, I have hope that thou wilt be the prophet of this people.'" Then she rose and gathered her garments about her and set forth to her cousin Waraqa b. Naufal b. Asad b. 'Abdu'l-'Uzzā b. Quṣayy, who had become a Christian and read the scriptures and learned from those that follow the Torah and the Gospel. And when she related to him what the apostle of God told her he had seen and heard, Waraqa cried, "Holy! Holy! Verily by Him in whose hand is Waraqa's soul, if thou hast spoken to me the truth, O Khadīja, there hath come unto him the greatest Nāmūs (Ṭ. meaning Gabriel) who came to Moses afore-time, and lo, he is the prophet of this people. Bid him be of good heart." So Khadīja returned to the apostle of God and told him what Waraqa had said. (Ṭ. and that calmed his fears somewhat.) And when the apostle of God had finished his period of seclusion and returned (to Mecca), in the first place he performed the circum-ambulation of the Ka'ba, as was his wont. While he was doing it, Waraqa met him and said, "O son of my brother, tell me what thou hast seen and heard." The apostle told him, and Waraqa said, "Surely, by Him in whose hand is Waraqa's soul, thou art the prophet of this people. There hath come unto thee the greatest Nāmūs, who came unto Moses. Thou wilt be called a liar, and they will use thee despitefully and cast thee out and fight against thee. Verily, if I live to see that day, I will help God in such wise as He knoweth." Then he brought his head near to him and kissed his forehead; and the apostle went to his own house.

Questions

1. What convinces Muhammad that his visions are truly from God?

2. What is the importance of texts and literacy to Muhammad's mission?

3. How is Muhammad's relation to previous prophets portrayed?

Pact of Umar (ninth century CE)

In the years immediately after the death of the prophet Muhammad Muslims launched a series of military expeditions against the Byzantine and the Persian Sassanian empires. Whether these were intended as wars of conquest or merely raids is not clear. However, they were fabulously successful. By the mid-seventh century CE the Muslims had defeated the Byzantines and destroyed the Persian Empire. Muslim rule extended from Afghanistan to North Africa, with Iran, Iraq, Syria, and Egypt all under their control. Within a very short time a small number of Muslims had become masters of millions of Jews, Christians, and Zoroastrians. One of the major tasks the Muslim community faced was working out its relationship with these groups. Eventually the Muslims devised an arrangement by which these "people of the book" became *dhimmis*. In return for payment of a special tax known as *jizya*, they were allowed to practice their religions. Various restrictions were also imposed on them. The following document reflects this process. According to traditional Islamic historiography, it was an arrangement reached by the Caliph Umar II (c. 682 CE–720 CE) with his Christian subjects. Most Western historians believe it was actually composed at a later time, probably in the ninth century, by jurists who attributed it to Umar. Spelling has been updated in the following excerpt to reflect modern orthography.

———

In the name of God, the Merciful, the Compassionate!

This is a writing to Umar from the Christians of such and such a city. When you [Muslims] marched against us [Christians], we asked of you protection for ourselves, our posterity, our possessions, and our co-religionists; and we made this stipulation with you, that we will not erect in our city or the suburbs any new monastery, church, cell or hermitage; that we will not repair any of such buildings that may fall into ruins, or renew those that may be situated in the Muslim quarters of the town; that we will not refuse the Muslims entry into our churches either by night or by day; that we will open the

SOURCE: Jacob R. Marcus, *The Jew in the Medieval World: A Source Book, 315–1791* (Cincinnati: Sinai Press, 1938), pp. 13–15.

gates wide to passengers and travellers; that we will receive any Muslim traveller into our houses and give him food and lodging for three nights; that we will not harbor any spy in our churches or houses, or conceal any enemy of the Muslims.

That we will not teach our children the Quran; that we will not make a show of the Christian religion nor invite any one to embrace it; that we will not prevent any of our kinsmen from embracing Islam, if they so desire. That we will honor the Muslims and rise up in our assemblies when they wish to take their seats; that we will not imitate them in our dress, either in the cap, turban, sandals, or parting of the hair; that we will not make use of their expressions of speech, nor adopt their surnames, that we will not ride on saddles, or gird on swords, or take to ourselves arms or wear them, or engrave Arabic inscriptions on our rings; that we will not sell wine; that we will shave the front of our heads; that we will keep to our own style of dress, wherever we may be; that we will wear girdles round our waists.

That we will not display the cross upon our churches or display our crosses or our sacred books in the streets of the Muslims, or in their market-places; that we will strike the clappers in our churches lightly; that we will not recite our services in a loud voice when a Muslim is present; that we will not carry palm-branches or our images in procession in the streets; that at the burial of our dead we will not chant loudly or carry lighted candles in the streets of the Muslims or their market-places; that we will not take any slaves that have already been in the possession of Muslims, nor spy into their houses; and that we will not strike any Muslim.

All this we promise to observe, on behalf of ourselves and our co-religionists, and receive protection from you in exchange; and if we violate any of the conditions of this agreement, then we forfeit your protection and you are at liberty to treat us as enemies and rebels.

Questions

1. What privileges do the Muslims have vis-à-vis Christians?

2. What restrictions are put on Christians in the practice of their religion?

3. How likely do you think it is that Christians actually wrote this document?

Bishop Daniel of Winchester, Advice to Boniface on the Method of Conversion (723–724 CE)

In the seventh and eighth centuries CE many Christian monks from Anglo-Saxon England went to the Continent to serve as missionaries. They were particularly interested in converting the Saxons in northern Germany, whom they regarded as their cousins. The best known of these is St. Boniface (c. 672–754 CE). He was born in the southern Anglo-Saxon kingdom of Wessex and entered a monastery when still a child. Determined to be a missionary, he left for the continent in 716 CE. Although he saw himself as a missionary, most of his career was devoted to reforming and organizing the Christian church in northwestern Europe. He became archbishop of Mainz and founded many monasteries and bishoprics east of the Rhine. In the 740s he played a major role in reforming the church in the Frankish kingdoms. He then set off to work as a missionary in Frisia, to the north of Francia. There he and his companions were killed, supposedly by thieves, in the summer of 754 CE. The preservation of much of Boniface's correspondence makes him one of the most knowable figures in eighth-century Europe. One of his correspondents was Daniel, bishop of Winchester (died 745 CE) in Wessex. In the following letter Bishop Daniel offers advice on how to convert pagans.

Great is my joy, brother and colleague in the episcopate, that your good work has received its reward. Supported by your deep faith and great courage, you have embarked upon the conversion of heathens whose hearts have hitherto been stony and barren; and with the Gospel as your ploughshare you have laboured tirelessly day after day to transform them into harvest-bearing fields. Well may the words of the prophet be applied to you: "A voice of one crying in the wilderness, etc."

* * * And so, moved by affection and good will, I am taking the liberty of making a few suggestions, in order to show you how, in my

---

SOURCE: *The Anglo-Saxon Missionaries in Germany*, edited and translated by C. H. Talbot (New York: Sheed and Ward, 1954), pp. 75–78.

opinion, you may overcome with the least possible trouble the resistance of this barbarous people.

Do not begin by arguing with them about the genealogies of their false gods. Accept their statement that they were begotten by other gods through the intercourse of male and female and then you will be able to prove that, as these gods and goddesses did not exist before, and were born like men, they must be men and not gods. When they have been forced to admit that their gods had a beginning, since they were begotten by others, they should be asked whether the world had a beginning or was always in existence. There is no doubt that before the universe was created there was no place in which these created gods could have subsisted or dwelt. And by "universe" I mean not merely heaven and earth which we see with our eyes but the whole extent of space which even the heathens can grasp in their imagination. If they maintain that the universe had no beginning, try to refute their arguments and bring forward convincing proofs; and if they persist in arguing, ask them, Who ruled it? How did the gods bring under their sway a universe that existed before them? Whence or by whom or when was the first god or goddess begotten? Do they believe that gods and goddesses still beget other gods and goddesses? If they do not, when did they cease and why? If they do, the number of gods must be infinite. In such a case, who is the most powerful among these different gods? Surely no mortal man can know. Yet man must take care not to offend this god who is more powerful than the rest. Do they think the gods should be worshipped for the sake of temporal and transitory benefits or for eternal and future reward? If for temporal benefit let them say in what respect the heathens are better off than the Christians. What do the heathen gods gain from the sacrifices if they already possess everything? Or why do the gods leave it to the whim of their subjects to decide what kind of tribute shall be paid? If they need such sacrifices, why do they not choose more suitable ones? If they do not need them, then the people are wrong in thinking that they can placate the gods with such offerings and victims.

These and similar questions, and many others that it would be tedious to mention, should be put to them, not in an offensive and irritating way but calmly and with great moderation. From time to time their superstitions should be compared with our Christian dogmas and touched upon indirectly, so that the heathens, more out of confusion than exasperation, may be ashamed of their absurd opinions and may recognise that their disgusting rites and legends have not escaped our notice.

This conclusion also must be drawn: If the gods are omnipotent, beneficent and just, they must reward their devotees and punish those who despise them. Why then, if they act thus in temporal affairs, do they spare the Christians who cast down their idols and turn away from their worship the inhabitants of practically the entire globe? And whilst the Christians are allowed to possess the countries that are rich in oil and wine and other commodities, why have they left to the heathens the frozen lands of the north, where the gods, banished from the rest of the world, are falsely supposed to dwell?

The heathens are frequently to be reminded of the supremacy of the Christian world and of the fact that they who still cling to outworn beliefs are in a very small minority.

If they boast that the gods have held undisputed sway over these people from the beginning, point out to them that formerly the whole world was given over to the worship of idols until, by the grace of Christ and through the knowledge of one God, its Almighty Creator and Ruler, it was enlightened, vivified and reconciled to God. For what does the baptizing of the children of Christian parents signify if not the purification of each one from the uncleanness of the guilt of heathenism in which the entire human race was involved?

Questions

1. What techniques does Bishop Daniel recommend for trying to convert heretics?

2. What do his recommendations tell us about his notions of human nature?

3. In Daniel's opinion, does correct belief have effects in this world?

Ahmad Ibn Fadlan, Journey to Russia (920 CE)

In 920 CE a Slavic king in what is today Kazan (along the Volga River in Russia's Republic of Tatarstan), wrote to the Abbasid caliph, asking for assistance and instruction in the Islamic faith. Sensing a chance to spread the faith and perhaps win useful military allies, the caliph sent an expedition that departed the next year, traveling through the lands of various mostly Turkic pastoralists on the way, and later encountering both Russians and people trading with them who were probably Vikings. A scribe on that mission, Ahmad Ibn Fadlan, left behind a lengthy record of his experiences and impressions.

The selection below records Ibn Fadlan's impressions of the Oghuz Turks. As with many of these peoples—both Muslim and pagan—Ibn Fadlan considered their customs crude, their material living standards low, and their religious understanding very limited; he was, after all, coming from one of the world's great cities, and the contrast between Baghdad and nomadic life sometimes shocked him. At the same time, he found much to admire in at least some of these people—particularly their honesty, straightforwardness, and hospitality.

After we had crossed, we reached a Turkish tribe, which are called Oghuz. They are nomads and have houses of felt. They stay for a time in one place and then travel on. One sees their dwellings placed here and there according to nomad custom. Although they lead a hard existence they are like asses gone astray. They have no religious bonds with God, nor do they have recourse to reason. They never pray, rather do they call their headmen lords. When one of them takes counsel with his chief about something he says: "O lord, what shall I do in this or the other matter?" Their undertakings are based upon counsel solely among themselves; when they come to an agreement on a matter and have decided to put it

SOURCE: *Ibn Fadlan's Journey to Russia: A Tenth-Century Traveler from Baghdad to the Volga River*, translated by Richard N. Frye (Princeton: Markus Wiener Publishers, 2005), pp. 33–36.

through, there comes one of the lowest and basest of them and disrupts their decision.

I have heard how they enounce: "There is no God but Allah and Muhammad is the prophet of Allah," so as to get close to any Muslims who come to them by these words, but not because they believe them. When one of them has been dealt with unjustly, or something happens to him which he cannot endure, he looks up to the sky and says: "*bir tengri*," that is in Turkish, "By the one God," because *bir* means one in Turkish and *tengri* is in the speech of the Turks God. The Oghuz do not wash themselves either after defecation or urination, nor do they bathe after seminal pollution, or on other occasions. They have nothing whatever to do with water, especially in winter.

Their women do not veil themselves neither in the presence of their own men nor of others, nor does any woman cover any of her bodily parts in the presence of any person. One day we stopped off with one of them and were seated there. The man's wife was present. As we conversed, the woman uncovered her pudendum and scratched it, and we saw her doing it. Then we veiled our faces and said: "I beg God's pardon." Her husband laughed and said to the interpreter: "Tell them she uncovers it in your presence so that you may see it and be abashed, but it is not to be attained. This, however, is better than when you cover it up and yet it is reachable."

Adultery is unknown among them; but whomsoever they find by his conduct that he is an adulterer, they tear him in two. This comes about so: they bring together the branches of two trees, tie him to the branches and then let both trees go and so the man who was tied to the branches is torn in two.

One of them said he heard [my recitation] from the Quran and found that this recitation was beautiful; he approached addressing the interpreter: "Tell him do not stop." One day this man said to me through the interpreter: "Ask this Arab if our God, mighty and glorious, has a wife?" I felt this an enormity and uttered the formulas: "Praise God" and "I beg God's pardon." And he praised God and begged forgiveness, as I had done. This was the custom of the Turks: every time when a Turk hears a Muslim [pronounce these formulas] he repeats them after him.

Their marriage customs are as follows: one of them asks for the hand of a female of another's family, whether his daughter or his sister or any other one of those over whom he has power, against so and so many garments from Khwarazm. When he pays it he brings her home. The marriage price often consists of camels, pack animals, or other things; and no one can take a wife until he has fulfilled the obligation on which he has come to an understanding with those who have power over her in regard to him. If, however, he has met it, then he comes with any ado, enters the abode where she is, [and] takes her in the presence of her father, mother, and brothers; these do not prevent him. If a man dies who has a wife and children, then the eldest of his sons takes her to wife if she is not his mother.

None of the merchants or other Muslims may perform in their presence the ablution after seminal pollution, except in the night when they do not see it, for they get angry and say: "This man wishes to put a spell on us for he is immersing himself in water," and they compel him to pay a fine.

None of the Muslims can enter their country until one of them has become his host, with whom he stays and for whom he brings garments from the lands of Islam and for his wife a kerchief and some pepper, millet, raisins, and nuts. When the Muslim comes to his friend, the latter pitches a tent for him and brings him sheep in accordance with his [the Turk's] wealth, so that the Muslim himself may slaughter the sheep. * * *

Should any of the Muslims wish to travel further and aught happen to some of his camels and horses, or if he needs resources, he leaves those [incapacitated] with his Turkish friend, takes from him camels, pack animals, and provisions, as much as he needs, and travels further. When he returns from where he went, he pays him [the Turk] money, and gives back his camels and pack animals. And in the same way, when a man stops off with a Turk whom he does not know, and he says to the Turk: "I am thy guest and I will have some of thy camels, [thy] horses, and thy *dirhams*," he gives him what he wishes. If the merchant dies in that region and the caravan returns, the Turk goes to meet them and says: "Where is my guest?" If they say: "He has died," then he stops the caravan and goes to the most prominent merchant whom he sees among the Muslims, opens his bales while he is looking, and takes of his *dirhams*, just the amount that he had claim upon the [deceased] merchant, without taking a grain more. In the same way, he takes some of the pack animals and camels and he [the Turk] says, "That one [the deceased] was thy cousin; thou art chiefly obligated to pay his debts." And if the [first merchant] has fled, the Turk does the same thing and tells him: "He is a Muslim just as thou art. You take from him." If he does not encounter his Muslim guest on the caravan trail, then he asks another [or a third] one: "Where is he?" If he receives an indication, he sets out to find him, journeying for days until he reaches him, and takes away from him what he had of his property and also what he has presented to the [Muslim].

Questions

1. What do Oghuz attitudes toward Islam seem to be? How does Ibn Fadlan feel about this?

2. What most surprises Ibn Fadlan about Oghuz marriage practices, family life, and gender roles? Does he have an opinion about these practices? How can you tell?

3. The last part of this selection describes how the Oghuz lend provisions to traveling merchants, thus facilitating trade. How do lending and repayment work? What ideas of personal and collective responsibility seem to underlie these practices? Do you think these norms could be effectively enforced?

Avicenna, The Life of Ibn Sina (early eleventh century CE)

Abu Ali Al-Husayn Ibn Sina (980–1037 CE) was one of the most famous and influential Islamic philosophers. He was born in Bukhara, in what is today Uzbekistan, and died in Isfahan in Iran. Known to the Arabs as *Al-Sheikh al-Rais*, the "Chief and Leader (of thinkers)" and in the West as Avicenna, he wrote between 100 and 200 works on various subjects including his autobiography, excerpted below. He was a follower of Neoplatonism, a philosophical school originated by Plotinus (205–270

CE), who combined Plato's philosophy with religious, Pythagorean, and other classical ideas. In Neoplatonism the universe is the eternal emanation of the Good, a transcendental and unknowable object of desire and worship. In the twelfth century Ibn Sina's work was translated into Latin and had immense influence on the medieval Latin Christian philosophical tradition known as Scholasticism. Spelling has been updated in the following excerpt to reflect modern orthography.

My father was a man of Balkh; he moved from there to Bukhārā in the days of Amīr Nūh ibn Mansūr, during whose reign he worked in the administration, being entrusted with the governing of a village in one of the royal estates of Bukhārā. [The village,] called Kharmaythan, was one of the most important villages in this territory. Near it is a village called Afshanah, where my father married my mother and where he took up residence and lived. I was born there, as was my brother, and then we moved to Bukhārā. A teacher of the Quran and a teacher of literature were provided for me, and when I reached the age of ten I had finished the Quran and many works of literature, so that people were greatly amazed at me.

My father was one of those who responded to the propagandist of the Egyptians and was reckoned among the Ismā'īliyya [a Shi'ite sect]. From them, he, as well as my brother, heard the account of the soul and the intellect in the special manner in which they speak about it and know it. Sometimes they used to discuss this among themselves while I was listening to them and understanding what they were saying, but my soul would not accept it, and so they began appealing to me to do it [to accept the Ismā'īlī doctrines]. And there was also talk of philosophy, geometry, and Indian calculation. Then he [my father] sent me to a vegetable seller who used Indian calculation and so I studied with him.

SOURCE: *The Life of Ibn Sina*, edited by William E. Gohlman (Albany: State University of New York Press, 1974), pp. 17, 19, 21, 23, 25, 27.

At that time Abū 'Abd Allāh al-Nātilī, who claimed to know philosophy, arrived in Bukhārā; so my father had him stay in our house and he devoted himself to educating me. Before his arrival I had devoted myself to jurisprudence, with frequent visits to Ismā'īl the Ascetic about it. I was a skillful questioner, having become acquainted with the methods of prosecution and the procedures of rebuttal in the manner which the practitioners of it [jurisprudence] follow. Then I began to read the *Isagoge* ["Introduction" to Aristotle's "Categories" by Porphyry of Tyre (234–c. 305 CE), a pagan Neoplatonist philosopher who lived much of his life in Athens, Rome, and Sicily] under al-Nātilī, and when he mentioned to me the definition of genus, as being that which is predicated of a number of things of different species in answer to the question "What is it?", I evoked his admiration by verifying this definition in a manner unlike any he had heard of. He was extremely amazed at me; whatever problem he posed I conceptualized better than he, so he advised my father against my taking up any occupation other than learning.

I continued until I had read the simple parts of logic under him; but as for its deeper intricacies, he had no knowledge of them. So I began to read the texts and study the commentaries by myself until I had mastered logic. As for Euclid, I read the first five or six figures under him; then I undertook the solution of the rest of the book in its entirety by myself. Then I moved on to the *Almagest*, and when I had finished its introductory sections and got to the geometrical figures, al-Nātilī said to me, "Take over reading and solving them by yourself, then show them to me, so that I can explain to you what is right with it and what is wrong." But the man did not attempt to deal with the text, so I deciphered it myself. And many a figure he did not grasp until I put it before him and made him understand it. Then al-Nātilī left me, going on to Gurgānj.

I devoted myself to studying the texts—the original and commentaries—in the natural sciences and metaphysics, and the gates of knowledge began opening for me. Next I sought to know medicine, and so I read the books written on it. Medicine is not one of the difficult sciences, and therefore I excelled in it in a very short time, to the point that distinguished physicians began to read the science of medicine under me. I cared for the sick and there opened to me some of the doors of medical treatment that are indescribable and can be learned only from practice. In addition I devoted myself to jurisprudence and used to engage in legal disputations, at that time being sixteen years old.

Then, for the next year and a half, I dedicated myself to learning and reading; I returned to reading logic and all the parts of philosophy. During this time I did not sleep completely through a single night nor devote myself to anything else by day.

Questions

1. How widely spread was philosophic and mathematical knowledge in tenth-century Bukhara?

2. How did Ibn Sina acquire his education?

3. From what regions was tenth- and eleventh-century Bukhara receiving cultural influences?

Abû Ûthmân al-Jâhiz, On the Zanj (c. 860 CE)

Abû Ûthmân al-Jâhiz (781–c. 869 CE) was born in Basra (then in the Abbasid caliphate). The grandson of a Zanj (East African) slave, he gained prominence as a scholar, writing prose and learned commentary on history, botany, zoology, politics, Islamic philosophy, and Arabic literature. He moved to Baghdad after the Abbasid caliphs founded the House of Wisdom, where he engaged with leading intellects and the caliph's family. It is said al-Jâhiz authored over 200 books, of which thirty survived to modern times. In this excerpt he defends peoples of sub-Saharan Africa. Long-standing trade relationships between the Persian Gulf and the East African coast intensified with the arrival of many East Africans in southern Iraq as slaves in the seventh and eighth centuries CE. As al-Jâhiz's life shows, some of their descendants married into local families.

In this passage, al-Jâhiz is countering the "curse of Ham," which claims that black-skinned people are descended from the disgraced Ham (one of Noah's sons) and bear the mark of God's displeasure. This myth was used by both Arab and European slave traders to justify enslaving

Africans. This passage addresses social tensions, which later erupted as Zanj rebellions (869–883 CE) that happened near Basra.

Everybody agrees that there is no people on earth in whom generosity is as universally well developed as the Zanj. * * * These people have a natural talent for dancing to the rhythm of the tambourine, without needing to learn it. There are no better singers anywhere in the world, no people more polished and eloquent, and no people less given to insulting language. * * * No other nation can surpass them in bodily strength and physical toughness. One of them will lift huge blocks and carry heavy loads that would be beyond the strength of most Bedouins or members of other races. They are courageous, energetic and generous, which are the virtues of nobility, and also good-tempered and with little propensity to evil. They are always cheerful, smiling and devoid of malice, which is a sign of a noble character. * * *

The Zanj say to the Arabs: You are so ignorant that during the *jāhiliyya* you regarded us as your equals [when it came to marrying] Arab women, but with the advent of the justice of Islam you decided this practice was bad. Yet the desert is full of Negroes married to Arab wives, and they have been princes and kings and have safeguarded your rights and sheltered you against your enemies.

* * *

[The Zanj] say that God did not make [them] black in order to disfigure [them]; rather it is our environment that has made [them] so. The best evidence of this is that there are black tribes among the Arabs, such as the Banū Sulaim b. Manṣūr, and that all the peoples settled in the Ḥarra besides the Banū Sulaim are black. These tribes take slaves from among the Ashbān to mind their flocks and for irrigation work, manual labour and domestic service, and their wives from among the Byzantines; and yet it takes less than three

---

SOURCE: *The Life and Works of Jāḥiẓ*, translated by Charles Pellat and D. M. Hawke (Routledge & Kegan Paul, 1969).

generations for the Ḥarra to give them all the complexion of the Banū Sulaim. This Ḥarra is such that the gazelles, ostriches, insects, wolves, foxes, sheep, asses, horses and birds that live there are all black. White and black are the results of environment, the natural properties of water and soil, distance from the sun and intensity of heat. There is no question of metamorphosis, or of punishment, disfigurement or favour meted out by [Allah]. Besides, the land of the Banū Sulaim has much in common with the land of the Turks, where the camels, beasts of burden and everything belonging to these people is similar in appearance: everything of theirs has a Turkish look.

Questions

1. How would you characterize al-Jâhiz's description of Africans? Which elements of the description are most believable, and which might be exaggerations?

2. Is al-Jâhiz in favor of marriage between Arabs and Zanj?

3. How do you interpret al-Jâhiz's claim that "everybody agrees" on the generosity and skills of people from Zanj, given that many Zanj familiar to peoples living along the Persian Gulf or between the Tigris and Euphrates rivers would have been slaves?

Chapter 10

BECOMING "THE WORLD," 1000–1300 CE

The Rise of Chinggis Khan (c. 1206)

Chinggis Khan (c. 1162–1227) was the founder of the Mongol Empire, which ultimately became the largest contiguous land empire ever known. The construction of this empire began in Chinggis's reign, with successful military campaigns in China, central Asia, and Persia. Despite these successes, Chinggis's early life was beset with troubles. Fatherless, deserted by his kinsmen, at times a fugitive from his enemies in the wilderness, he nevertheless managed by 1206 to make himself master of the peoples of the East Asia steppe. The first text below comes from *The Secret History of the Mongols*, probably composed sometime between 1228 and 1252. This is the best source we have for Chinggis's early life. The excerpt describes the capture and execution of one of Chinggis's greatest rivals, Jamuqa, in 1206. Before he turned against Chinggis, Jamuqa had been the Khan's blood brother. The second text comes from Rashid-al-Din's *Jami' al-tawarikh* (Compendium of Chronicles), which he was commissioned to write by Ghazan Khan (1271–1304), the Mongol ruler of Persia. Rashid, a Jewish convert to Islam, and his sons were Ghazan Khan's most trusted advisers. However, he fell out with one of Ghazan's successors and was executed in 1318. Spelling has been updated in the following excerpts to reflect modern orthography.

THE SECRET HISTORY OF THE MONGOLS

When Chingis Khan defeated the Naiman army
Jamugha had been with the Naiman
and in the battle all of his people were taken away.
He had escaped with only five followers
and become a bandit in the Tangnu Mountains.
One day he and his companions were lucky enough to kill a great
    mountain sheep,
and as they sat around the fire roasting the mutton

* * *

his five followers seized him,
and binding Jamugha they brought him to Chingis Khan.
Because he'd been captured this way, Jamugha said:
"Tell my anda, the Khan,
'Black crows have captured a beautiful duck.
Peasants and slaves have laid hands on their lord.
My anda the Khan will see this and know what to do.
Brown vultures have captured a mandarin duck.
Slaves and servants have conspired against their lord.
Surely my holy anda will know how to respond to this.'"
When he heard Jamugha's words Chingis Khan made a decree:
"How can we allow men who lay hands on their own lord to live?
Who could trust people like this?
Such people should be killed
along with all their descendants!"
He brought before Jamugha the men who had seized him,
these men who had betrayed their own lord,
and in their lord's presence their heads were cut off.
Then Chingis Khan said:
"Tell Jamugha this.

SOURCE: "The Secret History of the Mongols": from *The Secret History of the Mongols*, trans. Francis Woodman Cleaves. "A maxim of Chinggis Khan": from Timothy May, *The Mongol Art of War: Chinggis Khan and the Mongol Military System* (Yardley, PA: Westholme, 2007), p. 77.

'Now we two are together.
Let's be allies.
Once we moved together like the two shafts of a cart,
but you thought about separating from me and you left.
Now that we're together again in one place
let's each be the one to remind the other of what he forgot;
let's each be the one to awaken the other's judgment whenever it
    sleeps.
Though you left me you were always my anda.
On the day when we met on the battlefield
the thought of trying to kill me brought pain to your heart.'"

* * *

Jamugha answered him:
"Long ago when we were children in the Khorkhonagh Valley
I declared myself to be your anda.
Together we ate the food which is never digested
and spoke words to each other which are never forgotten,
and at night we shared one blanket to cover us both.
Then it was as if people came between us with knives,
slashing our legs and stabbing our sides,
and we were separated from each other.
I thought to myself,
'We've made solemn promises to each other'
and my face was so blackened by the winds of shame
that I couldn't bring myself to show my face,
this shameful windburned face,
before the warm face of my anda, the Khan.

* * *

And now my anda, the Khan wants to favor me,
and says to me, 'Let's be allies.'
When I should have been his ally I deserted him.
Now, my anda, you've pacified every nation;
you've united every tribe in the world.
The Great Khan's throne has given itself to you.
Now that the world is ready for you

what good would I be as your ally?
I'd only invade your dreams in the dark night
and trouble your thoughts in the day.
I'd be like a louse on your collar,
like a thorn under your shirt.

* * *

Having been born a great hero,
he has skillful young brothers.
Having many fine men by his side,
he's always been greater than I am.
As for me,
since I lost both my parents when I was young,
I have no younger brothers.
My wife is a babbling fool.
I can't trust the men at my side.
Because of all this
my anda, whose destiny is Heaven's will,
has surpassed me in everything.
My anda, if you want to favor me,
then let me die quickly and you'll be at peace with your heart.
When you have me killed, my anda,
see that it's done without shedding my blood.
Once I am dead and my bones have been buried high on a cliff
I will protect your seed and the seed of your seed.
I will become a prayer to protect you."

* * *

Hearing this Chingis Khan spoke:
"Though my anda deserted me
and said many things against me,
I've never heard that he ever wanted me dead.
He's a man we all might learn from
but he's not willing to stay with us.
If I simply ordered him to be killed
there isn't a diviner in the world who could justify it.
If I harmed this man's life without good reason
it would bring a curse on us.

* * *

Now I say 'Let's be allies' but you refuse me.
When I try to spare your life you won't allow it.
So speak to Jamugha and tell him,
'Allow this man to kill you
according to your own wishes,
without shedding your blood.'"
And Chingis Khan made a decree, saying:
"Execute Jamugha without shedding his blood
and bury his bones with all due honor."
He had Jamugha killed and his bones properly buried.

[A maxim of Chinggis Khan:] Just as *ortaqs* [merchants engaged in commerce with capital supplied by the imperial treasury] come with gold spun fabrics and are confident of making profits on those goods and textiles, military commanders should teach their sons archery, horsemanship, and wrestling well. They should test them in these arts and make them audacious and brave to the same degree that *ortaqs* are confident of their own skill.

Questions

1. How important is loyalty to one's master in *The Secret History*?

2. What is Chinggis Khan's opinion of merchants? What status does he ascribe to them?

3. How can you account for the differences in the description of Chinggis Khan between *The Secret History* and Rashid's text?

Yuan Cai, The Problems of Women (twelfth century)

Yuan Cai (c. 1140–c. 1195) was an official and scholar best known for writing an advice book on how members of the scholar-gentry class should manage family matters. Such books had already appeared in China many centuries before, but with the boom in woodblock printing during the Song dynasty (960–1279 CE) and a marked increase in literacy rates, they became far more popular and influential. Increased social mobility also made such books more important, as successful people found themselves occupying roles that they had not had the opportunity to observe their parents handling.

The passages selected here deal with various aspects of the lives of women (though the presumed reader is a male household head). The Song dynasty was a period of major changes in the status of women, with most modern scholars concluding that the choices available to at least elite women narrowed considerably. (One formulation has it that in the Tang dynasty a young female aristocrat might be out horseback riding when her suitor came to call; by the Song dynasty she would not have learned to ride horses, would not have gone out on her own, and would not have seen her suitor prior to marriage.) But recent scholarship has suggested a more complex picture, with women losing ground in some areas but gaining in others.

WOMEN SHOULD NOT TAKE PART IN AFFAIRS OUTSIDE THE HOME

Women do not take part in extrafamilial affairs. The reason is that worthy husbands and sons take care of everything for them, while unworthy ones can always find ways to hide their deeds from the women.

Many men today indulge in pleasure and gambling; some end up mortgaging their lands, and even go so far as to mortgage their houses without their wives' knowledge. Therefore, when husbands are bad, even if wives try to handle outside matters, it is of no use. Sons must have their mothers' signatures to mortgage their family properties, but there are sons who falsify papers and forge signatures, sometimes borrowing money at high interest from people who would not hesitate to bring their claim to court.

* * * Therefore, when sons are bad, it is useless for mothers to try to handle matters relating to the outside world.

SOURCE: *Chinese Civilization: A Sourcebook*, 2nd ed., edited by Patricia Buckley Ebrey (New York: The Free Press, 1993), pp. 166–68.

* * * If husbands and sons could only remember that their wives and mothers are helpless and suddenly repent, wouldn't that be best?

WOMEN'S SYMPATHIES SHOULD BE INDULGED

Without going overboard, people should marry their daughters with dowries appropriate to their family's wealth. Rich families should not consider their daughters outsiders but should give them a share of the property. Sometimes people have incapable sons and so have to entrust their affairs to their daughters' families; even after their deaths, their burials and sacrifices are performed by their daughters. So how can people say that daughters are not as good as sons?

Generally speaking, a woman's heart is very sympathetic. If her parents' family is wealthy and her husband's family is poor, she wants to take her parents' wealth to help her husband's family prosper. If her husband's family is wealthy but her parents' family is poor, then she wants to take from her husband's family to enable her parents to prosper. Her parents and husband should be sympathetic toward her feelings and indulge some of her wishes. When her own sons and daughters are grown and married, if either her son's family or her daughter's family is wealthy while the other is poor, she wishes to take from the wealthy one to give to the poor one. Her sons and daughters should understand her feelings and be somewhat indulgent. But taking from the poor to make the rich richer is unacceptable, and no one should ever go along with it.

ORPHANED GIRLS SHOULD HAVE THEIR MARRIAGES ARRANGED EARLY

When a widow remarries she sometimes has an orphaned daughter not yet engaged. In such cases she should try to get a respectable relative to arrange a marriage for her daughter. She should also seek to have her daughter reared in the house of her future in-laws, with the marriage to take place after the girl has grown up. If the girl were to go along with the mother to her stepfather's house, she would not be able to clear herself if she were subjected to any humiliations.

For Women Old Age Is Particularly Hard to Bear

* * * For women who live a long life, old age is especially hard to bear, because most women must rely on others for their existence. * * * For this reason women often enjoy comfort in their youth but find their old age difficult to endure. It would be well for their relatives to keep this in mind.

It Is Difficult for Widows to Entrust Their Financial Affairs to Others

Some wives with stupid husbands are able to manage the family's finances, calculating the outlays and receipts of money and grain, without being cheated by anyone. Of those with degenerate husbands, there are also some who are able to manage the finances with the help of their sons without ending in bankruptcy. Even among those whose husbands have died and whose sons are young, there are occasionally women able to raise and educate their sons, keep the affection of all their relatives, manage the family business, and even prosper. All of these are wise and worthy women. But the most remarkable are the women who manage a household after their husbands have died leaving them with young children. Such women could entrust their finances to their husbands' kinsmen or their own kinsmen, but not all relatives are honorable, and the honorable ones are not necessarily willing to look after other people's business.

When wives themselves can read and do arithmetic, and those they entrust with their affairs have some sense of fairness and duty with regard to food, clothing, and support, then things will usually work out all right. But in most of the rest of the cases, bankruptcy is what happens.

Before Buying a Servant Girl or Concubine, Make Sure of the Legality

When buying a female servant or concubine, inquire whether it is legal for her to be indentured or sold before closing the deal. If the girl is impoverished and has no one to rely on, then she should be brought before the authorities to give an account of her past.

After guarantors have been secured and an investigation conducted, the transaction can be completed. But if she is not able to give an account of her past, then the agent who offered her for sale should be questioned. Temporarily she may be hired on a salaried basis. If she is ever recognized by her relatives, she should be returned to them.

HIRED WOMEN SHOULD BE SENT BACK WHEN THEIR PERIOD OF SERVICE IS OVER

If you hire a man's wife or daughter as a servant, you should return her to her husband or father on completion of her period of service. If she comes from another district, you should send her back to it after her term is over. These practices are the most humane and are widely carried out by the gentry in the Southeast. Yet there are people who do not return their hired women to their husbands but wed them to others instead; others do not return them to their parents but marry them off themselves. Such actions are the source of many lawsuits.

How can one not have sympathy for those separated from their relatives, removed from their hometowns, who stay in service for their entire lives with neither husbands nor sons. Even in death these women's spirits are left to wander all alone. How pitiful they are!

Questions

1. Which kinds of women seem to have the most control over their lives? Which ones have the least? What circumstances create openings for women to make their own choices?

2. The Song dynasty was a period in which commercial activity increased rapidly. What role do markets and money play in these documents?

3. What differences does Yuan Cai see between men and women? What capacities do they share? What moral significance, if any, does he attach to the differences?

Two Views of the Fall of Jerusalem (1099 CE)

In 1095 the Byzantine emperor, hard-pressed by the Seljuk Turks, wrote to Pope Urban II to request military aid. What he got was the First Crusade. Urban's call for an armed pilgrimage, full of stories of Muslim atrocities against Christians and promises of remission of sins for those who took part, touched off a wave of enthusiasm in western Europe. In 1096 large numbers of nobles and crowds of enthusiastic peasants set off to liberate Jerusalem from Muslim control. The three-year journey to Jerusalem was frightful, accompanied by massacres of Jews and Muslims, starvation, cannibalism, and near defeat and destruction. On July 15, 1099, those crusaders who had survived the frightful three-year long journey captured Jerusalem. They then proceeded to massacre the Muslim population of the city, an atrocity whose memory is still alive in Muslim consciousness. The following excerpts give two different perspectives on this event: one Christian, the other Muslim. The first is from the cleric Raymond d'Aguilers, who appears to have been a chaplain of Raymond, count of Toulouse, one of the leaders of the crusade. He was present at the siege and final storming of Jerusalem. The second is a lament for the destruction of Jerusalem written by the Arab poet, Abu l-Musaffar al-Abiwardi (1064–1113), who held important administrative positions in Baghdad under the Seljuks.

THE FIRST CRUSADE

When our efforts were ended and the machines completed, the princes held a council and announced: "Let all prepare themselves for a battle on Thursday; in the meantime, let us pray, fast, and give alms. Hand over your animals and your boys to the artisans and carpenters, that they may bring in beams, poles, stakes, and branches to make mantlets [movable shelters designed to protect

---

SOURCE: August C. Krey, *The First Crusade: The Accounts of Eye-Witnesses and Participants* (Princeton: Princeton University Press, 1921), pp. 258–61, and *Arab Historians of the Crusades*, translated from Arabic by Francesco Gabrieli, translated from Italian by E. J. Costello (Berkeley: University of California Press, 1969), p. 12.

soldiers assaulting a fortress]. Two knights should make one mantlet and one scaling ladder. Do not hesitate to work for the Lord, for your labors will soon be ended." This was willingly done by all. * * *

Meanwhile, the Saracens in the city, noting the great number of machines that we had constructed, strengthened the weaker parts of the wall, so that it seemed that they could be taken only by the most desperate efforts. Because the Saracens had made so many and such strong fortifications to oppose our machines, the * * * [leaders] spent the night before the day set for the attack moving their machines, mantlets, and platforms to that side of the city which is between the church of St. Stephen and the valley of Josaphat. You who read this must not think that this was a light undertaking, for the machines were carried in parts almost a mile to the place where they were to be set up. When morning came and the Saracens saw that all the machinery and tents had been moved during the night, they were amazed. Not only the Saracens were astonished, but our people as well, for they recognized that the hand of the Lord was with us. * * *

But why delay the story? The appointed day arrived and the attack began. However, I want to say this first, that, according to our estimate and that of many others, there were sixty thousand fighting men within the city. * * * At the most we did not have more than twelve thousand able to bear arms, for there were many poor people and many sick. There were twelve or thirteen hundred knights in our army, as I reckon it, not more. I say this that you may realize that nothing, whether great or small, which is undertaken in the name of the Lord can fail. * * *

Our men began to undermine the towers and walls. From every side stones were hurled from the *tormenti* and the *petrariae* [that is, catapults], and so many arrows that they fell like hail. The servants of God bore this patiently, sustained by the premises of their faith, whether they should be killed or should presently prevail over their enemies. The battle showed no indication of victory, but when the machines were drawn nearer to the walls, they hurled not only stones and arrows, but also burning wood and straw. * * * Thus the fight continued from the rising to the setting sun in such splendid fashion that it is difficult to believe anything more glorious was ever done.

Then we called on Almighty God, our Leader and Guide, confident in His mercy. Night brought fear to both sides. * * * [O]n both sides it was a night of watchfulness, labor, and sleepless caution: on one side, most certain hope, on the other doubtful fear. We gladly labored to capture the city for the glory of God, they less willingly strove to resist our efforts for the sake of the laws of Mohammed. * * *

When the morning came, our men eagerly rushed to the walls and dragged the machines forward, but the Saracens had constructed so many machines that for each one of ours they now had nine or ten. * * *

By noon our men were greatly discouraged. They were weary and at the end of their resources. There were still many of the enemy opposing each one of our men; the walls were very high and strong, and the great resources and skill that the enemy exhibited in repairing their defenses seemed too great for us to overcome. But, while we hesitated, irresolute, and the enemy exulted in our discomfiture, the healing mercy of God inspired us and turned our sorrow into joy, for the Lord did not forsake us. * * * [A] knight on the Mount of Olives began to wave his shield to those who were with the Count and others, signalling them to advance. Who this knight was we have been unable to find out. At this signal our men began to take heart, and some began to batter down the wall, while others began to ascend by means of scaling ladders and ropes. Our archers shot burning firebrands, and in this way checked the attack that the Saracens were making upon the wooden towers of the Duke and the two Counts. * * * This shower of fire drove the defenders from the walls. Then the Count quickly released the long drawbridge which had protected the side of the wooden tower next to the wall, and it swung down from the top, being fastened to the middle of the tower, making a bridge over which the men began to enter Jerusalem bravely and fearlessly. * * *

[N]ow that our men had possession of the walls and towers, wonderful sights were to be seen. Some of our men (and this was more merciful) cut off the heads of their enemies; others shot them with arrows, so that they fell from the towers; others tortured them longer by casting them into the flames. Piles of heads, hands, and feet were to be seen in the streets of the city. It was necessary to pick one's way over the bodies of men and horses. But these were small matters compared to what happened at the Temple of Solomon, a place where religious services are ordinarily chanted. What happened there? If I tell the truth, it will exceed your powers of belief. So let it suffice to say this much, at least, that in the Temple and porch of Solomon, men rode in blood up to their knees and bridle reins. Indeed, it was a just and splendid judgment of God that this place should be filled with the blood of the unbelievers, since it had suffered so long from their blasphemies. * * *

Now that the city was taken, it was well worth all our previous labors and hardships to see the devotion of the pilgrims at the Holy Sepulchre. How they rejoiced and exulted and sang a new song to the Lord! For their hearts offered prayers of praise to God, victorious and triumphant, which cannot be told in words. A new day, new joy, new and perpetual gladness, the consummation of our labor and devotion, drew forth from all new words and new songs. This day, I say, will be famous in all future ages, for it turned our labors and sorrows into joy and exultation; this day, I say, marks the justification of all Christianity, the humiliation of paganism, and the renewal of our faith. "This is the day which the Lord hath made, let us rejoice and be glad in it," for on this day the Lord revevealed Himself to His people and blessed them.

ABU L-MUZAFFAR AL-ABIWARDI, [DESTRUCTION OF JERUSALEM]

We have mingled blood with flowing tears, and there is no room
    left in us for pity
To shed tears is a man's worst weapon when the swords stir up the
    embers of war.
Sons of Islām, behind you are battles in which heads rolled at your
    feet.
Dare you slumber in the blessed shade of safety, where life is as soft
    as an orchard flower?
How can the eye sleep between the lids at a time of disasters that
    would waken any sleeper?
While your Syrian brothers can only sleep on the backs of their
    chargers, or in vultures' bellies!

Must the foreigners feed on our ignominy, while you trail behind
    you the train of a pleasant life, like men whose world is at peace?
When blood has been spilt, when sweet girls must for shame hide
    their lovely faces in their hands!
When the white swords' points are red with blood, and the iron of
    the brown lances is stained with gore!
At the sound of sword hammering on lance young children's hair
    turns white.
This is war, and the man who shuns the whirlpool to save his life
    shall grind his teeth in penitence.
This is war, and the infidel's sword is naked in his hand, ready to
    be sheathed again in men's necks and skulls.
This is war, and he who lies in the tomb at Medina seems to raise
    his voice and cry: "O sons of Hashim [an ancestor of the
    prophet Muhammad]!
I see my people slow to raise the lance against the enemy: I see
    the Faith resting on feeble pillars.
For fear of death the Muslims are evading the fire of battle,
    refusing to believe that death will surely strike them."
Must the Arab champions then suffer with resignation, while the
    gallant Persians shut their eyes to their dishonour?

Questions

1. What is Raymond's attitude toward the massacre of the inhabitants of
   Jerusalem?

2. To what does Raymond attribute the success of the crusaders?

3. What is al-Abiwardi's purpose in writing his poem? How does he try to
   motivate his fellow Muslims to take action?

Joseph Ben Abraham, Letter from Aden to Abraham Yijū (c. 1130)

Dispersed communities of merchants who shared language, religion, or
ethnic identity facilitated thriving long-distance trade in the twelfth

century. Many records of Jewish merchants working in Mediterranean and Indian Ocean networks were preserved in the Cairo Geniza. According to Jewish custom, text inscribed with the name of God should not be destroyed. So writings—from small scraps to complex documents—were stored in a dedicated room in a synagogue. Since God's blessing was frequently invoked in letters and commercial contracts, many of these ordinary documents connecting individual merchants were preserved. The synagogue in old Cairo accumulated documents and fragments from about 800 CE through the nineteenth century, at which point scholars began to work with this unparalleled collection of medieval sources to investigate aspects of Jewish life and the thick web of connections that linked communities across great distances.

Partnerships, many of them life-long, cemented connections between ports and served to spread the risks of long-distance trade. Ongoing correspondence, the exchange of presents, and sometimes the exchange of slaves or dependents created bonds between traders who might never have met in person. The following letter is a glimpse into one such relationship between Joseph ben Abraham in Aden, on the Arabian Peninsula, and Abraham Yijū in Mangalore, in southwestern India.

A. LOSSES AND ARRIVALS

In (Your) name, O Merci(ful).

The letter of your excellency, the illustrious elder, my master, has arrived. It was the most pleasant letter that came and the most delightful message that reached me. I read and understood it, etc. (another three lines).

You, my master, may God make your honored position permanent, wrote that you kindly sold the silk and sent goods for its proceeds and that you sent them in the ships of *Rāshmit*. I learned, however, that *Rāshmit's* two ships were lost completely. May *the H(oly one, be) he b(lessed)*, compensate me and you. Do not ask me, my master, how much I was affected by the loss of the cargo belonging

SOURCE: *Letters of Medieval Jewish Traders*, translated by S. D. Goitein (Princeton: Princeton University Press, 1973), pp. 192–96.

to you. But the Creator will compensate you soon. In any case, there is no counsel against the decree of God.

All the "copper" (vessels, *naḥās*), which you sent with Abū 'Alī, arrived, and the "table-bowl" also arrived. It was exactly as I wished—may God give you a good reward and undertake your recompensation (for only he is able to do it adequately).

B. EXCOMMUNICATION OF A TARDY DEBTOR

You, my master, mentioned that you approached the *kārdāl* gently in order to get something for us back from him. Perhaps you should threaten him that here in Aden we excommunicate anyone that owes us something and does not fulfill his commitments. Maybe he will be afraid of the excommunication. If he does not pay, we shall issue an official letter of excommunication and send it to him, so that he will become aware of his crime.

C. VARIOUS ORDERS, ESPECIALLY FOR BRONZE VESSELS

The re(d) betel-nuts arrived, as well as the two washbasins—may God give you a good reward. Please do not send me any more red betel-nuts, for they are not good. If there are any white, fresh betel-nuts to be had, it will be all right.

Please do not send me anything either betel-nuts or any other goods you acquire for me, in partnership with anyone, but specify each person and every item of merchandise.

I am sending you a broken ewer and a deep washbasin, weighing seven pounds less a quarter. Please make me a ewer of the same measure from its copper (or bronze, *ṣufr*) for it is good copper. The weight of the ewer should be five pounds exactly.

I am also sending 18¼ pounds of good yellow copper (*ṣufr aṣfar*, hardly "brass") in bars and five pounds of Qal'ī "lead" in a big mold and a piece of Egyptian "lead" (in the form of) a shell. Please put the bars, the "lead," and what remains from the manufacture of the ewer together and have two table-bowls for two dishes made for your servant, each table-bowl being of seventeen *fil(l)*, of the same form as the table-bowl you sent me; they should be of good workmanship.

D. Detailed description of a lamp ordered

Make me a nice lamp from the rest of all the copper (*ṣufr*). Its column should be octagonal and stout, its base should be in the form of a lampstand with strong feet. On its head there should be a copper (*naḥās*) lamp with two ends for two wicks, which should be set on the end of the column so that it could move up and down. The three parts, the column, the stand and the lamp, should be separate from one another. If they could make the feet in spirals, then let it be so; for this is more beautiful. The late *Abu 'l-Faraj al-Jubaylī* made a lamp of such a description. Perhaps this will be like it.

E. Additional orders

This year, I did not succeed in sending gold or silk. Instead, I am sending currency, 20 Malikī dinars, old dinars of good gold. Please pay with it the price of the labor of the coppersmith and for the rest buy me a quantity of "eggs" (a kind of cardamom) and cardamom, and if this is not to be had, anything else which God, be he praised, makes available. And, please, send everything with the first ship sailing.

Please buy me two washbasins of middle size, somewhat larger than those you previously sent me, and a large washbasin, which holds two waterskins of water, measuring two *siqāyas*.

F. Presents sent

I am sending you some things of no importance or value, namely two ruba'iyyas of white sugar; a bottle, in a tight basket, entirely filled with raisins; and in a *mazza* a pound of Maghrebi kohl, a pound of costus, a pound of vitriol, half a pound of litharge, three ounces of '*ilk* gum, and five sets of Egyptian paper; furthermore, in a little basket seven molds of "kosher" cheese; five packages altogether. Furthermore, all the copper (*naḥās*) sent by me is in a canvas. This makes six packages. I wrote on each: "*Abraham Yijū, shipment of Joseph*," and sent the whole together with the 20 dinars with the Sheikh *Aḥmad, the captain, son of Abu 'l-Faraj*.

Furthermore, in a bag there are two linen *fūṭas* for the children and two network veils dyed with carthamus. Please accept delivery and forward them to the Sheikh *Abu 'l-Surūr b. Khallūf al-Ṭalḥī*, as well as the letter destined for him. His name is on the bag.

My lord mentioned that there remained from last year copper to manufacture two bowls for drinking water. Kindly send them with the other copper.

Altogether there are seven packages with the bag of *Abu 'l-Surūr al-Ṭalḥī*.

May my master receive for his honored self the best greetings. And *upon you be peace!*

Questions

1. Which passages in this letter suggest to you that Ben Abraham and Yijū have an ongoing business relationship? What can you infer about twelfth-century Indian Ocean trade from the specificity of Ben Abraham's requests?

2. What kinds of trade goods are moving between Mangalore and Aden? How do these items compare to the trade goods mentioned in *The Periplus of the Erythraean Sea* (see Chapter 6)? What does this suggest to you about change or continuity in long-distance trade over centuries?

3. What does this letter tell us about production in Yijū's bronze factory? What does the letter tell us about the relationship between the value of the materials, the utility of the items produced, their workmanship, and aesthetics?

Letters between Pope Innocent IV and Güyük Khan (1245–1246)

In 1236 Batu, a grandson of Chinggis Khan, embarked on the conquest of Russia. By late 1240 the Mongols had subdued all of Russia and pressed on into eastern Europe. Separate columns destroyed an army of Germans and Poles at Liegnitz on April 9 and the army of the kingdom of Hungary at Mohi on April 11, 1241. For the next year the Mongols occupied Hungary. One of their armies reached the Adriatic on the coast of what is today Montenegro. Panic spread through central and western Europe. But Batu, in order to influence the impending election of a new Great Khan in Mongolia, withdrew his forces to the Volga. In 1245 Pope Innocent IV sent two Franciscan friars, John of Plano Carpini and Benedict the Pole, east to evaluate the situation. After an exhausting journey they reached Karakorum, the Mongol capital, in time to be present at the election of Güyük as Great Khan in August 1246. After delivering two letters from the pope and meeting with Güyük, they made a return journey to the Volga in the dead of winter. The first two selections below are excerpts from Innocent's letters to the Great Khan; the third is the message Güyük sent back with the Franciscans.

THE MONGOL MISSION

Wherefore we, * * * turn our keen attention, before all else incumbent on us in virtue of our office, to your salvation and that of other men, and on this matter especially do we fix our mind, sedulously keeping watch over it with diligent zeal and zealous diligence, so that we may be able, with the help of God's grace, to lead those in error into the way of truth and gain all men for Him. But since we are unable to be present in person in different places at one and the same time * * * in order that we may not appear to neglect in any way those absent from us we send to them in our stead prudent and discreet men by whose ministry we carry out the obligation of our apostolic mission to them. It is for this reason that we have thought fit to send to you our beloved son Friar Laurence of Portugal and his companions of the Order of Friars Minor, the bearers of this letter, men remarkable for their religious spirit, comely in their virtue and gifted with a knowledge of Holy Scripture, so that following their salutary instructions you may acknowledge Jesus Christ the very Son of God and worship His glorious name by practising the Christian religion. * * * We have thought fit to send to you the

SOURCE: *The Mongol Mission: Narratives and Letters of the Franciscan Missionaries in Mongolia and China in the Thirteenth and Fourteenth Centuries*, edited by Christopher Dawson (New York: Sheed and Ward, 1955), pp. 74–76, 85–86.

above-mentioned Friars, whom we specially chose out from among others as being men proved by years of regular observance and well versed in Holy Scripture, for we believed they would be of greater help to you, seeing that they follow the humility of our Saviour: if we had thought that ecclesiastical prelates or other powerful men would be more profitable and more acceptable to you we would have sent them.

Lyons, 5th March 1245

Seeing that not only men but even irrational animals, nay, the very elements which go to make up the world machine, are united by a certain innate law after the manner of the celestial spirits, * * * it is not without cause that we are driven to express in strong terms our amazement that you, as we have heard, have invaded many countries belonging both to Christians and to others and are laying them waste in a horrible desolation, and with a fury still unabated you do not cease from stretching out your destroying hand to more distant lands, but, breaking the bond of natural ties, sparing neither sex nor age, you rage against all indiscriminately with the sword of chastisement. We, therefore, following the example of the King of Peace, and desiring that all men should live united in concord in the fear of God, do admonish, beg and earnestly beseech all of you that for the future you desist entirely from assaults of this kind and especially from the persecution of Christians, and that after so many and such grievous offences you conciliate by a fitting penance the wrath of Divine Majesty, which without doubt you have seriously aroused by such provocation; nor should you be emboldened to commit further savagery by the fact that when the sword of your might has raged against other men Almighty God has up to the present allowed various nations to fall before your face; for sometimes He refrains from chastising the proud in this world for the moment, for this reason, that if they neglect to humble themselves of their own accord He may not only no longer put off the punishment of their wickedness in this life but may also take greater vengeance in the world to come. * * *

Lyons, 13th March 1245

GUYUK KHAN'S LETTER TO POPE INNOCENT IV (1246)

We, by the power of the eternal heaven,

Khan of the great Ulus [Community]

Our command:—

This is a version sent to the great Pope, that he may know and understand in the [Persian] tongue, what has been written. The petition of the assembly held in the lands of the Emperor [for our support], has been heard from your emissaries.

If he reaches [you] with his own report, Thou, who art the great Pope, together with all the Princes, come in person to serve us. At that time I shall make known all the commands of the *Yasa* [Mongol laws and statutes].

You have also said that supplication and prayer have been offered by you, that I might find a good entry into baptism. This prayer of thine I have not understood. Other words which thou hast sent me: "I am surprised that thou hast seized all the lands of the Magyar and the Christians. Tell us what their fault is." These words of thine I have also not understood. The eternal God has slain and annihilated these lands and peoples, because they have neither adhered to Chingis Khan, nor to the Khagan [supreme ruler], both of whom have been sent to make known God's command, nor to the command of God. Like thy words, they also were impudent, they were proud and they slew our messenger-emissaries. How could anybody seize or kill by his own power contrary to the command of God?

Though thou likewise sayest that I should become a trembling Nestorian Christian, worship God and be an ascetic, how knowest thou whom God absolves, in truth to whom He shows mercy? How dost thou know that such words as thou speakest are with God's sanction? From the rising of the sun to its setting, all the lands have been made subject to me. Who could do this contrary to the command of God?

Now you should say with a sincere heart: "I will submit and serve you." Thou thyself, at the head of all the Princes, come at once to serve and wait upon us! At that time I shall recognize your submission.

If you do not observe God's command, and if you ignore my command, I shall know you as my enemy. Likewise I shall make you understand. If you do otherwise, God knows what I know.

At the end of Jumada the second in the year 644 [November 1246].

Questions

1. What does Innocent IV want the Khan to do? Why might he think the Khan would actually do what he wants?

2. Why does Güyük refuse to accede to the pope's requests?

3. How does each party understand heavenly favor and how it manifests itself in politics?

Francesco Pegolotti, Advice to Merchants Bound for Cathay (c. 1340)

The rise of the Mongol Empire in the thirteenth century greatly facilitated contacts across Eurasia. For a long time the Mongols were able to maintain good order along the Silk Route that ran from China to the Mediterranean. Indeed, under their rule a new branch of the Silk Road opened that ran north of the Caspian Sea to the Black Sea, where the Italian cities of Genoa and Venice had trading colonies. European envoys visited the court of the Great Khan in Mongolia. Catholic missionaries reached China; for a time there was even a Franciscan archbishop in Beijing. Dominican missionaries were even allowed into Muslim Iran. Merchants, the most famous of whom were the Polos, traveled to China. The following document (c. 1340) comes from a commercial handbook titled the *Book of Descriptions of Countries and of Measures of Merchandise*, written by the Florentine merchant Francesco Balducci Pegolotti (c. 1310–c. 1340). Among other things it describes markets, trade goods, exchange rates, and customs duties from the Atlantic to China.

This book is called the Book of Descriptions of Countries and of measures employed in business, and of other things needful to be known by merchants of different parts of the world, and by all who have to do with merchandise and exchanges; showing also what relation the merchandise of one country or of one city bears to that of others; and how one kind of goods is better than another kind; and where the various wares come from, and how they may be kept as long as possible.

*　*　*

In the first place, you must let your beard grow long and not shave. And at Tana [at the mouth of the Don River on the Sea of Azov in modern Russia] you should furnish yourself with a dragoman [translator]. And you must not try to save money in the matter of dragomen by taking a bad one instead of a good one. For the additional wages of the good one will not cost you so much as you will save by having him. And besides the dragoman it will be well to take at least two good menservants, who are acquainted with the Cumanian tongue. And if the merchant likes to take a woman with him from Tana, he can do so; if he does not like to take one there is no obligation, only if he does take one he will be kept much more comfortably than if he does not take one. Howbeit, if he do take one, it will be well that she be acquainted with the Cumanian tongue as well as the men.

And from Tana travelling to Gittarchan [Astrakhan on the Caspian Sea] you should take with you twenty-five days' provisions, that is to say, flour and salt fish, for as to meat you will find enough of it at all the places along the road. And so also at all the chief stations noted in going from one country to another in the route, according to the number of days set down above, you should furnish yourself with flour and salt fish; other things you will find in sufficiency, and especially meat.

SOURCE: *Cathay and the Way Thither,* H. Yule, ed., 2nd ed. H. Cordier (London: Hakluyt Society, 1916).

The road you travel from Tana to Cathay is perfectly safe, whether by day or by night, according to what the merchants say who have used it. Only if the merchant, in going or coming, should die upon the road, everything belonging to him will become the perquisite of the lord of the country in which he dies, and the officers of the lord will take possession of all. And in like manner if he die in Cathay. But if his brother be with him, or an intimate friend and comrade calling himself his brother, then to such an one they will surrender the property of the deceased, and so it will be rescued.

And there is another danger: this is when the lord of the country dies, and before the new lord who is to have the lordship is proclaimed; during such intervals there have sometimes been irregularities practised on the Franks, and other foreigners. (They call "Franks" all the Christians of these parts from Romania [the Byzantine empire] westward.) And neither will the roads be safe to travel until the other lord be proclaimed who is to reign in room of him who is deceased.

Cathay is a province which contains a multitude of cities and towns. Among others there is one in particular, that is to say the capital city, to which is great resort of merchants, and in which there is a vast amount of trade; and this city is called Cambalec [Beijing]. And the said city hath a circuit of one hundred miles, and is all full of people and houses and of dwellers in the said city.

You may calculate that a merchant with a dragoman, and with two menservants, and with goods to the value of twenty-five thousand golden florins, should spend on his way to Cathay from sixty to eighty sommi of silver, and not more if he manage well; and for all the road back again from Cathay to Tana, including the expenses of living and the pay of servants, and all other charges, the cost will be about five sommi per head of pack animals, or something less. And you may reckon the sommo to be worth five golden florins. You may reckon also that each ox-waggon will require one ox, and will carry ten cantars Genoese weight; and the camel-waggon will require three camels, and will carry thirty cantars Genoese weight; and the horse-waggon will require one horse, and will commonly carry six and a half cantars of silk, at two hundred and fifty Genoese pounds to the cantar. And a bale of silk may be reckoned at between one hundred and ten and one hundred and fifteen Genoese pounds.

You may reckon also that from Tana to Sara[i] the road is less safe than on any other part of the journey; and yet even when this part of the road is at its worst, if you are some sixty men in the company you will go as safely as if you were in your own house.

Anyone from Genoa or from Venice, wishing to go to the places above-named, and to make the journey to Cathay, should carry linens with him, and if he visit Organci [Urgench in modern Turkmenistan] he will dispose of these well. In Organci he should purchase sommi of silver, and with these he should proceed without making any further investment, unless it be some bales of the very finest stuffs which go in small bulk, and cost no more for carriage than coarser stuffs would do.

Merchants who travel this road can ride on horseback or on asses, or mounted in any way that they list to be mounted.

Whatever silver the merchants may carry with them as far as Cathay the lord of Cathay will take from them and put into his treasury. And to merchants who thus bring silver they give that paper money of theirs in exchange. This is of yellow paper, stamped with the seal of the lord aforesaid. And this money is called balishi; and with this money you can readily buy silk and all other merchandise that you have a desire to buy. And all the people of the country are bound to receive it. And yet you shall not pay a higher price for your goods because your money is of paper. And of the said paper money there are three kinds, one being worth more than another, according to the value which has been established for each by that lord.

And you may reckon that you can buy for one sommo of silver nineteen or twenty pounds of Cathay silk, when reduced to Genoese weight, and that the sommo should weigh eight and a half ounces of Genoa, and should be of the alloy of eleven ounces and seventeen deniers to the pound.

You may reckon also that in Cathay you should get three or three and a half pieces of damasked silk for a sommo; and from three and a half to five pieces of nacchetti [cloths] of silk and gold, likewise for a sommo of silver.

Questions

1. What does Pegolotti see as the chief dangers for merchants traveling to China?

2. What role does the city of Urgench play in the flow of trade across Eurasia as it is described by Pegolotti?

3. How well informed does Pegolotti seem to be about mercantile affairs in the lands he discusses?

Mobilizing for War in the Age of the Mongols

Although military technology did not differ dramatically across Afro-Eurasia in the eleventh through the fourteenth centuries, there were significant differences in the ways armies were conscripted, organized, and fielded. Moreover, armies related to their societies differently. For example, in settled societies military training is a distraction from the pursuit of other forms of economic productivity, but in a nomadic society, a horseman is more integral to general social and economic pursuits, so there can be less differentiation between martial and other goals. In most societies, the elites saw themselves as participants in military culture, and many hunted and rode horses as leisure—Chinese elites were a notable exception. Nevertheless, China wanted a skilled cavalry and at times recruited horsemen from central Asia.

Regardless of differences, all societies had to find ways of feeding and equipping the military, and motivating and disciplining the troops. As you will see from the following documents, various societies found different approaches to these problems. Another commonality across most of Afro-Eurasia was the influence of the Mongols. The painting of Sir Geoffrey Luttrell is the only source in this group that comes from the period after the Mongol threat had been eclipsed. The other sources are all either about Mongols or people who were worried about central Asian nomads.

These documents show multiple adaptations to shared sets of problems. As you read, pay attention both to questions of military effectiveness as well as to the material and cultural consequences of mobilization on society at large.

Images of Mongol Horsemen and a Medieval European Knight (fourteenth and fifteenth centuries)

The two images below show different ways of depicting, and perhaps conceptualizing, warriors in the fourteenth century. The first comes from the Luttrell Psalter (a psalter is a book containing psalms from the Old Testament). This was commissioned by an English knight, Sir Geoffrey Luttrell, and produced sometime between 1320 and 1340. The image shows Sir Geoffrey mounted on his war horse with his wife handing him his great helm and lance, while his daughter-in-law holds his shield. Both the shield and the horse's trapper (the cloth placed over the horse) bear the Luttrell family's coat of arms, a diagonal silver line between six silver swifts. The second image is from a fifteenth-century manuscript copy of the *Jami' al-tawarikh* (Compendium of Chronicles) by Rashid al-Din (1247–1318). He was commissioned to write this by Ghazan Khan (1271–1304), the Mongol ruler of Persia (see The Rise of Chinggis Khan, in Chapter 10). It shows dismounted Mongol warriors with their recurved bows fighting mounted opponents with small round shields.

Sir Geoffrey Luttrell on his war horse and in armor

SOURCE: Luttrell Psalter, in the collection of the British Library. HIP/Art Resource, NY.

Mongolian warriors

Questions

1. Compare the equipment shown in the Luttrell Psalter illustration with that in the illustration from the *Jami' al-tawarikh*. What differences or similarities do you see?

2. Which of these warriors would have cost more to equip? Which could move faster? Which would have an advantage in close-range fighting?

SOURCE: Rashid-al-din, *Jami' al-tawarikh*. AKG Images.

3. What makes Luttrell more identifiable as an individual than the Mongol soldiers? How does this reflect different ideas about warfare in medieval Afro-Eurasia?

'Ala-ad-Din 'Ata-Malik Juvaini, Genghis Khan: The History of the World Conqueror (mid-thirteenth century)

The Mongol army that carried out the great conquests of the thirteenth century was organized very differently from those of the settled peoples of Afro-Eurasia. In Afro-Eurasia armies were recruited in a great variety of ways. Some men served for pay; some received land in return for military service; and in some Muslim countries slaves were used as soldiers. When these armies assembled, their members often differed greatly in armament, training, and organization. Discipline, both on and off the battlefield, was often not very good. The following description of the Mongol military is from 'Ala-ad-Din 'Ata-Malik Juvaini's *History of the World Conqueror*. Juvaini (1226–1283) was a Persian historian and administrator. In the 1240s and 1250s he made two trips to Mongolia, where he began writing his history. In 1256 he entered the service of the Mongol Hülügü and accompanied him on the conquests of Persia and Iraq, which culminated with the destruction of Baghdad and the death of the last Abbasid caliph in 1258. Thereafter he became a provincial governor for the Mongols.

What army in the whole world can equal the Mongol army? In time of action, when attacking and assaulting, they are like trained wild beasts out after game, and in the days of peace and security they are like sheep, yielding milk, and wool, and many other useful things. In misfortune and adversity they are free from dissension and opposition. It is an army after the fashion of a peasantry, being

SOURCE: 'Ala-ad-Din 'Ata-Malik Juvaini, *Genghis Khan: The History of the World Conqueror*, translated from the text of Mizra Muhammad Qazvini by J. A. Boyle (Seattle: University of Washington Press, 1997), pp. 30–32.

liable to all manner of contributions (*mu'an*) and rendering without complaint whatever is enjoined upon it, whether *qupchur*, occasional taxes (*'avāriẓāt*), the maintenance (*ikhrājāt*) of travellers or the upkeep of post stations (*yam*) with the provision of mounts (*ulagh*) and food (*'ulūfāt*) therefor. It is also a peasantry in the guise of an army, all of them, great and small, noble and base, in time of battle becoming swordsmen, archers and lancers and advancing in whatever manner the occasion requires. Whenever the slaying of foes and the attacking of rebels is purposed, they specify all that will be of service for that business, from the various arms and implements down to banners, needles, ropes, mounts and pack animals such as donkeys and camels; and every man must provide his share according to his ten or hundred. On the day of review, also, they display their equipment, and if only a little be missing, those responsible are severely punished. Even when they are actually engaged in fighting, there is exacted from them as much of the various taxes as is expedient, while any service which they used to perform when present devolves upon their wives and those of them that remain behind. Thus if work be afoot in which a man has his share of forced labour (*bīgār*), and if the man himself be absent, his wife goes forth in person and performs that duty in his stead.

The reviewing and mustering of the army has been so arranged that they have abolished the registry of inspection (*daftar-i-'arẓ*) and dismissed the officials and clerks. For they have divided all the people into companies of ten, appointing one of the ten to be the commander of the nine others; while from among each ten commanders one has been given the title of "commander of the hundred," all the hundred having been placed under his command. And so it is with each thousand men and so also with each ten thousand, over whom they have appointed a commander whom they call "commander of the *tümen*." In accordance with this arrangement, if in an emergency any man or thing be required, they apply to the commanders of *tümen*; who in turn apply to the commanders of thousands, and so on down to the commanders of tens. There is a true equality in this; each man toils as much as the next, and no difference is made between them, no attention being paid to wealth or power. If there is a sudden call for soldiers an order is issued that so many thousand men must present themselves in such and such a place at such and such an hour of that day or night. *"They shall not retard it* (their appointed time) *an hour; and they shall not advance it."* And they arrive not a twinkling of an eye before or after the appointed hour. Their obedience and submissiveness is such that if there be a commander of a hundred thousand between whom and the Khan there is a distance of sunrise and sunset, and if he but commit some fault, the Khan dispatches a single horseman to punish him after the manner prescribed: if his head has been demanded, he cuts it off, and if gold be required, he takes it from him.

How different it is with other kings who must speak cautiously to their own slave, bought with their own money, as soon as he has ten horses in his stable, to say nothing of when they place an army under his command and he attains to wealth and power; then they cannot displace him, and more often than not he actually rises in rebellion and insurrection! Whenever these kings prepare to attack an enemy or are themselves attacked by an enemy, months and years are required to equip an army and it takes a brimful treasury to meet the expense of salaries and allotments of land. When they draw their pay and allowances the soldiers' numbers increase by hundreds and thousands, but on the day of combat their ranks are everywhere vague and uncertain, and none presents himself on the battle-field. A shepherd was once called to render an account of his office. Said the accountant: "How many sheep remain?" "Where?" asked the shepherd. "In the register." "That," replied the shepherd, "is why I asked: there are none in the flock." This is a parable to be applied to their armies; wherein each commander, in order to increase the appropriation for his men's pay, declares, "I have so and so many men," and at the time of inspection they impersonate one another in order to make up their full strength.

Another *yasa* is that no man may depart to another unit than the hundred, thousand or ten to which he has been assigned, nor may he seek refuge elsewhere. And if this order be transgressed the man who transferred is executed in the presence of the troops, while he that received him is severely punished. For this reason no man can give refuge to another; if (for example) the commander be a prince, he does not permit the meanest person to take refuge in his company and so avoids a breach of the *yasa*. Therefore no man can take liberties with his commander or leader, nor can another commander entice him away.

Questions

1. What strikes Juvaini as most remarkable about the Mongol army?

2. What does he mean by the comments that "it is an army after the fashion of a peasantry" and "a peasantry in the guise of an army"?

3. How does Juvaini compare the Mongol military organization to those he was familiar with in Persia and Iraq?

Ouyang Xiu and Fan Zhen, Conscription and Professional Soldiers in Song China (960–1127 CE)

The northern Song dynasty (960–1127 CE) was the largest empire on earth, and also the richest; its army often had well over 1 million men—far more than any other state of that era. But most of the time it was on the defensive against nomadic invaders from the north, to whom it succumbed in 1127.

The Song could not raise enough high quality horses themselves, and had to import them from central Asian pastoralists. The large infantry forces they could raise were not fast enough to contend with nomadic cavalry, and were prohibitively expensive to feed if stationed along the semi-arid northern frontier. Moreover, after a mutiny had nearly destroyed the previous (Tang) dynasty, the Song had strengthened civilian control of its armies—but at the cost of weakening them. Defense and defense costs were central issues in debates that ran throughout the dynasty's life.

The two brief texts excerpted here come from high-ranking, reform-minded civilian politicians who favored reducing reliance on professional soldiers and relying more on conscription. There had been a universal draft in the Qin and early Han dynasties, and various modified draft systems in other periods. Although farmers could quickly learn the skills needed for local self-defense tasks, or serve the army as porters, learning the sophisticated horsemanship and archery needed on the northern frontiers would have required a long, very burdensome service period. The professional army, however, attracted many of the "wrong" people, and cost a great deal even during peacetime. Spelling has been updated in the following excerpts to reflect modern orthography.

FROM A MEMORIAL BY OUYANG XIU, c. 1040

The weakness of our forces has been exposed recently by the defeat sustained on the western frontier by our troops under Qi Zongju. If only the troops were hardy and efficient it might be considered justifiable to expend the resources of the farming class upon their maintenance. But what reason have we for maintaining the mere pretence of an army, composed as it is of such proud, lazy, and useless men?

The ancient practice was to give the strong and robust fellows of the farming class military drill and instruction in the intervals between the agricultural seasons, keeping them free for their farming work at other times. But this practice no longer obtains. The recruiting officers go out in times of dearth, measuring the height of the men, testing their strength, and enrolling them in the standing army. Those of better physique are drafted into the Imperial Army, while those of inferior standard are allocated to the Provincial Corps. The recruiting officers are rewarded according to the number of recruits they enrol. In times of dearth and poverty it is only natural that there should be competition to enter the army. So it has come about that after every period of famine, the strong and robust have been found in the army, while the older and feebler folk have been left on the fields.

I am not unaware of the criticism that if such men were not received into the army at such times they might turn to banditry for a living. But the pity is that while such critics are conscious of

---

SOURCE: H. R. Williamson, *Wang An-shih: A Chinese Statesman and Educationalist of the Song Dynasty* (London: Arthur Probsthain, 1935), vol. 1, pp. 187, 189–90.

the danger that these men might become robbers for a short period, they seem completely to overlook the fact that once they are enrolled in the regular army they become robbers for practically the whole of their lives.

FROM A MEMORIAL BY FAN ZHEN, C. 1260

Though taxation is heavy the revenue remains insufficient. The chief cause for this is to be found in the size of our standing army. It is said that this is essential to our frontier policy, as we must be prepared for the Qitans. But, as a matter of fact, the Qitans have made no incursion southwards for over fifty years. Why? Because it is much more to their advantage to go on receiving our handsome tribute gifts of money and silk, and to maintain the peace. But supposing they were to decide to launch an attack. In that case I venture to predict that the only defenders of our cities north of the Yellow River would be found to be composed of women and girls. For the soldiery who are stationed in the districts, and who engage in no farming or other productive work, would be found quite useless.

And yet we continue to maintain them at the expense of the people. The policy of creating and maintaining a standing army leads to a great decrease in the numbers of those engaged in agriculture. This, of course, means that great areas of arable land lie fallow. This in its turn involves the people in heavier taxation and an increase of the burden of public services. So the loyalty of the people gets strained, and cannot be relied upon.

On the contrary, the policy of raising Militia or People's Corps, making soldiers of them while they continue their work of farming, tends to eliminate these evils. The number engaged in farming operations is not decreased, more land gets tilled, taxation is lighter, and the loyalty of the people remains staunch and true.

It is surely preferable to prepare to meet the Qitans by a policy which ensures the loyalty of the people than by pressing a policy which tends to deprive the State of such an asset. I am convinced that if we pursue our present policy our resources both in money and men will be exhausted before the enemy appears. Whereas our revenue will be sufficient and our military strength more than adequate, if we adopt a policy of making soldier-farmers of our people.

Questions

1. What do each of these officials object to about the professional standing army?

2. What advantages do they see in training and mobilizing farmer-soldiers?

3. What assumptions do these writers make about how people think and act? What assumptions are made about the sources of their state's strength and weakness?

Ziya' al-Din Barani, The Challenges of Raising an Army (1357)

Alauddin Khilji (ruled 1296–1316), part of the second Muslim dynasty to rule the Delhi Sultanate, is best remembered for his attack on Chittor. Legend has it that Alauddin seized the city in order to posses the beautiful queen Rani Padmini, a story recounted in the epic poem *Padmavat*—though more recent scholarship emphasizes the strategic importance of the city. The sultanate was always vulnerable to attacks from central Asia, and the Khilji dynasty was engaged in territorial conquest of the south, so the military was an important part of the dynasty's success.

The following passage makes explicit some of the challenges of maintaining political power in a turbulent era. Like the Mongols and the Song, Alauddin had to worry about the caliber of his soldiers. Also like the Song, the sultanate faced real financial constraints to support the large army necessary to protect itself from the threat of Mongol invasion.

Ziya' al-Din Barani (1285–1357) was a Muslim political thinker from an aristocratic family that served the Delhi Sultanate. He wrote a history of thirteenth- and early fourteenth-century India and an important tract on Muslim social hierarchies in South Asia. Spelling has been updated in the following excerpt to reflect modern orthography.

After Sultan Alauddin had taken care to make these preparations against another inroad of the Mongols, he used to have discussions with his councillors both by day and night as to the means
of effectually resisting and annihilating these marauders. * * *

The Sultan then took counsel with his advisers, everyone of
whom was unequalled and eminently distinguished, saying: "To
maintain an immense picked and chosen force well mounted, so
that they may be fully equipped and efficient at all times, is impossible, without the expenditure of vast treasures; for one must give
regularly every year whatever sum is fixed upon at first; and if I
settle a high rate of pay upon the soldiery, and continue to disburse
money to them at that rate annually, at the end of a few years, not
withstanding all the treasure I possess, nothing will be left, and
without treasure it is of course impossible to govern or deliberate.

"I am accordingly desirous of having a large force, well
mounted, of picked and chosen men, expert archers, and well
armed that will remain embodied for years; and I will give 234
tankahs to a *Murattab* and 78 *tankahs* to a *Du-aspah*; from the
former of whom I shall require two horses with their corresponding equipments, and from the latter one with its usual gear. Consider now and inform me how this idea that has entered into my
mind about raising a large force, and maintaining it permanently,
may be carried into execution."

The councillors, endowed with abilities like those of Āśaf, exercised their brilliant intellects, and after some reflection unani-
mously expressed the following opinion before the throne: "As it
has entered into your Majesty's heart, and become implanted there,
to raise a large force and permanently maintained on small allowances such can never be accomplished unless horses, arms and all
the equipments of a soldier, as well as subsistence for his wife and
family, become excessively cheap, and are reduced to the price of
water; for if your Majesty can succeed in lowering the price of pro-

SOURCE: Ziya al-Din Barani, *The Reign of Alauddin Khilji*, translated by
A. R. Fuller and A. Khallaque (Calcutta: Pilgrim Publishers, 1967), pp.
100–103, 128–29.

visions beyond measure, a large force can be raised and permanently maintained according to the idea that has entered your august mind; and by the aid of this vast force all fear of danger from the Mongols will be averted."

The Sultan then consulted with his trusty and experienced councillors and ministers, as to what he should do, in order that the means of livelihood might be made exceedingly cheap and moderate, without introducing capital punishment, torture, or severe [coercion]. The Sultan's ministers and advisers represented, that until fixed rules were established, and permanent regulations introduced for lowering prices, the means of livelihood would never get exceedingly cheap. First then, for the cheapening of grain, the benefit of which is common to all, they proposed certain measures, and by the adoption of these measures, grain became cheap, and remained so for years.

* * *

As soon then the cheapness of all necessaries of life had been secured, and a large standing army could be entertained, the Mongols were defeated each time they invaded Delhi or the Delhi territory, and were slain, or captured, and the standard of Islam obtained one signal victory after the other over them. Several thousand Mongols with ropes on their necks were brought to Delhi and trampled to death by elephants. Of their heads, they formed a large platform or made turrets of the Mongol skulls, and the stench in the city of the dead bodies of such as had been killed in battle or had been executed in Delhi, was very great. The army of Islam gained in fact such victories over the Mongols that a *Duaspah* would bring in ten Mongols with ropes on their necks, or a single Muslim trooper would drive one hundred Mongols before himself.

Questions

1. What was Alauddin's biggest constraint in fielding an army adequate to defend against the Mongols?

2. What strategy did Alauddin and his advisers pursue to address this

challenge? Whom else would this policy have benefited? Who might have opposed it?

3. What differences do you note between the concerns of Mongol, Chinese, and Indian rulers in this period? What can account for the similarities and the differences you note?

Chapter **11**

CRISES AND RECOVERY IN AFRO-EURASIA, 1300s–1500s

Giovanni Boccaccio, The Decameron (1353)

The establishment of the Mongol Empire in the thirteenth century greatly promoted trade across Afro-Eurasia. The Black Death, known to the Europeans who lived through it as the Great Pestilence, was transmitted westward from the empire into Afro-Eurasia. It entered Sicily in September 1347. In the next five years it spread across Europe. The most common estimates are that it killed one-third to one-half of the population of Europe, a demographic catastrophe without parallel in European history. One of the most vivid descriptions of it was written by Giovanni Boccaccio (1313–1375) as an introduction to his *Decameron*, a collection of one hundred short stories which he portrays as being told by ten people who have fled the city of Florence to the countryside to escape the plague.

———

[In 1348] when in the illustrious city of Florence, there made its appearance that deadly pestilence, which, whether disesminated by the influence of the celestial bodies, or sent upon us mortals by God in His just wrath by way of retribution for our iniquities, had had its origin some years before in the East. * * *

SOURCE: Giovanni Boccaccio, *The Decameron*, translated by J. M. Rigg (London, 1903), pp. 5–11.

In Florence, despite all that human wisdom and forethought could devise to avert it, as the cleansing of the city from many impurities by officials appointed for the purpose, the refusal of entrance to all sick folk, and the adoption of many precautions for the preservation of health; despite also humble supplications addressed to God, and often repeated both in public procession and otherwise, by the devout; towards the beginning of the spring of the said year the doleful effects of the pestilence began to be horribly apparent by symptoms that [showed] as if miraculous.

* * * [I]n men and women alike it first betrayed itself by the emergence of certain tumours in the groin or the armpits, some of which grew as large as a common apple, others as an egg, some more, some less, which the common folk called gavoccioli. From the two said parts of the body this deadly gavocciolo soon began to propagate and spread itself in all directions indifferently; after which the form of the malady began to change, black spots or livid making their appearance in many cases on the arm or the thigh or elsewhere, now few and large, now minute and numerous. And as the gavocciolo had been and still was an infallible token of approaching death, such also were these spots on whomsoever they [showed] themselves. * * * [N]ot merely were those that recovered few, but almost all within three days from the appearance of the said symptoms, sooner or later, died, and in most cases without any fever or other attendant malady.

Moreover, * * * not merely by speech or association with the sick was the malady communicated to the healthy with consequent peril of common death; but any that touched the clothes of the sick or aught else that had been touched or used by them, seemed thereby to contract the disease.

*　　*　　*

In which circumstances, * * * divers[e] apprehensions and imaginations were engendered in the minds of such as were left alive, inclining almost all of them to the same harsh resolution, to wit, to shun and abhor all contact with the sick and all that belonged to them, thinking thereby to make each his own health secure. Among whom there were those who thought that to live temperately and avoid all excess would count for much as a preservative against seizures of this kind. Wherefore they banded together, and, dissociating themselves from all others, formed communities in houses where there were no sick, and lived a separate and secluded life, which they regulated with the utmost care, avoiding every kind of luxury, but eating and drinking very moderately of the most delicate viands and the finest wines, holding converse with none but one another, lest tidings of sickness or death should reach them, and diverting their minds with music and such other delights as they could devise. Others, the bias of whose minds was in the opposite direction, maintained, that to drink freely, frequent places of public resort, and take their pleasure with song and revel, sparing to satisfy no appetite, and to laugh and mock at no event, was the sovereign remedy for so great an evil: and that which they affirmed they also put in practice, so far as they were able, resorting day and night, now to this tavern, now to that, drinking with an entire disregard of rule or measure, and by preference making the houses of others, as it were, their inns, if they but saw in them aught that was particularly to their taste or liking. * * * Thus, adhering ever to their inhuman determination to shun the sick, as far as possible, they ordered their life. In this extremity of our city's suffering and tribulation the venerable authority of laws, human and divine, was abased and all but totally dissolved, for lack of those who should have administered and enforced them, most of whom, like the rest of the citizens, were either dead or sick, or so hard bested for servants that they were unable to execute any office; whereby every man was free to do what was right in his own eyes.

Not a few there were who belonged to neither of the two said parties, but kept a middle course between them, neither laying the same restraint upon their diet as the former, nor allowing themselves the same license in drinking and other dissipations as the latter, but living with a degree of freedom sufficient to satisfy their appetites, and not as recluses. They therefore walked abroad, carrying in their hands flowers or fragrant herbs or divers[e] sorts of spices, which they frequently raised to their noses * * * because the air seemed to be everywhere laden and reeking with the stench emitted by the dead and the dying. * * *

Some again, the most sound, perhaps, in judgment, as they were also the most harsh in temper, of all, affirmed that there was no medicine for the disease superior or equal in efficacy to flight; following which prescription a multitude of men and women, negligent of all but themselves, deserted their city, their houses, their estates, their kinsfolk, their goods, and went into voluntary exile, or migrated to the country parts, as if God in visiting men with this pestilence in requital of their iniquities would not pursue them with His wrath wherever they might be, but intended the destruction of such alone as remained within the circuit of the walls of the city; or deeming, perchance, that it was now time for all to flee from it, and that its last hour was come.

* * * Tedious were it to recount, how citizen avoided citizen, how among neighbours was scarce found any that [showed] fellow-feeling for another, how kinsfolk held aloof, and never met, or but rarely; enough that this sore affliction entered so deep into the minds of men and women, that in the horror thereof brother was forsaken by brother, nephew by uncle, brother by sister, and oftentimes husband by wife; nay, what is more, and scarcely to be believed, fathers and mothers were found to abandon their own children, untended, unvisited, to their fate, as if they had been strangers. Wherefore the sick of both sexes, whose number could not be estimated, were left without resource but in the charity of friends (and few such there were), or the interest of servants. * * *

It had been, as to-day it still is, the custom for the women that were neighbours and of kin to the deceased to gather in his house with the women that were most closely connected with him, to wail with them in common, while on the other hand his male kins-folk and neighbours, with not a few of the other citizens, and a due proportion of the clergy according to his quality, assembled without, in front of the house, to receive the corpse; and so the dead man was borne on the shoulders of his peers, with funeral pomp of taper and dirge, to the church selected by him before his death. Which rites, as the pestilence waxed in fury, were either in whole or in great part disused, and gave way to others of a novel order. For not only did no crowd of women surround the bed of the dying, but many passed from this life unregarded, and few indeed were they to whom were accorded the lamentations and bitter tears of sorrowing relations; nay, for the most part, their place was taken by the laugh, the jest, the festal gathering; observances which the women, domestic piety in large measure set aside, had adopted with very great advantage to their health. Few also there were whose bodies were attended to the church by more than ten or twelve of their neighbours, and those not the honourable and respected citizens; but a sort of corpse-carriers drawn from the baser ranks, who called themselves becchini and performed such offices for hire, would shoulder the bier, and with hurried steps carry it, not to the church of the dead man's choice, but to that which was nearest at hand, with four or six priests in front and a candle or two, or, perhaps, none; nor did the priests distress themselves with too long and solemn an office, but with the aid of the becchini hastily consigned the corpse to the first tomb which they found untenanted. The condition of the lower, and, perhaps, in great measure of the middle ranks, of the people [showed] even worse and more deplorable; for, deluded by hope or constrained by poverty, they stayed in their quarters, in their houses, where they sickened by thousands a day, and, being without service or help of any kind, were, so to speak, irredeemably devoted to the death which overtook them. Many died daily or nightly in the public streets; of many others, who died at home, the departure was hardly observed by their neighbours, until the stench of their putrefying bodies carried the tidings; and what with their corpses and the corpses of others who died on every hand the whole place was a sepulchre.

It was the common practice of most of the neighbours, moved no less by fear of contamination by the putrefying bodies than by charity towards the deceased, to drag the corpses out of the houses with their own hands, aided, perhaps, by a porter, if a porter was to be had, and to lay them in front of the doors, where any one who made the round might have seen, especially in the morning, more of them than he could count; afterwards they would have biers brought up, or, in default, planks, whereon they laid them. * * * And times without number it happened, that, as two priests, bearing the cross, were on their way to perform the last office for some one, three or four biers were brought up by the porters in rear of them, so that, whereas the priests supposed that they had but one corpse to bury, they discovered that there were six or eight, or sometimes more. Nor, for all their number, were their obsequies honoured by either tears or lights or crowds of mourners; rather, it was come to this, that a dead man was then of no more account than a dead goat would be to-day.

Questions

1. What are the physical symptoms of the plague as described by Boccaccio? What possible causes does he give for its outbreak?

2. How do the people of Florence try to deal with the outbreak in their city? How effective are their efforts?

3. What is the impact of the plague on the behavior of the people of Florence?

Jean Froissart, On the Jacquerie (1358)

The fourteenth and fifteenth centuries saw major peasant revolts in Europe. The population collapse following the Black Death forced down rents and drove up wages. The peasantry deeply resented efforts by the nobility to halt these processes. At the same time large-scale warfare became a fixture of European politics, often resulting in destruction of peasant property. One of the bloodiest revolts was the Jacquerie (whose name comes from "Jacques," or in English "Jack" or "John," a slang term for peasant used by the upper classes). This took place in May and June 1358. It followed a massive defeat of the French and the capture of their king by the English at the Battle of Poitiers in 1356, which left in its wake quarrels among the French ruling elite, a revolt by the people of Paris, the ravaging of the countryside by mercenary bands, and heavy war taxation. All these factors sparked a revolt of the peasants living north of Paris. Jean Froissart (c. 1337–c. 1404) describes the revolt in his *Chronicles*. From a merchant background, Froissart became a cleric and writer catering to the interests of the nobility. His *Chronicles*, despite its imprecision, is one of the best sources for the first part of the Hundred Years War between France and England.

Anon after the deliverance of the king of Navarre there began a marvellous tribulation in the realm of France, as in Beauvoisin, in Brie, on the river of Marne, in Laonnois, and about Soissons. For certain people of the common villages, without any head or ruler, assembled together in Beauvoisin. In the beginning they passed not a hundred in number: they said how the noblemen of the realm of France, knights and squires, shamed the realm, and that it should be a great wealth to destroy them all; and each of them said it was true, and said all with one voice: "Shame have he that doth not his power to destroy all the gentlemen of the realm!"

Thus they gathered together without any other counsel, and without any armour saving with staves and knives, and so went to the house of a knight dwelling thereby, and [broke] up his house and slew the knight and the lady and all his children great and small and [burned] his house. And then they went to another castle, and took the knight thereof and bound him fast to a stake, and then violated his wife and his daughter before his face and then slew the lady and his daughter and all his other children, and then slew the knight by great torment and [burned] and beat down the castle. And so they did to divers[e] other castles and good houses; and they multiplied so that they were a six thousand, and ever as they went forward they increased, for such like as they were fell ever to them, so that every gentleman fled from them and took their wives and children with them, and fled ten or twenty leagues off to be in surety, and left their houses void and their goods therein.

These mischievous people thus assembled without captain or armour robbed, [burned] and slew all gentlemen that they could lay hands on, and forced and ravished ladies and damosels, and did such shameful deeds that no human creature ought to think on any such, and he that did most mischief was most praised with them and greatest master. I dare not write the horrible deeds that they did to ladies and damosels: among other they slew a knight and after did

SOURCE: *The Chronicles of Froissart*, translated by John Bourchier and Lord Berners, edited by G. C. Macaulay (London: Macmillan and Co., 1895), pp. 136–37.

put him on a broach and roasted him at the fire in the sight of the lady his wife and his children; and after the lady had been enforced and ravished with a ten or twelve, they made her perforce to eat of her husband and after made her to die an evil death and all her children. They made among them a king, one of Clermont in Beauvoisin: they chose him that was the most ungraciousest of all other and they called him king Jaques Goodman, and so thereby they were called companions of the Jacquerie. They destroyed and [burned] in the country of Beauvoisin about Corbie, Amiens and Montdidier more than threescore good houses and strong castles. In like manner these unhappy people were in Brie and Artois, so that all the ladies, knights and squires of that country were fain [compelled] to fly away to Meaux in Brie, as well the duchess of Normandy and the duchess of Orleans as divers[e] other ladies and damosels, or else they had been violated and after murdered. Also there were a certain of the same ungracious people between Paris and Noyon and between Paris and Soissons, and all about in the land of Coucy, in the county of Valois, in the bishopric of Laon, Noyon and Soissons. There were [burned] and destroyed more than a hundred castles and good houses of knights and squires in that country.

Questions

1. What does Froissart identify as the causes of the peasant uprising?

2. How organized do the peasants appear to be?

3. How does Froissart characterize the rebellious peasants' behavior?

Chihab Al-ʿUmari, The Pilgrimage of Mansa Musa (1342–1349)

The following account of Mansa Musa's 1324 visit to Cairo has circulated widely since the fourteenth century. The author, Chihab Al-ʿUmari (1300–1384), was born in Damascus and visited Cairo shortly after Mansa Musa's highly visible stay. Mansa Musa, king of Mali, traveled with a large, well-supplied caravan to perform the *hajj*—the pilgrimage to Mecca incumbent upon all Muslims who can afford the journey. When Al-ʿUmari arrived in Cairo, people were still talking about the extraordinary visit of a monarch who brought so much wealth that his spending and alms-giving undermined the price of gold in Egypt for the next decade. The following selections provide descriptions of the Malian kingdom, the tribute system that provided abundant gold for the Malian king, Mansa Musa's piety, and the effect of his retinue's presence on the Cairene economy. As you read, remember that Al-ʿUmari, writing at least two decades later, relied on what people who met Mansa Musa had to say. The fact that he was not a direct witness does not make his account unreliable, but it does raise questions about how information was relayed from one person to the next in the fourteenth century.

———————

[S]ultan Mūsā the king of [Mali] * * * came to Egypt on the Pilgrimage. He was staying in [the] Qarāfa [district of Cairo] and Ibn Amīr Ḥājib was governor of Old Cairo and Qarāfa at that time. A friendship grew up between them and this sultan Mūsā told him a great deal about himself and his country and the people of the Sūdān who were his neighbours. One of the things which he told him was that his country was very extensive and contiguous with the Ocean. By his sword and his armies he had conquered 24 cities each with its surrounding district with villages and estates. * * * He has a truce with the gold-plant people, who pay him tribute.

Ibn Amīr Ḥājib said that he asked him about the gold-plant, and he said: "It is found in two forms. One is found in the spring and blossoms after the rains in open country. It has leaves like grass and its roots are gold. The other kind is found all the year round at known sites on the banks of the Nīl and is dug up. There are holes there and roots of gold are found like stones or gravel and gathered up." * * * Sultan Mūsā told Ibn Amīr Ḥājib that gold was his prerogative and he collected the crop as a tribute except for what the people of that country took by theft.

———————

SOURCE: *Corpus of Early Arabic Sources for West African History*, translated by J. F. P. Hopkins, edited by V. Levtzion and J. F. P. Hopkins (Cambridge: Cambridge University Press, 1981), pp. 267–71.

But * * * in fact he is given only a part of it as a present by way of gaining his favour, and he makes a profit on the sale of it, for they have none in their country. * * *

[I]t is a custom of his people that if one of them should have reared a beautiful daughter he offers her to the king as a concubine and he possesses her without a marriage ceremony as slaves are possessed, and this in spite of the fact that Islam has triumphed among them and that * * * this sultan Mūsā was pious and assiduous in prayer, [Quran] reading, and mentioning God.

"I said to him (said Ibn Amīr Ḥājib) that this was not permissible for a Muslim, whether in law or reason and he said: 'Not even for kings?' and I replied: 'No! not even for kings! Ask the scholars!' He said: 'By God, I did not know that. I hereby leave it and abandon it utterly!'

"I saw that this sultan Mūsā loved virtue and people of virtue. He left his kingdom and appointed as his deputy there his son Muḥammad and emigrated to God and His Messenger. He accomplished the obligations of the Pilgrimage, visited [the tomb of] the Prophet [at Medina] (God's blessing and peace be upon him!) and returned to his country with the intention of handing over his sovereignty to his son and abandoning it entirely to him and returning to Mecca the Venerated to remain there as a dweller near the sanctuary; but death overtook him, may God (who is great) have mercy upon him.

* * *

"This sultan Mūsā, during his stay in Egypt both before and after his journey to the Noble Ḥijāz, maintained a uniform attitude of worship and turning towards God. It was as though he were standing before Him because of His continual presence in his mind. He and all those with him behaved in the same manner and were well-dressed, grave, and dignified. He was noble and generous and performed many acts of charity and kindness. He had left his country with 100 loads of gold which he spent during his Pilgrimage on the tribes who lay along his route from his country to Egypt, while he was in Egypt, and again from Egypt to the Noble Ḥijāz and back. As a consequence he needed to borrow money in Egypt and pledged his credit with the merchants at a very high rate of gain so that they made 700 dinars profit on 300. Later he paid them back amply. He sent to me 500 mithqals of gold by way of honorarium.

* * *

"This man flooded Cairo with his benefactions. He left no court emir nor holder of a royal office without the gift of a load of gold. The Cairenes made incalculable profits out of him and his suite in buying and selling and giving and taking. They exchanged gold until they depressed its value in Egypt and caused its price to fall."

* * *

[W]hen he made the Pilgrimage * * * the sultan was very open-handed towards the pilgrims and the inhabitants of the Holy Places. He and his companions maintained great pomp and dressed magnificently during the journey. He gave away much wealth in alms. * * *

Gold was at a high price in Egypt until they came in that year. The mithqal did not go below 25 *dirhams* and was generally above, but from that time its value fell and it cheapened in price and has remained cheap till now. The mithqal does not exceed 22 *dirhams* or less. This has been the state of affairs for about twelve years until this day by reason of the large amount of gold which they brought into Egypt and spent there.

Questions

1. How does Al-'Umari choose to document Mansa Musa's piety?

2. What is Al-'Umari's attitude toward Mansa Musa's incredible wealth?

3. Al-'Umari's retelling of a conversation between Mansa Musa and the governor of Cairo suggests that gold was the product of plants. Does this fanciful description undermine the reliability of other aspects of this account? Why or why not?

Galileo Galilei, Letter to Madame Cristina di Lorena, Grand Duchess of Tuscany (1615)

Galileo Galilei (1564–1642) was born to a relatively poor noble family. Sent to the University of Pisa to study medicine, he instead became interested in physics and mathematics. He became a professor of mathematics at Padua in 1592. He made important discoveries about falling objects that called Aristotelian physics into question, about the motion of the pendulum, and in several other areas. He also developed an improved water pump and other practical implements. He is best known, however, for inventing a telescope. The observations he made with it in 1610 confirmed the arguments of Copernicus (1473–1543) that the sun is the center of the solar system, and the earth and other planets move around it.

This position conflicted with the doctrine of the Catholic Church; Galileo was denounced in 1614, tried by the Inquisition in 1616, and warned against publicly advocating Copernicanism. Still, he persisted. Various powerful people, including the Pope, tried to arrange a compromise in which Galileo would be protected so long as he was relatively quiet in his support of heliocentrism; Galileo, however, continued to publish. In 1632 he was tried and convicted of heresy, and spent the rest of his life under house arrest.

In the letter excerpted below, Galileo addresses Cristina di Lorena (1565–1636), Grand Duchess of Tuscany—a descendant of French royalty who married into the Medici family, which had patronized Galileo. Although Galileo had not yet been condemned by the Inquisition, and this letter was not made public until much later, it represents a forceful statement of views on the relationship between science and religious authority that the Catholic Church of his time was unwilling to accept. The Catholic Church stopped prohibiting books advocating heliocentrism in 1758, but it did not formally absolve Galileo until 1992.

———

Some years ago, as your Serene Highness well knows, I discovered many things in the heavens that had remained unseen until our own era. Perhaps because of their novelty, perhaps because of certain consequences which followed from them, these discoveries conflicted with certain propositions concerning nature which were commonly accepted by the philosophical schools. Hence no small number of professors became stirred up against me—almost as though I, with my own hand, had placed these things in heaven in order to disturb and obscure nature and the sciences. Displaying greater affection for their own opinions than for true ones, and, at the same time, forgetting that the multitude of truths contribute to inquiry by augmenting and establishing science, and not by diminishing and destroying it, these professors set about trying to deny and abolish these new discoveries. Although their very senses, had they seen fit to heed them attentively, would have rendered these things as certain, they nonetheless alleged various things and published various writings full of empty reasoning and containing—a still graver error— scattered testimonies from Holy Scripture. The latter were not only cited out of context, but had little to do with the matter at hand. * * *

Thus it is that these men persist in their primary objective, which is to try, by every means imaginable, to destroy me and all that is mine. They know that, in my astronomical and philosophical studies concerning the structure of the world, I maintain that the Sun, without moving, remains stationary in the center of the revolution of celestial orbs; and that the Earth, turning about its own axis, revolves around the Sun as well. They are aware, moreover, that I proceed to confirm the above hypothesis (*posizione*), not simply by condemning the account of Ptolemy and Aristotle, but by bringing forward much conflicting evidence—in particular, certain natural effects, the causes of which cannot be explained in any other manner, and certain celestial effects, determined by the concordance of many new astronomical discoveries, which clearly confute the Ptolemaic system, and which admirably agree with and support the other hypothesis. Now, perhaps they are confused by the fact that certain other propositions, contrary to common opinion but affirmed by me, have been recognized as true. And thus unsure of their defenses on the battlefield of philosophy, they have sought to make a shield

SOURCE: *Introduction to Contemporary Civilization in the West*, 2nd ed., edited by the Contemporary Civilization Staff of Columbia College, Columbia University (New York: Columbia University Press, 1954), vol. 1, pp. 724–27.

for their fallacious arguments out of the mantle of simulated piety and the authority of Scripture, applied by them with little intelligence to combat arguments which they have neither thought about nor understood. * * *

But who could with all certainty insist that the Scripture has chosen rigorously to confine itself to the strict and literal meaning of words when it speaks incidentally of the Earth, water, the Sun, and other creatures? And above all when it asserts something about these creatures which in no way touches upon the primary purpose of Holy Writ, which has to do with the service of God, the salvation of souls, and things far removed indeed from vulgar apprehension? Considering this, then, it seems to me that, when discussing natural problems, we ought to begin with sensory experience and logical demonstrations, and not with the authority of passages in Scripture. For both Nature and the Holy Scripture proceed alike from the Word of God, the latter being the dictate of the Holy Spirit, and the former being the utterly obedient executrix of Divine Law. Now, it is the case that Scripture finds it convenient, in order to accommodate itself to the understanding of everyone, to say many things which, from the bare meaning of the words it employs, differ in aspect from the absolute truth. But in just the opposite way, Nature is inexorable and immutable, never transcending the limits imposed upon her by law; and it is as though she feels no concern whether her deep reasons and hidden modes of operation shall ever be revealed to the understanding of humankind or not. From this it would seem that natural effects, either those which sensory experience sets before our eyes or those which are established by logical demonstration, ought never on any account to be called into question, much less condemned, on the basis of Scriptural passages whose words may appear to support a conflicting opinion. For not every Scriptural dictum is connected to conditions as severe as those which hold with respect to effects of Nature; nor does God reveal Himself less excellently to us in the effects of Nature than He does in the sacred utterances of Scripture. It is this, perchance, that Tertullian meant when he wrote: *We conclude that God is first cognized in Nature, then recognized in Doctrine: in Nature through His works; in Doctrine through His word preached.* * * *

I should judge that the authority of Scripture was intended principally to persuade men of certain articles and propositions which transcend the powers of human reason, and which could be made credible by no other science and by no means other than the very voice of the Holy Spirit. * * * But I do not feel it necessary to believe that God, Who gave us senses, reason, and intellect, should have wished us to postpone using these gifts; that He has somehow given us, by other means, the information which we can obtain with our own senses, reason, and intellect; nor that He should want us to deny the senses and reason when sensory experience and logical demonstration have revealed something to our eyes and minds! And above all I do not feel it necessary to believe this where a science [like astronomy] is concerned, only a tiny part of which is written about (and then in contradictory ways) in Scripture. * * *

Experience plainly indicated that, concerning the rest and motion of Sun and Earth, it was necessary for Scripture to assert what it did, in order that the popular capacity [for understanding] should be satisfied. For even in our own day, individuals far less rude still persist in the same opinion for reasons which, if they were well weighed and examined, would be found to be completely specious, and which experiment would show to be wholly false or altogether beside the point. Nor can we attempt to remove their ignorance, for they are incapable of grasping the contrary reasons, which depend upon the most delicate observations and the most subtle demonstrations, involving abstractions the comprehension of which demands a more vigorous imagination than they possess. And though the stability of the Sun and the motion of the Earth are more than certain and demonstrated to the wise, it is nonetheless necessary, in order to maintain belief amongst the innumerable vulgar, to assert the contrary. If a thousand ordinary men were interrogated on this matter, perhaps not a single one would be found who would not respond by saying that he thinks, and firmly believes, that the Sun moves and the Earth stands still. But such common popular assent must in no way be taken as an argument for the truth of what is being affirmed. For if we were to question the same men about the causes and motives which provide the basis for their belief, and then to contrast what they say with the experiments and reasons which lead a few to believe otherwise, we would find the former to have been persuaded by simple appearances and the shallowest and silliest objections, and the latter to have been persuaded by the most substantial reasons. It is obvious, then, how necessary it was [for Scripture] to attribute motion to the Sun and stability to the Earth. It was necessary in order not to confuse the limited understanding of the vulgar, and in order not to render them obstinate and antagonistic, and in order that they should have faith in the principal doctrines which have altogether to do with Faith. And if this had to be done, it is not at all to be wondered at that it was done with such consummate wisdom in divine Scripture.

Questions

1. How does Galileo think people should read the Bible? What should they do when it appears to conflict with evidence observed in nature?

2. Does Galileo believe that his position is consistent with Christian faith and church authority? Why or why not?

3. What do you think Galileo was trying to accomplish with this letter?

Ibn Battuta, Visit to Mombassa and Kilwa, Rhila (c. 1358)

Ibn Battuta (1304–c. 1368) was born in Tangier, Morocco. He studied Islamic law and in 1325 embarked on his first *hajj* to Mecca. The pilgrimage should have taken about a year and half—but Ibn Battuta traveled for twenty-four years, moving through the extensive *Dar-al-Islam* (areas ruled by Muslims) including Africa, Southwest Asia, central Asia, and India. His travels took him to places as diverse as Constantinople, Baghdad, and the Maldive Islands. He supported himself as a *qadi* (jurist) and so found work in numerous places. When he finally returned to Morocco, the sultan asked him to dictate his adventures. Whether due to the faulty memories of an aging man or deliberate fabrication, some segments of the *Rhila* (travels) do not correlate with other sources. Nevertheless, the work as a whole sheds light on the extensive world of the race of men outside the window of the dead man's room, the overwhelming, commonplace mystery of life in the restless light of dawn . . .

He had reached the big trees: fir trees already drowned in darkness, with a raindrop still sparkling on the end of every needle; linden trees chattering with sparrows. The loveliest were two walnut trees: he was reminded of the statues in the library.

The magnificence of the venerable trees was due to their great bulk, but the strength with which the twisted branches sprang from their enormous trunks, the bursting into dark leaves of this wood which was so heavy and so old that it seemed to be digging down into the earth and not sprouting from it, created at the same time an impression of free will and of endless metamorphosis. Between them the hills rolled down to the Rhine; they framed Strasbourg Cathedral far off in the smiling twilight, as so many other trunks framed other cathedrals in the meadows of the West. And that tower standing erect like a cripple at prayer, all the human patience and labour transformed into waves of vines reaching right down to the river, were only an evening decoration round the venerable thrust of the living wood, the two sturdy, gnarled growths which dragged the strength out of the earth to display it in their boughs. The setting sun cast their shadows across to the other side of the valley, like two broad furrows. My father was thinking of the two saints, and of the Atlas. Instead of supporting the weight of the world, the tortured wood of these walnut trees flourished with life everlasting in their polished leaves under the sky and in their nuts that were almost ripe, in all their venerable bulk above the wide circle of young shoots and the dead nuts of winter. "Civilisations or the animal, like statues or logs. . . ." Between the statues and the logs there were the trees, and their design which was as mysterious as that of life itself. And the Atlas, and St. Mark's face consumed with Gothic passion, were lost in it like the culture, like the intellect, like everything my father had just been listening to—all buried in the shadow of this kindly statue which the strength of the earth carved for itself, and which the sun at the level of the hills spread across the sufferings of humanity as far as the horizon.

There had been no war in Europe for forty years.

III

I

JUST under a year later—on 11th June 1915—my father was waiting in the ante-room of General Von Spitz's command post on the Vistula front.

The clerks were busily writing, bothered by the flies. The command post overlooked a broad landscape flecked with sunflower blooms; after the last attack my father had walked through scarred fields of them, their thick petals stuck together with blood. Where the specks of yellow stopped was the end of the German line: the Russians used to cut them down to eat their seeds. From time to time the drawn-out whistle of the trains bringing the German reinforcements up from Lodz sounded across the summery plain; there was not a trench in sight, no firing, the weather was as fine as before the war.

"Isn't Captain Wurtz with you, sir?" an orderly enquired.

"No. Why?"

"You were ordered to report together."

Captain Wurtz was head of the Intelligence Service in this sector.

My father had never had any dealings with the General. He had been posted to an Officers' Training School four days after mobilisation and from there he had been sent to the eastern front at his own request. Not that he pinned his hopes on France, as a number of Alsatians had; his mother was German. But in the realm of the arts and the intellect at least, France and Germany were both necessary to him; Russia did not matter.

When he had come back from Asia as a civilian, the people he used to meet knew him by reputation; now that he was a soldier, no one outside the Wilhelmstrasse knew anything about him. Men have only to be lifted out of their environment to become quite ignorant except of a few names and words. In his colleagues' eyes he was a university professor, a bit of an explorer and—God knows why!—something of a journalist. Saying nothing during their arguments (he regarded most of them as illiterates in the intellectual field), talkative and full of stories about the East during the dull hours of the day, showing an exemplary indifference to promotion, he earned—with the help of "shamanism" —the popularity that is achieved by anyone who can dispel gloom. Stripped of his past, he had lost all social personality, and this he would not have minded at all if the result had only been the crude, fundamental relationship that fighting sometimes entails; and if he had not realised the quickly inverted passion men have for mistaking an appointment for a personality, a colonel educated, urbane elites connected through a shared belief in Islam. The following selections describe Ibn Battuta's visit to the Swahili coastal towns of East Africa.

Manbasā [Mombasa] is a large island with two days' journey by sea between it and the land of the *Sawāḥil*. It has no mainland. Its trees are the banana, the lemon, and the citron. They have fruit which they call the *jammūn*, which is similar to the olive and its stone is like its stone except that it is extremely sweet. There is no cultivation of grain among the people of this island: food is brought to them from the *Sawāḥil*. The greater part of their food is bananas and fish. They are Shāfiʿī [a practice within Sunni Islam] by rite, they are a religious people, trustworthy and righteous. Their mosques are made of wood, expertly built. At every door of the mosques there are one or two wells. The depth of their wells is a cubit or two. They take water from them in a wooden container into which a thin stick of a cubit's length has been fixed. The ground around the well and the mosque is level. He who wants to enter the mosque washes his feet and enters. There is at its gate a piece of thick matting upon which he rubs his two feet. He who wants to make the ablution holds the pot between his thighs and pours water upon his hands and carries out the ablutions. All the people walk barefoot. We spent the night on this island and travelled by sea to the city of Kulwā [Kilwa]. [Kilwa is] a great coastal city. Most of its people are Zunūj, extremely black. They have cuttings on their faces like those on the faces of the Līmiyyīn of Janāda. * * * The city of Kulwā is amongst the most beautiful of cities and most elegantly built. All of it is of wood, and the ceiling of its houses are of *al-dīs* [reeds]. The rains there are great. They are a people devoted to the Holy War because they are on one continuous mainland with unbelieving Zunūj. Their uppermost virtue is religion and righteousness and they are Shāfiʿī in rite.

*　　*　　*

SOURCE: Said Hamdun and Noël King, *Ibn Battuta in Black Africa* (Princeton, N.J.: Markus Weiner, 1975), pp. 21–22, 24–25.

DESCRIPTION OF THE SULTAN OF KULWĀ

Its sultan at the time of my entry into Kulwā was Abū al-Muẓaffar Ḥasan whose *kunya* [honorific title] was Abū al-Mawāhib [father of gifts] because of his many gifts and deeds of generosity. He was much given to razzias upon the land of the Zunūj; he raided them and captured booty. He used to set aside one fifth of it, which he spent in the ways indicated in the book of God the Exalted. He put the share of the kindred [of the prophet, the *sharīfs*] in a treasury by itself. When the *sharīfs* came to him he gave it to them. The *sharīfs* used to come to him from ʿIrāq and Ḥijāz and other places. * * * This sultan is a very humble man. He sits with the poor people [*faqīrs*] and eats with them, and gives respect to people of religion and of prophetic descent.

A STORY CONCERNING THE SULTAN OF KULWĀ'S DEEDS
OF GENEROSITY

I was present with him on a Friday when he came out from the prayer and was returning to his house. He was confronted on the road by one of the Yemeni *faqīrs*. He said to him, "O father of gifts." He replied, "At your service, O *faqīr*, what is your need?" He said, "Give me these clothes which you are wearing." He replied, "Yes, I will give them to you." He said to him, "This very moment." He said, "Yes, this very moment." He went back to the mosque and went into the house of the preacher [*khaṭīb*]. He put on other clothes and took off those clothes. He said to the *faqīr*, "Enter and take them." So the *faqīr* went in, tied them in a piece of cloth and put them on his head and went away. The gratitude of the people to the sultan increased at the evidence of his humility and graciousness. His son and heir-apparent took that suit of clothes from the *faqīr* and compensated him for it with ten slaves. When the news reached the sultan of the gratitude of the people to him for that deed he ordered the *faqīr* to be given in addition ten head of fine slaves and two loads of ivory. (The greater part of their gifts are ivory and seldom do they give gold.) When this honourable and generous sultan was gathered to God (may God have mercy on him), his brother Dā'ūd succeeded him. He was the opposite from him. When a beggar came to him he said to him, "He who used to give has died, and he did not leave anything after him to be given."

Questions

1. This description of the sultan of Kilwa presents a ruler both belligerent and generous. How does Ibn Battuta reconcile these two different facets of a ruler?

2. As in many other passages of the book, Ibn Battuta's description of Mombassa is disjointed, with little apparent connection between the elements he chooses to mention. What captures his attention in Mombassa? Why might Ibn Battuta want to tell readers about these features of Mombassa and emphasize different things about Kilwa?

3. What social and religious values does this passage emphasize?

Kabir, Three Poems (fifteenth century)

Kabir (1398–1448) was probably illiterate, and his mysticism earned him passionate enemies among both Muslims and Hindus during much of his lifetime. He was born to a family of Muslim weavers, but lived an itinerant life. By the end of his life, however, he was renowned as one of India's great religious poets and teachers; Hindus and Muslims both attempted to claim him, and still do. There is also a Kabir sect of people who revere him as a holy man.

In part, Kabir made enemies during his lifetime by an uncompromising insistence on what he considered to be honesty, and scathing criticisms of those whom he thought robbed religion of its deep, ecstatic meaning. Scholars and clergy whom he felt focused on the details of textual and ritual correctness and missed the physical experience and intense emotions that went with true insight were one of his favorite targets; priestly sacrifices and attempts to picture gods in physical forms were another; rules and customs that restricted women in particular were a third. He often went out of his way to behave publicly in ways that religious and political authorities would find scandalous.

54

She went with her husband to the in-laws' house
but didn't sleep with him,
didn't enjoy him.
Her youth slipped away like a dream.
Four met and fixed the marriage date,
five came and fixed the canopy,
girlfriends sang the wedding songs
and rubbed on her brow the yellow paste
of joy and sorrow.
Through many forms her mind turned
as she circled the fire.
The knot was tied, the pledge was made,
the married women poured the water.
Yet with her husband on the wedding square
she became a widow.
She left her marriage without the groom.
On the road the father-in-law explained.
Kabir says, I'm off to my real marriage now.
I'll play the trumpet
when I cross with my lord.

84

Qazi, what book are you lecturing on?
Yak yak yak, day and night.
You never had an original thought.
Feeling your power, you circumcise—
I can't go along with that, brother.
If your God favored circumcision,
why didn't you come out cut?

Source: *The Bijak of Kabir*, translated by Linda Hess and Shukdev Singh (San Francisco: North Point Press, 1983), pp. 59, 69–70, and *Songs of Saints of India*, translated by J. S. Hawley and Mark Juergensmeyer (Oxford: Oxford University Press, 2004), pp. 50–51.

If circumcision makes you a Muslim,
what do you call your women?
Since women are called man's other half,
you might as well be Hindus.
If putting on the thread makes you Brahmin,
what does the wife put on?
That Shudra's touching your food, pandit!
How can you eat it?
Hindu, Muslim—where did they come from?
Who started this road?
Look hard in your heart, send out scouts:
where is heaven?
Now you get your way by force,
but when it's time for dying,
without Ram's refuge, says Kabir,
brother, you'll go out crying.

[*Untitled*]

Go naked if you want,
Put on animal skins.
   What does it matter till you see the inward Ram?

If the union yogis seek
Came from roaming about in the buff,
   every deer in the forest would be saved.

If shaving your head
Spelled spiritual success,
   heaven would be filled with sheep.

And brother, if holding back your seed
Earned you a place in paradise,
   eunuchs would be the first to arrive.

Kabir says: Listen brother,
Without the name of Ram
   who has ever won the spirit's prize?

Pundit, how can you be so dumb?
You're going to drown, along with all your kin,
   unless you start speaking of Ram.

Vedas, Puranas—why read them?
   It's like loading an ass with sandalwood!
Unless you catch on and learn how Ram's name goes,
   how will you reach the end of the road?

You slaughter living beings and call it religion:
   hey brother, what would irreligion be?
"Great Saint"—that's how you love to greet each other:
   Who then would you call a murderer?

Your mind is blind. You've no knowledge of yourselves.
   Tell me, brother, how can you teach anyone else?
Wisdom is a thing you sell for worldly gain,
   so there goes your human birth—in vain.

You say: "It's Narad's command."
   "It's what Vyas says to do."
   "Go and ask Sukdev, the sage."
Kabir says: you'd better go and lose yourself in Ram
   for without him, brother, you drown.

Questions

1. What does the first poem suggest about what is and is not important in marriage? How can you tell?

2. What complaints against both Muslims and Hindus can you find in the second poem? How does the third poem extend those complaints?

3. What hints do you get in these poems of what Kabir thinks would constitute genuine religious experience? What might some Hindus find particularly objectionable about this? What might some Muslims object to?

Leo Africanus, On Timbuktu (1526)

Leo Africanus (c. 1494–c. 1554) was born al-Hasan ibn Muhammad al-Wazzan al-Fasi in Granada. Given the difficulties for Muslims in Spain after the expulsion of the Moors, his family joined relatives in Fez, where al-Hasan grew up and studied at the university. As a young man he traveled with his uncle throughout the Maghreb, going as far south as Timbuktu, then part of the Songhai Empire. He later performed the *hajj* to Mecca, and traveled across the Mediterranean to Istanbul. In 1518 his ship was captured by pirates; he was eventually taken to Rome and presented to Pope Leo X. As a man of letters with extensive diplomatic knowledge, he was welcomed at the papal court. He was baptized as Leo Africanus in 1520.

The historical geography of Africa is Africanus' best known scholarly work. It was quickly translated from Italian and had several printings in the sixteenth century. Although he was well-traveled, it is unlikely that Africanus visited all the places he described. Like other early modern writers, he probably relied on relayed oral descriptions from other travelers. When Leo Africanus visited Timbuktu, it was a vibrant commercial city famous for its wealth and learning.

This name was in our times (as some think) imposed upon this kingdom from the name of a certain town, so called, which (they say) king Mansa Suleiman founded in the year of the Hegira 610 [1213 CE] and it is situated within twelve miles of a certain branch of the Niger. All the houses are now changed into cottages built of chalk, and covered with thatch. Howbeit there is a most stately temple [mosque] to be seen, the walls whereof are made of stone and lime; and a princely palace also built by a most excellent workman of Granada. Here are many shops of artificers [craftspersons], and merchants, and especially of such as weave linen and cotton cloth.

SOURCE: Leo Africanus, *The History and Description of Africa and of the Notable Things Therein Contained*, translated by Robert Brown (London: Hakluyt Society, 1896), vol. 3, pp. 824–26. Text modernized by Norton authors for this edition.

And hither do the Barbary [North African] merchants bring cloth of Europe.

All women of this region go with their faces covered, except maid-servants who sell all necessary victuals. The inhabitants and especially strangers there residing, are exceedingly rich, insomuch as the king that now is, married both his daughters to two rich merchants. Here are many wells containing most sweet water; and so often as the river Niger overflows, they convey the water thereof by certain sluices into the town. Grain, cattle, milk, and butter this region yields in great abundance, but salt is very scarce here. It is brought hither by land from Taghaza [also in modern-day Mali], which is five hundred miles distant. When I myself was here, I saw one camel load of salt sold for 80 ducats.

The rich king of Timbuktu has many plates and scepters of gold, some whereof weigh 1300 pounds. He keeps a magnificent and well furnished court. When he travels he rides upon a camel which is led by some of his noblemen. He does likewise when he goes to war, and all his soldiers ride upon horses. Whosoever will speak to this king must first fall down before his feet, and then taking up earth must sprinkle it upon his own head and shoulders. This custom is ordinarily observed by them that never saluted the king before, or come as ambassadors from other princes. He always has three thousand horsemen, and a great number of footmen that shoot poisoned arrows, attending on him. They often have skirmishes with those that refuse to pay tribute, and so many [prisoners] as they take they sell to the merchants of Timbuktu.

Very few horses are bred here. The merchants and courtiers keep certain little nags which they use to travel upon, but their best horses are brought out of Barbary. As soon as the king hears that any merchants are come to town with horses, he commands a certain number to be brought before him. Choosing the best for himself, he pays a most liberal price for them.

He so deadly hates all Jews that he will not admit any into his city. Any merchants he understands have dealings with Jews, he presently causes their goods to be confiscated.

Here are a great store of doctors, judges, priests, and other learned men that are bountifully maintained by the king's cost and charge.

And hither are brought diverse manuscripts or written books out of Barbary; they are sold for more money than any other merchandise.

The coin of Timbuktu is of gold without any stamps or superscription. In matters of small value they use certain shells brought out of Persia, four hundred of which shells are worth a ducat. Six pieces of their golden coin with two thirds parts weigh an ounce.

The inhabitants are people of a gentle and cheerful disposition, and spend a great part of the night in singing and dancing through all the streets of the city. They keep a great store of men and women slaves. Their town is in much danger of fire; at my second visit, half the town was almost burned in five hours time. Without the suburbs there are no gardens or orchards at all.

Questions

1. What features of a sophisticated economy are evident in this description of Timbuktu?

2. What connection did Timbuktu have to other regions?

3. Both Leo Africanus and Ibn Battuta (see Ibn Battuta, Visit to Mombassa and Kilwa, in this chapter) left records of their visits to Muslim cities in Africa. Compare their descriptions. What explains the similarities and differences in their accounts?

TEXT PERMISSIONS